D1288620

CONSTRUCTION PROJECT MANAGEMENT:
A Complete Introduction

Alison Dykstra, AIA, CSI

LCCN: 2010909115
Dykstra, Alison
Construction Project Management:
A Complete Introduction

Printed in the United States of America
10 9 8 7 6 5 4

ISBN: 978-0-9827034-9-6

Cover and book design by Andrea Young
Author photo by Andrea Young

Kirshner Publishing Company
Production Offices:
PO Box 14132
Santa Rosa, CA 95404
www.kirshnerbooks.com
www.kirshnerpublishing.com

This book is dedicated to the extraordinary California Community College system and to my equally extraordinary students at Santa Rosa Junior College

THANK YOU

To the industry experts who very generously gave their time in the classroom to share their wisdom with my students and me, to those who reviewed the manuscript of this book as it was being developed as a class reader, and to those who gave me invaluable suggestions, opinions, and guidance as it became a comprehensive textbook: Dave Buckle, Alan Butler, Michael Chambers, Don Shaw, Scott Thomas, Jay True, Bryan Varner, Dixon Wright, and Jerry Yudelson.

To Curt Groninga (retired) and Tim Bosma at Santa Rosa Junior College, who took time to educate me about the programming, design, procurement and construction processes used to develop campus facilities.

To Andrea Young who was able to take my vision of this book and create the perfect artistic response; to Stephanie Marohn for her careful editing; to Reny Slay, Gretchen Dykstra, Willis Eschenbach, Linda Lange, Christina Mead, and Pam Ward for their encouragement and willingness to read the manuscript and offer suggestions.

To my daughter, Marisol, for putting up with my constant distractions, and, finally, the most heartfelt and profound thanks to my brilliant, insightful, and loving husband, Andrew Schulman. For so many reasons, I couldn't, and wouldn't, have done it without you.

There are many good books on construction project management and I would like to recommend several that I think are especially helpful for those new to the subject:

Management of Construction Projects: A Constructor's Perspective, by John Schaufelberger and Len Holm

Construction Management JumpStart, by Barbara Jackson

Managing the Construction Process: Estimating, Scheduling and Project Control, by Frederick Gould

Computer Integrated Construction Project Scheduling, by John Buttelwerth

TABLE OF CONTENTS

PART 1—Context: The Industry, the Projects, the Players

PART 2—A Project Begins

PART 3—Bidding and the Contractor

PART 5—Construction

PREFACE

Background

This textbook is a direct outgrowth of years spent teaching college courses in planning and organizing construction projects. My students range from young people not long out of high school to seasoned contractors with decades of experience in the field. In my first years in the classroom, all my students were men. Every year after that brought an increasing number of women and students whose first language is not English. Some of my students now are in the industry, some are not, and they range in age from 18 to 50. My teaching challenge is to convey the basics of a complex subject and yet address the needs of a student body with diverse life and professional experiences.

Anyone who teaches introductory classes understands a fundamental truth: basics are not always simple. Often the concepts and ideas that seem most obvious are the ones that need to be the most thoroughly explained.

Equally challenging to the task of conveying complicated information is the critical choice of which textbook to assign. There are many excellent books on construction management. My frustration has been that many skip too lightly over the necessary basics or fail to address adequately the ways in which students absorb introductory information. Sometimes even superior textbooks gloss over the very concepts that deserve the most in-depth explanatory background information. For example, it is not difficult to find information on the various types of owner-contractor construction contracts – their characteristics, strengths, and weaknesses. It's more difficult to find basic details that can help explain the context: What, exactly, is a contract? Why is the type of contract important? How do different construction contracts shift risk on a job? What kind of potential problems might arise for a contractor (or an owner) in the absence of a contract or an enforceable contract? Why is it in the contractor's interest to have a contract in writing? Similarly, the subject of delivery systems presents persistent student confusion and warrants a detailed explanation not typically provided to students. The goal of *Construction Project Management: A Complete Introduction* is to deconstruct complex information such as this and present it in a highly accessible, readable, and understandable way.

Who is the reader?

This book is a suitable textbook for a baccalaureate or associate degree program. The anticipated readers are likely to have different backgrounds and interests: they are laborers, apprentices and licensed contractors, aspiring architects and engineers, owners and property managers. The book is directed at those unfamiliar with the construction industry as well as experienced professionals interested in broadening their understanding of development and management processes. Some will pick up the book as a way to make sense of the questions: How, exactly, do projects happen? And, importantly, where might I – a carpenter, specification writer, designer, or owner – fit into the picture?

Organization of the book

The coordination and management of the construction stage of a project is the responsibility of the general contractor, and this books looks primarily through the GC's lens. But the GC's work does not happen in a vacuum. Construction is a team effort and it is helpful, sometimes critical, that those involved, in any role, understand the context. Therefore this text takes a broad perspective by reviewing how projects get started; the roles of the owner and designer, as well as other players such as regulatory agencies, funders, and insurers; programming, design, and the role of building codes, zoning ordinances, and standards; how contractors find jobs and make assessments regarding risk; hiring and managing subcontractors; sustainable construction, estimating, and scheduling; and much more.

The book is organized into five parts, with chapters roughly following the natural sequence of project development. Although each chapter builds on those that come before (and not all activities fit neatly into a chronological order), the reader can use individual chapters as stand-alone descriptions of various aspects of project development and management.

Part 1: The Context introduces the reader to the players – who they are and their various roles in the construction process – and the various stages of construction, from development through occupancy. Sustainable, or green, construction is a reality for most designers, and Part 1 covers the history of this exciting new approach, what makes something "green," major industry standards, and how contractors can adapt.

Part 2: A Project Begins looks at the early stages of a project: how an owner makes the decision to develop a project, the potential problems, and how to balance risk with possibility. The reader is introduced to the concept of project delivery systems, the different ways that projects are organized and administered, and is provided with a look at programming and design.

Part 3: Bidding and the Contractor provides an overview of how contractors identify, assess, and get jobs. Readers are introduced to cost estimating: what estimates are, who creates them and when, their different types, and how they are used.

Part 4: The Contract Documents explores the basics of the legal agreement between the owner and the general contractor and between the general contractor and subcontractors. Although this text does not pretend to provide legal advice, Part 4 introduces the reader to the ingredients required to make a contract, the difference between a legal contract and an enforceable contract, how various construction contracts distribute risk between the parties, and what documents make up a construction contract.

Part 5: Construction focuses on the general contractor's many management activities, which start before the physical work begins and extend throughout construction and occupancy. This part describes the contractor's typical management activities before the physical work begins: clarification of project goals and objectives; putting a team together and assigning responsibilities; assessing ways to accomplish the work; determining time and money constraints and developing budgets and schedules; identifying potential problems and possible solutions; and clarifying the resources (money, labor, and equipment) that will be needed to complete the job.

The construction section reviews the coordination, management, and administrative tasks assumed by the contractor once construction begins: managing subcontractors; monitoring, evaluating and controlling time, costs, and quality of the work; administering changes; communication; payment and more. This part also looks at the contractor's role after the completion of construction; the close-out tasks and procedures for addressing problems, and the mechanisms for tracking warranty work.

To reinforce student-learning objectives, each chapter ends with a glossary of terms (which are also included in a complete glossary at the end of the book) and review questions. Explanatory notes or comments regarding additional important concepts are enclosed in boxes throughout the text.

PART 1

Context: The Industry, The Projects, The Players

- Chapter 1: The Construction Industry – Overview and Trends
- Chapter 2: Green Construction – A Builder's Opportunity
- Chapter 3: Construction Projects and Players
- Chapter 4: Project Stages – An Overview

Andrea Young

CHAPTER 1

The Construction Industry: Overview and Trends

Construction is big business. A typical year sees about $1 trillion in construction in the United States alone. Nearly seven million people work as carpenters, plumbers, electricians, painters, and the like. Several hundred thousand others – designers, engineers, manufacturers, suppliers – work indirectly in the industry and in the many fields and professions associated with construction. It's not hard to understand that when construction activity is strong, employment in many non-construction sectors also tends to be strong. This makes a lot of sense; when construction is booming, not only will those directly involved in completing buildings and other projects have work, but all the money pumped into the community supports other industries and businesses as well. The reverse is also true. When construction is slow, there is a weakening of sectors throughout the entire economy.

Construction sectors

Construction is diverse. The construction industry includes everything from small projects easily handled by a single worker to huge power plants or skyscrapers that require decades of planning and construction, and hundreds of people to complete. Some projects require extensive community and regulatory review, whereas others can be constructed by an owner without so much as a building permit.

Although the construction industry is complex and employs people across a wide spectrum of our economy, not all construction work is equally complex, requires the same skills, or has an equal impact on our economy. Construction is generally grouped into one of four broad sectors: *residential, commercial, industrial,* and *infrastructure.* These four sectors typically differ in several ways: complexity, size, and type of project; the technology and equipment required; and how the project is funded. As a result of these differences, many designers, contractors (or constructors as they are often called), manufacturers, and suppliers specialize in only one or perhaps two project types or sectors. Let's look briefly at what distinguishes each of the sectors.

Residential

The residential sector includes both new construction and renovation of single- and multi-family residential properties including single-family homes, small condominiums, and apartments.

Buildings in the residential sector are often wood frame and fairly low-tech; sophisticated and complex equipment or construction methodologies are not typically used. Residential projects include projects that are designed and built by the contractor but are more typically designed by architects with the support of engineers. Much of the residential sector is built by small general contracting and specialty trade contracting companies; there are well over 500,000 such companies in the United States. These small companies account for the majority of employment in the industry.

Most residential projects are privately funded, that is, they don't use government dollars and are financed by the owner or an institution such as a bank.

Commercial

Commercial buildings are typically more complicated than residential projects. This sector includes offices, large apartment complexes, theaters, schools, hospitals, and other such facilities. As with residential construction, commercial projects are usually designed by architects with engineers' support.

Often commercial projects use more sophisticated materials and systems than residential projects and therefore lend themselves to specialization by the team that designs them and the team that builds them. Hospitals and laboratories, with complicated and costly equipment and very specific design requirements, are good examples of this.

Most commercial projects are privately owned and privately funded, but this is not always the case. Public buildings – such as schools, municipal buildings, prisons, and libraries – also typically fall into this sector and they are publicly funded, which means that the government funds the project, using taxpayer money. That, in turn, means there are generally extra regulatory requirements that must be followed. For example, the criteria used for hiring contractors to work on public projects are highly regulated (including a requirement that contractors have certain qualifications and that they provide a fixed price for the work).

Industrial

Industrial projects include refineries, electrical stations, chemical processing plants, factories, and similar facilities. These projects are typically highly technical and specialized and are defined less by the aesthetics of the structure than by what goes on inside them. A significant amount of the construction process for industrial projects is devoted to equipment installation.

Industrial projects are often privately owned and financed and, due to their complexity, require close cooperation between the designers and builders. As a result of complicated equipment, systems, and specialized machinery, industrial projects are typically designed by engineers (not architects) and require specialized construction expertise and licensing.

Infrastructure (heavy or horizontal construction)

Construction isn't just about buildings. The category of construction referred to as infrastructure includes transportation and service projects such as roads, tunnels, bridges, ferries, and subways. Infrastructure is typically publicly owned and funded. These projects are designed by engineers and require specialized licensing of the contractors.

Trends

The construction industry is in a state of flux, due not only to economic instability, but also to long-term changes – in the workforce, in technology, in costs, in types of materials, and in technology. These long-term trends are the result of both internal and external forces and are affecting virtually all aspects of the industry. The challenge for the American construction industry and its workers is to understand the opportunities presented by these changes.

Let's look at several of the changes affecting the construction industry.

Photo by Kaye Richey

A changing workforce

Typically, about seven million people in the United States are directly employed in construction[1] as carpenters, electricians, plumbers, and so on. As we have discussed, several hundred thousand more are indirectly employed in construction-related fields such as manufacturing, lumber, transportation, and mining.

These figures don't describe the ongoing demographic changes in the industry. Although construction remains a white, male-dominated field, changes are taking place and increasing numbers of non-traditional workers, especially women and immigrants, are entering the field.

Estimates indicate that women account for approximately 10 percent of the construction industry, up from about 7 percent in the early 1980s. It appears that more women are finding their way to the management side of the business. In 1980, approximately 13 percent of all women in construction were in management or professional positions. In 2000, that number rose to 33 percent. Racial minorities also make up approximately 10 percent of the construction workforce, with 12 percent of those employed in management.

Worker demographics are changing in other ways too. Since the 1980s, fewer young people have been entering the industry. A lack of enthusiasm for construction has been due, in part, to the industry's reputation as dirty and dangerous. As a result, young people began going into other fields, leaving an understaffed and aging workforce in construction.

In addition, there has been a trend away from workers moving up in the ranks. Workers interested in advancing their careers must be proficient in reading, writing, and computer skills. Today's project superintendent or project manager is likely to have a degree in construction management or business, as well as years of field experience.

Unions–Trade and industrial unions arose in the nineteenth century primarily to lobby for an eight-hour workday and collective bargaining. From modest beginnings, unions evolved into an important and powerful voice for the worker, lobbying for better wages, health benefits, and safer working conditions. Despite hostility from government and business, unionism was a widely accepted force by the turn of the century and reached its largest membership in the mid-twentieth century.

For a variety of reasons, this strength has been seriously reduced in recent decades. The roots of the reduced influence of unions are complex and there are a variety of theories that attempt to explain it. Although organizations such as the Business Roundtable and others have successfully pushed to weaken worker-protection laws and reduce collective bargaining, and sponsored non-union projects, other causes include the fluctuating economy, impact of globalization, expansion of the workforce, reduced union access to the workplace, and changes in national politics. Importantly, the unions themselves contributed to their reduced impact through tolerance of corruption.

Today, union contractors no longer dominate construction in the United States. According to the U.S. Department of Labor, in 2006 only 12 percent of all employed wage and salary workers were unionized (down from 20.1 percent as recently as 1983). Of this total, union membership for construction was down to 13 percent.[2]

Changes in technology and materials

Technology is playing an ever-increasing role in construction projects of all sizes; even commonplace computer technology has revolutionized design and construction. Buildings are becoming "smart": computers can control access, lighting, and communication and make it possible to incorporate "green" components, including recycled products, into structures of all sizes. Technology has also made it possible to create buildings that, until recently, would have been impossible to design or construct. The massive curvilinear buildings by Frank Gehry, such as the Walt Disney Concert Hall shown here, for example, are defined by innovative forms and materials that did not exist or would not have been possible to utilize in the pre-computer world.

Figure 1.1. Walt Disney Concert Hall
Photo by Andrew Schulman

Technology has also revolutionized construction management: how designers and contractors plan and organize for construction, and then manage, track, and control the process. Computer technology has revolutionized the way various management tasks are conducted and have made it possible to design more complex projects that can be built more efficiently than in the past. For example, there are software programs for developing estimates and monitoring costs, preparing and updating schedules, standardizing information, tracking labor and other performance indicators, and communicating with those working to complete the job. When this software is "integrated", information entered once can automatically be used for multiple functions; changing a single number can immediately modify the drawings, schedule, and cost estimate, for example.

Today's construction personnel–especially the field superintendent and project manager who assume the primary roles in the construction process–can choose from many excellent software packages. Some popular programs include Microsoft Project,[3] Prolog Manager,[4] and Primavera.[5] These types of software packages can do complicated calculations for scheduling workers and equipment, track supplies and information, monitor costs, and maintain documentation for multiple purposes.

New technology enters the workplace almost daily and continually becomes more sophisticated. The industry now uses global positioning systems, robotics, and virtual-reality environments. Various types of building modeling software (building information modeling or BIM) create 3D models from which both graphic and non-graphic information can be extracted. Drawings can be produced quickly and accurately, and embedded data let designers and contractors analyze code and installation requirements (including the optimum sequence for installing building components), manufacturers' specifications, cost data, and scheduling information. When changes or adjustments are made, the model and the accompanying data change too.

The wide use of electronic technology in construction has made it mandatory for today's construction manager to be computer literate. The rapidly changing nature of systems and products in the industry also requires informed and sophisticated builders. The days are fast disappearing when the contractor was just a guy with a tool belt.

Finally, technology and environmental necessity have driven the development of thousands of new products and materials. This trend has been accelerated by rising energy prices and concerns over the impact of greenhouse gases. Buildings can be constructed from materials produced using less energy, less waste, and fewer harmful chemicals. Some of these new materials are futuristic: a concrete product that reportedly traps carbon dioxide, zero-carbon drywall, energy-harvesting glass, panels made from sorghum stalks, and paint that helps clean the air. Today's contractors are training to become familiar with this new generation of innovative and unfamiliar materials and products.

Costs are climbing

Over the last several years, prices for construction have risen substantially. This increase was fueled, in part, by a worldwide scarcity of certain building materials. Prices skyrocketed for copper, iron, steel products, sheet rock, and cement, among other materials. Although prices settled back down for certain materials, long-term trends are for continued price increases. If, as many expect, oil prices continue to climb in the future, the impact on construction costs, and therefore on the industry, will be extreme.

Several factors can lead to increases in the cost of materials and therefore in general project costs:

- When energy costs go up, the result is higher transportation costs, which are passed on to the consumer.
- 9/11 resulted in increased inspections and regulations that have had a ripple effect on project costs.
- Expansion of environmental and other regulations has also contributed to increased costs.
- Huge overseas demand (especially in China and India) absorbs materials and labor, causing shortages elsewhere.
- Reconstruction following natural disasters, including Hurricane Katrina, the tsunami of 2004, and the earthquakes in Haiti, has competed for labor and materials.

Globalization

Although the term globalization is somewhat vague, it implies a fluidity of skills and experience between countries. The historical model of the master builder, spending his entire professional life working on a few local projects that are owned locally, is over. Today's large project is apt to be a global effort that might be owned by a multinational conglomerate, for a site in New York City, designed in Holland, engineered in India, using steel fabricated in Japan, and built by a construction company owned by Germans.

Globalization is occurring within individual construction companies as well, as indicated by the recent surge in the consolidation and globalization of general contracting and subcontracting construction companies. Some of the largest U.S. firms have been bought by overseas companies; almost all compete with other huge firms from overseas for domestic projects here in the United States. The Turner Construction Company is one example of consolidation and globalization of the industry. From its beginnings in 1902 as a modest company in Maryland, Turner grew to become one of the largest and richest construction companies in the country. It was responsible for such buildings as Lincoln Center, Madison Square Garden, and the United Nations Secretariat in New York City. Over the years, Turner acquired other construction companies. With 44 U.S. offices and activities in 20 countries, Turner is involved annually with hundreds of projects around the globe, generating construction volume over $10 billion per year. Turner Construction Company is now owned by a German construction conglomerate, Hochtief AG.

Globalization has an impact on U.S. companies of all sizes. Even small local firms are finding it harder to retain customers who may now be able to hire construction services elsewhere for less.

Although the majority of construction companies remain small, the biggest ones can work on highly complex projects and shift workers wherever the "hot spots" are, both domestically and abroad. The presence of these huge firms, competing for projects worldwide, exerts pressure on the entire industry.

Transition to green building

One of the most exciting trends in the construction industry is the social, economic and environmental movement for **green building** (also called **sustainable construction**). The increasing use of new technologies and demand for contractors who are experienced in their use presents significant implications and opportunities for the industry.

Figure 1.2 Santa Rosa Junior College Doyle Library
Courtesy of SRJC School District

What is a "green building"? There are several evolving sets of standards. In general, the term refers to projects that minimize the use of resources and eliminate the negative impacts on the natural and human environment. Green includes putting solar heating panels on a roof or installing geothermal heating and cooling systems, using recycled materials, capturing rainwater for irrigation, and choosing products that maximize long-term energy savings.

In January 2007, Santa Rosa Junior College, in Santa Rosa, California, completed a 145,000-square-foot library that is an example of how one public building integrated green principles and components.

- Solar panels on the roof are expected to generate enough electricity to save the college between $20,000 and $30,000 per year in energy costs.
- The air conditioning system makes 350 tons of ice at night (when energy costs are lowest), then circulates water through the ice during the day to chill it before sending the water through the building to reduce AC costs.
- The computer monitors used generate less heat than standard monitors.
- Tiles, carpeting, and fabrics are made of recycled materials.
- Lights turn off automatically when users leave the room.
- Windows and skylights were placed to maximize the use of natural sunlight

As demand for green construction grows, so will demand for contractors who are well informed about and specially trained and experienced in various aspects of sustainable construction. The skills required by contractors will expand. We'll discuss green building in more detail in the next chapter.

---

1 See www.census.gov/construction-spending

2 News, Thursday, January 25, 2007,U.S. Dept. of Labor, Bureau of Labor Statistics

3 www.microsoft.com/project

4 www.meridiansystems.com/products/prolog

5 www.primavera.com

Chapter Vocabulary

Commercial sector – a sector of the construction industry that includes offices, large apartment complexes, theaters, schools, hospitals, and other such facilities. As with residential construction, commercial projects are usually designed by architects with engineers' support.

Green building (**sustainable construction**) – projects that seek to minimize or eliminate negative impacts on the natural and human environment.

Industrial sector – a sector of the construction industry that includes refineries, electrical stations, chemical processing plants, factories, and similar facilities. Industrial projects are typically highly technical and specialized.

Infrastructure – a sector of the construction industry that includes transportation and service projects such as roads, tunnels, bridges, ferries, and subways. Infrastructure is typically publicly owned and funded. These projects are designed by engineers and require specialized licensing of the contractors.

Residential sector – a sector of the construction industry that includes both new construction and renovation of single- and multi-family residential properties such as houses, condominiums, and apartments. Buildings are often wood frame and fairly low-tech.

Sustainable construction (**green building**) – projects that seek to minimize or eliminate negative impacts on the natural and human environment.

Union – an organization of workers who have joined together to achieve common goals such as better working conditions and higher wages.

Test Yourself

1. You have a small construction company and do simple, low-tech buildings. In which of the four sectors of the industry is it likely that you work?
2. Why might it be that some projects in the commercial sector lend themselves to specialized designers and contractors?
3. Why are many projects in the industrial sector designed by engineers?
4. How are demographics changing the construction industry?
5. What sort of educational background do today's project managers often have?
6. Identify two ways that computer technology has impacted the construction industry.
7. What is the impact of development in China on construction in the United States?
8. How is globalization of the construction industry affecting smaller U.S. construction companies?
9. What is meant by a green building?
10. Why is the green building movement good for contractors?

Andrea Young

CHAPTER 2

Green Construction: A Builder's Opportunity

The world is at the beginning of an unprecedented global movement to reduce energy use and to make adjustments in how we think about and design our built environment. This is producing major changes in the construction industry and, with those changes, major opportunities.

Recent confirmation by the scientific community regarding the catastrophic impact of global warming (brought on, in part, by our use of energy), the increased dependence on Middle East – supplied fossil fuels, and an expanded awareness of environmental health has resulted in various worldwide responses. In the United States, one way we are responding is by making changes in the way we plan, design, and construct our buildings and our communities, including a growing emphasis on energy conservation and alternative sources of power (such as solar, wind, and geothermal). An increasingly sophisticated environmental movement has also contributed to a deepening appreciation and understanding of the relationship between buildings and the health of human beings and our environment.

Only recently have we begun to understand the degree to which our buildings are sinkholes: they gobble up resources during construction and occupancy; they produce waste when they're built and when they're demolished; and they are often built in places that destroy critical natural habitats. Sometimes they are plain unhealthy (ever walked into a newly carpeted space and smelled the chemical off-gassing?). We haven't always been smart about our developments, but we're beginning to understand what makes our buildings unsuccessful and how to make them better. This is what green building is all about.

In this chapter, we'll review what green building is and how contractors can position themselves to take advantage of the new opportunity green building presents. This chapter will:

1. Provide an overview of what it means for a building to be "green."
2. Describe why green building is important.
3. Build a case for why green building skills are important for contractors.
4. Describe how contractors can educate themselves about the field.

Andrea Young

What's all the fuss about, what does green mean?

There is no single accepted definition of what it means to be "green." As we learned in Chapter 1, at its simplest we can say that a **green** or **sustainable building** is one that seeks to minimize or eliminate negative impacts on the natural and human environment. A house that gets its power from photovoltaic solar panels on its roof might be called green. A green building can also be a 500,000-square-foot skyscraper that has a high-performance geothermal heating system, uses materials and products with high recycled content, recycles water for landscaping, and meets green certification criteria.

Early definitions of green focused on individual components or systems: a house that used some kind of alternative heating system was considered green; switching to longer-life light bulbs was called green; an office building that specified Low-E windows called itself green. Though it's true that these measures are all on the right track – indeed, they *are* green – we are finding that such isolated actions are too narrow. Many designers and builders working in the field have broadened their approach. Instead of indicating a specific component – a building's heating system, or the type of windows specified, or how many water-conserving toilets are used – being green now implies a more complex approach requiring an analysis of the entire structure and its context.

In this expanded approach, designers analyze the links between each component and each stage of a building's life cycle – design, construction, use, operation and maintenance, and final decommissioning. They also take into account the economic, social, and cultural impacts of design choices. An example of this is the complicated impacts of using a rare wood, harvested through clear-cutting, from a rain forest in South America. A few of the questions that might now be raised when considering such a product include the following: What are the social and cultural costs to the communities whose forests are destroyed? What will be the impact on global warming if the land is deforested? What are the economic costs involved in transporting the wood to the building site? How would using this product affect human health?

Greenwashing is a term most often used to refer to the practice of misrepresenting or "spinning" the environmental benefits of a product (or structure). Sometimes the misrepresentation is based on unsubstantiated facts ("Buy this green widget – it's biodegradable!") and sometimes the green claim is based on a single green attribute ("Our widget is green – we use biodegradable packaging"). Owners, designers, and contractors should be on alert for exaggerated claims.

This broader perspective was new for most of us, but in the past decade, it has become more common. Now there is a growing sensitivity to the fact that the choices we make with respect to the design and construction of our buildings – construction methodologies, equipment, systems and material choices, and where we choose to locate them – trigger chains of events and impacts that can have real and profound effects on the well-being of people and the planet. Building green is now marked by a comprehensive approach that explores long-term costs, building functions, occupant productivity, and the health, environmental, and social impacts of design and construction approaches.

High performance is a term that is increasingly used, as it is more understandable and familiar to the business world than "green" or "sustainable building." Some use these three terms interchangeably, but high performance tends to focus on energy systems. Buildings, products, or systems can all be high performance, even if they are not certifiably "green."

Choosing green

There are many green systems and approaches that designers are incorporating into their design work. Although not a comprehensive list, some of the approaches that define green are cited in the following sections.

Systems

- Proper orientation of the structure to take advantage of passive solar heating in winter and to minimize unwanted solar gain in other seasons
- Improved glazing and insulation to control heat gain or loss
- Use of high-efficiency mechanical and plumbing equipment
- Use of renewable energy systems such as solar, wind, and others
- Efficient lighting
- High-performance, energy-saving appliances
- Water conservation measures
- Use of recycled and durable materials
- Use of materials that can be recycled after a building's useful life

Site considerations

- Access to public transportation and alternative systems (such as bike paths)
- Increased open space
- Restoration or conservation of natural habitats

Indoor quality

- Access to natural ventilation
- The use of non-toxic materials
- Maximization of light and views

Economic and social impact costs

- Life-cycle costs from production to operation and maintenance
- Costs of transporting products to the construction site and disposing of construction wastes
- Impact of decommissioning a building at the end of its useful life
- Impact on communities where products are harvested or manufactured
- Ability of a product to be rapidly renewed (e.g., bamboo, which can be harvested in only a few years)

It has been said that a truly sustainable building, one that embraces the broader definition of green, is subtle and often hard to detect. Jerry Yudelson, who writes often about sustainability, has an elegant way of describing the feel of a building that is truly well designed. Such a structure "feels right on the site rather than obtrusive; there is abundant daylighting; nature is both within and outside; as a design element, water flows naturally from the building into ... a natural drainage feature; the building is comfortable without a huge rush of moving air; internal spaces create expansiveness and delight; and the overall effect is beautiful."[1]

A short history

The green building revolution is, in many ways, an outgrowth of the environmental movement that was kicked off by the 1963 publication of Rachel Carson's *Silent Spring*. This groundbreaking book exposed the hazards of the pesticide DDT, and created a new public awareness that nature was vulnerable to human intervention. Carson's proposal, very radical for the time, was that sometimes technological progress is so fundamentally at odds with natural processes that it must be curtailed. In post World War II America, few people cared much about conservation or worried about the disappearance of wilderness. But the chemical threats that Carson outlined in her book, including the contamination of the food chain, cancer, genetic damage, and the deaths of entire species, horrified the public and, for the first time, large numbers of people began to understand and think about the relationship between human actions and the environment.

Carson's book was one of the triggers that started an environmental movement that became, in just a few years, mainstream. This process was accelerated by the success of the first U.S. Earth Day in 1970. This event (which is still celebrated around the world every April) helped solidify public concern and forced environmentalism onto the political agenda. At the same time, the Arab oil embargo against the West that began in 1973 shifted thinking: natural resources and energy no longer seemed "free." Suddenly, energy use and production became powerful issues.

As concern mounted over both the dwindling sources of fossil fuels and the increased dependence of the United States on oil controlled by unfriendly nations, concern also grew throughout the 1980s and '90s regarding the human contribution toward global warming. This period also saw the creation of influential organizations and initiatives on national and worldwide energy use and, in 1993, the formation of the best-known group in green building, the U.S. Green Building Council (USGBC). A key player in the evolution of a sustainable future, the USGBC has proven to be perhaps *the* key player in the "greening" of America. Here's why.

Standards

It would be very cumbersome to have to specify all the qualities and provisions for every product and system incorporated into a project. Not only would the specifications be huge, but there would also inevitably be enough variation between how specification writers described products that manufacturers would have to custom fabricate everything. Standards are a way to avoid this problem.

Various agencies and organizations, nonprofits, and manufacturers have established product and material standards that provide descriptive uniformity. Several commonly referenced non-governmental agencies that provide standards or information regarding standards are ASTM International (formerly-American Society for Testing and Materials), UL (Underwriters Laboratory), and ANSI (American National Standards Institute). How would one use these standards? ASTM steel standards, for example, classify and evaluate various types of and uses for steel. If the specification writer wants to specify a welded wire mesh fence, he can specify a particular ASTM designation and be confident that the correct product will be supplied.

A standard may be required. An example of a required standard is a building code. A standard may also be voluntary. An example of that is the LEED standards for sustainable buildings. Here we look at the LEED standards in some detail.

USGBC and the development of LEED

The USGBC is a nonprofit group made up of other nonprofits, businesses, universities, government agencies, and individuals. In less than 20 years, USGBC gained enormous credibility and, by early 2010, had more than 18,000 member organizations and companies.[2]

The USGBC's goal is, within a generation, to make green buildings and communities accessible to everyone.[3] The centerpiece of its approach was the development of the Leadership in Energy and Environmental Design (LEED) program in 1994. **LEED** is a rating system that provides a way to measure and give clarity to the definition of what makes a building green. USGBC hoped that this system, the first of its kind, would help to promote a more comprehensive and understandable way of looking at sustainability.

LEED is a voluntary standard for rating and certifying all types of buildings that focuses on five key areas of human and environmental health:

1. Sustainable site development
2. Water efficiency
3. Energy and atmosphere
4. Materials and resources
5. Indoor environmental quality

How a project meets the performance goals of LEED is left to the designers. Certification is based on attaining a minimum number of points, and a project may be certified under four progressive levels: LEED Certified, LEED Silver, LEED Gold, or LEED Platinum (the highest rating). Projects are typically registered before detailed design begins and are certified upon completion.

Figure 2.1. Bank of America Tower
Cook + Fox Architects

LEED has become the premier rating system for green buildings in the United States, and its impact has been spectacular. Within 10 years of its introduction, nearly 3.2 *billion* square feet of commercial building space had been registered or certified under the LEED Green Building Rating System.[4] All over the world, people have been jumping on the LEED bandwagon and a new attitude has emerged: it's cool to go green. More than this, there is a growing appreciation that LEED buildings also make economic sense. A study by the CoStar Group found that green buildings have higher occupancy rates and command higher sales and rental prices than their non-green peers,[5] because there is now an appreciation of the tremendous benefits that result from implementing a green approach. Green buildings use fewer resources, reduce gas emissions that contribute to global warming, are healthier for the occupants and increase worker productivity, reduce waste, and are better for the social, cultural, and natural environments.

Because of the many benefits resulting from using a LEED-type approach and the current sense of urgency regarding energy use, state and local governments across the country are adopting LEED for both publicly funded and privately owned buildings; some have woven green standards into their building codes. There are LEED initiatives in federal agencies, including the Departments of Defense, Agriculture, Energy, and State; there are LEED-certified skyscrapers like New York's Bank of America Tower[6] (Fig. 2.1) and LEED-certified private homes, LEED offices, and LEED municipal and state buildings throughout the nation. There isn't a state that doesn't have a LEED building. And it's not just in the United States–LEED is represented in 69 countries.[7]

Other energy standards

Although LEED is the most important standard, it is not the only one. Some standards (such as LEED and Energy Star) rate the performance of buildings[8]; others only rate products such as boilers, dishwashers, plastic pipe, and so on; and some standards rate both products and buildings. Energy Star (developed as a joint program of the U.S. Environmental Protection Agency and the U.S. Department of Energy) is one such example. The blue Energy Star seal, familiar to many people, means that a product or building meets strict energy efficiency standards such that it performs in the top 25 percent of its category. Consumers can find the Energy Star label on air conditioners, hot water tanks, and washing machines. For homes, the Energy Star rating means that the house uses 20 percent less energy than comparable new homes. Since the program's inception in 1995, more than one million homes have received the Energy Star designation.

Some individual products carry their own rating. Wood products that are made from lumber harvested in a sustainable way, for example, may be certified by one of several groups, including the Forest Stewardship Council (FSC), the Sustainable Forestry Initiative (SFI), and the Canadian Standards Association (CSA).

The Green Home Building Guidelines (developed by the National Association of Home Builders whose members build more than 80 percent of new homes in this country) is another common system designed to rate homes. The guidelines were developed in collaboration with the International Code Council and form the basis of certification programs run by local home builder associations across the country. The guidelines are part of the National Green Building Program.[9]

Some of these standards have met with criticism. Critics of LEED, for example, fault it for not adequately differentiating local conditions. Points given for water conservation are the same in Phoenix as they are in Portland, Maine, for example, even though local conditions and need for water conservation vary. In part to address this weakness and in part to provide a more simplified approach to certification, local standards have been developed in several states. California, for example, has a program called California Green Builder, which was developed by the building industry; another called GreenPoint is administered by the Build It Green organization. LEED version 3, introduced in 2009, addresses this very issue of regionalization.[10]

Who's going green?–projects around the country

We've been talking about non-regulatory green standards that provide guidelines for designers and builders, not regulatory requirements. In most jurisdictions, a building isn't required to meet LEED standards. In other words, an owner can decide whether to adopt green standards. A code, however, is a regulatory *requirement* that must be met. Examples are the strength of the concrete used in a foundation, when glass must be tempered, or how many exits a room must have. The increasing presence and use of green standards is providing an impetus for the incorporation of green standards into building codes.

As one example, in January 2010, California's Building Standards Commission adopted the first statewide green building code, CALGREEN, covering all new building construction in the state. Set to go into effect in January 2011, the code is designed to help the state meet stringent energy and water reduction goals, including 20 percent reduction in water consumption in all new buildings and the diversion of 50 percent of construction waste from landfills to recycling. It also mandates the assessment of energy systems (such as furnaces and air conditioning) for all buildings over 10,000 square feet to ensure that they are working at their maximum efficiency.[11] CALGREEN will be incorporated into existing state building codes and inspection infrastructure, making verification by local inspectors as simple as possible.

Another important example is the International Code Council's 2009 release of the International Green Construction Code.[12]

In addition, hundreds of municipalities and communities are embarking on a broad variety of innovative programs for residential and commercial projects, such as the following:

- Chicago has been a model for creatively addressing the need to reduce energy usage. Projects include the retrofit of over 15 million square feet of its municipal buildings to make them more energy efficient and the installation of 4 million square feet of rooftop gardens (including on City Hall) that act to cool the roofs down so that summer air conditioning loads are greatly reduced. In 2008, Mayor Richard Daley announced the Chicago Climate Action Plan, a comprehensive strategy using many energy-saving approaches for lowering greenhouse gases.[13]
- In January 2007, New York Mayor Michael Bloomberg signed the Green City Buildings Act, which requires that new or renovated municipal buildings meet strict energy standards. It is anticipated that this act will affect approximately $12 billion in construction during New York City's 10-year capital plan.[14]
- Seattle Mayor Greg Nickels spearheaded a national effort to organize America's cities to cut carbon dioxide pollution. By 2009, the resulting U.S. Mayors' Climate Protection Agreement had over 930 signatories, representing more than 83 million Americans.[15]
- The Solar for Schools Program was launched in Austin, Texas, in

2006 as a way to promote solar energy use and educate children about the benefits. Part of this effort is to retrofit schools across the city.

- Numerous cities have developed landfill methane recovery programs. Passaic, New Jersey; Portland, Oregon; Kansas City, Missouri; and New York City are among the cities that have installed energy-efficient LED traffic lights and have realized significant cost savings.[16]
- The State of California passed legislation permitting cities and counties to create financing districts for energy improvement projects. As a result, Sonoma County, as one example, launched the Energy Independence Program in March 2009. This program allows property owners to borrow money at 7 percent interest for energy-efficient improvements and pay it back in installments on their property tax bills. In its first year, the program approved nearly 900 applications for projects worth over $19 million.[17]
- The U.S. Department of Energy has issued a voluntary challenge to builders, called the Builders Challenge, to build 220,000 high-performance homes by 2012 to spur demand for green homes. DOE's vision is that, by 2030, a consumer will be able to buy an affordable net zero energy home – a home that annually produces as much energy as it consumes.[18]

Green building and the contractor

A zero energy building (also called a net zero energy building) is one that provides all of its own energy on an annual basis from onsite renewable resources or offsite renewable energy purchases. In this way, it can still be connected to the existing energy grid, providing power to the grid when it has excess and drawing from the grid when it needs power. In practice (and depending on the microclimate) net zero energy is not too difficult for small structures to achieve; the use of solar energy for heating, passive solar design, natural ventilation, and proper orientation on a site are all typical components.

The green building industry is young and growing. This means there are both enormous challenges as well as opportunities for contractors. As new technologies and systems are developed and implemented in our building projects, it will become critical for the construction industry to adapt.

The need for contractors who understand the principles of green building will be magnified when we consider what is about to happen to the *volume* of construction in the United States. As we saw in Chapter 1, the increase in population, coupled with an aging and mobile population, is going to require more housing and commercial buildings. It has been predicted that over the next 25 years, the United States can expect a $25 *trillion* construction binge to meet the anticipated need.[19] Current patterns indicate that a significant amount of this will be green and contractors will need to be prepared with new skills. Some of these new skills and opportunities will include:

- Understanding how to specify, install, and maintain new types of high-performance energy systems
- Understanding the use of new, high-tech materials
- Expanded estimating and scheduling skills
- Providing owners with **constructability reviews** of sustainable buildings (a process by which the contractor reviews a building design during pre-construction to determine if it is practical to construct with the means, methods, and products available at the proposed time of construction, within the owner's budget)
- Willingness and ability to adapt to new construction methodologies, including, for example, the reduction of environmental impacts caused by the construction process. This might include such things as reducing soil compaction during construction, the recycling of construction waste, and the use of durable, salvaged, recycled, and recyclable building materials.
- Ability to provide owners and designers with effective reviews and cost estimates for new types of products and systems
- Broader and more comprehensive understanding of the health issues that construction and buildings present for workers and occupants
- Understanding of the use of local, low-tech, indigenous materials and methods to avoid the high energy consumption and costs associated with transportation
- Skill to provide **commissioning** services, a practice involving a formal review of all parts of a building's systems to ensure that the project meets (and will continue to meet) certain energy objectives. (LEED-certified buildings already require commissioning.)

There are also contradictions implied by the use of green systems and products about which contractors should be aware. An example is the value of using salvaged materials to reduce waste and avoid the environmental impact of producing new materials versus the improved energy efficiency of some new products. Beautiful but single-glazed turn-of-the-century French doors may look terrific and satisfy an urge to re-use but they are also likely to be extremely energy-inefficient.

Getting ready

According to McGraw-Hill Construction and the National Association of Home Builders (NAHB), a significant percent of buyers would like a green home yet have trouble finding one. Part of this limitation is due to the hesitation of residential builders who may be unfamiliar with green building. Builders have lacked expertise or interest in a field that seemed at first to be only a fad. As the field has matured and it has become clear that green building is here to stay, more contractors have become interested in improving their skills and there has been a growth in educational opportunities.

Several independent groups–NAHB, the National Association of the Remodeling Industry, and the U.S. Dept. of Housing and Urban Development among them–offer building guidelines, education and certification programs, and interactive educational software to help contractors. Companies such as General Electric and utilities such as Pacific Gas & Electric provide short- and long-term programs to teach builders the techniques for green construction.

Certification programs are offered through several organizations, including the Green Building Certification Institute that administers the LEED Accredited Professional program. The LEED-AP certification is national, as is the LEED Green Associate (LEED-GA) certification, which many find easier to achieve than LEED-AP. In 2008, NAHB launched the NAHB National Green Building Program, an education, verification, and certification program.

There are other local and state programs, such as the California Home Energy Efficient Rating Services (CHEERS) and GreenPoint, also in California. In addition, community colleges, private organizations, and public agencies around the country provide educational programs and classes. There are also several informative journals and magazines as well as excellent conferences and expositions such as the annual Solar Power Conference & Exposition that can provide individuals with information and guidance about getting into the field.

The unions go green

Though unions are nonexistent in residential construction and are weakened in commercial construction in many cities, unions around the country are playing constructive roles in advocating for the creation of green jobs. In July 2008, Teamsters' General President Jim Hoffa, for example, announced the unions withdrawal from the Arctic National Wildlife Refuge Coalition, a group advocating drilling, citing the need to build a green economy that fosters the development of alternative energy sources and creates good union jobs. Roger Toussaint, president of Transport Workers Local 100 in New York is another official who has identified the need for union involvement in the green economy. He states:

> "We have to rise to the challenge of climate change by making it a key priority for our unions. A trade union agenda, rooted in the organized strength of workers and day-to-day engagement in affected communities, can help transition our society to a low-carbon future ... I firmly believe all leaders of America's working people must take immediate steps to familiarize themselves and their organizations with the issues involved and figure out the obligations of their appropriate job sectors. Nationally, the union movement must take the lead in shaping policy and legislation needed in this area. We need meaningful engagement and decisive action. We are on borrowed time, but the chance to make our mark on the process is there for the taking."[20]

In 2008, the United Steelworkers (USW) and the Sierra Club formed the Blue Green Alliance to focus on the goal of creating renewable energy sources and hundreds of thousands of green jobs. The USW has also joined Al Gore's We Campaign to participate in town hall meetings to discuss strategies for developing new green jobs. Another example is a photovoltaic (PV) apprenticeship provided by the International Brotherhood of Electrical Workers (IBEW) and the National Electrical Contractors Association (NECA).

There is union activity at local levels as well. One example is in Oakland, California, where the electrical union, as part of the local Oakland Apollo Alliance, helped raise $250,000 from the city government to create a union-supported training program for green jobs.

Hiring a green contractor

As with conventional construction, an owner contemplating a green project will expect that a potential contractor will have the necessary knowledge to do the job. What sort of special concerns might such an owner have when interviewing contractors for a potential job? Some possibilities are:

Experience

What is the contractor's experience with green building? Can the contractor point to specific projects in his or her portfolio and provide references? Does the contractor understand green products–their benefits and drawbacks, their initial and life cycle costs, their installation and operation? Can the contractor suggest local examples of high-quality green buildings that the owner might visit? Does the contractor understand the contradictions sometimes present in green building and have an approach to dealing with these contradictions?

The contractor's level of interest in the subject

What kind of specialized education or training in green building does the contractor have? Does the contractor's office have books, periodicals, and product information on green products and buildings? Does the contractor have any specialized certifications such as LEED-AP or LEED-GA? Is the contractor a member of any organizations that are involved in green building such as the U.S. Green Building Council?

Does the contractor practice what he preaches?

How is the contractor's business operated? Are there green elements in the contractor's office? Examples of this might be energy-saving light fixtures or employee bicycle racks out front. Not long ago, the author interviewed a contractor for work on a green building and he arrived in a Hummer. The author considered this a pretty good indicator that his heart wasn't really in it; he didn't get the job.

---

1 Jerry Yudelson, *Green Building A to Z*, Gabriola Island, BC: New Society Publishers, 2007.

2 US Green Building Council, Washington DC, 2010.

3 Ibid.

4 "LEED for Homes FAQ for Homebuilders," Sept. 2008, *www.usgbc.org/ShowFile aspxDocument ID=3910*. It has since risen to over 5.5 billion square feet registered or certified under LEED.

5 Andrew C. Barr, "CoStar Study Finds LEED, EnergyStar Buildings Outperform Peers," *www.costar.com/News*, March 26, 2008.

6 Cook+Fox Architects, New York, NY

7 USGBC, 2008.

8 See *www.energystar.gov*.

9 See *www.nahbgreen.org*.

10 See LEED Version 3, *www.usgbc.org/DisplayPage.aspx?CMSPageID=1970.*
11 Office of the Governor, "Governor Schwarzenegger Announces First-in-the-Nation Statewide Green Building Standards Code," press release, Jan. 12, 2010.
12 See ICC, *www.iccsafe.org/cs/igcc/Pages/default.aspx.*
13 City of Chicago. Department of Environment. Chicago Climate Action Plan, 2008.
14 Business Bulletins, Construction Weblinks, January 15, 2007,
15 Office of the Mayor, Office of Sustainability & Environment, Dept. of Planning & Development Summary Report, Seattle Green Building Initiative, April 22, 2009.
16 "Cool Ca$h: How Local Governments are Using Smart Energy Solutions to Save Taxpayer Dollars and Curb Global Warming," Sierra Club, Coolcities, http://virginia.sierraclub.org/greatfalls/docs/Cool_Cash_Factsheet.pdf
17 Bleys Rose, "Sonoma County energy loan program gets state money–and restrictions," *Press Democrat*, March 7, 2010.
18 US Department of Energy, Building Technologies Program.
19 Barry B. Le Patner, *Broken Buildings, Busted Budgets*, Chicago: University of Chicago Press, 2007.
20 *http://blog.aflcio.org/2008/02/23/green-the-color-of-good-jobs*

Chapter Vocabulary

Commissioning – a practice that involves a formal review of all parts of a building's systems to ensure that the project meets (and will continue to meet) certain energy objectives.

Constructability review – review of materials, systems, and installation methodologies by experienced contractors to ensure that a project can be built efficiently.

Green building (sustainable construction) – projects that seek to minimize or eliminate negative impacts on the natural and human environment.

Greenwashing – misrepresenting the environmental benefits of a product or structure.

High performance – a term sometimes used interchangeably with "green" or "sustainable" but which tends to focus on energy systems.

LEED (Leadership in Energy and Environmental Design) – a voluntary rating system developed by the U.S. Green Building Council that provides a way to measure and give clarity to the definition of what makes a building green.

Standards – formal regulatory requirements (such as a building code) or a voluntary rating system (such as LEED).

Sustainable construction (green building) – projects that seek to minimize or eliminate negative impacts on the natural and human environment.

U.S. Green Building Council (USGBC) – the developers of the LEED rating system, a 501(c)(3) nonprofit community of leaders working to make green buildings available to everyone within a generation.

Zero net energy building – building that provides all of its own energy on an annual basis from onsite renewable resources or offsite renewable energy purchases.

Test Yourself

1. What does the term green building mean?
2. How has the definition of green building expanded?
3. Why is it useful for LEED to incorporate regionalization?
4. What has been the major contribution of the US Green Building Council?
5. What are the different certification levels for LEED buildings?
6. How did Americans adjust their thinking regarding resources and energy after the 1973 Arab oil embargo?
7. What has been the impact of LEED?
8. Identify three things an owner interested in hiring a green contractor might be interested in knowing about the contractor.
9. You are a builder and are interested in learning about green building. Identify a program near where you live that could offer you training; briefly describe the program.
10. A candidate who speaks out strongly for "green" legislation lives in a 30,000-square-foot home, which has photovoltaic cells and uses recycled water for landscaping. Do you see a problem here?

Andrea Young

CHAPTER 3

Construction Projects and Players

As we saw in Chapter 1, construction is diverse and involves everything from power stations to houses. *All* construction, however, from the simplest to most complex, has in common creating a product that is distinct, and requires some level of management or direction.

Construction management – the process of coordinating, monitoring, evaluating, and controlling a construction project – is what this text is about. But before we can define and discuss what we mean by this, we need to have an understanding of what it is that needs to be managed. In other words, what is a **project** and *why does it require management?*

What is a project?

The construction of a new college library is considered a *project*, but running the construction company that built it is not. When a homeowner adds a bathroom to her house, she's working on a *project*; building shelves in the garage is a *project*. It is not only in construction that projects are found: the software company that designs a new piece of software is involved with a *project*; the dentist who creates a crown for your tooth has taken on a *project*; the development of a new car is one of GM's *projects*.

What do all of these examples have in common? What makes them projects? We can begin to answer this question by looking at how these undertakings are similar, as all projects, in any field of endeavor, share certain characteristics:

- Projects have a *defined goal or objective*; they represent something specific that needs to be accomplished. (This is an outcome called a deliverable.) For example, constructing a new house, renovating a bathroom, and installing an irrigation system are all project goals.
- Projects represent a *specific task*, which is not routinely done. A house will only be built once (so it is a project), but running the construction company that built it is an ongoing task (so it is not a project). Projects are typically made up of a series of smaller, targeted tasks or activities that are also projects. For example, roofing the house and painting the interior are both small projects with specific goals and time frames within the larger project of building the entire house.
- Projects take a certain amount of time to complete, have a specific *beginning* and *end*, and have their own *schedule*. A project begins with planning, continues through design and construction (or production), and is finally completed. Projects can be accomplished quickly or can continue for years. In the case of a complex project, such as a power station, the design, approvals, and construction can last for decades.
- Projects *use resources* such as labor, money, and/or equipment. The cost of these resources can be measured and tracked in dollars (and/or labor hours) on a budget.

In construction, there is typically a general contractor hired by the owner to coordinate and be responsible for the physical work required to complete a project (a house, an office building, a new bathroom). As we'll learn, the work required to complete a project is usually divided into smaller segments of work such as the excavation, the roofing, and the electrical system. These portions of the whole project are themselves projects. The overall project requires management by the general contractor to make sure that everyone's work is coordinated and properly completed. Typically, subcontractors manage the smaller project segments. All contractors will be concerned with controlling costs, construction time, and project quality. The extent of management activities and the management tools used vary depending on whether one is the general contractor or a subcontractor and on the size and complexity of the project.

Who are the players?

Today's projects are developed and built by individuals, agencies, organizations, and companies that, in most cases, come together for a specific project and move on at its completion. The fact that this group of people typically changes from project to project is a defining feature of construction. On large projects there may be hundreds of individuals involved in planning, designing, approving, and constructing a building or facility. Some of these people, such as the architect and the bankers, for example, may be involved from the very beginning of a project; others, such as building inspectors and the fire department, aren't involved until the project is under construction; and still others, such as real estate agents, may play a role only at or just before completion.

Generally, the individuals and agencies involved in projects can be grouped into three primary groups or teams, each with distinct responsibilities and obligations:

- The *owner's team*, which establishes the project goals, determines the budget and finances the cost, identifies key dates, provides the site, and selects the other major players.
- The *designer's team*, which provides planning and design services, and administers the construction contract between the owner and the contractor.
- The *contractor's team*, which coordinates and is responsible for the physical work as well as the performance of subcontractors and product suppliers.

Although the roles of the owner, the designer, and the contractor have been established over time and are fairly standard on every project, contractual relationships and owner preferences can result in adjustments and shifts in roles.

Let's look briefly at each of these three teams.

The owner's team

The **owner** comes up with the project concept or idea, establishes the time and budget constraints, provides the site, figures out how to pay for the project, and hires many of the people who will help make it happen. Owners may be private individuals, organizations, corporations, or businesses, or they may be public agencies such as school districts, transportation departments, and the like.

Most commonly, the owner has separate contracts with the designer and with a general contractor. Owners may or may not have other people or companies working with them. On small private jobs such as a renovation project or a simple house, the owner may work alone, directly with the contractor. On larger projects the owner will have the assistance of a team, typically made up of both employees and consultants, and including:

- A project manager/business manager who is responsible for coordinating and managing the owner's interests.
- Someone who is verifying that the contractor is performing. This may be the designer, a construction manager, or (on public jobs) a clerk of the works. This person typically administers the construction contract between the owner and the contractor and verifies payment requests.
- Attorneys to assist in putting legal documents together.
- Accountants to track money dispersals and issue checks.
- Insurance agents to provide coverage advice and policies.
- Financiers to help fund the work. (Construction projects are expensive and owners need funds for many things: funds to secure the building site, pay designers and contractors, and deal with unexpected situations and conditions. Private owners rarely have the money to fund these costs themselves and must therefore obtain loans. The individuals or agencies financing a project are typically important (and sometimes active) members of the team.)

The owner's team might also include other parties such as the eventual users of the facility (end users), real estate agents, and marketing personnel.

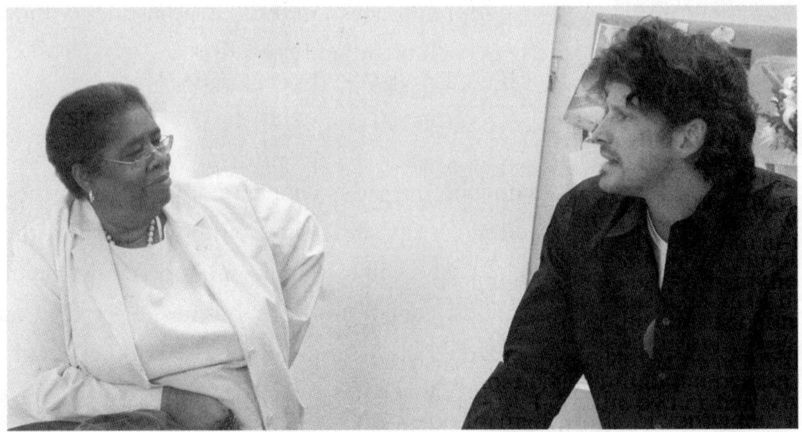

Andrea Young

Public vs. private owners – There are two basic types of owners: public owners and private owners. They are distinguished primarily by the type of financing used on a project.

Public owners include all public entities such as local, state, and federal governments, as well as some educational institutions, public hospitals, and other institutions. Publicly owned projects are paid for with public funds (typically, bonds or general tax revenues). A new library built at a community college is an example of a project owned and built by the public and paid for with public funds. A new highway through town, the replacement of old sewer and water lines, and the construction of a local park are other examples.

Because public projects are paid for with taxpayer money, they have layers of oversight that private projects typically do not. One primary example of this is that most public jobs must be *publicly bid* (lots of contractors can compete to get the job) and the qualified contractor who promises to complete the work for the best price generally gets to do the work. Public jobs may also have to meet regulatory requirements such as environmental standards.

Private owners have more latitude than public owners; there are fewer regulations governing what they can do. This is because they are paying for the project themselves (typically through short-term construction loans) and do not use public dollars. Private owners have no rules regarding how they hire contractors and they are free to hire pretty much whomever they choose. Funding for privately owned projects is by the owners themselves or through lending institutions such as banks. Private owners include ordinary citizens, organizations, agencies, institutions, companies, and businesses.

The designer's team

Designers provide planning, design, and construction administration services to the project. The designer is sometimes referred to as the **A/E**, an acknowledgment that both architects and engineers can be the primary designer on a project. Architects typically design buildings; engineers design infrastructure and complex commercial and industrial projects such as roads and power plants. Both are licensed professionals whose accreditation is typically administered through the state. In this text, we will assume that the designer is an architect.

The designer (sometimes an individual but more often a company) is hired by and responsible to the owner. The job of the designer is not just that of sitting at a drafting table (or a computer monitor) and drawing. Architects (and engineers) have the training to help create solutions that meet an owner's goals within the framework of budget, schedule, and regulatory requirements such as building codes. (We'll discuss the construction drawings developed by the architect in Chapter 7.) The architect can provide the owner with a range of services, including assistance in getting the project bid and hiring a contractor, and is typically the owner's representative during construction. As the administrator of the owner's contract (the legal agreement) with the general contractor, the architect approves payment requests by the contractor and monitors the contractor's performance. The designer reviews submittals (such as product information) and substitution requests, and works with the contractor to answer questions that may come up regarding the contract drawings and the specifications.

Like the owner's team, the designer's team varies, depending on the complexity of the project and the size and organization of the designer's company. Sometimes the architectural firm is small and one person serves several roles; other firms are large and have many in-house personnel. On large projects, members of the designer's team typically include:

- A principal-in-charge who assumes overall responsibility for the project and may be called on to make major decisions or when there are problems.
- A project architect who takes primary responsibility for generating a design that meets the owner's vision and budget and for developing the documents that the contractor uses to bid and then build the project. This person is the primary contact with the owner.
- A project manager (PM) who is responsible for ensuring that the work progresses adequately. The PM visits the site regularly and works with the contractor to resolve any questions that arise.
- A job captain who is responsible for organizing the drawings and coordinating with the engineers and other consultants.

The designer's team includes consultants (hired by the architect) to assist in the completion of planning and design. These consultants typically include:

- Engineers (such as structural, civil, and mechanical) to provide the design, drawings, and written specifications for specific technical aspects of the project.
- Estimators to develop cost projections at various points in the design process.
- Specification writers to assist in the development of the material and workmanship requirements for the project.
- Suppliers and product representatives to assist in the selection of specific products, materials, and systems.

The contractor's team

Contractors (also called **constructors** or **builders**) are individuals or firms who agree to construct a project in accordance with contract documents (the drawings and other documents that make up the contractor's legal agreement with the owner).

Of the three primary players, the contractor assumes the greatest responsibility. In addition to ensuring that all the physical work (no matter who performs it) meets the requirements of the contract, the contractor is responsible for managing and controlling cost and schedule requirements, administering payment and contract modification procedures, securing necessary permits, coordinating testing and inspections, and much more.

Contractors may be hired to perform a range of services including: a preconstruction constructability review, (as we learned in the last chapter, this is a process by which the contractor reviews a building design during pre-construction to determine if it is practical to construct with the means, methods, and products available at the proposed time of construction, within the owner's budget), cost estimating, scheduling, comprehensive management, as well as the physical work. Construction services are either bid or negotiated with the owner.

On most (but not all) projects, the owner has a contract with a single contractor who assumes responsibility for all the work. This is typically a general contractor, (also called a GC). On most jobs the general contractor doesn't actually *do* all the work himself.

Historically, the contractor hired subcontractors (**subs**) for specialized work on a project; the general contractor did the vast majority of the work with his own crews. On small projects, this is still the case. The general contractor – typically working with one or two others – may do all the work himself: pour the foundation, frame and finish the walls, even do the plumbing and electrical work. (When contractors use their own crews, it is called self-performing.) But this has become the exception; on most projects, general contractors hire specialty (trade) contractors to do a large part of the work. Specialty contractors are experts in specific areas of construction: electrical, plumbing, concrete, framing, and so on. Because the work of specialty contractors is more narrowly focused than that of the general contractor, they are typically very efficient and, for this and other reasons, it is not unusual for the majority of a job to be done with subcontracted crews. Sometimes the general contractor subcontracts *all* the work and acts only as project coordinator.

Some projects have multiple layers of subcontractors. A specialty contractor who is hired by the general contractor is referred to as a first-tier subcontractor. On many projects (especially large ones), **first-tier subcontractors** are allowed to hire subcontractors to perform part of *their* work. These are **second-tier subcontractors** (sometimes called sub-subcontractors).

Here's an example of how this works: Superior Construction Company has been hired to do the construction of a retail project near town. Superior hires ABC Mechanical Contractors to complete all the mechanical and plumbing work on the project. ABC is a first-tier subcontractor to Superior. This is a complex project and ABC doesn't have sufficiently skilled crews to install the fire sprinkler system, although this is part of their contractual obligation. What do they do? They hire their own specialty contractor – Fire Systems Installation (FSI). FSI's contract is with ABC, not with Superior; they take direction from ABC and are paid by ABC – they are a second-tier subcontractor. It is the general contractor, Superior Construction, however, that is ultimately responsible to the owner for the work of FSI.

Licensing of general and specialty contractors – To protect public health, safety, and welfare, most states have enacted laws that specify licensing requirements for various professions, occupations, and businesses. Construction is one of these. Requirements regarding *who* needs to be licensed, *when* a license is required, and *how* one gets licensed vary greatly from state to state. In many states, candidates for a contractor's license are required to take a written examination and meet certain standards of experience and age. Sometimes contractors are required to be bonded for the benefit of consumers who may be damaged as a result of defective construction or other license law violations, and for the benefit of employees who have not been paid wages that are due them. Contractors are required to have the appropriate license in the jurisdiction where they intend to work; failure to be properly licensed can result in financial or disciplinary action.

Typically, the type and dollar value of a project are what determine whether a contractor needs to be licensed. Commercial projects usually have different requirements than residential projects, for example. In some states, any project that costs more than a few hundred dollars will require a licensed contractor; in other states, the threshold value of work is many thousands.

Most states differentiate between general building contractors and specialty contractors, but, not surprisingly, this too is variable between jurisdictions. A few states have many different specialty license categories. (California is an extreme example with three classifications for general contractors and over 40 specialty classifications including everything from ironworkers and plumbers to glazers and awning installers.) Other states require licenses in only a few categories; the most common classifications are electrical, mechanical, and plumbing.

Those contemplating doing construction work should educate themselves regarding local and state licensing requirements.

As with the owner and the designer, the general contractor's (GC) team for a project varies depending on the size and complexity of the project and the size and organization of the contractor's firm. Small jobs may require few individuals. Larger jobs require a greater number of individuals; some are in the contractor's employ, others are hired for the duration of a specific project.

In addition to subcontractors, the general contractor's team, typically led by an executive of the construction company, includes the following:

- A **project manager** (PM) is responsible for the business end of a project and for ensuring that the team is in compliance with all of the contract requirements. The PM assembles the team, works with the superintendent to determine work sequence and scheduling milestones, submits monthly progress payments, and is typically the person who evaluates, negotiates, and awards subcontracts and purchase orders. The project manager interacts frequently with the owner and the designer. Today's PMs are often highly educated, with advanced degrees in construction management or business, and typically work out of the contractor's home office.
- A **superintendent** is at the jobsite ("in the field") and is responsible for coordinating all the production work and the daily activities, whether conducted by the general contractor or by subcontractors. As a key person on the team, the superintendent is responsible for coordinating and managing the work, monitoring progress, and instituting management strategies for ensuring that work progresses as intended. The superintendent works closely with subcontractors and is typically the safety officer on the job.
- A **foreman** is responsible for direct supervision of the contractor's workers. Foremen lay out the work, verify that the correct tools and equipment are at the site, ensure that work conforms to contract requirements, and prepare daily time sheets. Each subcontractor has a foreman for his portion of the work.
- Assistants such as **field engineers** or project engineers or assistant superintendents are responsible for documents and making sure that information gets communicated. They prepare field questions, maintain submittal and tracking logs, and review invoices and other documents.

To summarize: The owner typically has separate contracts with the designer and the general contractor. Each hires various consultants to assist with their portion of the work; the architect hires consulting engineers such as civil, structural, electrical, and mechanical engineers, and the contractor hires specialty contractors. The general contractor (or other contractors) hires and pays the subcontractors and is responsible to the owner for their work. Figure 3.1 is a graphic depiction of these relationships.

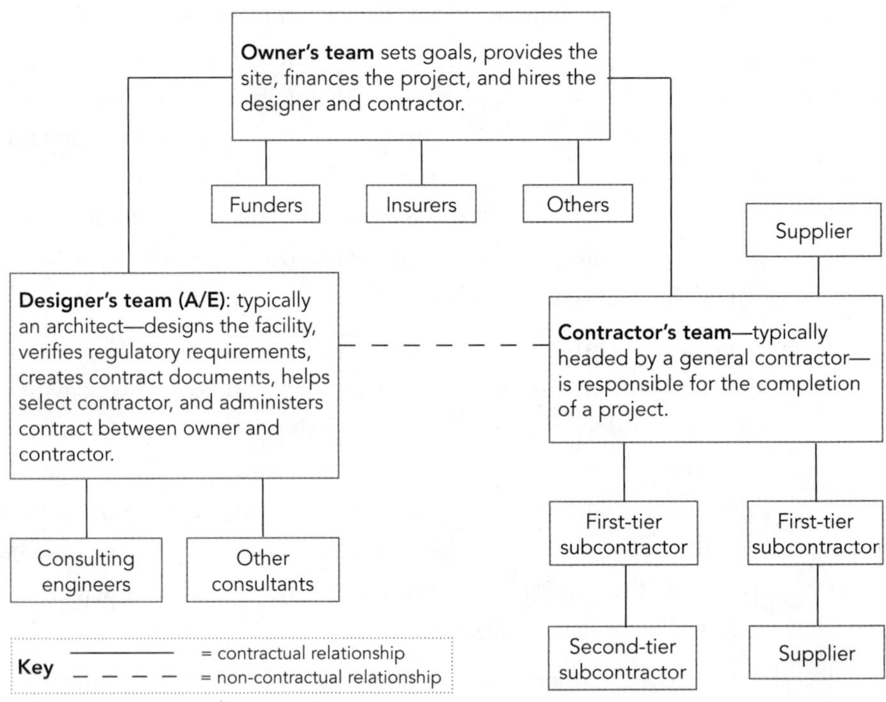

Figure 3.1. Players

Prime contractors – Contractors who have contracts with owners are called **prime contractors** ("prime" means first rank). Contractors who are hired by and have contracts with other contractors are called **subcontractors** ("sub" means "under"). We tend to refer to specialty contractors as subcontractors, but if they have a contract with the owner, they too are considered prime contractors.

Other important players

These are not the only important players. There are at least three other groups that interact with owner, architects, and contractors and play key roles at various stages of a project.

Authorities having jurisdiction

Every project exists within a regulatory environment particular to its location. Building, zoning, and environmental regulations are typical (although not the only) examples and vary substantially from state to state and within local jurisdictions. Various agencies, called **authorities having jurisdiction** (AHJs), have responsibility for ensuring that projects comply with these health, safety, and public welfare regulations. Multiple jurisdictions often have authority. For example, an urban project might be governed by the city building department, the county health department, and the state fire marshal.

The authorities having jurisdiction review documents, issue permits, and inspect the work for compliance. Each AHJ that has authority over a project must certify that requirements have been met before the structure can be used. Local building departments that issue building permits and sign off on the completed project are typically the primary AHJ for private projects; they typically issue the final certificate of occupancy, which allows use of the structure. A local public works department might be the AHJ for a local road.

Manufacturers/fabricators/product representatives and suppliers

The individuals and companies that make up the product manufacturing and supply segment of the industry play important roles during design as well as construction. Product representatives provide information and assistance to owners and designers to help them make good product selection decisions that meet project goals and budget constraints. The suppliers and distributors, who furnish products (but typically not labor) to contractors and subcontractors, are sources for up-to-date cost data and, once construction is under way, can provide a range of services to the contractor. These services might include technical assistance as well as installation advice and inspections, and operational and maintenance training to the owner's facility manager. Submittals such as shop drawings and product data sheets are often provided by fabricators.

Testing and inspecting agencies

Before the AHJ (or multiple AHJs) can sign off on a project and certify it for occupancy, all the regulatory agencies require verification that the project and its components are in full compliance. In addition to testing required by law (such as steel bolt connections or welds), the contract documents may specify additional tests or inspections (such as a wind test), and the contractor may require still others as part of his quality control measures.

Testing is typically done by independent testing agencies and may be based on calculations or analysis, or on tests conducted during manufacturing (such as steel strength tests) or in the field (such as slump tests to measure concrete design mix). Agencies such ASTM International (formerly known as the American Society for Testing and Materials) may certify performance criteria for specified products or materials (e.g., flame spread criteria).

Commissioning agents

Many projects include commissioning agents, who are hired by the owner to verify that specific systems, or the whole project, meet design intentions. Commissioning agents ensure that specific systems have been installed properly and are working as designed. They often review operations and maintenance information for the owner and may review drawings and other documents. When total project commissioning is part of the project, the agent is on board throughout construction. Projects that are seeking LEED certification are required to have total project commissioning.

Chapter Vocabulary

Authority having jurisdiction (AHJ) – an agency with designated authority to provide compliance inspections and approval for a project. Local building departments are often the AHJ.

Commissioning – a practice that involves a formal review of all parts of a building's systems to ensure that the project meets (and will continue to meet) certain energy objectives.

Constructability review – review of materials, systems, and installation methodologies by experienced contractors to ensure that a project can be built efficiently.

Construction management – the process of coordinating, monitoring, evaluating, and controlling a construction project; also a project delivery method; not to be confused with the specific delivery method known as Construction Management.

Contractors (constructors or builders) – individuals or firms that agree to construct something in accordance with contract documents.

Designer – licensed professionals (architects or engineers-A/E) who provide planning, design, and construction administration services for a project. Architects are typically the designers of buildings; engineers typically design infrastructure and complex commercial and industrial projects.

Estimator – one who calculates the probable cost of something.

First-tier subcontractor – a specialty contractor hired by a general contractor to perform specialty work on a project. First-tier subcontractors may hire their own specialty contractors (second-tier subcontractors).

Foreman – the person responsible for direct supervision of a contractor's workers.

General contractor (GC) – an individual or firm hired by and responsible to an owner for coordinating the completion of a construction project. The GC hires subcontractors and suppliers.

Owner – an individual, organization, corporation, business(es), or public agency that comes up with a project concept or idea, establishes the time and budget constraints, provides the site, figures out how to pay for the project, and hires many of the people who will help make it happen.

Prime contractor – a contractor who has a direct contract with an owner.

Private owner – an individual, organization, corporation, or business(es) that pays for a project (typically, through short-term construction loans) without using public dollars.

Project – a unique activity that has a beginning and an end, uses resources, is not routinely done, and requires managing.

Project manager – the member of a construction team who is responsible for the business end of a project, in contrast to the superintendent who is responsible for production.

Public owner – a public entity such as a local, state, or federal government, or a certain institution, whose project is paid for with public funds.

Schedule – a timetable, typically shown in graphic form, that describes the order in which project activities will happen, details how long each activity will take, and tracks the progress of the work.

Second-tier subcontractor – a contractor hired by a subcontractor to perform specialty work on a project. Second-tier subcontractors may hire their own specialty contractors (third-tier subcontractors).

Specialty contractor (trade contractor) – a contractor who performs specialized activities.

Subcontractor (sub) – a person who has a contract with another contractor. In construction, subcontractors are specialty trade contractors.

Superintendent – the person responsible for the production of the project.

Supplier (vendor) – a company that manufactures, distributes, or supplies products and services to a contractor.

Test Yourself

1. Give three reasons why building a library is considered a project but running the company that did the construction is not.
2. What are the general responsibilities of the owner's team?
3. What are the general responsibilities of the designer's team?
4. What are the general responsibilities of the contractor's team?
5. In what major way does funding differ on public and private projects?
6. What is the difference between a prime contractor and a subcontractor?
7. An electrician is required on a project. Who would hire this specialty contractor?
8. Who is the person on the contractor's team responsible for the business end of the project?
9. Who is the person on the contractor's team responsible for production?
10. Who is ultimately responsible to the owner if a subcontractor does unacceptable work?

Andrea Young

CHAPTER 4

Project Stages: An Overview

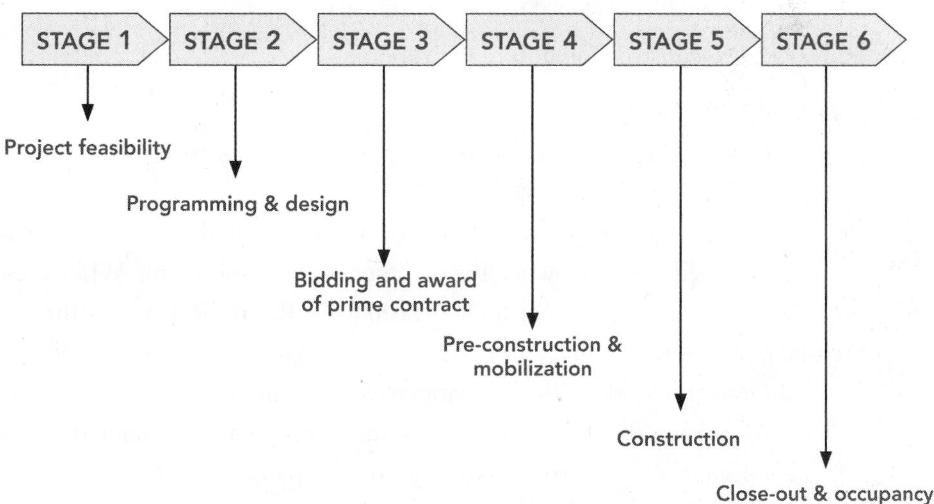

In Chapter 1, we learned that there are four broad categories of construction projects: residential, commercial, industrial, and infrastructure. Although the projects represented by these four sectors can be quite different (a single family house bears little resemblance to a power station), the process of construction for most projects is systematic and predictable. First there has to be an idea, the idea needs to be examined and analyzed, a specific design is created in response to that examination and analysis, a contractor is hired to do the work, and the work proceeds in a logical order to completion, at which time the building is occupied or used. This process of moving from an idea to use is called a project's **chronology** or stages.

On most (but not all) projects, these stages are sequential – they happen one after the other and they take various lengths of time depending on the complexity of the project. Although the concept of construction activities occurring in distinct stages is useful, it is also a bit misleading, as several occur within more than one stage. Estimating, for example, is done in the feasibility stage by the owner and again during design as part of the designer's role; a detailed estimate is developed by the contractor during the bidding phase, and again at the start of construction. Scheduling is another example of an activity that happens throughout a project. For clarity, we have assumed that activities occur in a single stage. With the understanding that there are overlaps, the six primary stages can be identified as follows:

1. Project feasibility
2. Programming and design
3. Bidding and award of prime contract
4. Pre-construction and mobilization
5. Construction
6. Close-out and occupancy

We know from Chapter 3 that the three principal players on most construction projects are the owner, the designer, and the contractor. While these players work together in a coordinated fashion as the project moves through different stages, the primary responsibility shifts between them. Let's look briefly at these stages to identify what happens at each and which of the primary players – the owner, the architect, or the contractor – has the major responsibility at each stage. As you progress through the chapters for each stage, you will note a graphic that identifies the activities linked to that stage.

Project feasibility | 2 | 3 | 4 | 5 | 6

Stage 1: Project feasibility

- **Goal of the project feasibility stage**: to assess the risk, and potential of a project so that the owner can decide whether to move ahead with the project.
- **Primary responsible party**: the owner
- **Outcomes**: project and site analyses and reports; identification of major project goals, initial budget, and schedule requirements; financing commitments; selection of a project delivery approach
- **Chapter in text:** 5

People sometimes think that the process of putting up a building starts and ends with the physical construction. This is hardly the case! Before a shovelful of dirt is dug or a single nail driven, much work has already been done. Not only that, but often this work happens before the contractor is even hired.

The earliest part of the process of developing a project is to define *why* the project is being developed and to clarify the project goals and objectives. What is the owner's vision? What is to be accomplished? Is there a need for the project and is it affordable? Who is going to be involved? Where will the facility be located? The owner answers these and other questions during the feasibility stage. For a simple and straightforward job (say an addition to a house), a feasibility analysis can happen quickly; for complex or controversial projects, it can take months or even years.

Let's look at an example of what is involved during the feasibility stage of a moderate-size project. A major housing developer is thinking about building a large new housing subdivision in his town. Before committing substantial funds toward such a project, he looks at and analyzes several issues: the economic condition of the community, who lives there (its demographics), whether there are sufficient jobs so that people can afford the new housing, the existing supply of competing homes, local construction costs, and land prices. He prepares an estimate projecting costs, identifies funding sources, and develops a rough timeline for the project, including important dates (milestones). Such information helps determine whether the idea is economically sound and has the potential to produce a satisfactory profit for the **developer**. (A developer is a private owner who coordinates the tasks required to create a project.)

At the conclusion of the feasibility phase, the owner has important information regarding the potential risks and possible rewards of proceeding with the proposed project. Outcomes from this stage include a project analysis sufficient to lead the owner to proceed as planned, abandon the project idea, or adjust his or her vision.

A final, important outcome of the feasibility stage is the owner's determination, based on project goals and needs, of a project delivery system: how the project design and construction will be organized. Project delivery determines at what point the designer and the contractor will be hired and several other important issues.

Stage 2: Programming and design

- **Goal of programming and design:** to define specific project requirements
- **Primary responsible party:** the owner typically takes the lead during programming and the architect is responsible during design.
- **Outcomes:** the identification of project requirements; updated estimates and schedules; the documents to be used by contractors to price and build the project
- **Chapter in text:** 7

In the first part of this stage – **programming** – the project goals are identified and recorded in a document called a **program**, which gives direction to the designer. The owner is usually the primary responsible party during programming, although an architect or others may be hired to assist.

During programming, project goals are defined and the owner clarifies specifics about the project such as space sizes and uses and aesthetic preferences. The result provides the architect with sufficient information so that design work can begin. The programming stage can happen rapidly or, for a complex project, may take years to develop.

A program can be very simple. For example, the program for a new house might, in part, read: "A 2,000 SF single-story wood-frame ranch house with two bedrooms and two bathrooms that is as energy efficient as possible and maximizes light and natural ventilation; a carport should be located within easy access to the kitchen; kitchen and dining areas should have direct access to a deck." A program for a large and complex structure can be extremely extensive, very detailed, and take years to develop. In Chapter 7, there's an example of a program for a library, which will give the reader a more complete understanding of what a program is.

During the design stage, the designer (let's say it's an architect, as it typically is) moves to center stage and assumes primary responsibility. The architect (who is hired by the owner) engages consultants such as structural, mechanical, or civil engineers and is responsible for coordinating their work. **Design** takes the project from an idea to the point where an accurate estimate for construction costs can be made, and a contractor can be hired by the owner to complete the work. During this stage, the architect translates the objectives outlined in the program into a form that meets the owner's goals, follows applicable safety and code requirements, and is sufficiently detailed so that the project can be priced and built. At the conclusion of this stage, there is a complete set of construction documents: drawings (plans), specifications, and other documents required to price (and build) a project.

Stage 3: Bidding and award of prime contract

- **Goal of the bidding and award stage:** selection of a contractor
- **Primary responsible party:** the designer
- **Outcomes:** bid package; bid submittals by contractors; award of the construction contract
- **Chapter in text:** 8

The architect is typically responsible for coordinating the process of selecting a contractor for the job. The bid documents completed during the previous stage are presented as a package to contractors interested in competing (bidding) for the opportunity to do the work. The **bidding period** itself – when various contractors are putting prices together – typically lasts several weeks and operates under strict procedural guidelines.

Bidding—On most jobs, contractors are hired through a process called competitive bidding wherein several contractors compete to get a job. Based on bid documents developed by the designer's team, interested contractors provide the owner with a price quote for doing the job. Usually, the contractor who promises to do the work for the best price gets the job.

At the completion of the bidding process, the owner and the architect analyze the contractor's quotes (bids) and select a winning contractor (often, but not always, the lowest bidder), and the owner and the contractor enter into a construction contract. The process of identifying and hiring the contractor is called awarding the job, or procurement. (This term is also used to identify the award of subcontracts and the purchase of materials.)

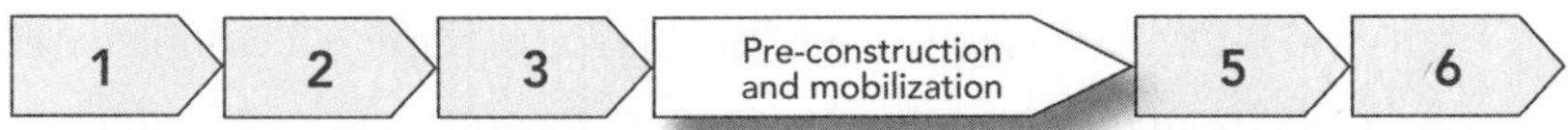

Stage 4: Pre-construction and mobilization

- **Goal of pre-construction and mobilization:** to organize for construction; move onto the worksite
- **Primary responsible party:** the contractor
- **Outcomes:** the plan for how the contractor intends to complete the job; jobsite layout plan; move onto the jobsite
- **Chapter in text:** 17

Once the winning contractor has been selected, he moves to the forefront and assumes responsibility for all the tasks required to get the facility built. Often there is a delay between signing a contract and the actual start of construction. But the contractor is hardly idle as he or she must organize a construction team, finalize a schedule for the work, determine which subcontractors will be involved, determine a strategy of administering and managing the project, and secure permits. All of these tasks are important **pre-construction** activities. (This period is also referred to as the project *start-up*.)

Another important pre-construction activity is the contractor's plan for how the site will be laid out: Where will the office be located? How will trucks and pedestrians access the site? Where will power and water be located? Where will trucks be parked and materials stored? These questions, and more, are answered on a jobsite layout plan.

The contractor doesn't take physical possession of the jobsite – move trailers and equipment onto the site or begin construction – until he or she gets the go-ahead from the owner. The owner sends the contractor a document called a notice to proceed, which not only alerts the contractor that mobilization can begin, but also marks the beginning of contract time (how long the contractor has to complete the work). The reason for this delay is that if something should go wrong and the project doesn't move ahead, the contractor might not get paid for the expenses incurred in moving onto the site. (What might prevent an owner from going ahead? Failure to get financing is a common cause; failure to get certain permits is another.)

Once notification is received from the owner, **mobilization** onto the jobsite can begin: the office is set up (typically, a mobile trailer that can be easily moved onto the site), temporary water and power are brought to the site, tools and equipment are collected, and construction begins.

Stage 5: Construction

- **Goal of construction:** to complete the physical work safely and on time, on budget, and according to the quality requirements of the contract
- **Primary responsible party:** the contractor
- **Outcomes:** completion of the physical work; substantial completion
- **Chapter in text:** 18

The physical work of construction can proceed as soon as mobilization occurs and all required permits are in hand. (Permits are approvals from authorities having jurisdiction over the project, which typically include the local building department.)

As is true with all the members of the team, including the owner and the architect, the general contractor (who we will refer to simply as "the contractor") has specific rights and responsibilities during construction. Contractor obligations have been determined by tradition, but they are also spelled out in the legal documents that are part of the contract with the owner.

The contractor has many responsibilities during construction, but in broad terms, he is responsible for determining *how* to complete the work (called the means, methods, and techniques of construction) and for coordinating all the work, whether completed by his crews or by subcontractors. During pre-construction, the contractor has figured out how to proceed: who will do the work, how the work will proceed, and how it will be directed and coordinated.

On most projects, the owner and the contractor have agreed to a specific time frame or schedule for completion of the work. As noted, the amount of time the contractor has for construction is called contract time, and often there are financial consequences if the contractor fails to complete construction on time. Similarly, the contractor is under an obligation to complete the work on budget or pay for cost overruns. Managing costs is a high priority.

Organizational and management activities that occur during the construction phase are described in various chapters throughout this text.

Stage 6: Close-out and occupancy

- **Goal of close-out and occupancy:** complete all the requirements of the construction contract; owner move-in
- **Primary responsible party:** the contractor
- **Outcomes:** completion of contract terms and final payment to contractor; building occupancy
- **Chapter in text:** 25

The fulfillment of all the terms of the construction contract and turnover to the owner is called **close-out**. This phase is marked by three primary stages: construction close-out, which marks the end of the physical work; contract close-out, which marks the completion of all contract requirements and final payment to the contractor; and contractor's close-out, which includes post-job evaluation by the contractor's team. The contractor has primary responsibility for all stages.

The conclusion of the physical work is marked by the issuance of a certificate of substantial completion by the architect, which basically says the work is done. As we'll see later in the text, this is an important document with many implications: the owner assumes responsibility for the structure, the warranty period begins, the contractor is no longer at risk for liquidated damages, and more.

One thing that this certificate does not do, however, is provide legal cover for the owner to move in. That must wait for a sign-off from the authority having jurisdiction that issued the building permit. The certificate of occupancy certifies the work is in compliance with regulatory requirements, and the owner may move in. This event marks the start of the owner's ongoing maintenance program. But the contractor isn't off the hook just yet.

The completion of the contract – the contract close-out – means the contractor has completed all the requirements in addition to the physical work. This might include submitting certain additional drawings, providing spare parts and operations manuals, and possibly training the owner's facility manager.

Once construction is complete, the owner wants some assurance that the building was built as intended. The owner won't know immediately if all is well on a project; it takes some period of building occupancy and use before problems might appear. Typically, contractors have a one-year correction period during which they are required to correct deficiencies and complete any work not previously noted. Warranties are also required from subcontractors and product manufacturers. Extended warranties may also be required for certain equipment and products.

The correction period may or may not be stipulated in the contract; in most states, there is a statutory requirement for this period. Manufacturers of products that are incorporated into the building (such as a pump, carpeting, roofing tiles, and so on) provide their own warranties. The method for completing warranty work is typically identified in the contract between the owner and the contractor.

During this stage of a project, the owner assumes full responsibility for the use and maintenance of the facility.

The final piece of close-out involves the important task of evaluating how it all went. The construction team will want to know how they performed: Was the budget accurate? Any problems with the schedule? How could they have done better and what are the lessons for next time?

Chapter Vocabulary

Authority having jurisdiction (AHJ) – an agency with designated authority to provide compliance inspections and approval for a project. Local building departments are often the AHJ.

Bidding – a process in which several contractors compete to get a job.

Bidding period – the period of time during which contractors develop bids.

Chronology (or stages) – the process of moving a project from an idea to use.

Close-out – the process of completing the terms of a contract. In construction, close-out includes completion of the physical work (construction close-out), completion of fulfilling the terms of a contract (contract close-out), and final evaluation by the contractor (contractor close-out).

Construction – the execution of physical work as outlined by contract documents.

Design – the process of developing a project plan that meets an owner's vision within budget, site, regulatory requirements, and other constraints.

Developer – a private owner who coordinates the tasks required to create a project.

Feasibility – the process of assessing the desirability, cost, and potential of a project so that a decision can be made regarding whether to move ahead.

Mobilization – the process of moving personnel, equipment, and materials onto a jobsite so that the physical work can begin. Mobilization typically follows the owner issuing to the contractor a notice to proceed.

Pre-construction – the period between award of the construction contract and the start of construction and marked by intense planning by the contractor.

Program – document that provides design objectives & requirements as guidance to a project's designer.

Programming – the process of identifying specific project goals and objectives.

Test Yourself

1. Identify three questions an owner might ask and seek to answer during the feasibility stage of a new housing development project.
2. What purpose does programming serve? What are the general responsibilities of the designer's team?
3. In which stage(s) does the owner have the primary responsibility?
4. During which stage does the contractor assemble his team? What is the difference between a prime contractor and a subcontractor?
5. What is a bid? What is the purpose of bidding?
6. Give two activities that happen during mobilization.
7. In which stage(s) does the contractor have the primary responsibility?
8. Why doesn't the contractor begin work until the owner gives him the go-ahead?
9. Who is responsible for the means, methods, and techniques of construction?
10. What is the purpose of a warranty period?

PART 2

A Project Begins

- Chapter 5: Owner's Feasibility: Does This Project Make Sense?
- Chapter 6: Project Delivery
- Chapter 7: Programming and Design

Andrea Young

CHAPTER 5

The Owner's Feasibility: Does this Project Make Sense?

- **Goal of the project feasibility stage:** to assess the risk and potential of a project so that the owner can make a go/no-go decision
- **Primary responsible party:** the owner
- **Outcomes:** project and site analyses and reports; identification of major project goals; budget and schedule requirements; financing commitments; selection of a project delivery approach

We all have examples in our lives of mistakes that happened because we jumped into something without thinking it through. In construction, the stakes can be very high indeed and an owner who plows ahead with a project without understanding if the objectives are reasonable may find him or herself in serious trouble. Similarly, contractors who take on a job without understanding its implications may wish they hadn't! (In Chapter 9, we'll see how important it is for a contractor to use care in selecting projects, and turn some down.)

In this chapter, we'll take a look at the efforts an owner might make before committing to move ahead with a project. Like contractors, some owners would do well to abandon a potential project. The work done at the earliest stage of a project to determine the viability of moving ahead is called **feasibility**. (This phase is also called the **conceptual phase**.)

Feasibility is the process of finding out whether a project is likely to be successful (as defined by the owner). During feasibility, the potential problems and possibilities of a project are analyzed so that a sound decision can be made regarding how (or even whether) to proceed. (This is referred to as making a go/no-go decision.) The end result of this stage is that the owner will decide to do one of the following:

- Move ahead with the project
- Make adjustments in the scope, schedule, and/or budget
- Abandon the idea

Although the owner is responsible for project feasibility, on many projects he or she hires consultants, including, perhaps, architects, contractors, estimators, marketing personnel, and others. Feasibility begins with a rough idea and, usually, a tentative budget, and provides the owner with answers to important questions: Is the idea a good one? Is there a need for the project? Can the expected occupants afford the building? Can construction happen in a timely manner? Is the anticipated budget sufficient? Will the project be profitable?

Careful work by the owner during feasibility can prevent terrible mistakes that can occur because of incomplete information. For example, imagine the financial disaster that might befall a developer who puts up an expensive office building without investigating whether there is a market for the space at the rents he will need to charge. Or consider this: you are a homeowner and you have bought a piece of land on which to build your dream house. Unhappily, you failed to fully investigate and discovered, too late, that local regulations won't let you build on the property because it is not only mostly a wetland and therefore undevelopable, but it also isn't zoned for residential use.

There are six broad issues that an owner might review during the feasibility phase. The complexity of the project determines the extent to which they are analyzed. The six issues are:

1. Needs assessment
2. Site selection

3. Financial feasibility
4. Schedule feasibility
5. Regulatory requirements
6. Community values

Let's look at each of these in more detail.

Needs assessment

This portion of the process defines the project goals: What is the owner trying to do? The answer might be fairly simple. As a homeowner, you might be assessing a relatively narrow problem, such as whether the needs of your family would best be served by turning the garage into a family room. Larger or more complex projects, such as those built on **speculation** (for an unknown buyer or user), may require a much more extensive needs analysis. In the case of the latter, the owner would want answers to the following questions:

- What are the needs of the local market and are those needs currently being met? If there is no need for the project, then the project may remain unsold or unrented.
- Who are the potential users? The developer will be able to create a more appropriate product if there is clarity regarding this question. If an apartment building consists of nothing but 700 square-foot one-bedroom units and likely buyers are young families with children, the project is likely to fail.
- What services or amenities will be required? What would be required to make the project competitive in the marketplace? For example, an office building in an upscale market may require facilities such as a fitness center or especially large conference spaces.
- Do the numbers work? In other words, when all is said and done, is there money to be made and is the budget appropriate?

Site selection

A site is a piece of land on which something has been or will be located. There are many issues that affect a piece of land's suitability for development. These include characteristics related to topography and geography, utilities, access and easements, size, and regulatory requirements such as zoning, building codes, and environmental laws. An owner will want to be sure that the site is appropriate for the proposed use.

In addition to the suitability of a site, the owner will balance the cost to buy and develop a piece of property against its possible use. A housing developer for example, would be unlikely to buy a piece of property that would result in homes with final sales prices that are far higher than the local housing market can bear. Our developer would likely look for a different site. On the other hand, the same piece of land might be suitable for a different type or size of project.

Financial feasibility

How much is the project going to cost? Can the owner afford to move ahead? Where is the money coming from? What kind of financial risk does the project carry? Will there be sufficient profit? These are all important questions that are answered during the feasibility phase. In order to do so, the owner develops an outline budget that assesses costs for the project, identifies possible income sources (for example, bank loans), and makes projections regarding anticipated future revenues. In addition to providing critical information to an owner, financial projections are required by whoever is lending the owner the money to develop the project.

Rough cost estimates, based on minimal design information, are completed during feasibility. These estimates (called conceptual estimates) are used to do preliminary cash flow projections of costs and revenues.

Financial planning is important to anyone contemplating a project. Like those embarking on large projects, the homeowner undertaking a small project would be smart to figure out before starting the project how much the job will cost and where the funds will come from.

Remember—money isn't free It costs money to borrow money, and the cost is called **interest**. The interest rate varies depending on several factors, but an owner includes the cost of paying interest as part of the overall project budget and cash flow projections. It makes sense that the longer construction takes the more interest the owner will have to pay (because the longer he'll be borrowing the money.) For very large projects, interest payments can be millions of dollars!

Schedule feasibility

Some projects have very strict time frames: a school needs to ready on the first day of classes; a ski resort wants to be open at the first snow; a homeowner has to move into his new home immediately after the sale of his current home. Scheduling constraints can have implications that might make a proposed project unfeasible.

Financial feasibility is closely linked to a potential schedule because costs are impacted by how long and when construction takes place. If, for example, an owner determines during feasibility that the scale of the proposed project means that construction will extend into multiple winters and therefore require additional protection from bad weather and a resulting decrease in worker productivity, costs will rise.

Regulatory requirements

An owner must determine whether the proposed project is allowable under local zoning laws and if there are any extraordinary building code requirements that might significantly impact costs.

Zoning

Most local governments (such as counties and municipalities) regulate land use through a system called **zoning**. The primary purpose of zoning is to separate uses that are thought to be incompatible and to prevent new development from harming existing residents or businesses. This is why you don't see sewage treatment plants or car manufacturers downtown!

New developments are of concern to a community because they can change the character of a neighborhood. Developments might result in the removal of existing buildings and replace them with larger buildings, different architectural styles, new uses, or a greater intensity of activity. Changes can impact traffic congestion, air quality, water consumption, shadows, housing affordability, and neighborhood businesses, and can result in changes that dramatically alter existing neighborhoods. Zoning regulations can also encourage the replacement of unsafe or outmoded buildings and can provide for neighborhood revitalization and growth.

Zoning regulations vary from state to state. Let's look at an example of zoning in California, to see how it works there. State law requires that each city and county in California have a general plan consisting of several elements including land use, traffic circulation, housing, and conservation (among other issues). The general plan acts as a guide for all future development within individual zoning districts. The zoning ordinance translates the general plan into a specific development standard and set of regulations. There are two parts to the zoning ordinance: the map and the written ordinance.

The **zoning map** graphically identifies allowable uses for every piece of land within a zoning district (such as a city or county). The written **zoning ordinance** describes in detail what additional uses are allowed and what restrictions apply (such as maximum height and parking requirements) and establishes the process by which development applications are considered.

Permitted uses of land are shown on zoning maps such as that shown in Figure 5.1, which represents a portion of Sebastopol, California. Each parcel of land is shown in outline and its location is included in one of several shaded zoning districts such as: RSF (Residential Single Family), CO (Commercial Office), SOS (Scenic Open Space), and CF (Community Facility), among others. In each of these zoning designations, some uses are allowed and some are not. For example, you can't build a residential project in an area that is designated CO and you can't put a McDonald's in a zone that is designated RSF. An owner's first step in his zoning review is to determine in which zoning district the project's site is located.

Selected Zoning Designations:

CG: General Commercial
CH: Heavy Commercial
O/LI: Office/Light Industrial
RSF-1: Low Density Single Family Residential
RSF-2: Med. Density Single Family Residential

Once the zoning designation has been determined, the zoning ordinance needs to be reviewed. This written document describes in detail the additional allowable and restricted uses. The owner checks both the map and the written ordinance to get a thorough understanding of what is allowed on a site. For example, let's say you are interested in building a new home and operating a small day care center on a parcel of land you own in Sebastopol. How will you determine if these two uses are allowed?

Zoning review step 1

Find your parcel on the zoning map (available at the City Planning Department) and see what the zoning designation is. For our example, let's assume that your property is located in zoning district with a RSF-2 designation. You verify on

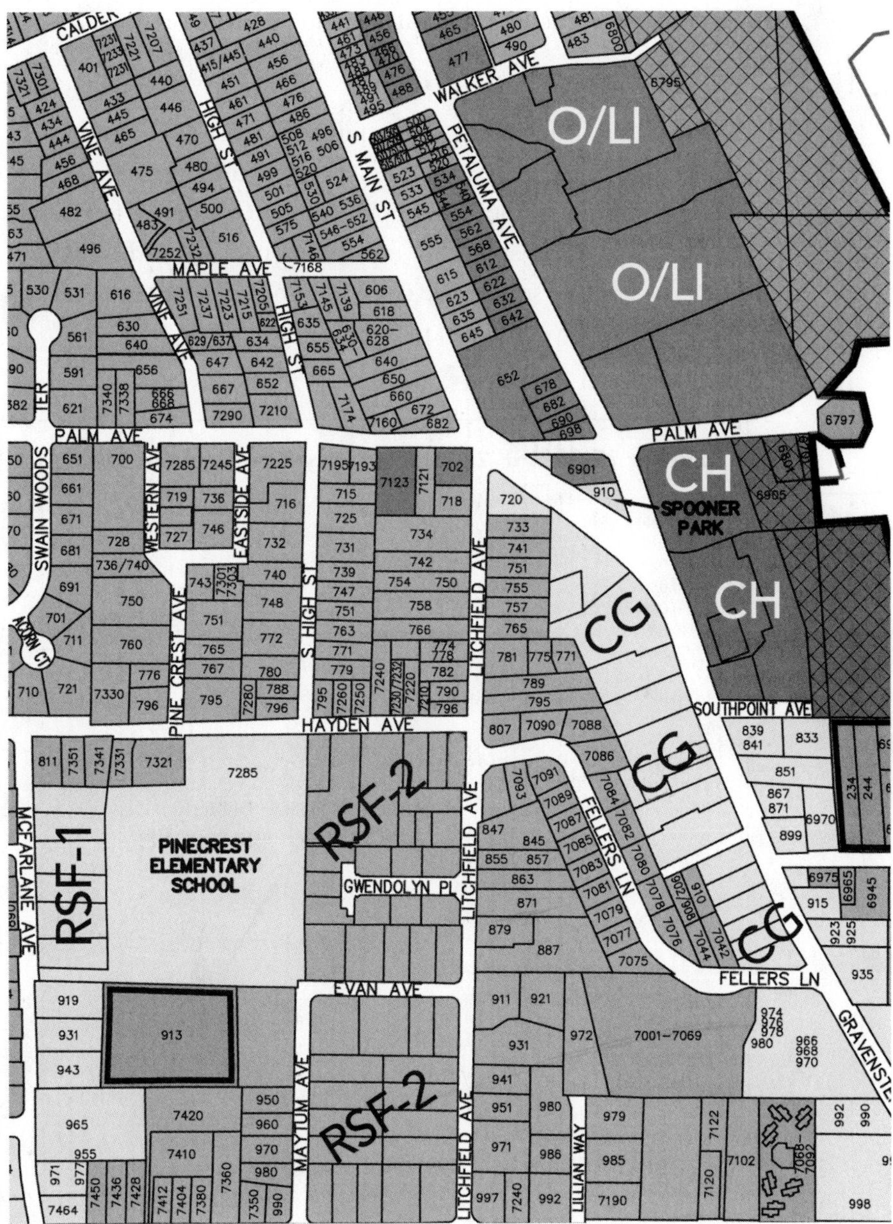

Figure 5.1. Excerpt, City of Sebastopol, CA zoning map

the map that RSF-2 means Single Family Residential-2. That sounds promising, but what exactly does it mean? You can see from the map that there are several different residential districts, with different designations, so you correctly assume they're not all alike. It looks like you'll be okay building a home, but the question remains about whether you can have a day care center on the same parcel.

To answer the question you will need to do further research.

Zoning review step 2

The next step is to review the zoning ordinance to define exactly what RSF-2 means and, more specifically, identify restrictions and allowed uses. Figure 5.2 shows a portion of the Sebastopol Zoning Ordinance for parcels with RSF-2 zoning. As you can see, there are several uses allowed on RSF-2 – – zoned property; happily, small-scale day care is one of them. This means that, from a zoning perspective, you can move ahead.

Chapter 17.30 RSF-2 Single Family Residential-2 District

Sections:

17.30.010	Purpose/Applicability
17.30.020	Permitted Uses
17.30.030	Conditionally Permitted Uses
17.30.040	Minimum Lot Area/Width
17.30.050	Maximum Building Height
17.30.060	Minimum Yards/Setbacks
17.30.070	Maximum Lot Coverage
17.30.080	Small Lot Subdivisions

17.30.010 Purpose/Applicability

The purpose of the RSF-2 District is to implement the "Medium Density Residential" land use category of the General Plan. This District is applicable to single-family residential areas at the mid-higher end of the allowable General Plan density range.

17.30.020 Permitted Uses

A. The following Residential Uses:

1. Single Family Dwellings (maximum one single-family dwelling unit per parcel of land).
2. Second Dwelling Units
3. Small Community Care Residential
4. Small Family Day Care Homes

B. Home Occupations

C. Accessory Uses, Structures and Buildings

D. Non-commercial Minor Antenna that meet the requirements of sections 17.100.010(B) through (F), and comply with the following, as appropriate:

1. Ground mounted antenna may not exceed 20 feet in height, except that citizens band radio antenna or a ground- or tower-mounted antenna operated by a federally licensed radio operator as a part of the Amateur Radio Service, may not exceed 30 feet in height.
2. Building mounted antenna may not exceed 15 feet (including any mast height) on a building that does not exceed 35 feet in height.

Figure 5.2. Excerpt, City of Sebastopol zoning ordinance

Building codes

The purpose of building codes is somewhat different from those of zoning ordinances; building codes are concerned with public safety within and around a structure. The earliest building codes were primarily fire protection codes concerned with the escape or rescue of the building occupants. Additional hazards are now recognized, such as earthquakes and hurricanes as well as other issues pertaining to public welfare such as sanitation, ventilation, and lighting.

Building codes are local building laws put in place to promote safe practices in the design and construction of a building. These codes cover everything from ceiling height requirements to structural requirements, width of stairs, number of exits, and much more. Most of the codes that regulate design and construction are not written by the government entity itself but are adapted from model codes that are written by code-writing organizations such as the International Code Council (ICC) and the National Fire Protection Association (NFPA). Local jurisdictions adopt the appropriate codes, often amending them to take into account local requirements. The codes are enforced by the government having jurisdiction (such as a city or a county; as we learned in Chapter 3, this agency is referred to as the authority having jurisdiction). Although most building codes are similar, they do differ depending on type, use, and location, and the designer must comply with the code applicable to the particular project.

During the early conceptual phase of a project, detailed analysis of building codes is probably not necessary. If, however, the proposed project is unusual (for example, you want to build a house made out of straw bales), early discussions with building officials would be wise. Detailed analysis of all code requirements occurs during the design phase. That said, an owner will want to be sure that there are no major building code requirements that might impact the proposed project.

Other codes and regulations may also be required for the project such as local or state health, fire, and transportation department requirements; and utility, water, sewer, and possibly environmental quality laws. If a project is in a special area – a historic district, for example – special reviews such as design review might also be required.

Community values

The final step in the feasibility process might be to investigate any potential political or community issues that could arise. Sometimes a project is theoretically allowable, but controversial. Community objection to a project has the potential to cause delays and increase costs. Those contemplating a potentially controversial project should make sure they understand what they might be facing and be prepared to accept possible delays and increased costs. For example, a developer is intending to build several houses on a large piece of property. He wants to subdivide the property so that the finished houses can be sold separately. In order to do this, the city could require a public hearing and approval by the planning commission. The owner will want to understand how local property owners are likely to react to the plan. Maybe there will be objection based on the fact that there will be increased traffic congestion and noise. Maybe one of the properties will be a halfway house, and a NIMBY ("not in my backyard") attitude is present. Community opposition can cause an owner time and money and, in some cases, can derail a project entirely.

Once an owner has completed a thorough feasibility review of the problems and possibilities of a proposed project (often referred to as doing **due diligence**), then wise decisions can be made regarding how to proceed. Perhaps the analysis has shown that costs are too high, or there is no market, or there is likely to be resistance from the community that could cause delays – all issues that might lead an owner to adjust the project scope or vision. In some cases, an owner might determine that the wisest course of action is to abandon the proposed project.

We'll see in Chapter 9 that a contractor goes through a similar (although less extensive) process when determining whether to pursue a job. Not all jobs are equal: a contractor might determine, after completing his or her own feasibility analysis, that a job may not be right.

Once the owner has decided to move ahead, major decisions need to be made regarding how the project will be realized: What is the time frame for hiring the designer and the contractor? What will the process be for getting a team together? Will it be beneficial to have a contract manager on board? Is the general contractor going to be hired through competitive bidding or does it make sense to negotiate a price with a preferred contractor? The choices made by the owner regarding these issues will define the method used to move a project from feasibility through construction to occupancy. This method is called project delivery and is the subject of the next chapter.

Chapter Vocabulary

Building codes – local building laws put in place to promote safe practices in the design and construction of a building.

Feasibility – the process of assessing the desirability, cost, and potential of a project so that a decision can be made regarding whether to move ahead.

Financial feasibility – a process of assessing a project's potential from a cost perspective.

Interest – the money a lender charges to borrow money.

Site – a piece of land on which something has been or will be located.

Speculation – something completed (such as a building) for an unknown buyer or user.

Zoning – a system of land use regulations.

Zoning map – a map of a specific zoning district that graphically identifies allowable uses for every piece of land within a zoning district.

Zoning ordinance – a law that describes what uses are allowed and what restrictions apply (such as maximum height and parking requirements) in a specific zoning jurisdiction.

Test Yourself

1. What is the purpose of project feasibility?
2. Who is responsible for the feasibility stage of a project?
3. An owner is considering building a 120-house development outside of town. Identify three separate issues that he will analyze before committing to moving ahead with this project.
4. You have determined that zoning allows you to put a house on a piece of property you own in town. How will you find out if you can have horses on the property?
5. What is the purpose of zoning regulations?
6. What is the purpose of building codes?
7. How does an owner (and his designer) know which building codes apply to a project?
8. You are going to need a bank loan to build your new house. What is interest? How does interest affect feasibility?
9. Explain the link between the schedule and project costs.
10. Why do community values matter to a developer? Give an example of a specific community value that might impact a project.

Andrea Young

CHAPTER 6

Project Delivery

What is project delivery?

To *deliver* something (a package, a pizza, a piece of software) is to distribute or complete something; the end product, the outcome, is called a **deliverable**. The expectation is that the deliverable will accurately reflect the client's goals: the post office makes every attempt to deliver the correct package to the correct address; the pizza shop cooks what was ordered and serves it to the correct customer; the software is in the stores on schedule and capable of meeting its manufacturer's claims. These things – the package, the pizza, and the software – are all deliverables and they are distributed using a specific method of delivery (such as a postal carrier or a pizza delivery van).

Almost anything can be thought about in terms of deliverables. Let's say you've volunteered to host this year's Thanksgiving dinner; the dinner is the deliverable. There are several ways to provide the meal: you could cook the entire meal yourself; family members could be enlisted to bring dishes; you could eat out. Although each of the choices provides the same deliverable – dinner – each reaches that goal in slightly different ways and has implications regarding cost, effort, and management. Each is a different delivery method. To decide how to proceed, you weigh the pros and cons of each approach and eventually settle on the one that meets your budget and your vision of what the dinner should be.

In construction, we talk about the delivery of *projects*. At an early stage, the owner makes decisions regarding how to manage a project to best meet his or her situation and goals. For example: Will a contractor be hired to both design and build the project? Would it be better for the project if an architect did the design and then for different contractors to compete for the work? Perhaps the owner feels it is necessary to hire a contractor who will be responsible for managing the whole process. Each of these represents an alternative delivery method and each has implications regarding responsibilities and risk.

The decision of how to organize a construction project is important, and the owner considers several issues when making this decision:

- How can time and money restraints best be protected and risk reduced? In other words, are there time and/or money issues that favor a particular type of delivery method?
- How will the team will be organized and administered?
- How and when will the designer and the contractor be selected?
- How much of a role will the owner assume?

The answers to these and other important management questions result in the choice of delivery method.

Let's look at our Thanksgiving dinner as an example of what this means. You are responsible for providing the meal. There are several ways for the dinner to happen and each has its good and bad points. If you cook the meal yourself, you can be confident that dinner will be just as you want it to be. But doing the whole thing yourself will be a lot of work and, because of your schedule, you're not sure you'll have the time or energy. On the other hand, you could ask various family members to contribute parts of the meal. This would make less work, but you can be pretty sure, given your family, that you'll lose control over both the timing and quality of the meal. Another possibility is that you could eat out. This approach has real merit because it would make it easy for everyone, but the cost would be prohibitive and, besides, you don't like the idea of celebrating Thanksgiving at a restaurant. Maybe you decide on a combination: purchase part of the meal and assign specific tasks to selected family members. The details of how the meal will happen will be determined by which approach you select. No matter what you choose, each of these ways will result in dinner being served, and each describes a different organizational technique, a **delivery method**.

A similar process occurs in construction. An owner weighs the situation and the needs of the project and selects an approach that she feels will best meet project goals and minimize risk. There are several different delivery method types: design-bid-build, design-build, construction management, and their variations. Each represents a different way of organizing a project.

In this chapter, we'll look at each of these alternative approaches and at some of the advantages and disadvantages of each method.

Before we jump into a discussion about the specific delivery methods, however, it would be helpful to first understand some of the issues on a construction project that are determined by the choice of delivery method. They include:

- **The point at which the contractor gets hired.** The most familiar type of delivery method is one in which several contractors compete for a job that has already been designed. But this is not the only way that contractors are hired. It might be of great value to the project to have the contractor hired *before* the design is finished so that he or she can provide feedback to the owner and the designer. When the contractor is hired (either before or after design completion) is linked to which delivery method is used.
- **The number of contracts the owner executes**. For most projects, the owner has two contracts, one with the architect and a separate one with the general contractor. This is typical of one type of delivery method. But other delivery methods operate with different contractual relationships: sometimes the owner has a single contract with the architect and the contractor; sometimes the owner has multiple contracts with multiple contractors. Each of these is a condition of a different type of delivery method and each has implications regarding legal obligations and administration of the project.
- **The roles of the team members and how the project will be administered.** The roles of the team members are also linked to the type of delivery method chosen. In some approaches, the architect administers the contract between the owner and the contractor; in other cases, a construction manager ensures that the contractor is meeting the contract requirements. The roles and responsibilities of the team members differ depending on how the project is organized.
- **The speed with which the project can be completed**. A project with a delivery method that hires the general contractor at the

conclusion of design may take longer to complete than a project that hires the contractor during design. Some types of delivery methods provide the option to accelerate the schedule. An owner concerned about quick completion is likely to select one of these.

Delivery methods in construction

There are different delivery method (DM) types in construction, but each is a variation on three basic types:

- **Design-bid-build (also called traditional DM)**
- **Design-build**
- **Construction management (CM)**

A fourth type of project delivery, **integrated project delivery**, is a new DM that is gaining in popularity. We'll take a look at this one at the end of the chapter.

Let's look at how these different delivery methods vary and in what situations they might be used.

Design-bid-build (traditional) delivery method

Design-bid-build (DBB) is the delivery method that results in a design and construction process that is linear and straightforward: the owner hires a designer who completes the design and the construction documents; the project then goes out to bid; a contractor is hired; and, finally, the facility is built. The name design-bid-build reflects this timeline. The contractor has no input into the design; the first time he or she sees the project is at the bid phase, when design has already been completed. The assumption in the design-bid-build delivery method is that once the contract documents are completed, any qualified contractor can do the work. The contractor who promises to complete the project for the least cost typically gets the job.

The traditional DM is the most common method of organizing a project, in part because it is so familiar to everyone. There are other advantages too; projects that are organized in this way result in competitive bidding, which often results in the lowest cost to the owner. Because project costs are known at the beginning of construction, the owner's financial risk is reduced. It is therefore the best way to organize a project when an owner has a fixed budget. In addition, payments to the contractor are usually straightforward, typically based on a rough percentage of completed work. Most public jobs are required by law to use this type of delivery method

The traditional DM has several major disadvantages, however. Because the contractor is not hired until the design is complete, the owner and the architect do not have the advantage of the contractor's expertise early in the process when adjustments to the design can be made easily. To add to the problem, in this DM the architect is typically responsible to the owner for administering the contract between the owner and the contractor. This means that the architect oversees the contractor's performance and approves (or disapproves) of the owner's payments to the contractor. This can create an adversarial relationship between the architect and the contractor, which may impact the success of the project.

Projects that are organized using the DBB delivery method generally take the longest to complete. This is because only after the architect finishes the drawings and bid documents does the project go out to bid. If there are design problems or the price comes in too high, the architect might have to re-design parts of the project before construction can begin. An owner with a very tight time frame would probably not select this delivery method.

Another potential problem with design-bid-build is the possibility of expensive changes in the work after construction begins. If the design documents are not complete and thorough, the contractor will have many opportunities to increase overall project time and expenses by claiming that information is lacking. Projects with an incomplete design (for example, a renovation project) do not typically use this type of delivery method. Despite these drawbacks, DBB remains the most common delivery method and has the advantages noted earlier.

The traditional delivery method is *most suitable* for the following:

- Small and/or straightforward projects, such as a private house
- Projects that are formulaic (such as a fast-food restaurant), built the same way every time
- Projects with limited budgets
- Public jobs that require competitive bidding

As noted earlier, one component of all delivery methods is the nature of both the contractual and the administrative relationships between the owner, the architect, and the contractor. These relationships vary depending on the type of delivery method used. Let's see how this works with the DBB delivery method.

Figure 6.1 shows the relationships between the owner, contractor, and architect in a DBB delivery method. Solid lines with arrows indicate contractual (legally enforceable) relationships. In this DM, the owner has *two contracts*: one with the architect and one with the contractor. Each of these parties (the architect and the contractor) has their own separate contracts with consulting engineers (in the case of the architect) and subcontractors (in the case of the contractor). There is a link between the architect and the contractor indicated by a dotted line, because they have a relationship but *do not* have a contract with each other.

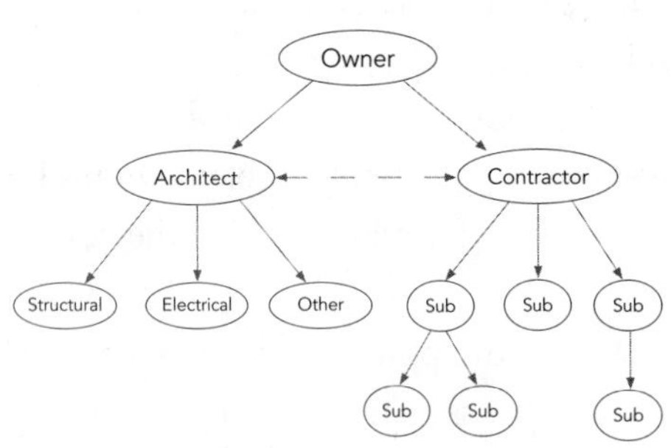

Figure 6.1. Design-bid-build delivery method

Why do contractual relationships matter? Contracts establish legal requirements between parties and determine administrative responsibilities. Obligations between the parties vary, depending on their contractual relationships. In addition, from the owner's perspective, fewer contracts mean less administrative oversight than that required with multiple contracts. On complex projects with multiple contracts, the owner must typically rely on others to manage them.

Note that Figure 6.1 does not tell us how much of the work will be completed by the contractor's own crews and how much will be subcontracted. The contractor is responsible, however, to the owner for *all* the work of the subcontractors (and *their* subcontractors), as well as the work performed by his own crews.

A design-bid-build delivery method is summarized in Figure 6.2.

Chapter 8 discusses the two ways that contractors are hired: through competitive bidding or through negotiation. Private owners may prefer to *negotiate* a fixed price with a contractor. In that situation, the delivery method is **design-negotiate-build** (DNB).

DNB operates like DBB: the owner has two contracts (one with the contractor and one with the architect); the architect administers the contractor-owner contract and reviews payment requests. The difference is that with DNB the contractor is on board earlier than with a DBB and can therefore provide expertise before design is complete. This results in a compressed time frame due to the elimination of re-design following bidding. The fixed price for the work is negotiated at the completion of the design phase and contractual relationships are as shown in Figure 6.1. Because of statutory requirements that competitive bidding be used, this delivery method is not used for jobs that utilize public funds.

D.M.	Advantages	Disadvantages	Characteristics	Project Types
Design-Bid-Build	Competitively bid	Can't fast-track	GC hired after design	Competitively bid jobs
	Familiar to the parties	No constructability reviews	Owner has 2 contracts	Private or public projects
	Cost known upfront	Not suitable when changes are needed	Arch. administers const. contract	Complete design info.
		Can be adversarial	Maximum time to complete	Residential
				Formulaic
				Projects with tight budgets

Figure 6.2. DBB Summary chart

Design-build delivery method

The fastest-growing delivery method is called design-build (DB). In this approach, the architect and contractor are hired as a team under a single contract with the owner. One appeal of design-build is that the traditional conflicts between the architect and the contractor are greatly reduced. With design-build, the assumption is that all members of the construction team will benefit from good communication. The improved communication between the design and construction portions of the project typically result in a more streamlined process that can accommodate changes in the work fairly easily.

The contractor/architect may be hired in different ways, but the most common is for several potential DB ventures to negotiate with the owner. Selection is made on a variety of factors including the overhead and profit, timeframe, and proposed team members. DB projects do not have final budgets at the time the contractor and designer are hired.

Figure 6.3 shows the contractual relationships between the primary players in the DB delivery method.

As with Figure 6.1, the arrows indicate contractual relationships. Note that with design-build, the owner has only *one contract* with a single company (or joint venture) that does both the design and the construction. This company hires the design consultants such as the engineers, and they perform as the general contractor and hire the subcontractors. Because the contractor and architect work closely together, communication is generally improved over a DBB delivery method. It also results in faster turn-around on questions from the contractor and subcontractors and on changes to the work. Ideally, design-build is a smooth and streamlined way of delivering a project.

Another of the primary advantages of using the design-build process is that the project can be **fast-tracked**. When a job is fast-tracked, construction starts before the design process is complete. Yes, you read that right: construction starts before the design of the building has been completed. Fast-tracking is a highly streamlined process that reduces the overall project schedule and thus reduces costs. This system, however, puts the owner at increased risk because costs are not known up front and critical pieces of the construction are set before the entire structure is designed. In the traditional DBB construction process, design, bidding, and construction occur one right after the other; none of the processes begin until the preceding process is complete. It's easy to see that this can take a long time, especially if problems arise in the bidding phase and require re-design.

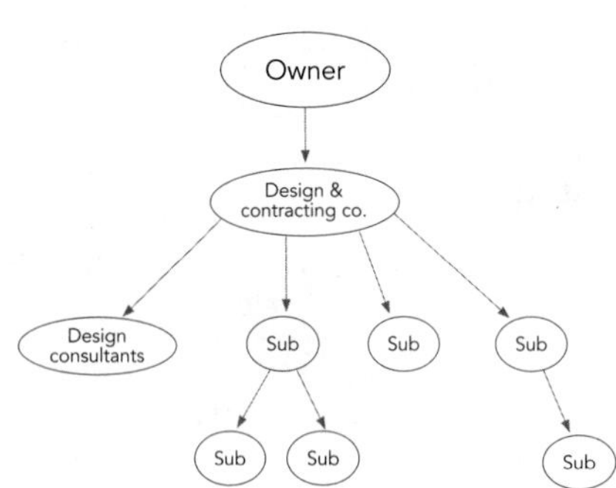

Figure 6.3. Design-build delivery method

When the series of project stages occur one right after the other (Design → Bidding →Construction →Completion) it is called **sequential construction**. It is the most common way of proceeding with a project. Sequential construction is *always* used with a design-bid-build delivery method; it may or may not be used with design-build.

Given the increasing costs of construction, there is growing interest in reducing construction time (and hence costs). Fast-tracking is therefore becoming a preferred approach on large and costly projects. This type of construction is not limited to the design-build delivery method. Construction management delivery methods can also be fast-tracked but, as with DB, do not *have* to be.

Although a design-build approach can offer budget savings if fast-tracking is used and improved communication because of the single contract, there are several potential *disadvantages*.

When a single firm or joint venture is hired to do all the work, there are no checks and balances and there is an increased possibility of fraud. Because an owner needn't be as involved in the process, he or she may be left out of the decision-making process.

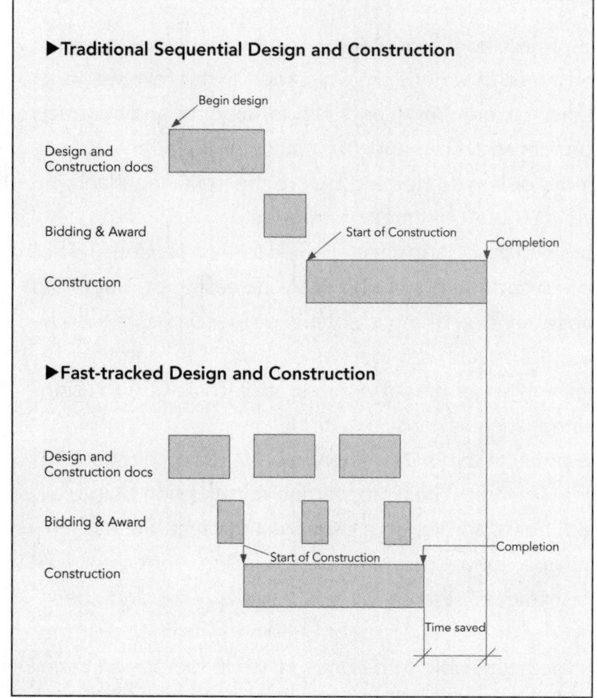

Figure 6.4. Comparison of sequential/fast-tracked construction

With a fast-tracked project design and bidding are phased. (Each phase obtains separate approvals from the AHJ.) Construction on each phase can begin while design is proceeding with other phases. Although the overall time required for design and bidding is longer than with a sequential project (because of the additional coordination and time necessary to assemble various packages) the completion date is earlier because of the earlier start of construction.

Projects for which the design-build delivery method may be suitable include:

- Highly technical projects requiring intensive designer-contractor communication (refineries, manufacturing plants, power plants, etc.)
- Projects with time constraints that would benefit from fast-tracking
- Projects where the owner is absent or, for various reasons, uninterested in being actively involved

D.M.	Advantages	Disadvantages	Characteristics	Project Types
Design-Build	Better communication btwn contractor/arch.	No price up front	GC hired same time as arch.	Projects with time restraints
	Contractor on board early	Owner may be out of loop	Owner has 1 contract	Specialized projects
	Flexibility	No checks/ balances btwn GC/Arch	Arch. administers contract	
			Owner typically less involved	

Figure 6.5. Design-build summary chart

Fast-tracking – The process of moving a project from a concept to use by the owner involves the completion of a series of activities performed in various project stages. In this text, we have identified these stages as: project feasibility, programming and design, bidding and contract award, pre-construction and mobilization, construction, and occupancy and warranty. On a typical project, each of these stages is more or less completed before the next stage (and its activities) begins. Each stage takes a certain amount of time to complete.

Sometimes the owner wants the project time shortened. How can this be done? The usual way of shortening the time required to complete a project is by increasing productivity, completing each stage as efficiently as possible: everything is done in proper order, as quickly as possible, and no time is wasted. There are several approaches open to the contractor to accomplish increased productivity: increasing the number of workers, adding crews, and using products and systems that can be expedited (such as modularization).

Another way of saving total elapsed project time is by *compression* of the time schedule, that is, by overlapping some of the stages. This translates into starting construction before all parts of the design have been completed. For example: on a sequential project, the excavation/foundation work doesn't begin until the contractor receives a building permit for the entire structure. If the same project is fast-tracked, the contractor submits plans and specifications sufficient to enable the building department to issue a building permit on just the excavation/foundation work. The contractor is thus able to begin work while the design team is still determining the details of the rest of the structure. Figure 6.4 shows how time saved by concurrent work will accumulate and appear at the end of the construction period in the form of early overall completion. Organizing the project stages to produce early completion by the technique of concurrent or overlapping time scheduling is called fast-tracking.

How does fast-tracking work? – A project that is fast-tracked has the contractor on board early to provide constructability and cost reviews during design. Before the design is complete, but when the size and character of the project are fairly well determined, the contractor begins the process of getting prices from potential subcontractors. As the design progresses, refinements are made to the cost estimates.

Construction documents are submitted to the authority having jurisdiction (AHJ) – typically, the building department – in segments identified by the designer and contractor. These segments more or less follow the ground-up progression of construction. The AHJ reviews, approves, and issues permits as they receive segments. The contractor can start construction as soon as the building permit is issued for each segment. Construction therefore starts before the final design work is complete.

Although the contractor provides cost and time estimates that are refined as design proceeds, a characteristic of fast-tracking is that the owner does not know the final costs before construction begins. As soon as practicable, the contractor gives the owner a price for the complete job.

Construction management (CM) delivery method

"Construction management" can be a confusing term. On the one hand, it defines all the processes involved in organizing, monitoring, and controlling a construction project. Many construction tasks – hiring subcontractors, scheduling the work, monitoring the cash flow – involve *management.* But construction management (CM) is also a specific delivery method in which management services are provided to the owner before construction has begun or a contractor has been hired. The construction manager becomes part of the team early in the design phase and assists the owner throughout the entire construction process. Sometimes the construction management company functions only as a consultant; in other cases, it acts as a consultant during design and as a general contractor during construction.

There are two types of CM delivery methods: agency CM and at-risk CM. The role of the CM during construction differentiates between the two. Both types of construction management can use either sequential or fast-track construction.

Agency construction management (agency CM)

In an agency construction management (agency CM) delivery method, a construction manager hired by the owner oversees the construction process but *does not use his own crews for labor* and is *not* financially responsible for construction costs. In contrast, with a design-bid-build delivery method, for example, a contractor is hired (at the completion of design) by the owner to complete a project for a set price. This means that the contractor is responsible for all the work and the associated costs. If the contractor has miscalculated and the costs are higher than what he promised they would be, he is responsible for paying those costs. On a project that uses an agency CM delivery method, a construction manager (who is typically also a general contractor) is hired by the owner early in the process to provide expertise. At the completion of the design, the CM coordinates the hiring of a separate general contractor who will complete the physical work. The CM manages the general contractor.

With an agency CM delivery method, the owner has at least three separate contracts: one with the architect, one with the CM, and one with the GC. The GC is responsible for the construction of the project and hires the subcontractors. These relationships are typically as shown in Figure 6.6.

Note that the construction manager and the general contractor do not have a contract with each other. Each of them has a separate contract with the owner. Because the CM oversees the GC's work they do, however, have a rela-

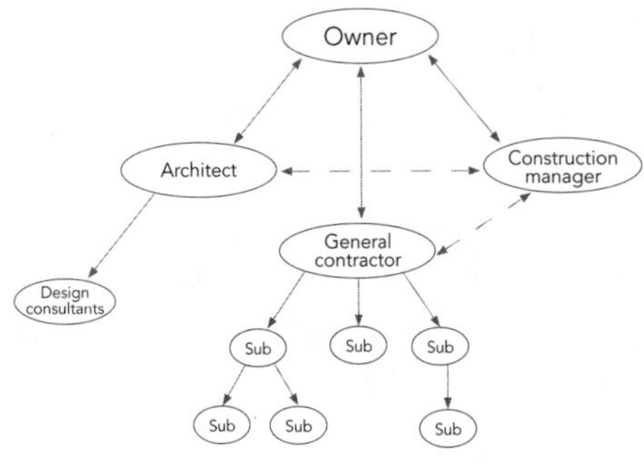

Figure 6.6. Agency CM

tionship and this relationship is depicted by a dotted line in the figure.

An agency construction management delivery method provides the owner with construction expertise early in the process, allows for fast-tracking, and gives the owner the cost benefits of competitive bidding for the construction work. But as with any delivery method, there are also disadvantages. Agency CM requires high owner input and a certain level of sophistication. It is most suitable for commercial or large projects that would benefit from increased levels of management.

D.M.	Advantages	Disadvantages	Characteristics	Project Types
Agency CM	Constructability reviews and value engineering	Typically requires sophisticated owner	CM coordinates hiring GC	Large and/or complex projects
	CM works in owner's interest only	Possible supervision confusion	Owner has at least 3 contracts	
	Can be fast-tracked	Owner may have many contracts	Arch or CM administers construction contract	
	Competitive bidding		Can be fast-tracked	
	Can use multi-prime contracts		CM not at risk financially	

Figure 6.7. Agency CM summary chart

At-risk construction management (at-risk CM)

Like agency CM, with an at-risk CM delivery method, the construction manager is hired early in the process. In agency CM, the construction management company does not do the construction work; this is not the case with at-risk CM. The construction manager acts as a consultant to the owner early in the process, then as the equivalent of a general contractor during the construction process. The CM carries some financial risk because he provides the owner with a price guarantee for the construction work. In at-risk CM, the owner has *two contracts*:

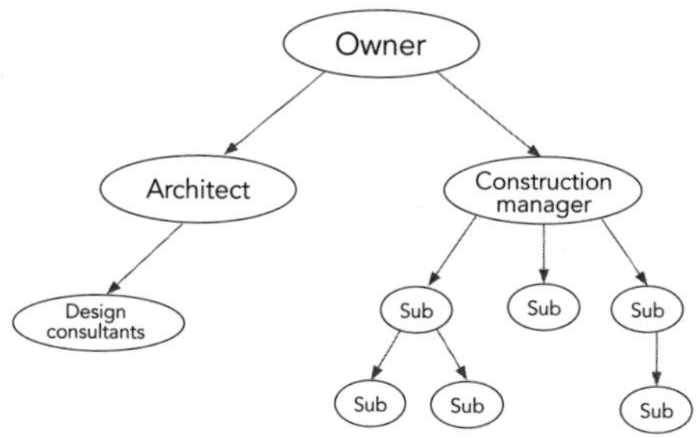

Figure 6.8. At-risk construction management

one with the architect and one with the CM. (These relationships are shown in Figure 6.8.) In his role as general contractor during construction, the CM hires the subcontractors. As with the GC in other delivery methods, the construction manager is responsible to the owner for all the construction work.

D.M.	Advantages	Disadvantages	Characteristics	Project Types
At-risk CM	Constructability reviews and value engineering	Typically requires sophisticated owner	GC hired early as the CM	Large and/or complex projects
	Can be fast-tracked	No competitive bidding for GC	Owner has 2 contracts	
	Owner only has 2 contracts		Arch. administers construction contract	
			Can be fast-tracked	
			CM during pre-construction/GC during construction	
			CM is at risk financially	

Figure 6.9. At-risk CM summary chart

Agency CM using multiple prime contractors Some projects benefit from having more than one *prime contractor* (remember, anyone with a contract directly with an owner is called a prime contractor.) In such a project, a construction management company typically coordinates the work of several contractors, each of which has a contract with the owner. These contracts are known as multiple prime or multi-prime contracts ("multi" means many). The CM is hired to provide help to the owner early in the design process, assists in the selection of the contractors who will complete the work, and manages the contractors and their work. This type of delivery method might be used when, for one reason or another, an owner prefers to break up the work into smaller units but can't coordinate the work him or herself. As is typical with an agency CM delivery method, the construction manager does not assume any financial risk.

Integrated project delivery

Another type of delivery method has recently been introduced: integrated project delivery (IPD). IPD employs a highly collaborative approach to project design and construction. All primary team members – the owner, architect, general contractor, engineers, and major subcontractors – are brought on board at the same time, during design, and, relying on sophisticated computer modeling and information sharing, are able to collaborate in unusually effective ways. As with any delivery method, the goal of IPD is to reduce inefficiencies and potential mistakes on a project, to eliminate misunderstandings and disputes, and to reduce costs and construction time. With IPD, the tool for doing this is to incentivize all team members through the sharing of profits and losses. For example, if costs in one area of the project exceed the anticipated budget, the additional costs are covered by a fund provided at the start of construction. Similarly, if the team performs well and there are excess funds at the completion of work, all share in the profits. The leverage for profit/loss sharing is formalized with contractual relationships.

Building information modeling

The success of IPD is dependent on transparent and open information that can be accessed and used by all team members. IPD projects use sophisticated computer modeling software called building information modeling (BIM), which enables members to share an extensive database.

Building information modeling is a computer-based system that creates three-dimensional cyber models of a structure's geometry (plans, elevations, sections, etc.). In addition to providing team members with full-scale models that can be assessed and adjusted, the program incorporates non-graphical data and links. This information further defines the structure and lets users analyze important data such as code and installation requirements, manufacturers specifications, cost data, installation requirements, and scheduling information. When changes or adjustments are made, the model and the accompanying data change too. The information provided by BIM means that team members can make smart design decisions early in the process, identify problems before construction starts, schedule efficiencies into construction sequencing, and get accurate cost estimates up front.

BIM makes the collaborative process of IPD possible in a way that traditional two-dimensional informational systems could not.

Summary

All projects can experience delays, cost overruns, changes, and other problems. Choosing the appropriate delivery method can greatly reduce the risk of such problems. As we have seen, there are advantages and disadvantages to each of the ways that a project can be delivered. An owner weighs these advantages and disadvantages against the project type, her willingness to tolerate risk, the budget and schedule requirements, and project goals to determine which method to choose. For example, if an owner is most concerned about knowing the construction cost up front, then a traditional (DBB) delivery method is a good choice. On the other hand, if the schedule is most important, then one of the methods that allow for fast-tracking, such as a design-build or a CM approach, is more suitable.

Chapter Vocabulary

Agency construction management – a type of construction project delivery method whereby the CM, who is hired early in the process, works as the owner's agent but does not do any of the physical work.

At-risk construction management – a type of construction project delivery method whereby the CM, who is hired early in the process, works as the owner's agent during pre-construction and as the general contractor during construction.

Building information modeling (BIM) – a process of gathering and managing information that uses virtual (typically, 3D) models as a tool for design, construction, and facilities management. BIM software enables information on systems, costs, and scheduling to be incorporated so that design, budget, and installation assumptions can be extensively evaluated and tested prior to construction.

Construction Management (CM) delivery method – a delivery method in which a contract manager is hired early in the process and acts as the owner's representative. CM may be agency CM in which the CM manages the construction but does not do the work, or at-risk CM in which the CM performs as the general contractor following completion of design.

Deliverable – an outcome; something specific that needs to be accomplished.

Delivery method – the organizational structure for completing a project.

Design-bid-build (traditional) – a delivery method in which the GC is hired at the completion of design.

Design-build – a delivery method in which the owner has one contract with a single construction/design firm.

Design-negotiate-build – a variation on design-bid-build, in which award of the general contract is made following negotiations between several general contractors and the owner.

Fast-track – a job in which construction starts before the design process is complete. Projects that are fast-tracked have compressed schedules and therefore can be completed faster than those that use sequential construction.

Integrated project delivery – a project delivery method in which all primary team members (the owner, architect, general contractor, engineers, and major subcontractors) are brought on board at the same time (during design), and, using sophisticated computer modeling and information sharing, are able to collaborate in unusually effective ways.

Multi-prime contract – a project in which the owner has contracts with several prime contractors.

Sequential construction – a job in which each stage of a project is completed before the next stage begins. Projects that are sequential take the longest to complete.

Traditional delivery method – see Design-bid-build.

Test Yourself

1. Who determines what delivery method will be used on a project and when is this decision made?
2. What are the four issues that influence which type of delivery method will be selected for a project?
3. When is the contractor hired in a design-bid-build delivery method?
4. Who does the owner have contracts with in a DBB delivery method?
5. What sort of projects might benefit from a DBB delivery method?
6. Why might an owner choose to fast-track a project?
7. Why can't a DBB project be fast-tracked?
8. Why might an owner want to hire the contractor before the design has been completed?
9. How does the DB delivery method help reduce conflicts between the architect and the contractor?
10. What is the primary difference between agency CM and at-risk CM?

Andrea Young

CHAPTER 7

Programming and Design

- **Goal of programming and design:** to define and organize project requirements
- **Primary responsible party:** the owner for programming; the architect for design
- **Outcomes:** a written description of project requirements; updated estimates and schedules; the documents that the contractors will use to price and build the project

After the owner has completed the feasibility phase and decided to proceed, a project moves into programming and design. During this stage, the project progresses from an idea or concept into usable plans and information so that the building or facility can be accurately priced and be built.

Programming

Just as contractors require drawings to construct a building, architects require information in order to produce those drawings in the first place. Design cannot happen in a vacuum. Before solutions to a design problem can be proposed, there needs to be an understanding of what the design problem is! What, exactly, are the owner's goals and objectives? This information is contained in a written document created by the owner called a **program** that serves as a design guide for the architect.

As part of the process of developing a program, the project goals and objectives that were outlined during feasibility are expanded and detailed. The owner, ideally in collaboration with the end users, identifies the building design requirements:

- The number and type of users (for example, young professionals, families with children, the elderly)
- Need for flexibility (will the use need to change?)
- Size and types of rooms
- Adjacency requirements (what spaces need to be near each other?)
- Preferred building materials
- Special requirements regarding security, circulation, media, and so on

Other relevant data, such as operational, maintenance, and replacement goals, are also identified and articulated during programming. Aesthetic considerations important to the team are defined (for example, the desire to have lots of natural light and space that opens to the outdoors). Requirements regarding energy efficiency and sustainability are articulated in the program.

In some cases, the proposed building is complex enough that the owner does not have the expertise to develop the program. In such cases, (including facilities such as laboratories, theaters, health care facilities, and so on) the owner is likely to use the services of a programming consultant. Most, but certainly not all, programming consultants are either architects or have architectural training, and architects typically perform programming as an additional service to their standard contracts.

Together with project feasibility, the programming phase can be extensive and can sometimes take years to complete. When Santa Rosa Junior College (SRJC) was investigating its need for a new library, for example, the process of planning and programming took almost 10 years! Before the program could be written, the college and its consultants, as well as teams of faculty and staff, developed key assumptions as a framework for the program. These assumptions included such items as the importance of group study and classroom space in the library, the desirability of electronic facilities that would accommodate future changes, and the inclusion of "green" components in the design. The team then determined basic layout requirements and specified needs such as the number of student seats, linear feet of shelf space, and the number and size of offices. The program was eventually reflected in the architect's design.

Figure 7.1 is a section from one piece of the program for the SRJC Library: it identifies the requirements for a department supervisor's office. Note the level of detail contained in the program: everything from the overall square footage requirement to the number of chairs, linear feet of shelving, and type of lighting. This level of detail (and more) was duplicated throughout the library program.

Program element: Circulation Supervisor's Office Adjacency requirements: Circulation Desk	
Square feet: 140	Acoustical requirements: Moderate
Lighting requirements: 50 f.c. combination of natural and fluorescent lighting; task lighting at workstation	HVAC requirements: Normal
Plumbing: None	Data, power, telecommunications requirements: workstation provides for 2 voice/2 data (quad) per workstation and 2 duplex and 1 isolated grounded duplex per workstation mounted at counter height or 12" AFF and supplied through systems furniture panels. One 110v utility outlet per 10 feet of wall space
Miscellaneous furniture: None	Floor, wall, window treatment: carpet; glass to circulation desk; natural light
Seating: 1 task chair 1 guest chair	Shelving requirements: 15 linear feet freestanding or wall mounted shelving
Filing cabinets: 1 four-drawer file cabinet, lockable	Tables: None
Equipment: 1 PC, 1 printer, 1 typewriter, 1 - 24" x 48" whiteboard	Workstations: 1 L-shaped workstation @ 30" deep with two 5' sections and one 36" corner unit, containing two lockable pedestal units: 1 stationary/box/file and 1 two-drawer file unit.

Figure 7.1. Santa Rosa Junior College Doyle Library, program excerpt

Design

Design cannot begin in earnest until the program is complete and the designer has sufficient information regarding the owner's expectations and goals. The goal of the design phase is to develop a project that meets the owner's vision within budget, site, regulatory requirements, and other constraints. The design team studies the program, researches applicable codes and regulations, proposes solutions, and develops the graphic and written documents that describe the project. The end product is a package of documents that enables contractors to price and build the structure and that describe the roles and responsibilities of the entire team.

During the design phase, the architect takes the lead and looks at different solutions to the requirements identified by the program. This is a back-and-forth process with the owner and there is lots of communication between the parties as different solutions are proposed and discussed.

In any project, design proceeds from conceptual planning that identifies the basic layout and form of the project to a completed set of construction documents that include detailed working drawings (plans) and written descriptions of the project. The process of moving a design forward occurs in three distinct phases, each of which is defined by an increasing level of detail:

1. Schematic design
2. Design development
3. Final design (construction documents)

Drawings

Before we explore what happens during each of the design stages, let's step back and look briefly at the drawings that are created as part of a project. (Most drawings are developed during design, but sketches are also done during construction to clarify a detail or make a change in the work.)

All projects require drawings to convey necessary information: how the structure rests on the site, how it's laid out and dimensioned, the details of how parts join together, and more. Different types of drawings convey different types of information and because most are scaled (which means they show actual dimensions but not actual size) the designer has the option of representing an entire building or the smallest detail as required.

There are four basic types of drawings: **plans, elevations, sections**, and

details. Each of these conveys specific levels of information and all are required in order to fully explain a project.

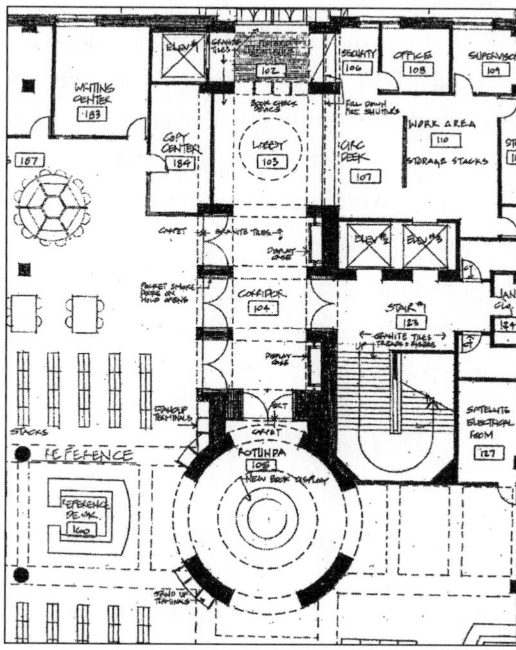

Figure 7.2. Floor plan

Plans show horizontal slices through the building. There is a plan for each level of a building – site, foundation, each floor, and the roof. The simplest projects, such as a small renovation project, have a single floor plan. Complex projects may have many different sheets of plans and, in addition to a separate sheet for each floor, might also have site plans, excavation and foundation plans, and plans that identify specific work such as the electrical and mechanical layouts. Figure 7.2 shows a typical floor plan.

Elevations show the building as if the viewer is looking straight at it at eye level. All four sides (north, south, east, and west) of the building are typically done in elevation. Several interior elevations are also drawn to explain necessary relationships (for example, the height of a counter or the location of wall lights). Figure 7.3 shows an elevation of a hallway.

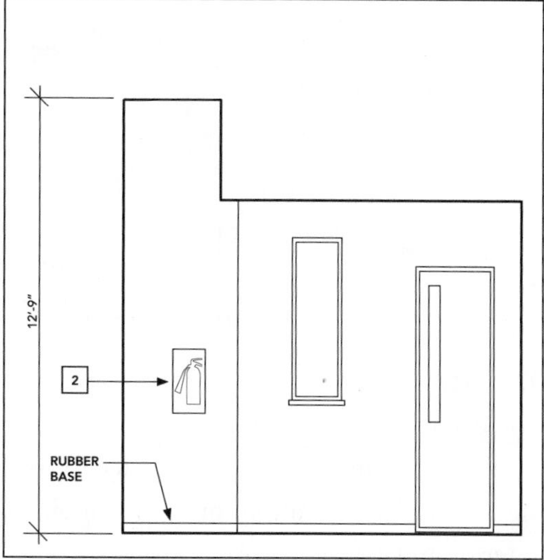

Figure 7.3. Elevation

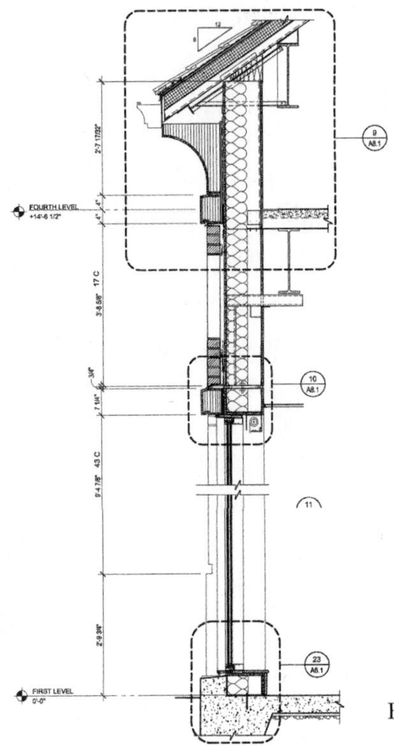

Sections provide a more detailed look at key areas of the plan. Unlike floor plans, which are horizontal slices through the building, sections are vertical slides through the entire building or a portion of the building. The architect typically draws several sections through a building. See Figure 7.4.

Figure 7.4. Section

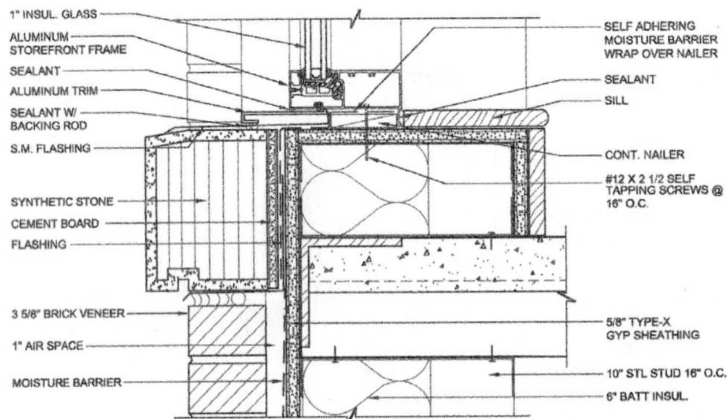

Figure 7.5. Detail

Details are blow-ups of specific elements to show how products or materials fit together. For example, the architect might draw a detail to explain how a skylight intersects with roof flashing, or how reinforcing steel should be located within a foundation. Details can be shown in plan, elevation, or sectional views. The detail above shows a window sill and its interior and exterior construction.

Plans, elevations, sections, and details are used during all stages of design. As the design progresses, the drawings become more complete with additional levels of information.

Let's return to the three stages of design: schematic design, design development, and final design and construction documents to see the progression of a design. We'll use the SRJC library as a continuing example.

Schematic design

Schematic design is the first design phase and focuses on developing a broad form and layout for the project. Schematic drawings are not detailed and are used for analyzing design alternatives. During "schematics" (as schematic design is also called), there is a lot of communication between the owner and the designer as alternative solutions to the owner's vision are explored and analyzed. Many possibilities and solutions are developed, studied, and considered.

At the completion of schematic design, the owner and the architect have reached an agreement regarding a rough floor plan, and decisions have been made regarding major materials and systems. A cost estimate is completed and design adjustments are made, if necessary.

A schematic design may start out as a simple and rough "bubble diagram" similar to the one shown in Figure 7.6. This early diagram of the SRJC library represents an initial layout of spaces as identified by the program. This is the main floor of the building and shows an entry lobby with various spaces leading off and connecting to a circulation spine and rotunda. This kind of a diagram will evolve into a more refined schematic plan such as that shown in Figure 7.7.

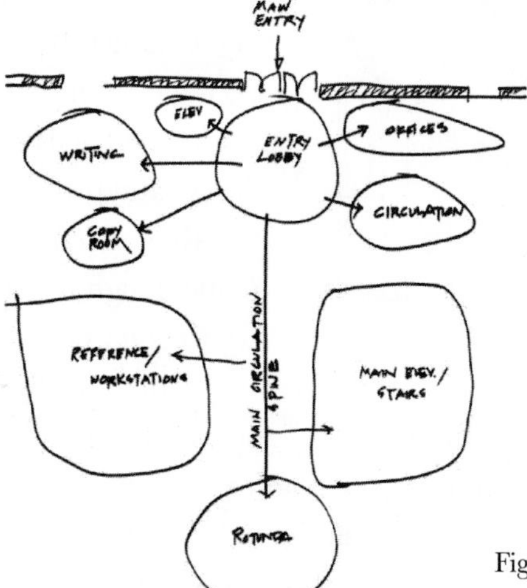

Figure 7.6. Bubble diagram

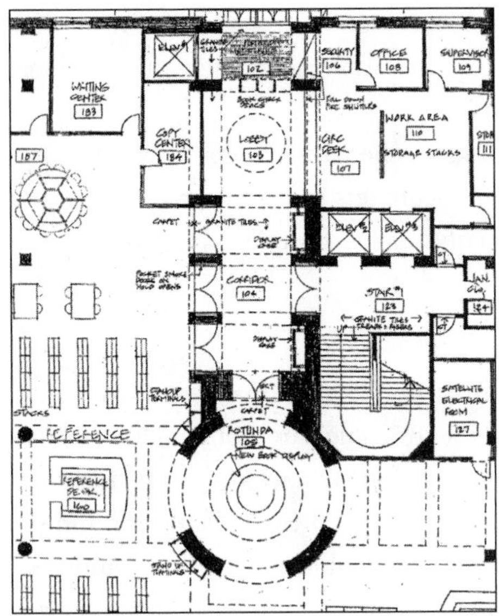

Figure 7.7. Schematic plan

By the conclusion of schematics, the architects and the school agreed on the general size and shape of the area shown in the bubble diagram as well as identified spatial and functional characteristics. We saw figure 7.7 earlier as an example of a typical floor plan. The spaces off the lobby and the circulation hallway are identified as functional (note the copy center and the circulation desk) and a staircase has been located across from elevator banks. Access is shown directly from the hallway into the reference and book areas.

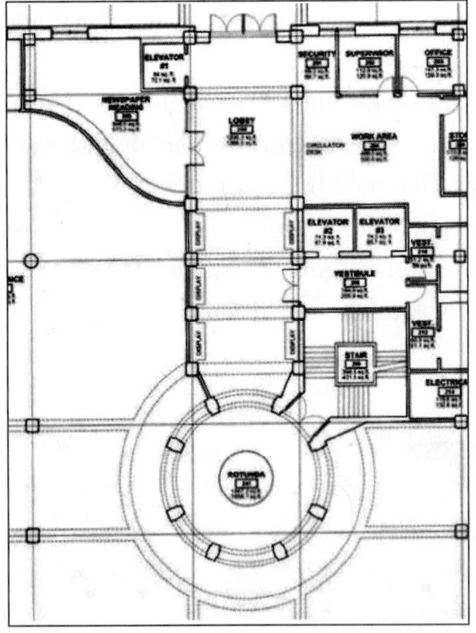

Figure 7.8. Design development

Design development

During **design development**, the architect refines the schematic design approved by the owner and makes decisions regarding layout, materials, and systems. In this next phase, there is detailing of forms, structures, systems, floor plans, and elevations and details are worked out. Many product and materials selections are made and outline specifications recorded (see Chapter 16 for information on specifications). A more refined budget estimate and work schedule is completed to ensure that the design and project budget are in sync.

Refinements for the SRJC Library schematic design resulted in an elimination of the copy center off the lobby and the substitution of a more socially oriented use of that area, a café. During this phase, the designers and owner decided to create a more controlled flow within the space and consequently re-oriented the staircase to funnel users into the rotunda at the heart of the building. Access from the central hallway into the library was tightened up as well.

Final design

Final design and the development of construction documents take the design to 100 percent completion. Although small or straightforward projects may require few drawings or other documents, this is not true of most projects, which typically require a variety of graphic and written documents to describe them fully. In the final design phase, these drawings and documents, together called the **construction documents**, are completed. The construction documents are made up of the following:

- Detailed construction drawings that graphically describe the final project design and provide the *quantitative* details and instructions regarding the facility
- Specifications that provide written details that describe the *quality* of the project
- Other written documents that outline the rights and obligations of the contractor and the owner

The construction documents are given to the authorities having jurisdiction over the project for review and are distributed to bidding contractors so that they can estimate the costs. Eventually, the construction documents form the basis for the legal contract between the owner and the contractor hired to do the work.

We'll be discussing many of the construction documents later in this text, for now, let's look briefly at what they are.

Construction documents: the drawings

During this final stage of design, every detail is worked out and complete plans, elevations, sections, and details – the **construction drawings** (sometimes referred to as just the *plans* or the *drawings*) – are produced. These drawings are more detailed than the design development drawings and are the instructions to the contractor regarding what to build. Most projects have separate drawings showing the floor plans overlaid with structural details, the electrical system, the mechanical and plumbing systems, and more. Some of the construction drawings are developed by the architect and some are developed by consultants (but coordinated by the architect).

Figure 7.9 represents the same area of the SRJC library as shown in the schematic and design development drawings (Figures 7.7 and 7.8). Though it

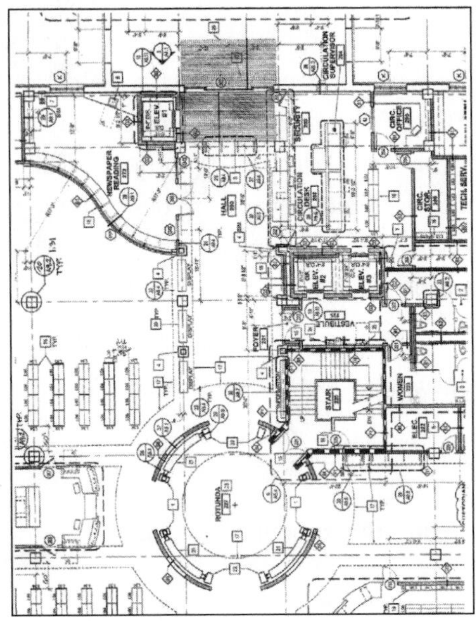

Figure 7.9. Design construction drawing

is apparent that this is the same area of the building (note the cafe, the location of the stairs, and the rotunda), the increased level of detailing is dramatic.

Drawings are done by hand or, more typically, by computer. A complete set of printed drawings for a complex structure can weigh many pounds. Today massive rolls of drawings are becoming increasingly unusual; drawings are much more likely to be produced electronically using computer aided design (CAD) programs or building information modeling (BIM). Drawings can now easily be transported on a CD, and may be electronically distributed. No matter whether drawn by hand or electronically, however, every line, symbol, and abbreviation on the drawings has meaning and a contractor's accurate reading of them is crucial if the project is to meet the conditions of the contract.

Construction documents: the specifications

A building cannot be priced, nor built, using the plans alone. Written specifications complement the drawings and expand on the information contained in them. The specifications explain the characteristics of materials, manufacturers, and workmanship and are necessary for purchase of the proper products and materials as well as accurate assessment of the installation requirements. For example, the drawings might specify concrete, but there are large variations in labor costs depending on curing methods, surface finish, color, and so on. The specifications give the contractor and the estimator this information.

As with the rest of the design stage, the architect is responsible for developing (or hiring someone to help develop) the specifications. As design decisions are made and products or performance requirements determined, the specifications are completed and finalized. They are a key part of the construction documents. (Specifications are discussed in Chapter 16.)

Construction documents: other bidding documents

In most projects, a contractor is hired at the completion of the design phase. As we've already learned, the contractor uses the drawings and specifications to price the job. At the completion of the design phase, the architect coordinates the development of other documents that, with the drawings and specifications, form what are called the bid documents. The bid documents are distributed as part of a bid package to contractors who are interested in being hired to do the work. We'll go into detail on the bidding documents in Chapter 8.

At the conclusion of design, a project has completed its first two stages: feasibility, and programming and design. The owner is now ready to hire a contractor, and this is the subject of the next chapter.

Figures. 7.2, 7.3, 7.4, 7.5, 7.7, 7.8, 7.9 courtesy of TLCD Architects, Santa Rosa, CA and Shepley Bulfinch Richardson & Abbott Inc., Boston, MA

Chapter Vocabulary

Bid documents – the collection of documents (including drawings, specifications, agreement forms, general conditions, and other documents) used to make and obtain bids and to define the requirements of the work and the process that the contractor must follow when submitting a bid. When a construction contract is executed, most of the bid documents become contract documents.

Construction documents – the written and graphic documents prepared or assembled by the architect for communicating the project design for construction and administering the construction contract.

Construction drawings (working drawings or plans) – the detailed plans developed by the architect that are part of the construction documents. These drawings identify the layout and dimensions of a project.

Design development – the stage of the design process in which a designer (an architect or an engineer) refines the design and makes decisions regarding layout, materials, and systems and takes the design to approximately 60 percent completion.

Design phase – the stage of a project in which a designer (an architect or engineer) develops a design that meets the owner's vision and goals and creates the documents necessary to estimate the cost for the project and to enable a contractor to build it.

Details – drawings that graphically represent blow-ups of specific elements to show how products or materials fit together.

Elevations – drawings that graphically represent a building as if the viewer is looking straight at it at eye level.

Floor plans – graphic representations of a building using horizontal slices through the structure.

Program – a document that provides design objectives and requirements as guidance to a project's designer.

Schematic design – the first phase of design, which focuses on developing an overall form and layout for the project. Schematic drawings are not detailed and are used for analyzing design alternatives.

Sections – drawings that graphically represent a structure by showing vertical cuts through the entire building or a portion of the building.

Specifications – written descriptions of the work that define the materials, the processes, and the quality of products and systems. The specifications and the drawings work together to provide the information contractors need in order to price and build a project.

Test Yourself

1. What is the purpose of a program? Who typically has major responsibility during this stage?
2. Give three examples of information that might be included in a project's program.
3. What is the goal of the design phase of a project?
4. Who has major responsibility during the design phase?
5. Which document does the designer use to find out what the owner's goals are?
6. At which design phase will the architect and owner come to agreement regarding floor plans?
7. What is the difference between a floor plan and an elevation?
8. What drawings does the contractor use to estimate the costs of a job?
9. What are specifications?
10. Who is responsible for coordinating the development of the construction documents?

PART 3

Bidding and the Contractor

- Chapter 8: Bidding and Awarding the Job
- Chapter 9: Contractors: Finding and Qualifying for the Right Jobs
- Chapter 10: Fundamentals of Estimating
- Chapter 11: Creating Estimates

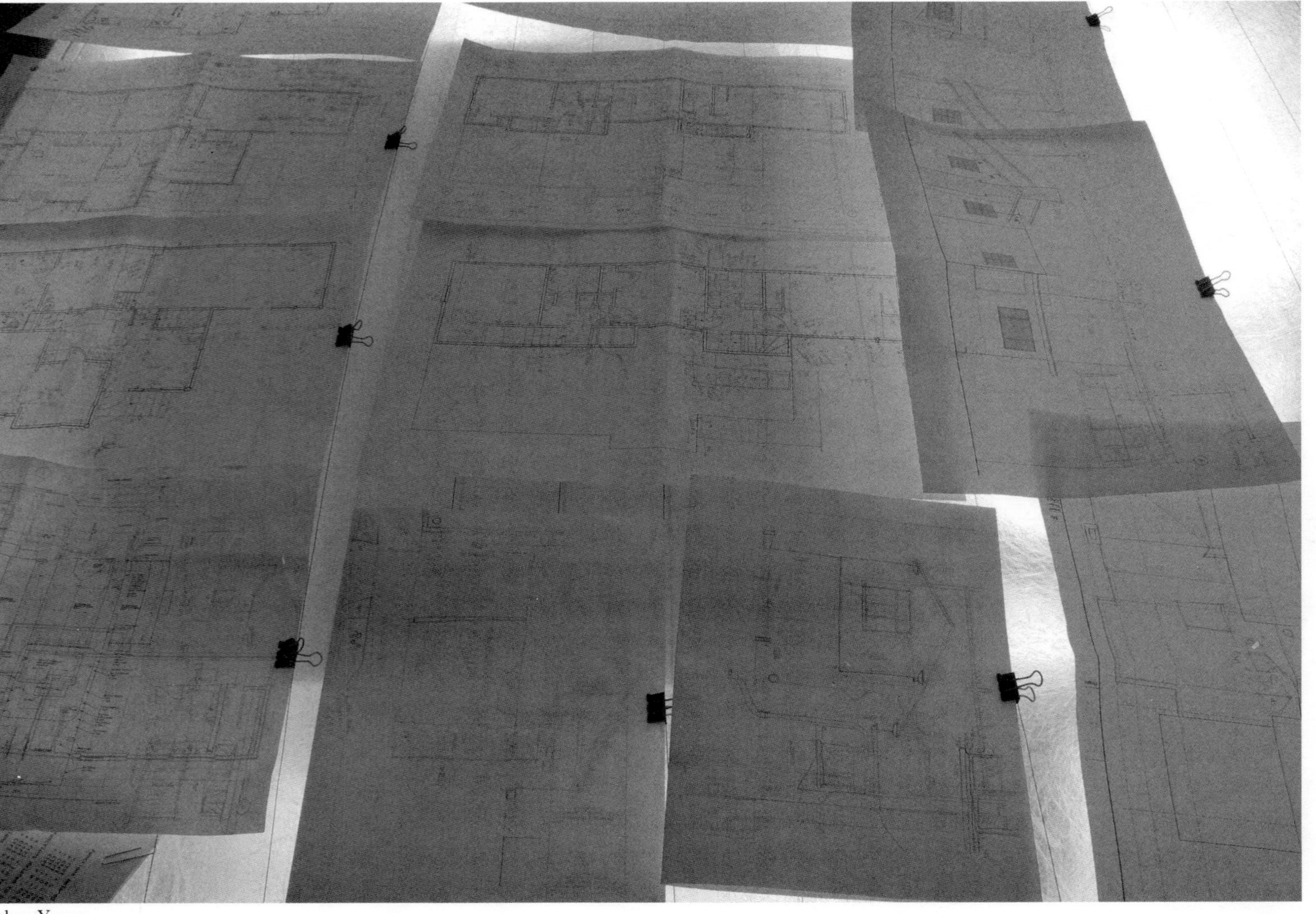

Andrea Young

CHAPTER 8

Bidding and Awarding the Job

Once programming and design (stage 2) are over and the construction drawings and specifications are complete and approved by the owner, the process of hiring a general contractor can begin.

The most common way for an owner to hire a contractor is through a process called competitive bidding, in which multiple contractors compete against each other to be hired. Competitively bid jobs require that information be there in the first place for them to bid on, however. This information is contained in a bid package, which is developed under the direction of the architect and defines and describes the work and identifies bidding and contracting requirements. When the bid package is complete and the owner and his team are ready to hire a contractor, the bid package is distributed to contractors so that they can submit a price to build it. This is called going out to bid.

The bid package is made up of different documents (the bid documents). The drawings and specifications are familiar (see Chapters 7 and 16), but they are not the only documents included in the bid package. Some of the documents provide direction for how bids are to be submitted; others describe the contractual obligations of the parties and form the basis for the legal obligations between the contractor and the owner should they enter into a contract.

In addition to a price for doing the work, the bid package typically requires that contractors submit a variety of back-up forms and documents. These documents might include a qualification questionnaire, a list of former clients, bonds, and more. The bid plus the back-up documentation are all submitted together and form the contractor's bid submittal. Instructions contained in the bid package outline the exact requirements for prospective contractors' bid submittals, including where and when they must be submitted. When all the bids are gathered, they are analyzed and the qualified contractor who promises to build the project for the lowest reasonable cost typically gets the job (although not always, as we'll learn).

Because many owners feel that the best price occurs when there is competitive bidding, it is often used. On public (government) jobs, competitive bidding is generally a requirement and all qualified contractors are expected to be given the opportunity to bid under the same terms and conditions.

Trade secrets On competitively bid jobs, potential contractors each submit a (secret) bid to the owner. In many cases, the prospective contractor makes public the bid amount, while the back-up information – the exact numbers that make up the bid – remain confidential. The reader might wonder why this is so. Established contractors use their own historical data to develop their bids and these data direct strategic decisions, such as how much they can or will pay for subcontracted work. If they let other contractors know how they calculated a bid, they may be giving away a competitive advantage.

Let's look at the process of bidding in more detail.

The process of bidding

Although every project is different, for most competitively bid projects the process of bidding is fairly consistent and includes the following steps:

Step 1. Architect completes bid package
Step 2. Owner solicits bids
Step 3. Contractors review bid information
Step 4. Contractors develop and submit bids
Step 5. Owner analyzes bids and awards contract

Step 1. Architect completes bid package

The bidding process is dependent on a bid package, which the architect provides to all bidding contractors. As noted, the bid package is made up of the bid documents, with information that enables potential contractors to price (i.e., estimate the cost of building) and, eventually, build the job; it forms the basis for the legal obligations of the contractor and the owner should they enter into a contract; and it provide rules for submitting a bid.

Although the documents vary depending on the complexity and needs of the project, they typically include the following:

- **Instructions to bidders**
- **Bidder's questionnaire**
- **Bonding requirements**
- **Blank agreement/contract form**
- **General and supplementary conditions**
- **Construction drawings and specifications**

Let's look briefly at these documents.

Instructions to bidders

The instructions to bidders contain specific information on the requirements with which bidders must comply before and during submission of bids. The instructions tell a bidder how to properly prepare and submit a bid, such as:

- The format to use for submitting a bid
- Where and when submittals are due
- Availability of documents, including where to get them, deposits or costs, and where documents can be examined
- How to prepare bids, including required forms to use
- Process for acceptance or rejection of bids
- Conditions or irregularities under which a bidder may be disqualified
- Procedures regarding subcontractors (for example, the requirement for the contractor to identify potential subcontractors to the owner)

- Special applicable laws such as licensing requirements or requirements for special permits
- Preliminary schedule information

Bidder's questionnaire

When a contractor has not been pre-qualified or invited to bid, a questionnaire is typically included in the bid package. This form is designed to provide the owner with detailed information regarding the experience and financial viability of a bidder.

Pre-qualification of bidders may be used on public or private jobs. Pre-qualification occurs following a process determined by the owner and results in a select list of bidders determined by the owner to have the necessary abilities to complete certain types of work. A public transportation department, for example, might have a roster of pre-qualified contractors capable of quickly responding to emergencies. Pre-qualifying bidders can eliminate problems in the bidding by eliminating those who lack the experience and financial resources to be successful. When pre-qualification is not done, bidding contractors typically fill out questionnaires outlining their competency, experience, and financial stability and include them with their bids.

Bonding requirements

All public jobs and most large private projects require various types of bonds. The contractor purchases bonds to assure the owner that, among other things, the project will be completed as required. Sometimes the owner stipulates the language, if not the precise form of the bonds; sometimes precise language is supplied by the companies that sell construction bonds. (These companies are called sureties). Bond forms may or may not be included as part of the bid documents. We'll talk about bonds in the next chapter.

Blank agreement/contract form

A copy of a blank agreement is included with the bid package. The type of agreement used is determined by the delivery and payment methods, and is the document that the owner and the winning contractor sign. Among other things, the agreement identifies the dollar amount of the contract, how payment will be made to the contractor, and when the work must be complete. Although often referred to as the contract, the agreement is only one of the documents that make up the legal contract between the owner and the contractor: the agreement includes the other documents by reference. We discuss the types of construction contracts in Chapter 13 and specifically the agreement in Chapter 14.

General and supplementary conditions

The general and supplementary conditions outline the terms and conditions relating to the project. The ground rules for the project are set out in these documents, including the rights and obligations of the parties, procedures for payment, dispute resolution, changes in the work, and much more. For information on the general and supplementary conditions, see Chapter 15.

Construction drawings and specifications

We know from the previous chapter that the owner provides a program from which the design team can create the graphic and written documents that describe the project. The construction drawings are graphic depictions of the job and provide information about the size, dimensions, layout, and detailing of the structure. The specifications are the written information that gives essential additional detail on the quality of materials, products, and workmanship.

The construction drawings and the specifications (Chapter 16) form the bulk of the bid package.

Addenda – Many bid packages also contain addenda. Addenda are formal changes or clarifications issued by the owner or architect during the bidding process. Although the design is supposed to be 100 percent complete at the time it goes out to bid, there are often adjustments that need to be made after the bid documents have been dispersed. For example, the specification writer may determine that a change in a particular material is required; this change is issued as an addendum to the drawings. All contractors receive information on any addenda, and procedures regarding them are spelled out in the instructions to bidders. Typically, no changes are permitted within several days of the bid are open.

Alternates are design adjustments that are priced as separate additions (or deductions) to the base bid. Owners sometimes ask bidders to price alternates so that a decision can be made regarding whether to go ahead with a piece of work or the use of a product. For example, an owner might want to have solar panels on the roof but is concerned about the cost; the panels could be priced as an alternate and rejected if the price is too high, or added if the price is acceptable. Often substitutions are priced as alternates. An alternate might be the substitution of slate for asbestos roofing, carpet instead of tile, or Corian counters instead of fiberglass. Alternates can either increase the cost of the base bid (these are called **additive alternates**) or reduce the cost of the base bid (these are called **deductive alternates**).

Most of the bid documents become known as contract documents once the owner and contractor enter into a contract. Together these documents make up the legal obligations and rights of the parties – the contract.

Once the architect has completed the bid package as the first step in the bidding process, the next step is to let potential contractors know about the project.

Step 2. Owner solicits bids

All projects are advertised in one form or another and contractors are notified about jobs in different ways depending on the type of work. There are local, state, and federal legal requirements that any qualified contractor should have an opportunity to compete for jobs that use public funds. Notice must be given to interested or qualified contractors in advance of the bidding. This notice – called a **notice** or **advertisement to bid** – is made in newspapers, journals, trade publications, and the like. The notice briefly identifies the work and the owner, and gives minimum additional information such as where and when the bids are due and how to obtain complete bidding information and documents. Sometimes the notice contains more specific information that will impact a contractor's ability to submit a bid, such as contractor qualification requirements, provisions for bonds, and minimum wage requirements. A brief notice might look like the sample in Figure 8.1, printed in the local newspaper.

NOTICE is hereby given that the Governing Board of the LOCAL SCHOOL DISTRICT of the County of –, State of – will receive up to, but no later than, January 15, 2011, at 2:00 p.m. and will then publicly open and read aloud sealed bids for the

TOWN HIGH SCHOOL LIBRARY

Such bids shall be received at Bailey Hall on the campus of Town High School, 22 Main St., Town

Two non-mandatory bidder's conferences will be held, the first on December 9, 2010, at 10:00 a.m. The second bidder's conference will be held on January 6, 2011, at 10:00 a.m. Prospective bidders shall meet at Facilities Operations Dept., 100 Main St., Town, State.

This will be a construction managed multi-primed contract. Bid documents are available to Contractors holding a class of license listed in the contract bid divisions, for a $700.00 per set refundable deposit. Contact ABC Architecture at 101-100-2000

Figure 8.1. Notice to bid

When a private owner solicits bids from a select number of contractors, an **invitation to bid** is issued by mail. As has been noted, private parties have no requirements (apart from anti-discrimination laws) regarding whom they can hire, and many owners prefer to choose who can bid. Figure 8.2 is an example of how this invitation might read.

Local Architects | Address | Telephone

October 1, 2010

Ace Contracting Company

(Address)

Re: Project No. 3813

Owner: Developers

(Address)

You are invited to bid on a General Contract, for a 10-unit condominium, approximately 85,500 square feet. Structure will be three-story, steel frame with brick exterior.

Bids shall be on a fixed price basis. Project is to be completed in 420 calendar days from the date of award of the contract. Start of construction is tentatively set for Dec. 1, 2010.

Owner will receive bids until 3:00 p.m. on Tuesday, November 4, 2010, at (address). Bids received after this time will not be accepted.

Bid Documents may be examined at the Architect's office or at the Plan Center (Address).

Copies of the Bid Documents may be obtained at the Architect's office in accordance with the Instructions to Bidders upon depositing the sum of $100.00 for each set of documents. Any bidder, upon returning the documents in good condition, shall be returned their deposit in full. Any non-bidder returning the documents in good condition will be returned the sum of $75.00.

A Bid Bond (or bid security) in the amount of 10 percent of the bid must accompany each bid in accordance with the Instructions to Bidders. The winning contractor will enter into a fixed-price contract with the owner no later than November 11, 2010.

The Owner reserves the right to waive irregularities and to reject bids.

A mandatory pre-bid conference will be held at the architect's office at 3 PM on October 15.

Sincerely,

John Doe

Local Architects

Figure 8.2. Invitation to bid

Once the architect has compiled the bid documents and potential contractors have been made aware of the project, the contractors review the documents to determine their interest in submitting a bid.

Step 3. Contractors review bid documents

As we've seen, the notice for bids identifies where interested contractors can obtain a limited number of copies of the bid documents. This is typically through the architect or engineer and a refundable deposit is usually required to check out the documents. As the bidding contractor typically gets only one or two copies, additional sets are generally made available for subcontractors at a trade association or local Builders Exchange.

Thorough review of the documents is necessary before a contractor can make a reasonable decision regarding whether to bid. Developing a bid submittal that is complete, accurate, and competitive is a time-consuming and expensive proposition not to be entered into lightly. (Contractors are typically given two to four weeks to develop a bid submittal.) We'll be talking about the critical decision on whether or not to put together a bid submittal, and about estimating (which is the core component of the bid) in Chapters 9 and 10, respectively.

As part of their pre-bid review, contractors typically visit the site to identify special challenges or potential problems. Sometimes the owner *requires* a site review. The contractor does everything possible to identify potential problems before committing to a bid price. Some conditions (a rock outcropping, for example) can be identified in advance and taken into account in the estimate. The contractor also reviews any geological data that might be available.

Sometimes the owner will hold a pre-bid conference to answer any questions the contractors may have about the process and the project. As with the site visit, some owners make the conference a requirement for all bidding contractors.

Step 4. Contractors develop and submit bids

Putting together a bid is a complicated process for the contractor that involves several steps:

- Planning
- Preparing the estimate and tabulating the costs
- Completing and submitting the bid

Let's look briefly at each of these steps.

Planning

A bid submittal is expensive, and the contractor's first step (after deciding to move ahead) is to identify the team and strategize how to develop a complete and accurate submittal that will both succeed in winning the job and result in a successful project. The contractor develops a checklist of the tasks required to ensure that all parts of the submittal are complete and accurate. Typical tasks during the planning phase include:

- Identify which construction activities will be done with the contractor's own workers, and which tasks will be subcontracted to specialty contractors
- Begin to collect information on possible subcontractors
- Develop bid packages for possible subcontracted work so that the subcontractors can begin to estimate their portions of the project
- Seek clarification from the owner or architect on any questions or issues that are identified during review of the documents. It's not uncommon for drawings and/or specifications to have contradictions or omissions. For example, the construction drawings show Spanish tile on the roof, but the specifications identify asphalt shingles. Bidding contractors need this confusion cleared up in order to price the job correctly.
- Note ideas regarding possible building procedures such as construction or manufacturing choices that might impact the cost estimate. For example, a contractor might determine that significant costs can be saved if the roof is built off-site and hoisted into place.

Preparing the estimate and tabulating the costs

The contractor estimates costs for the entire job, including anticipated subcontractor bids. The first step in estimating costs is completing **quantity takeoffs** – the process of determining, through measurement, the amount of materials required for a project.

Once all the quantities are determined, the contractor's estimator identifies costs for labor, materials, equipment, and taxes. Overhead and profit are added to the total. Anticipated subcontractor costs are included in the contractor's estimate as **plug numbers**. Plug numbers provide the general contractor with a guideline for what the subcontractors' sub-bids should be and act as a price "placeholder" in case no sub-bids are submitted.

The contractor has a detailed cost estimate for the entire job but, as noted earlier ("Trade secrets"), provides just the total cost to the owner as the bid amount. This final number is adjusted depending on the subcontractor's bids, which may be provided at the very last minute. There's an important and complex legal issue of whether subcontractors can be held to their sub-bids, but that is beyond the scope of this book.

We'll go into detail on estimating in Chapters 10 and 11.

Completing and submitting the bid

As already noted, there are additional documents that typically need to be submitted with the bid itself. These documents might include a bid bond, a contractor's qualification form or questionnaire, a list of proposed subcontractors, and insurance forms. Bids must be submitted exactly as required and by the bid deadline. Late bids are returned unopened to the contractor. Usually, a member of the contractor's team hand-delivers the bid to the designated location.

The close of bidding is often called, confusingly, the "bid opening," because this is when bid submittals are opened. At a public bid opening, where bids are read aloud, care is given to announce what is called the "apparent" low bidder. This provides the owner's selection team with time to review all the bids to verify responsiveness.

The final step in the bidding process is the analysis of bid submittals.

Responsible bidder and **responsive bid** – A **responsible bidder** is one who meets the bid requirements regarding qualifications, experience, and any other criteria deemed necessary by the owner. For example, there may be a requirement that contractors have a certain amount of experience doing similar work. Contractors without the required experience are not considered responsible bidders and are not considered for the job. A **responsive bid** is a bid submittal that meets all the bidding requirements as outlined in the bid package. For example, bids are typically required to be submitted at a certain time and place. A bid that is received late is considered unresponsive and is not likely to be considered. Thus a contractor without required experience might submit a "responsive" bid, but that contractor is not considered a "responsible" bidder, and will probably not be awarded the job.

Step 5. Owner analyzes bids and awards contract

Before awarding a contract, the owner and the architect carefully review all the bids to ensure they are responsive and that the contractors have submitted their bids according to the instructions. They verify that required attachments, such as the builders questionnaire and back-up documents, are all attached. If the owner is a public entity, the low bidder is awarded the job. As we've already learned, if competitive bidding is used on a private job, the owner may select any of the bidding contractors; the lowest price may not be the most important criterion.

The winning contractor is **awarded** the contract and is typically sent a **notice of award** (also called a letter of intent) alerting him that he has been awarded the job and that the owner intends to enter into a contract.

Negotiated jobs

Not all projects utilize competitive bidding. There is another way that contractors get hired: negotiation.

As noted previously, on privately funded projects the owner may use any non-discriminatory criteria he or she prefers for choosing a contractor. Although many private owners do select a contractor using competitive bidding, unlike publicly funded jobs there is no requirement for them to do so, nor is there a requirement that the contractor with the lowest bid be awarded the contract. They might select a contractor based on the fee she proposes charging for her services, the time frame for project completion, the contractor's management plan and workload, or her experience with similar projects.

Sometimes a few select contractors are invited to look at early design documents and put together proposals based on the owner's selection criteria. The owner then compares the proposals, interviews one or more of the contractors, and eventually awards a **negotiated contract**.

In some cases, a single contractor negotiates a price with the owner. In this situation, the contractor is typically involved during the design phase and provides expertise such as constructability reviews (which we've already learned is a process of reviewing construction processes from start to finish before construction begins).

There are several reasons why an owner might choose to use negotiation: maybe they have preferred contractors that they tend to work with; the design isn't far enough along to result in good bids; or the owner wants to have the contractor's expertise during the design process. When negotiation is used, the contractor and the owner can work together to determine the extent of the work and different design solutions can be explored and balanced against the budget, with final pricing determined at the completion of the design process. Many aspects of the contract can be negotiated with the contractor.

Time factors might also lead an owner to a negotiated job. Projects that are competitively bid typically require a sequential design/construction process. In contrast, negotiated projects provide an opportunity for design and construction to overlap, and hence to complete a project in less time than a competitively bid project.

While some delivery methods can use negotiation, some cannot. For example, all projects using a design-bid-build delivery method must use competitive bidding, because with this delivery method the three design, bid, and build stages are performed sequentially, and bidding does not affect the design. And, as noted, public jobs rarely use negotiation because laws require competitive bidding.

Open or closed projects – The reader may be familiar with the terms open or closed projects. Projects that allow any qualified contractor to bid are called open bid projects. These are, typically, publicly funded projects. Jobs that are negotiated or bid between a few select contractors are referred to as closed bid projects. Most privately funded projects are closed bid.

The delivery method selected for the job (see Chapter 6) will, in part, determine how the contractor is hired. Irrespective of whether a project is bid or negotiated, however, they both require clear processes and procedures.

Chapter Vocabulary

Addenda – formal changes or clarifications issued by the owner or architect during a bidding process.

Additive alternates – design adjustments that are priced as separate additions to a base bid.

Advertisement to bid (notice to bid) – a public solicitation for bids.

Award – procurement of a contract; selection of a winning bidder.

Bid – a price quote presented by a contractor that identifies the price for which the contractor offers to complete work.

Bidder's questionnaire – a form designed to determine a bidder's qualifications for a job.

Bid documents (bid package) – the collection of documents (including drawings, specifications, agreement forms, general conditions, and other documents) used to make and obtain bids and to define the requirements of the work and the process that the contractor must follow when submitting a bid. When a construction contract is executed, most of the bid documents become contract documents.

Bid submittal – a contractor's response to a bid package that typically includes the contractor's price for completing the work plus backup documentation. The bid submittal must be made exactly according to the requirements of the bid package.

Competitive bidding – the process of selecting a contractor that is based on several contractors competing against each other to be awarded a contract to do work. Typically (but not always), the contractor with the lowest bid gets the job.

Constructability review – review of materials, systems, and installation methodologies by experienced contractors to ensure that a project can be built efficiently.

Deductive alternates – design adjustments that are priced as separate cost reductions to a base bid.

Going out to bid – presenting a project to contractors so that they can submit a price to build it.

Instruction to bidders – one of the bid documents; it gives the exact requirements for prospective contractors' bids.

Invitation to bid – a solicitation for bids made by an owner to select contractors.

Negotiated contract – a method of selecting a contractor in which a few select contractors are asked to look at early design documents and put together a proposal. The owner then compares the proposals, interviews one or more of the contractors, and eventually selects a winning contractor.

Notice of award – notification made to a winning contractor that he or she has gotten the job and that the owner intends to enter into a contract.

Plug numbers – anticipated subcontractor expenses. Plug numbers provide the general contractor with a guideline for what the sub-bids should be and act as a price "placeholder" in case no sub-bids are submitted.

Pre-bid conference – a meeting, facilitated by the owner or architect, before bids are due, to answer any questions the contractors may have about the bid process and the project.

Pre-qualification – a determination by an owner that selected contractors have the necessary abilities to complete certain types of work.

Quantity take-off – the process of itemizing the amount of materials required for a job.

Responsible bidder – a contractor who meets the bid requirements regarding qualifications, experience, and any other criteria deemed necessary by the owner.

Responsive bid – a bid submittal that meets all bidding requirements as outlined in the bid package.

Test Yourself

1. What does it mean when a project goes out to bid?
2. Who is responsible for completing or coordinating the documents that the contractor uses to price a job?
3. What are the two ways that contractors are hired? How do they differ?
4. What types of costs are included in the contractor's bid estimate?
5. What is the difference between a bid and a bid submittal?
6. Why might it be helpful to an owner to pre-qualify contractors?
7. What happens if a contractor fails to submit his/her bid on time?
8. Why is it important that a contractor visit the site before submitting a bid?
9. When a contractor prepares a bid submittal, the first step is planning. What are the other two steps?
10. What is the pre-bid conference and why might it be important?

Andrea Young

CHAPTER 9

Contractors: Finding & Qualifying for the Right Job

Before a contractor can bid on a job, he or she first has to find it! So how do contractors identify possible work, and what are the issues that will determine if it's the *right* work or not? Not every job is an appropriate job for a particular contractor. Having decided that the job is right, the next question is whether the contractor can qualify for the job, which, in turn, may depend on whether the contractor can get bonded.

In this chapter, we'll look first at the process the contractor uses to decide whether to bid, and next at the process of getting bonded.

This chapter also applies to subcontractors: how they find and qualify for jobs from a general contractor. The flip side to this process – how the general contractor determines if prospective subs are qualified – is covered in Chapter 21.

How to find work

The construction industry has always been very competitive; with more sophisticated owners, tighter budgets, and more complicated projects, the competition is becoming more intense. Some contractors find the process of finding work a real hassle. The lucky ones have ongoing business with the same clients; others rely on word of mouth and good referrals. Most construction firms, however, need to be proactive in order to find work and win contracts.

A good first step is to keep up to date on what jobs are in the planning phase and what jobs will be going out to bid. Because all construction projects become public knowledge in one way or another, it's fairly easy for contractors to get information about upcoming projects. Public jobs (those that use taxpayer money) are listed in newspapers, trade journals, and various government publications. We learned in the last chapter that these notices serve as an announcement that all qualified contractors can submit a bid for an upcoming facility. Private jobs, while not required to advertise, may also be listed in newspapers and trade journals.

Many contractors subscribe to electronic news services that provide up-to-date information on the status of many projects. McGraw-Hill Construction Dodge Reports (*www.fwdodge.com*) is one of the best known of these services. Reed Construction (*www.reedconstructiondata.com*) provides hundreds of leads on commercial and civil construction projects nationwide through publications and online services. There are a variety of other online services such as *www.buildcentral.com* and *www.bidclerk.com*, which also provide lists. Many local Builders Exchanges publish lists of jobs that are about to go out to bid.

Often a contracting company identifies someone to be responsible for networking and making sure the firm has a presence in the community. It is important for contractors to be known by the community because many private owners prefer that only a select number of known contractors be offered an opportunity to bid.

Does this project make sense?

In Chapter 5, we learned that an owner should be careful not to jump into the wrong project. The same can be said for contractors; not all jobs are worth the time and cost to pursue. Submitting bids or proposals can be very time-consuming and expensive propositions for contractors, and it is not in a contractor's best interest to bid on every job. Understanding what projects are worth bidding on is a critical decision, as taking on the wrong job can have negative results. There are laws regulating the bidding process, and if an owner accepts a contractor's bid, a contract has been formed that now obligates both parties. (This may also be true when subs submit bids to GCs.) There's an old saying worth remembering: *Be careful what you bid on because you might get it!*

What are the issues a contractor considers when deciding whether to bid? Every contractor has his own list of factors; here are a few:

- Contractor's experience
- Quality of design information
- Other team members
- Type of contract
- Location of the job
- Time frame and liquidated damages
- Local economy and profit potential
- Desire for the job

Let's look at each of these to see why they might be important.

Contractor's experience

Most contractors specialize in certain types of work. Lack of experience can increase a contractor's risk of mis-estimating costs or being unable to meet the contract obligations. Inability to assess the costs on a job accurately can mean that the contractor might get the job, but then find there are inadequate funds to complete it because his estimate (and hence what the owner will be paying) was too low. Conversely, an unnecessarily high bid greatly reduces a contractor's chance of winning the job.

Here's an example of why experience (or **experiential information**) matters. A contractor is completing a cost estimate in preparation to submit a bid for a job with complicated concrete foundations. The designer has shown the extent of the foundation on the drawings and has described the quality of the concrete in the specifications. From this information, the contractor can accurately identify how much concrete will be needed and determine its purchase price. If the contractor is inexperienced in this type of work, however, it is difficult to arrive at an accurate estimate of the labor costs for forming and handling and finishing the concrete. One cost concern: Should the estimate include anything to cover spillage and waste? If so, how much? Only experience and the historical data that come with doing this type of work, coupled perhaps with published cost information, can really enable a contractor to produce an accurate estimate.

In addition, even if a contractor happens to put together a correct bid on the basis of insufficient experience (of the appropriate type), his lack of experience might later make it difficult for him to meet contractual obligations efficiently. Once the inexperienced contractor is on the job, he may discover that efficiency suffers, leading to higher costs and less profit.

Quality of design information

In addition to how much experience a contractor has, a contractor considering whether or not to bid on a project will carefully analyze the **design information**, which is the information about a construction project provided to bidders or contractors in the plans and specifications. The more complete and thorough this information, the less guessing the contractor has to do; a contractor cannot accurately estimate a project with incomplete or sloppy design information. When a contractor provides a cost figure to an owner for what a job is going to cost, both the contractor and the owner want to feel confident that the price is accurate.

For example: You are a roofing contractor and you are interested in submitting a bid for a new roof. The owner's house is old, and there is no way to know the condition of the sheathing or the ceiling joists until you remove the existing roofing. How can you provide the owner with a realistic cost estimate when you don't know the full extent of the work involved? You can do one of several things:

1. Pass on the opportunity to bid because a mistake could cost you dearly
2. Price the job as accurately as you can and hope for the best
3. Put language in the contract (and hope the owner agrees) that will cover you in case the work is more extensive than shown on the drawings

Poor design information, like inadequate experience, can result in an underbid job. If a contractor underbids a job and the costs for doing the work are greater than the bid amount, then the contractor typically has to absorb the difference. As a result, the contractor may attempt to cut corners, or to make up the costs if an owner asks for changes. Underbidding can result in the loss of a contractor's reputation and, in some cases, extreme financial hardship.

Other team members

Because outlays must be made for labor and materials before payment is received, and because of uncertainties such as weather, construction is financially risky. It is important that all members of the project team – the owner, the architect, and the contractor – function effectively as a group so that work can proceed smoothly, thus reducing risk. The GC will want to know who the owner is: Is he easy to work with or does he have a reputation for being difficult and litigious? Is the owner sophisticated and does he understand the building process? What is his reputation among other contractors? Similarly, is the architect someone who does quality work? Have her drawings for other jobs been clear and complete? Does she have a reputation for responding quickly to questions? Is she easy to work with? On many projects, the architect administers the contract between the owner and the contractor and acts as the owner's agent on a jobsite. This arrangement has the potential to be adversarial and it is complicated when any of the parties is uncooperative. Contractors need to think about who they're going to be "marrying" for the life of the project, before making a proposal.

Type of contract

The bid package identifies the contract type. Because different contract types impose varying levels of risk, the contract type is a factor in the contractor's decision whether or not to bid. Different contracts are distinguished primarily by how the contractor gets paid. A job requiring that the contractor guarantee his price (such as a lump-sum contract; see Chapter 13), for example, is riskier for the contractor than one stipulating that the contractor will be paid for whatever the job costs (cost plus contract). The contractor will want to be sure that any risks implied by the contract are balanced by potential profit.

Location of the job

A project close to home is easier for a contractor to manage and involves lower overhead than one which is located at a distance. Furthermore, when a contractor understands the local subcontractor and supplier markets, it is likely that cost and labor estimates will be more accurate and that she will be more successful at putting together a good construction team.

Time frame and liquidated damages

Not all projects happen at the right time. The contractor wants to be sure that his or her crews will be available and that a new project won't overstretch the business. Another consideration is that the owner's time frame for construction be reasonable. If the owner insists that the work be completed in 12 months and you're confident that the cost figures don't work unless you spend 13, it may not be the right job.

Sometimes a contract includes a **liquidated damages** clause that will assess fees against a contractor for failure to complete work on time according to the terms of the construction contract. In this situation, the prospective contractor will be concerned about the added financial risk, especially if the schedule is tight.

Here's an example of how liquidated damages might work. A project completion has been delayed by 20 days. If liquidated damages (which are determined and agreed to before the start of construction) are assessed at $1,000/day for every day the project is delayed, then the contractor would likely (if the liquidated damages were a reasonable up-front estimate of the owner's likely financial harm from a delay) owe the owner $20,000 (20 days x $1,000/day). The existence of a liquidated damages clause on a job with a tight construction schedule may prove too big a financial risk for the contractor. It's easy to see how liquidated damages might eat up a contractor's profit.

On the other hand, some projects have incentive payments for early completion (see the example of the Santa Monica Freeway and C. C. Myers in Chapter 19) and this might prove to be a powerful incentive for a contractor.

Local economy and profit potential

Contractors aren't in business only for the fun of it: is there sufficient money to be made from the job, given the amount of risk and other considerations? If it's a "hot" market and everyone has work, it may be difficult for the contractor to find good subcontractors. This can result in an inability to complete the work according to the required schedule or quality. Conversely, if the economy is slow and there is insufficient work to go around, then competition from other contractors will be stiff and bids will tend to be lower. This might result in significantly lower (or even zero) profit. When developing his or her bid, the contractor balances expected profit with the realities of the market.

Desire for the job

There are various reasons for wanting a job besides the potential for immediate profit. Maybe the contractor is trying to break into a new sector, or it is a high-profile job that would be good advertising for the contractor. Sometimes it's worth taking a job just to keep one's crews busy.

Once the contractor has studied the bid package and assessed the risks, he makes a decision either to move ahead with the development of a bid submittal or to pass. Spending too much time on bids for wrong projects can have serious negative long-term implications for a business.

Qualifying for the job: bonding

We've already noted that contractors typically need to have experience that matches the project. Other issues might also disqualify a contractor; bonding is one of these.

Bonding requirements

There are many different types of bonds. The most common types are those sold by federal, state, city, and other levels of government to raise money for projects such as roads and schools. These are called *municipal bonds*. Those who buy municipal bonds are doing so as a financial investment; they are lending money to the issuer of the bond. Investors who purchase a bond can expect to earn a certain amount of interest and be repaid by a certain date.

Bonds used in the construction industry (called **surety bonds**; also referred to as construction bonds or contract surety bonds) are different; they are used as a means to reduce an owner's risk on a project or, in the case of bonding by subcontractors, to reduce the GC's risk. The following are some of these risks:

- The risk that the low bidder won't enter into a contract and that the owner will be obligated to accept a higher price
- The risk that the contractor will not complete the work
- The risk that suppliers and/or subcontractors will not be paid by the general contractor and will take action against the owner

Surety bonds provide a way to reduce these risks. Surety bonds are three-party instruments (documents) between the issuer of the bond (typically called a surety), the contractor, and the beneficiary (typically the owner) – or, alternatively, between the surety, subcontractor, and beneficiary (in this case, the general contractor). Contract bonds are issued for specific projects.

A contractor's ability to purchase bonds is an important factor in determining the suitability of a contractor for a particular job. The size of a project determines the size of the bond. Because contractors must qualify to buy bonds (see the following detailed discussion of qualification), an inability to purchase them creates a limitation on the size and types of projects a contractor can do.

The surety sells bonds to a contractor in exchange for taking on or "assuming" the obligations of the contractor. This means that if the contractor doesn't pay subcontractors or gets into financial trouble and walks off the job, the surety will step in and the owner won't be left with the potentially devastating impact of an unfinished project.

Surety bonds are not the same as insurance. Insurance companies take in premiums and expect to pay out a certain amount every year to those who have bought policies. If you are a homeowner with a $100,000 fire insurance policy and your house burns down, the insurance company will pay you $100,000. In contrast, surety companies charge the person or company that purchases a bond (in our case, a contractor) a fee to offer them credit in case it is needed.

For example, Superior Construction Company is required by the terms of its contract with the owner to purchase a bond for a current project. Superior gets in over its head, however, and walks off the job before it is finished. Because Superior bought a construction bond, the owner is protected and the surety pays to have the work finished. In contrast to our home insurance example, though, Superior is not off the hook financially; it has to *repay the surety*.

Most large insurance companies have surety departments. There are also insurance companies that do nothing *except* surety work. In both cases, a company, which issues surety bonds, must be licensed by the state (typically the Department of Insurance or its equivalent). The state where the surety company is located conducts periodic examinations of the company to ensure its soundness.

The owner, not the contractor, makes the determination regarding whether bonds will be required on a job. Many large private projects require bonds; public jobs also have bonding requirements. When bonds are specified in the bid package, it is the contractor's obligation to obtain them; typically, their cost is included in the bid. If the contract price changes, the bond and the premium also change. For example, if a contractor has purchased a $100,000 bond for a project and there is a change in the job that adds $20,000 to the project cost, the value of the bond increases to cover this additional amount. The fee, or premium, that must be paid to the surety increases accordingly.

Not all projects require that bonds be provided, but on those that do, the general contractor typically requires the subcontractors to be bonded too. General contractors require bonds for much the same reason that owners do: to reduce their own risk in case a subcontractor fails to complete his or her work.

Again, the owner can require that the GC get a surety bond, to protect the owner. The GC can require that each subcontractor get a surety bond, to protect the GC.

Types of surety bonds in construction

Different types of surety bonds are designed to address different risks. There are several types of bonds in construction; the three primary types are:

- **Bid bonds**
- **Performance bonds**
- **Payment bonds**

Each of these bonds is purchased separately by the contractor and benefits the owner. Let's see how each reduces different types of risk.

Bid bonds

Bid bonds assure an owner that if a contractor wins a competitive bid, the owner will pay no more than that winning bid amount. If the low bidder fails to sign a contract with the owner, the surety may step in and pay the owner the difference between the low bid and the next lowest bid. The owner is saved from having to pay a higher price for the work. These bonds are typically issued for 5 to 10 percent of the total dollar value of the bid and are submitted with the bid.

Here's an example of how a bid bond works. Contractor A enters a bid amount of $1,000,000 for a job and includes a $100,000 bid bond (10 percent of the bid amount). The next lowest bid, from Contractor B, is for $1,050,000. Contractor A is awarded the contract but decides that he made a mistake in his bidding and would lose money at the bid price so decides against signing the contract. The owner has little choice but to accept the next lowest bid, that of Contractor B, at $50,000 more than Contractor A's bid ($1,050,000 – $1,000,000.) Under the bid bond, the surety is responsible for paying the owner up to the value of the bid bond (in this case, $100,000). The owner gets the difference between the two bids ($50,000) plus any related costs up to $100,000. The surety then pursues reimbursement from Contractor A; the whole point is that the owner is freed from fighting Contractor A to make good the owner's losses.

Performance bonds

Performance bonds assure the owner that work will be completed in accordance with the plans and specifications, at the bid price (plus any agreed changes). Performance bonds kick in if the contractor has **defaulted**, that is, has seriously failed to live up to the terms of a contract, also called breaching the contract. For example, if a contractor's business fails and he or she walks off the job before it is finished, the contractor is considered in default and the owner formally terminates the construction contract. The owner files a claim with the surety, which then steps in to make sure that the work is completed. There are several ways that sureties choose to respond to a default:

- The surety finances the original contractor or provides the support required to complete the work.
- A replacement contractor, agreeable to both the owner and the surety and managed by the owner, is hired to complete the work.
- The surety simply pays the owner what is necessary to complete the project (up to the bond amount); the surety thus gives up any control over the project, but it also assumes no further responsibility.
- The surety contests the owner's termination of the contractor.

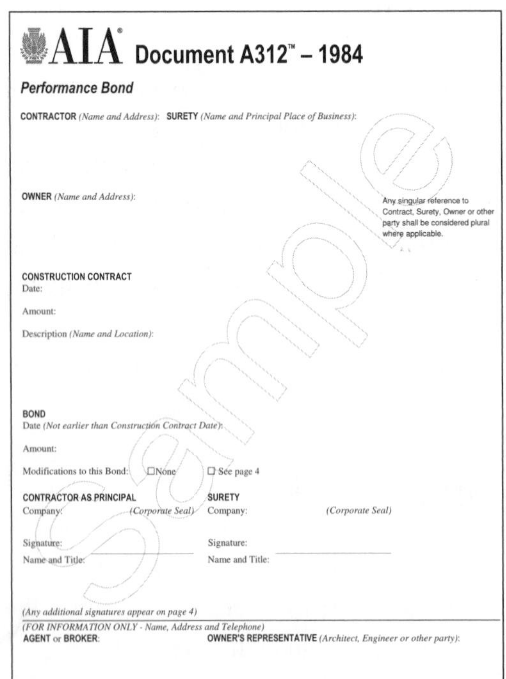

AIA® Document A312™ – 1984

Performance Bond

CONTRACTOR *(Name and Address)*: **SURETY** *(Name and Principal Place of Business)*:

OWNER *(Name and Address)*:

Any singular reference to Contract, Surety, Owner or other party shall be considered plural where applicable.

CONSTRUCTION CONTRACT
Date:

Amount:

Description *(Name and Location)*:

BOND
Date *(Not earlier than Construction Contract Date)*:

Amount:

Modifications to this Bond: ☐None ☐ See page 4

CONTRACTOR AS PRINCIPAL	**SURETY**
Company: *(Corporate Seal)*	Company: *(Corporate Seal)*
Signature:	Signature:
Name and Title:	Name and Title:

(Any additional signatures appear on page 4)

(FOR INFORMATION ONLY - Name, Address and Telephone)
AGENT or **BROKER**: **OWNER'S REPRESENTATIVE** *(Architect, Engineer or other party)*:

Figure 9.1. Performance bond
AIA Document A312 - 1984

Unlike bid bonds, performance bonds are typically issued for 100 percent of the bid amount and are purchased after the contract is awarded. The cost of the bond is based on the contract amount and the contractor's bond rating (see the section "Surety Program" to follow).

Payment bonds

Payment bonds (also called labor and material bonds) assure an owner that subcontractors and suppliers get paid. The owner pays the general contractor who, in turn, pays the subcontractors. If the GC fails to pay the subs, the owner is at risk of having the sub (or supplier) take action against him. This action is likely be in the form of a mechanic's lien, which is a financial claim that a person who has performed work or provided materials makes against title to the improved property. (We'll look more at mechanic's liens in Chapter 24.)

As with performance bonds, payment bonds are typically issued for 100 percent of the contract price and are provided at the time the contract is signed. They are typically issued with performance bonds.

Contractor license bonds – There is another specific type of bond, called a contractor license bond, which guarantees that a contractor will operate within the laws and regulations required by the state in which he works; the bond is filed with the contractor's license. The requirements for having these bonds differ from state to state. In California, for example, the Contractor's State License Board is the regulatory agency that oversees the construction industry. They require that contractors purchase a license bond at the time that they are issued (or reissued) a license. The bond costs the contractor about $100, and can pay out as much as $12,500 for the benefit of consumers who may be damaged as a result of defective construction or other license law violations, or for the benefit of subcontractors and suppliers who have not been paid.

How do contractors qualify to buy bonds?

Although construction bonds benefit an owner, it is the contractor who must qualify to purchase them. This makes sense because it is the work of the contractor that is being guaranteed. When a contractor needs to buy a bond, he therefore doesn't just go to a surety, fill out a form, and get a bond. A surety company takes a risk when it provides bonds and is therefore selective about which contractors it is willing to underwrite and for how much. Qualifying for bonds is a time-consuming process.

Each surety company has its own guidelines and underwriting criteria. Three factors are of concern to every surety, however. They are:

- The contractor's capacity
- The contractor's capital
- The contractor's character

The contractor's capacity

Capacity is the ability and skill to do a particular project. Factors that determine a contractor's capacity include his or her years of experience and types of prior work, amount of other work currently under way, the size and location of the proposed project, and the contractor's organization and management. The surety wants to be sure the contractor has the physical resources and experience to do the job.

The contractor's capital

Capital refers to the amount of cash the contractor has and therefore the ability to finance the work under the contract. Typically, the contractor must finance the costs for labor and materials between progress payments and the surety will want to be sure that there is sufficient money to do so. The surety will also want to know if the contractor has enough financial assets to weather unexpected financial storms, such as if the job costs more than expected. Basically, does the financial condition of the contractor justify the risk to the surety?

The contractor's character

Character refers to the integrity and honesty of the owners and the senior staff of the construction company and their proven willingness to meet their obligations and commitments. Is the contractor likely to perform the obligations contained in the contract? For some sureties, this is the most important of the three factors. In order to assess the contractor's character the surety may consult the local Better Business Bureau and the licensing board, and seek testimonials from the contractor's former clients.

In order to help determine the capacity, capital, and character of a contractor, the surety requires the contractor to complete a lengthy qualification form. Information such as current and past work, dollar value of past and current projects, types of work completed, bank statements, current financial statements, references, and more are required.

Surety program (rating)

Typically, the contractor is provided with a **surety "program"** (sometimes referred to as a **rating**), which specifies the contractor's maximum bond amount for a single job and a maximum aggregate amount (total value of the contractor's current bonds). For example, Contractor A has a \$5 million single job rating and a \$10 million aggregate rating from his surety. The contractor has \$8 million of bonded work just started and wants to bid \$4 million for a new job. Although the new job amount is less than the amount of his single job rating (\$5 million), the total amount of current plus proposed work – the aggregate – is too high. It is unlikely that Contractor A will get the bond. The aggregate limit is based on cost to complete open projects, however, not the total contract value of open projects. If the $8 million dollar job had only $5 million left to complete, the aggregate work to complete would be less than $10 million and the contractor is likely to get the bond even though the total of the bonds is $12 million.

Once a surety gets involved in a project, it's understandable that it will take an interest in how the project is progressing. At the very least, it will require approval before the project costs can be increased through change orders.

To summarize, contractors weigh many factors before deciding to assume the lengthy and expensive task of submitting a bid. The requirement that bidding contractors purchase bonds immediately eliminates anyone with an insufficient bond rating. Even if a contractor qualifies to purchase the required bonds, there may be other good reasons not to submit a bid, however. These reasons include current workload and available labor; insufficient experience or design information to enable the contractor to develop a complete, accurate, and competitive bid; the required time frame for completion; type of contract and other team members; location of the project; and potential for profit. Finally, the contractor assesses whether he or she really wants the job for some long-term reason despite insufficient short-term profits on the particular job.

Chapter Vocabulary

Bid bond – a construction bond that insures an owner against the financial risk of a low bidder not executing a contract.

Capacity – the ability and skill of a contractor to complete a project; also, the competency or ability of a party to understand the terms of a contract.

Capital – the amount of cash available to a contractor.

Character – the integrity and honesty of the owners and the senior staff of the construction company and their proven willingness to meet their obligations and commitments.

Default (breach) – failure to live up to the terms of a contract.

Design information – the information about a construction project provided to bidders or contractors in the plans and specifications.

Experiential information – a person's level of experience with a type of work.

License bond (contractor license bond) – a bond that contractors are required to purchase as a condition to being licensed.

Liquidated damages – a previously agreed-upon amount of money the contractor is required to pay an owner if construction is not completed on time.

Payment bond – a construction bond that provides assurance to an owner that subcontractors and suppliers will get paid by the contractor; typically issued with performance bonds.

Performance bond – a construction bond that provides assurance to the owner that work will be completed in accordance with the plans and specifications at the bid price (plus any agreed changes).

Surety – a company (often an insurance company) that sells construction bonds.

Surety bond (construction bond) – a bond sold by a surety and used by an owner to manage risk on a project.

Surety program (rating) – a rating given by a surety that specifies the maximum bond amount that a contractor can qualify to purchase.

Test Yourself

1. Why might the type of project affect a contractor's ability to get a job?
2. Why is it important for contractors to network in their communities?
3. How does a local Builders Exchange assist contractors in finding work?
4. In what way do bonds impact a contractor's qualification for a job?
5. In what way does design information impact a contractor's bid amount?
6. How does experiential information impact a contractor's ability to get work?
7. Why does it matter to a contractor who the owner and architect are on a job?
8. What might be the consequences to a contractor of failing to complete a job on time?
9. Why might a contractor not bid on a job that is located far from his or her office?
10. Why might a contractor bid on a job that has no potential for profit?

Andrea Young

CHAPTER 10

Fundamentals of Estimating

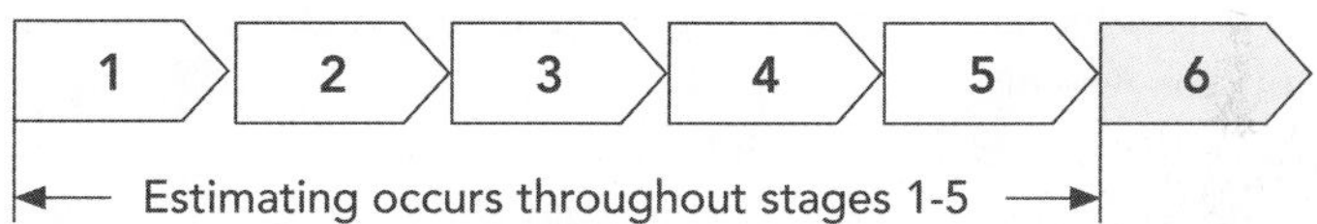

What are estimates and when are they done?

An **estimate** is an educated guess, based on the best available information, of what something is going to cost, usually in dollars or time. Most of us are familiar with getting estimates for repairing the car or painting the house. We make informal estimates ourselves almost daily – how long it will take to drive to Grandma's or how much the utility bill is going to be this month.

In construction, estimates are made to determine the probable real time – and, from that information, the probable cost – of building a project. The contractor's goal is to predict costs accurately and have this estimate low enough to win the job.

Because estimates are done before a project is built, they are, at best, an approximation of what the actual costs are going to be. The true costs of a project will not be known until the project has been completed and all the costs recorded. An estimate done before much design work is complete is very rough; an estimate done after the drawings and specifications are available is far more accurate. Both types of estimates are valuable and serve different purposes at different times during the development of a project.

Both owners and contractors need to know what a project will cost. The owner needs to balance project goals against costs and establish a realistic and workable budget and the contractor needs to establish an amount that the owner will pay for the work. For both parties, the stakes can be high, and an inaccurate or incomplete cost estimate can have serious implications.

Estimates are done throughout the life of a project, beginning at the feasibility phase, continuing throughout the design (during schematics, design development, and final design), before the general contractor is hired, and whenever changes occur during construction. Different types of estimates are done at different phases of a project as the amount of design information is refined. Estimates completed very early in the process are quicker to do but much less accurate than the detailed estimates developed when the drawings and specifications are complete.

Contractor and owner estimates – When we talk about a construction estimate, it's helpful to understand that the owner's project estimate is not the same as the contractor's project estimate. Let's see how they differ.

As we might expect, an owner is involved with, and responsible for, an entire project – from feasibility to occupancy or sale. The costs associated with actually constructing the project are only one piece of the project expenses. The owner is concerned with *all* the costs, which, in addition to the physical construction, might include: purchasing the property, paying for the design work, hiring marketing personnel, paying for attorneys and accountants, interest payments on loans, and other costs. All the anticipated project expenses are estimated and monitored by the owner throughout the process. Estimates are important to an owner because they are the major tools he or she will use to make key determinations about the project: its affordability, its size, and its quality.

The contractor's concern is narrower. The contractor's estimate includes only the expenses involved in the portion of the overall project for which he or she has been hired—typically, the labor, materials, equipment, and supervision necessary to complete the structure and fulfill the contract with the owner. The contractor's detailed estimate provides the basis for the bid price to the owner.

Considerations when developing an estimate

No matter at what stage of a project an estimate is created – whether at the earliest conceptual phase or at the completion of construction documents – there are several factors affecting costs that the estimator takes into account. These factors include the following:

- **Project size and complexity**
- **Quality of building materials**
- **Location of the project**
- **Schedule and time frame**
- **Market conditions**
- **Management**

Let's look at each of these factors.

Project size and complexity

Typically, the bigger the job the more it will cost in terms of materials and labor. But larger projects also provide an economy of scale not present in smaller projects. A larger project provides workers with an opportunity to find their rhythm. And once a contractor has mobilized onto a site – set up his tools and equipment, and prepared the area – it is generally cost effective to be there for a while rather than having to demobilize and move to another project. This is why, for example, painters charge a premium for using different colors: it costs time and money to clean the brushes, and close and open different cans. An additional factor is that repetition increases speed. If a tile setter has 5,000 square feet of floor tile to install, it typically takes longer to lay the first 1,000 square feet than the second 1,000, and so on. As square footage increases, cost per square foot decreases. The estimator must factor in these aspects of size and productivity.

Another characteristic that impacts worker productivity is project complexity. Anytime a structure has complications – a corner, oversized heights, bay windows, odd shapes – productivity goes down and labor costs go up. It is easier for an electrician to put fixtures in an 8-foot-high ceiling than to install them 15 feet up, for example. When complexity requires non-standard sizes, then the price climbs too. Straightforward, simple buildings are easier to build and cost less (that's why so many buildings are so plain!).

Quality of building materials

The quality of products plays a significant role in costs. It costs more to install specially sized wood with jamb extensions than off-the-shelf aluminum windows with drywall returns; Italian marble costs more than standard ceramic tile; 40-ounce nylon carpet costs more than 28-ounce. Some projects just meet code requirements and include very basic finishes; others include fine craftsmanship and superior materials. The estimator reviews the specifications for information regarding the quality requirements of a product.

Location of the project

Location impacts many aspects of an estimate. Labor costs vary from place to place. An inaccessible site (such as a house built in the mountains) means delivery costs are likely to be high, and if the project site is at a distance from the contractor's office, then overhead costs typically rise.

Location can impact the availability and cost of labor. It can also increase the contractor's difficulty in hiring qualified subcontractors who might be operating under different licensing requirements and with different viewpoints and experience. If there is a shortage of local workers, the general contractor might be obligated to bring them in, which can be expensive. Costs vary from area to area too, even when they're within a reasonable proximity to each other. It's more expensive to build something in Boston than in Worchester, Massachusetts, and more expensive in Denver than in Greeley. A contractor working outside his or her normal location adjusts for that in the estimate.

Two other problems associated with location are traffic and parking. Inner-city sites with vehicular and pedestrian traffic increase the costs of access and protection and sites without parking may require making costly alternative arrangements for workers and staff (such as renting spaces). These issues are factored into the estimate.

Schedule and time frame

If a project has an extremely tight time frame, the contractor might be forced to accelerate the work by adding crews or overtime, thus increasing labor and other costs. Extended schedule durations also increase supervision costs, which add indirect costs. Furthermore, if a contractor expects the project to extend over a long period of time, the estimate needs to take into account the likelihood that material prices will fluctuate. The time of year that work will take place also impacts the estimate, as there may be delays due to weather and the necessity for taking measures to protect materials from rain and/or cold.

Market conditions

If the local economy is in a slump and competition for jobs is tough, the estimator sharpens his bid and likely reduces the amount identified as profit. Sometimes a contractor accepts a job even though there's no profit to be had, in fact, simply to keep his crews busy. Conversely, if work is plentiful and it's more difficult to hire experienced crews, this will be reflected in higher bids.

Management

Management considerations include the general tone and effectiveness that might be expected on a project. Is the owner likely to be difficult? Does the architect respond quickly to requests for information? Is there skilled management among all the parties? Also, is the job likely to require additional paperwork such as one typically finds on a federal job? Extra work takes extra time and should be accounted for in the estimate.

Categories of Costs

In order to understand how a cost estimate is created, it's important to understand the different ways that job costs are categorized. To be sure that all costs are included and to organize the hundreds of costs associated with a project so that they can be tracked, costs are customarily identified as being in one of two categories:

- Direct project costs
- Indirect project costs

Every expense on a job is classified as one of these categories and assigned a cost code to enable it to be tracked and managed. In addition there is a third category of costs which include those that are not directly linked to specific projects but are necessary to maintain the contractor's business: indirect business costs. Let's take a look at all three of these types of costs.

Direct project costs

Direct project costs are the materials, labor, and equipment expenses directly associated with the items that become part of the physical structure. *Direct project costs are billable to a specific task and/or subcontractor*. Examples of direct project expenses include the cost of excavating for foundations, pouring concrete, building walls, supplying and laying kitchen tile, and installing the landscaping.

Let's look at how the estimator calculates direct costs.

Direct costs: materials

Materials are the easiest direct costs to calculate because they don't vary much from contractor to contractor (although suppliers can, and do, give variable price quotes to different contractors based on their history with the contractor and the contractor's ability to pay by specified discount dates).

The first step in pricing materials is to calculate how much is needed. The quantity of materials in a project is determined from the drawings. Each sheet of the drawings must be analyzed, with the materials identified and total amounts calculated.

The process of measuring plans to quantify materials is called doing the **take-off**. This process is completed in the same sequence as the building is built – from the ground up – to reduce the chance of missing something. Completing an accurate take-off is important because other costs are calculated based on quantities. For example, if the estimator calculates (through measurement) that 10,850 square feet (SF) of drywall is going to be required, when labor costs are assigned to the task of hanging the drywall, the numbers are based on an estimate of how many labor hours it is expected to take to hang 10,850 square feet. If the estimator has miscalculated the quantity of drywall, then the labor hours as well as the material costs will be wrong.

Andrea Young

Knowing just the quantity of materials isn't sufficient, however; the estimator also needs to know exactly what the product quality requirements are. The specifications provide the information necessary to price the correct product. In our drywall example, the quantity of drywall needed doesn't tell the estimator what grade of drywall the architect wants. For example, is it fire or water or mold resistant? The specifications provide this information.

Once the quantity and quality of the material has been determined, the cost can be calculated by multiplying the quantity of the materials times the **unit cost**. For example, a contractor is estimating the cost of an addition on a house. The take-off indicates that 2,050 linear feet (LF) of 2ft by 6ft redwood decking will be required. A quote from the supplier indicates that it will cost $2.15 per LF (a linear foot is the unit cost) for the decking. The total estimated cost for the lumber is therefore 2,050 LF x $2.15/LF = $4,407 (plus applicable taxes).

Direct costs: labor

Estimating labor costs is more difficult because these costs can vary substantially from contractor to contractor. Labor costs are calculated by multiplying an hourly **wage rate** (which includes costs such as social security, unemployment taxes, and health benefits in addition to the worker's direct pay) by **productivity** (how much a worker can accomplish in a given period of time). For example, let's assume a $40/hour wage rate for a drywaller who is likely to be on a two-person crew with a productivity rate of 2,000 square feet per 8-hour day. If the contractor's take-off indicates that there are 11,850 square feet of drywall, how much will the labor cost? The calculation is quite simple:

> *11,850 SF (total units of drywall) ÷ 2,000 SF (units installed per 8 hours) = 5.9 days (we'll round up to 6 days)*

> *Each worker's wage rate is $40/HR, therefore the cost is $80/HR x 8 HR/day = $640/day x 6 days = $3,840 total labor cost*

Determining labor costs isn't always so straightforward, however, because these costs are highly variable. As we've said, the productivity rate identifies the number of units of work (such as the square feet of drywall) a person is able to install in a specified period of time (usually hourly or daily). But productivity rates can vary greatly from contractor to contractor, and they are impacted by the skill and experience of the worker as well as the conditions in the field: Is there sufficient coordination and supervision? Is all necessary equipment in

The Davis-Bacon Act – Congress enacted the Davis-Bacon Act in 1931 to assure workers a fair wage, provide local contractors an equal opportunity to compete for local government contracts, and preserve the government's ability to distribute employment and federal money equitably through public works projects. Among other things, the law states that labor on federal projects or federally assisted projects must pay workers no less than the local prevailing wages and benefits. This ensures that contractors bidding on public works projects will not lower wages in order to achieve a lower bid.

Some organizations, including the Republican Party, have long tried to repeal the Davis-Bacon Act on the grounds that the regulations are outdated, expensive, and bureaucratic. There have also been several times when the act was temporarily suspended. After Hurricane Katrina, for example, President George W. Bush suspended the act *indefinitely* in designated areas along the Gulf Coast. After pressure from both Democrats and Republicans, Bush rescinded his emergency order and restored the prevailing wage requirement. For the most part, the Davis-Bacon Act continues to enjoy local support across the nation.

place? Is the job especially complicated or does it require working in less than optimal conditions? Are there efficiencies of scale in the work? All of these can impact a worker's productivity.

In addition, hourly labor rates are variable among the trades; electricians and plumbers are generally more highly paid than painters, for example. The "going rate" for a particular trade and worker is a function of whether the rate is based on prevailing wage rates, union rates, or on open shop rates. A **prevailing wage** is the hourly wage, plus benefits and overtime, paid to the majority of workers in the local area. Most workers on publicly funded jobs are paid a prevailing wage

Andrea Young

because of the Davis-Bacon Act. This act requires that most federal construction projects pay workers the local area's prevailing wage. **Union rates** are paid to workers who are members of a labor union and are paid a wage rate established by the union and a project's management, and workers who are not in a union are paid **open shop wages**. Open shop wage rates are agreed to by the individual worker and his employer. The estimator needs to understand how wages for each trade, on each job, have to be calculated.

Direct costs: equipment

Equipment can be rented or purchased; the contractor may or may not own it. If a contractor owns her equipment, the usual practice is to charge an hourly rate for its use. The cost for equipment includes the rental cost for the piece of equipment plus the operating cost (gas, set-up, maintenance, etc.) Equipment operators may or may not be rolled into base equipment costs; typically, when the equipment is owned by the contractor and rented to the job, the cost for operators is included under labor costs.

Direct costs: subcontractors

Subcontracted work is a direct project cost to the general contractor. All the labor, material, equipment, taxes, overhead, and profit are included as part of the subcontractors' bids to the GC. Typically, the general contractor itemizes the costs for subcontracted work and adds a markup to those costs.

The estimator has now calculated the costs of materials, labor, equipment, and subcontractors – the direct costs. Once these costs are known, the indirect project costs are calculated.

Indirect project costs

The second category of job cost is **indirect project costs** (also called general requirements or general conditions costs). These are the job expenses that are directly linked to the cost of the work as a whole but *not to a specific task or subcontract*. Indirect project costs include such items as the general contractor's job supervision, setting up a jobsite office (typically a trailer), temporary water and power for the job, scaffolding, cleaning the site, the costs incurred in organizing meetings, and much more. Some of these costs are required by the terms of the contract (an example would be a requirement that a full-time superintendent be at the jobsite), some are required by law (such as certain testing requirements), and some are the result of good construction practice (such as keeping the site clean). Indirect project costs are not physically incorporated into the structure.

The cost of the superintendent is an example of why a cost might be categorized as an indirect project cost rather than a direct cost. The general contractor's superintendent on a project is on the jobsite full-time, managing and coordinating the work. He works with *all* the subcontractors, facilitates meetings, updates the schedule, helps track costs, and works closely with both the contractor's project manager and the architect. The superintendent is involved with most, if not all, aspects of the work; the cost for his salary and benefits is therefore not billable to any one specific task. The superintendent is an indirect project cost. Compare this to the supervisory staff for the electrical subcontractor on the job. All *his* time is focused on the specific tasks involved with the electrical work and can be billed against this cost. This supervision is *not* an indirect project cost. Indirect project costs are typically, although not always, incurred only by the general contractor.

There is a direct time/cost relationship between indirect project costs and how long the work continues: the longer the job the higher the indirect project costs. Once the construction is over, the jobsite trailer is removed, the portable toilets are returned, and the general contractor's superintendent goes on to another job; the work is done and so are all indirect project costs.

Indirect business costs (overhead)

There is a second category of indirect costs that are critical to the success of a contractor's business but are not classified as job costs: **indirect business costs,** more commonly referred to as **overhead**. These are the costs associated with running the contractor's business and *have no direct relationship with any specific job*. Overhead expenses include the cost of staffing the home office, telephone and fax machines, office rent, and so on.

Although overhead costs occur away from the jobsite, they are critical contractor expenses and must be paid for with proceeds from each job. How they are calculated is highly variable and depends on the contractor's fixed costs (such as rent and home office staff), the number of projects the office is working on, and other factors. Sometimes contractors pro-rate overhead according to their volume of work; sometimes they charge a set percentage on all jobs. Typically, indirect business costs are simply added to the total estimated direct and indirect project costs. All the contractors and subcontractors have overhead expenses that are at least partially funded through individual jobs.

Let's look at a simple comparison of how different costs might be classified as either direct, indirect project, or overhead costs.

Expense	Direct project cost	Indirect project cost	Overhead
Roofing	√		
Superintendent		√	
Home office			√
Telephone at jobsite		√	
Telephone at homeoffice			√
Contractor's attorney			√
Site excavation	√		
Solar panels on the new building	√		
Solar panels on the home office			√
Drinking water at the jobsite		√	
Meeting minutes		√	

Figure 10.1. Comparison of costs

Now that we understand in general terms how estimates are created, let's look at where contractors get their numbers and what makes a good estimate.

Where does the estimator get the numbers?

We know the types of costs the estimator needs to calculate, but where, exactly, does he or she get the numbers? There are three basic sources:

- In-house data from previous jobs (field-generated data)
- Purchased cost data
- Subcontractors and suppliers

The data a contractor gets from his own experience, called in-house data, are the best way to estimate costs. These are a contractor's tested, real costs, using known crews. This historical data – how much the same task for a similar project cost the contractor in the past – are the best way for the contractor or his estimator to price labor costs accurately.

There are sometimes items in an estimate for which the contractor does not have adequate data. Several companies specialize in compiling and publishing cost data. Although not as reliable as a contractor's own field data, purchased data can be accurate, as costs may be adjusted for project conditions and location. One commonly used source of published data is RSMeans, a division of Reed Construction Data. RSMeans is one of North America's leading suppliers of construction cost information and publishes estimating guides for all sectors of the industry and for different types of projects – residential, industrial, commercial, and institutional. They publish several dozen cost estimating and reference books that are readily available. We'll examine some of the Means data in the next chapter.

Finally, estimators can get pricing help from subcontractors and suppliers. Companies that supply materials, called vendors, gladly provide material and equipment costs to the estimator, as do potential subcontractors.

What makes a good estimate?

Sometimes it doesn't matter too much if an estimate is not absolutely accurate. For example, if you are adding a bathroom in your house, miscalculate the plumbing costs, and end up spending more than you had planned, it could be expensive, but the loss may not make a substantial difference in your life. But if you're a subcontractor for all the plumbing in a 500,000-square-foot skyscraper and you make a mistake on your estimate, it could have catastrophic implications for your business, with lost reputation, litigation, and, in extreme cases, bankruptcy.

The goal of the estimate is to include *everything*, and for everything to be priced *accurately* so that the estimated cost is as close as possible to the final, actual costs for the work. Because the contractor typically bears any cost overruns caused by errors or omissions in the estimate, it is crucial that the bid estimate be both accurate and complete. To ensure this, the estimator asks the following questions:

1. Has everything been accounted for and priced?
2. Are labor costs and material prices based on accurate data that reflect local conditions?
3. Are the quantity, quality, model numbers, and color of all products correct?
4. Does the price of materials and equipment include taxes and delivery?
5. Will the owner pay for materials that need to be stored before they're installed or used? (Note: Sometimes an owner will only pay for materials once they have become part of the structure.)
6. Do the manufacturer's warranties match what is required by the specifications? If not, the contractor will need to purchase an extended warranty.

7. Does the supplier offer a price discount for speedy payment? If the contractor can pay promptly for materials, many suppliers offer price breaks.
8. Have risks been carefully analyzed and does the estimate reflect this? (An example of a risk is escalating material costs for projects with a long construction time.)
9. Is there adequate overhead and sufficient profit?

Value engineering – The increasing cost of materials, labor, overhead, and maintenance is making it necessary to get the most value out of our construction, and reducing costs is increasingly important. Many projects – from small houses to large industrial and commercial buildings – may be "value engineered" to minimize overall costs. Value engineering (VE) is not the same as "cost cutting" but is a methodical analysis of ways to reduce the costs of a project or structure over its entire life. Value engineering can be done at any time but is best done during the design phase when it's easier to make design adjustments. VE is a systematic process of analyzing specific building components and systems to find ways to perform the same function(s) at a lower life cycle cost without sacrificing reliability, performance, and design goals. It is possible that the initial cost for something (an expensive geothermal cooling system, for example) will be higher than a conventional system but will save costs over the life of the project. Value engineering must balance the up-front costs with the long-term cost savings – and the budget and vision of the owner.

Now that we have a basic understanding of the components of and reasons for estimating, we're ready, in the next chapter, to take a look at different types of estimates.

Chapter Vocabulary

Davis-Bacon Act – a law stating that labor on federal projects or federally assisted projects must pay workers no less than the local prevailing wages and benefits.

Direct project costs – the labor, materials, and equipment expenses directly associated with the items that will become part of a physical structure.

Estimate – an educated guess, based on the best available information, of what something is going to cost, usually in dollars or time.

Fee – the amount paid as remuneration for services. In construction, the fee is typically overhead plus profit.

General conditions costs (general requirements costs, indirect project costs) – expenses that are directly linked to the cost of the work but not to a specific task or subcontract.

General requirements costs (general conditions costs, indirect project costs) – expenses that are directly linked to the cost of the work but not to a specific task or subcontract.

Indirect business costs (overhead) – costs associated with running the contractor's business and not directly billable to any specific job expense.

Indirect project costs – see General conditions costs.

Open shop wage rate – wages paid to workers who are not in a union or on a federal project, and as agreed to by the individual worker and his or her employer.

Overhead (indirect business costs) – costs associated with running the contractor's business and not directly billable to any specific job expense.

Prevailing wage – pay rates set by the Department of Labor based on wages in a specific locality.

Productivity – how much a worker can accomplish in a given period of time.

RSMeans – a product line of Reed Construction Data, and a primary supplier of construction cost data.

Take-off ("doing the take-off") – the process of measuring construction drawings in order to quantify materials.

Union rates – wages paid to workers who are members of a labor union and whose pay rate is established by the union and a project's management.

Unit cost – the cost of materials based on a typical unit for that product such as tons, square feet, linear feet, or cubic yards.

Value engineering – a methodical analysis of ways to reduce the costs of a project or structure over its entire life.

Wage rate – rate (typically, by the hour) for labor, including costs such as social security, unemployment taxes, and health benefits in addition to the worker's direct pay.

Test Yourself

1. What is a cost estimate?
2. Why are estimates done at different phases of a project?
3. Name three examples of direct costs.
4. Name three examples of indirect project costs.
5. Why would a superintendent be categorized as an indirect project cost and not a direct cost?
6. What is a take-off and when is it used?
7. Explain how project complexity can impact a cost estimate.
8. Why does an estimate have to be complete and accurate?
9. Why are labor costs more difficult to calculate than material costs?
10. A contractor who is putting an estimate together is inexperienced with doing foundation work and therefore has no in-house cost data. What other two ways might she use to get cost figures for this portion of the job?

Andrea Young

CHAPTER 11

Creating Estimates

Estimates are based on design information. When the design of a project is incomplete, it is still possible to estimate what it will cost to build, but the estimate will, of course, be approximate. In the last chapter, we defined an estimate as an educated guess. As the owner and architect move ahead in the planning and design of a project, progressively more detailed estimates are generated and the educated guess becomes increasingly accurate. These early estimates are tools for the owner and architect to make adjustments in the program while it's still relatively easy. It is always cheaper and less stressful to make changes during the design process than to find out, after contractors' bids come in, that the project is unaffordable and needs to be changed.

Types of estimates

There are three basic types of estimates: two are developed before the design is 100 percent complete, and one is a very detailed estimate based on complete design information. Each of these exhibits a different level of accuracy and completeness.

- **Conceptual estimates** are based on very little design information and use gross unit pricing to determine the project cost. Estimates using gross unit costs might quote a cost per room (for a hotel), a cost per pupil (for a school), a cost per bed (for a hospital), and so on. These estimates are used during the early phase of a project when there are no drawings; they assist the owner in making program choices. A common conceptual estimate is called a rough-order-of-magnitude (ROM) estimate.

- **Preliminary estimates** are developed after some design is known and decisions are still being made. There are several types of preliminary estimates; in this text, we'll look at square foot estimates in which costs are projected based on area. These estimates are more accurate than ROM estimates.
- **Detailed estimates** (also called **final, bid**, or **unit price** estimates) are based on the most detailed design information and are developed by the contractor (or bidding contractors) after the design drawings and specifications are completed. A detailed bid estimate is prepared by determining the price of labor, materials, and equipment necessary for the work and includes subcontracts, overhead costs, taxes, and the contractor's profit. The contractor prepares the detailed estimate prior to submission of the bid to the owner.

Conceptual and preliminary estimates can be sufficiently accurate for the owner to evaluate design alternatives (for example, the project size and configuration) and to provide initial cost data. But they are insufficient for the very detailed cost estimate that a contractor develops at the completion of design, which forms the basis for the amount the contractor will be paid for the work.

Let's look at rough-order-of-magnitude, square foot, and detailed estimating in a bit more detail.

Conceptual/rough-order-of-magnitude estimates

A rough-order-of-magnitude estimate is completed early in the planning phase (typically during feasibility) by the owner to determine if the project is affordable and to help define the scope of work. As noted, this type of estimate is done before many details are known; the estimate can be completed very quickly. But because conceptual estimates are based only on broad design projections before many specific decisions have been made, they are, by necessity, very rough. A ROM estimate is useful primarily as a planning tool.

How might the owner develop a ROM estimate? If the owner is familiar with the type of project being estimated, she will use her own in-house data to complete the conceptual estimate. Otherwise, she must rely on a consulting estimator or on published data. Once the cost per unit is known, this number is multiplied by the anticipated quantity.

Let's say an owner is interested in developing a 42-room hotel and wants to get a rough idea of the financial feasibility of the project. She determines that the unit cost is $84,000 per room (including all costs except those to purchase the site). The total ROM estimate can be as simple as the following:

Number of rooms x cost per room = total cost
42 rooms x $84,000/room = $3,528,000 total cost

Added to this figure are adjustments that might be made such as non-standard room sizes, unusual building configuration, location, or expected construction date.

The conceptual estimate can be completed quickly and without drawings. Although a conceptual estimate is very rough, with limited accuracy, it can serve an important function. Conceptual estimates provide an owner with early data regarding project budgets and programs and can be used to set broad development goals and cost projections.

What does an owner do when the conceptual estimate is too high? Take our hotel as an example: The owner has experience with similar projects and makes a rough projection that a 42-room hotel will cost in the range of $3,530,000. She is going to depend on bank financing for the project and doesn't think she can get loans for more than $3 million, however. What might she do? She has four options: 1) abandon the idea; 2) cut back the size of the proposed project to lower the overall cost; 3) reduce the quality of the work, thereby lowering the square-foot cost and meeting the lower budget; or 4) some combination of 2 and 3. Although the final actual costs for the hotel will be different, the conceptual estimate should be close enough to enable the owner to make a reasonable decision regarding how to proceed.

Preliminary/square foot estimates

A **square foot estimate**, which is completed after some design detail is available but before the entire design is complete, uses a cost per square foot to calculate totals (size in square feet x cost per SF = total cost). The cost *per unit* includes labor, equipment, material, overhead, and profit but does not calculate these numbers separately. This type of estimate is therefore more detailed and hence more accurate than the rough-order-of-magnitude estimate. The square foot estimate is used to define the project budget further; depending on the amount of detail available, square foot estimates are significantly more accurate than conceptual estimates.

Square foot estimates are typically completed by contractors or architects using the estimator's own experience or published data such as the cost data guides printed by the RSMeans Company (introduced in the last chapter). Let's look at how a contractor might use an RSMeans guide to price a private residence that has not yet been completely designed but about which major decisions regarding layout, materials, and amenities have been determined. (In addition to residential projects, the RSMeans guide also has data for industrial, commercial, and institutional structures. Here we'll focus on residential work, however.)

Problem to solve

What is the estimated cost of a 1,400 SF one-story house in Tampa, Florida, with one and a half baths, a one-car detached garage, and textured ceilings? Assume the exterior wall system is stucco over wood frame and that the quality of the structure is average.

Price is linked to quality: the higher the quality the higher the price. So, in order to maximize pricing accuracy, the estimator needs to understand what quality is anticipated. RSMeans addresses this through their classes of residential construction: from economy to average, custom, and, finally, luxury. Each classification has specific characteristics. In our problem, we are pricing a house of "average" quality, which, according to Means, is a house with a simple design built from standard plans. Features include one bathroom, asphalt roofing, and no garage; there are some distinctive features to the house, and the workmanship typically exceeds minimum code requirements. (Our house is slightly different from the "average" identified by Means because of the extra half-bath and the garage. There will be an opportunity later to take these facts into account.)

Pricing is also affected by the number of stories a house has. Means provides cost breakdowns for seven different *categories* of housing defined by the number of stories. The estimator needs to select the cost data sheet that matches the *quality* of the project (economy, average, custom, or luxury) plus the residential *category*. For our problem we have been asked to price an average one-story house. Figure 11.1 is therefore the appropriate RSMeans Cost Data Sheet.

RESIDENTIAL | **Average** | **1 Story**

- **Simple design from standard plans**
- **Single family – 1 full bath, 1 kitchen**
- **No basement**
- **Asphalt shingles on roof**
- **Hot air heat**
- **Gypsum wallboard interior finishes**
- **Materials and workmanship are average**
- **Detail specifications on p. 27**

Note: The illustration shown may contain some optional components (for example: garages and/or fireplaces) whose costs are shown in the modifications, adjustments, & alternatives below or at the end of the square foot section.

©Home Planners, Inc.

Base cost per square foot of living area

	Living Area										
Exterior Wall	600	800	1000	1200	1400	1600	1800	2000	2400	2800	3200
Wood Siding - Wood Frame	135.60	122.45	112.70	104.85	98.30	94.05	91.75	88.85	83.15	78.95	76.10
Brick Veneer - Wood Frame	152.80	138.85	128.50	120.05	112.95	108.35	105.95	102.75	96.70	92.20	89.10
Stucco on Wood Frame	141.80	129.05	119.55	112.00	105.65	101.50	99.35	96.50	91.05	86.95	84.20
Solid Masonry	166.85	151.40	139.85	130.30	122.25	117.10	114.35	110.65	103.95	98.90	95.30
Finished Basement, Add	33.95	32.80	31.25	29.85	28.75	27.95	27.60	27.00	26.10	25.50	24.90
Unfinished Basement, Add	13.90	12.50	11.55	10.65	9.95	9.50	9.20	8.85	8.30	7.90	7.60

Modifications

Add to the total cost

Upgrade Kitchen Cabinets	$ + 3521
Solid Surface Countertops (Included)	
Full Bath - including plumbing, wall and floor finishes	+ 5993
Half Bath - including plumbing, wall and floor finishes	+ 3570
One Car Attached Garage	+ 12,676
One Car Detached Garage	+ 16,871
Fireplace & Chimney	+ 5234

Adjustments

For multi family - add to total cost

Additional Kitchen	$ + 6796
Additional Bath	+ 5993
Additional Entry & Exit	+ 1640
Separate Heating	+ 1409
Separate Electric	+ 1915

For Townhouse/Rowhouse - Multiply cost per square foot by

Inner Unit	+ .92
End Unit	+ .96

Alternatives

Add to or deduct from the cost per square foot of living area

Cedar Shake Roof	+ 3.85
Clay Tile Roof	+ 4.55
Slate Roof	+ 6.65
Upgrade Walls to Skim Coat Plaster	+ .41
Upgrade Ceilings to Textured Finish	+ .48
Air Conditioning, in Heating Ductwork	+ 4.19
In Separate Ductwork	+ 8.02
Heating Systems, Hot Water	+ 2.16
Heat Pump	+ 2.66
Electric Heat	- 1.01
Not Heated	- 3.80

Additional upgrades or components

Kitchen Cabinets & Countertops	Page 58
Bathroom Vanities	59
Fireplaces & Chimneys	59
Windows, Skylights & Dormers	59
Appliances	60
Breezeways & Porches	60
Finished Attic	60
Garages	61
Site Improvements	61
Wings & Ells	37

28 **Important: See the Reference Section for Location Factors (to adjust for your city) and Estimating Forms**

Figure 11.1. Square foot cost data

The RSMeans data sheet shows national average costs *per square foot* depending on the exterior wall system and the size of the house. For residential projects, there are four possible exterior wall systems (wood, brick, stucco, and masonry; see the vertical column on the left side of the chart) and a range of sizes from 1,000 to 3,800 square feet. Basements may also be added and the estimator can adjust costs for various modifications such as extra bathrooms, garages, and upgraded materials and systems such as tile roofing and air conditioning.

To determine the cost for our house, the estimator locates the house's exterior wall system; in our case, this is stucco over wood frame. Next, we read across to the square footage that matches the proposed building size; in our problem, it is 1,400 square feet. Reading down at the intersection of exterior wall and building square footage shows a cost of $105.65 per square foot. (Interpolation is necessary if the square footage is different from what is presented in the cost sheet. For example, if the building is 1,500 square feet, the cost per square foot is ($105.65 + $101.50) ÷ 2 = $103.58.)

The base square foot cost represents a national average cost and can be increased, or reduced, depending on the complexity of the building, whether it has a basement, and if there are any features that deviate from the average house.

To find the total base cost for our house, we multiply the square footage of the building by the cost per square foot as shown in the data sheet.

1400 SF x $105.65/SF = $147,910

To get our estimate as close as possible to what the building will cost, we need to add in the upgrades. The upper left of the cost sheet indicates what is included in the average house. Our house has upgrades of an extra half-bath, a garage, and textured ceilings. If we refer to Figure 11.1 we can see that the following costs need to be added to the base cost:

½ bath...Add $ 3,570
One-car detached garage..Add $16,871
Upgrade ceilings to textured finish ($.48/SF x 1,400 SF)..............Add $ 672
Total modifications = ...$21,113

To get the total estimated project cost, we add the upgrades to the base price:

$147,910 + $21,113 = $169,023 adjusted base cost

But we're not quite done.

The Means cost sheets are all based on *average national* costs so an additional adjustment must be made to take into account that the house will be built in Tampa, Florida. Location adjustments are done by multiplying the project cost by a *city location factor* (Figure 11.2). The location factor assumes that the *average* city cost is 100, and costs in Tampa (and elsewhere) are expressed as a percentage of this average.

Location Factors

Costs shown in *RSMeans Square Foot Costs* are based on national averages for materials and installation. To adjust these costs to a specific location, simply multiply the base cost by the factor for that city.

The data is arranged alphabetically by state and postal zip code numbers. For a city not listed, use the factor for a nearby city with similar economic characteristics.

STATE/ZIP	CITY	Residential	Commercial
ALABAMA			
350-352	Birmingham	.86	.88
354	Tuscaloosa	.77	.80
355	Jasper	.72	.80
356	Decatur	.77	.81
357-358	Huntsville	.83	.85
359	Gadsden	.74	.80
360-361	Montgomery	.75	.80
362	Anniston	.77	.83
363	Dothan	.75	.77
364	Evergreen	.73	.78
365-366	Mobile	.81	.84
367	Selma	.72	.77
368	Phenix City	.73	.79
369	Butler	.73	.77
ALASKA			
995-996	Anchorage	1.26	1.21
997	Fairbanks	1.27	1.21
998	Juneau	1.25	1.20
999	Ketchikan	1.29	1.27
ARIZONA			
850,853	Phoenix	.86	.89
851,852	Mesa/Tempe	.81	.84
855	Globe	.77	.82
856-857	Tucson	.84	.86
859	Show Low	.79	.83
860	Flagstaff	.84	.88
863	Prescott	.77	.82
864	Kingman	.81	.84
865	Chambers	.77	.82
ARKANSAS			
716	Pine Bluff	.79	.82
717	Camden	.67	.71
718	Texarkana	.72	.74
719	Hot Springs	.68	.72
720-722	Little Rock	.83	.84
723	West Memphis	.77	.79
724	Jonesboro	.76	.80
725	Batesville	.73	.75
726	Harrison	.75	.76
727	Fayetteville	.70	.75
728	Russellville	.75	.76
729	Fort Smith	.76	.80
CALIFORNIA			
900-902	Los Angeles	1.08	1.08
903-905	Inglewood	1.01	1.00
906-908	Long Beach	1.00	1.01
910-912	Pasadena	1.00	1.01
913-916	Van Nuys	1.03	1.03
917-918	Alhambra	1.04	1.02
919-921	San Diego	1.03	1.05
922	Palm Springs	1.00	1.00
923-924	San Bernardino	1.01	.99
925	Riverside	1.07	1.05
926-927	Santa Ana	1.02	1.01
928	Anaheim	1.07	1.06
930	Oxnard	1.08	1.06
931	Santa Barbara	1.07	1.06
932-933	Bakersfield	1.06	1.05
934	San Luis Obispo	1.03	1.02
935	Mojave	1.01	1.00
936-938	Fresno	1.09	1.06
939	Salinas	1.11	1.08
940-941	San Francisco	1.26	1.24
942,956-958	Sacramento	1.12	1.08
943	Palo Alto	1.14	1.10
944	San Mateo	1.22	1.15
945	Vallejo	1.15	1.11
946	Oakland	1.22	1.16
947	Berkeley	1.20	1.13
948	Richmond	1.23	1.13
949	San Rafael	1.21	1.14
950	Santa Cruz	1.14	1.11
951	San Jose	1.21	1.17
952	Stockton	1.08	1.06
953	Modesto	1.08	1.06

STATE/ZIP	CITY	Residential	Commercial
CALIFORNIA (CONT'D)			
954	Santa Rosa	1.16	1.12
955	Eureka	1.10	1.06
959	Marysville	1.09	1.06
960	Redding	1.09	1.06
961	Susanville	1.09	1.06
COLORADO			
800-802	Denver	.92	.94
803	Boulder	.89	.90
804	Golden	.87	.91
805	Fort Collins	.86	.90
806	Greeley	.76	.84
807	Fort Morgan	.89	.90
808-809	Colorado Springs	.87	.91
810	Pueblo	.89	.91
811	Alamosa	.85	.89
812	Salida	.87	.90
813	Durango	.87	.90
814	Montrose	.84	.88
815	Grand Junction	.88	.90
816	Glenwood Springs	.87	.90
CONNECTICUT			
060	New Britain	1.09	1.08
061	Hartford	1.09	1.09
062	Willimantic	1.10	1.08
063	New London	1.09	1.06
064	Meriden	1.09	1.07
065	New Haven	1.10	1.09
066	Bridgeport	1.10	1.09
067	Waterbury	1.10	1.09
068	Norwalk	1.10	1.09
069	Stamford	1.11	1.12
D.C.			
200-205	Washington	.96	.99
DELAWARE			
197	Newark	1.03	1.04
198	Wilmington	1.04	1.04
199	Dover	1.02	1.04
FLORIDA			
320,322	Jacksonville	.81	.84
321	Daytona Beach	.88	.88
323	Tallahassee	.78	.81
324	Panama City	.75	.79
325	Pensacola	.82	.86
326,344	Gainesville	.81	.86
327-328,347	Orlando	.89	.89
329	Melbourne	.88	.91
330-332,340	Miami	.88	.91
333	Fort Lauderdale	.87	.89
334,349	West Palm Beach	.87	.86
335-336,346	Tampa	.92	.92
337	St. Petersburg	.79	.84
338	Lakeland	.89	.91
339,341	Fort Myers	.87	.87
342	Sarasota	.90	.89
GEORGIA			
300-303,399	Atlanta	.88	.89
304	Statesboro	.71	.78
305	Gainesville	.77	.81
306	Athens	.76	.82
307	Dalton	.75	.81
308-309	Augusta	.82	.83
310-312	Macon	.80	.83
313-314	Savannah	.80	.82
315	Waycross	.79	.81
316	Valdosta	.74	.81
317,398	Albany	.77	.82
318-319	Columbus	.81	.83
HAWAII			
967	Hilo	1.19	1.15
968	Honolulu	1.21	1.17

Figure 11.2. Location factors

On the location factor sheet, find Tampa and go across to the residential column. We can see that Tampa is valued at .92 of the national average. This means it's cheaper to build in Tampa than it is in the average American city.

Multiplication of the adjusted project cost by the location factor for Tampa gives us the total estimate for building our house:

$169,023 (base costs plus additives) x .92 (location factor) = $155,501 total cost

If we compare the cost of building the house in Tampa ($155,501) with the national average for the same building ($169,023), we can see that Tampa is less costly.

What if we were to build the same building in San Francisco? How would *that* cost compare to the national average and to the cost in Tampa? To determine this, we do exactly what we did for Tampa: calculate an adjusted base cost and multiply by the location factor for San Francisco (1.26):

$169,023 x 1.26 = $212,968

So it appears that the cost to build our house in San Francisco is a lot higher than both the national average ($169,023) and the cost in Tampa ($155,501).

The final adjustment that might have to be made is for time. We computed our examples based on the 2010 Means data indices. A project set to begin sometime in the future needs to be adjusted for expected increases in labor and material. This can be accomplished by using an anticipated inflation figure or by referring to *Means Historical Data*, which suggests an escalation rate for future years.

As already discussed, conceptual and square foot estimating are approximate estimates completed before the design is complete. For the most accurate and detailed estimating, the owner looks to the detailed estimate developed by the contractor at the completion of design and before the bid submission. Not surprisingly, these estimates are far more difficult and time-consuming to complete and their accuracy is more critical.

Detailed/bid estimates

Bid estimates (also called **final estimates** or unit **price estimates**) are prepared at the end of design to finalize the construction budget. They are developed by bidding contractors attempting to be hired for the work. (Subcontractors also develop detailed estimates to put *their* bids together for the general contractors.) These estimates are accurate because they are based on complete design information. Unlike conceptual and preliminary estimates, the detailed estimates put together by bidding contractors break down all the separate costs for construction – direct and indirect project costs (including subcontractor costs), overhead, and profit.

What steps does the contractor take to generate all the detailed price data for a bid estimate? Estimating is a systematic process that mimics the sequence of construction: the estimator begins at the foundation and works his or her way up to the roof. The first thing the estimator does is quantify every work item through a measurement process called a take-off (discussed in the previous chapter). The take-off generates a list of products and materials and the quantity of each (the number of windows, square feet of roofing materials, tons of gravel, cubic yards of concrete, board feet of decking, etc.). For a detailed estimate, most costs are separated into units of labor, material, and equipment and the contractor calculates a cost for each. Let's generate a detailed estimate for a small task as an example of how this process might work.

Problem to solve

What is the total cost for 5/8" fire resistant gypsum board on both sides of four 15' high x 32' long partitions, with no openings and no finish?

How are the costs for the gypsum board calculated? The estimator's take-off determines that there are 3,840 square feet of drywall (the common name for gypsum board) used on the partition.

15'H x 32'L x 2 (sides) x 4 (partitions) = 3,840 SF

Once the quantity of material is known the estimator determines the cost for the materials plus installation labor. Typically, the estimator uses in-house historical data along with square foot cost data from suppliers to complete the calculation. We will use published data from RSMeans to assist us, as we did with the residential calculations. Because in this problem we have a greater amount of design information, the appropriate Means reference will be the *Cost Construction Data*, which breaks down costs more completely than does the square foot price data sheets.

The *Cost Construction Data* index provides the page location for gypsum board. A detail from that page is shown in Figure 11.3. Let's see how the data is presented.

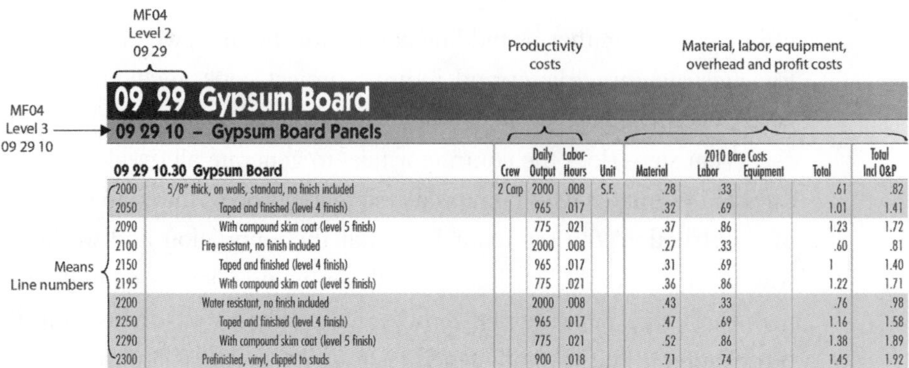

09 29 Gypsum Board

09 29 10 – Gypsum Board Panels

09 29 10.30 Gypsum Board		Crew	Daily Output	Labor-Hours	Unit	Material (2010 Bare Costs)	Labor (2010 Bare Costs)	Equipment (2010 Bare Costs)	Total (2010 Bare Costs)	Total Incl O&P
2000	5/8" thick, on walls, standard, no finish included	2 Carp	2000	.008	S.F.	.28	.33		.61	.82
2050	Taped and finished (level 4 finish)		965	.017		.32	.69		1.01	1.41
2090	With compound skim coat (level 5 finish)		775	.021		.37	.86		1.23	1.72
2100	Fire resistant, no finish included		2000	.008		.27	.33		.60	.81
2150	Taped and finished (level 4 finish)		965	.017		.31	.69		1	1.40
2195	With compound skim coat (level 5 finish)		775	.021		.36	.86		1.22	1.71
2200	Water resistant, no finish included		2000	.008		.43	.33		.76	.98
2250	Taped and finished (level 4 finish)		965	.017		.47	.69		1.16	1.58
2290	With compound skim coat (level 5 finish)		775	.021		.52	.86		1.38	1.89
2300	Prefinished, vinyl, clipped to studs		900	.018		.71	.74		1.45	1.92

Figure 11.3. Construction cost data gypsum board (excerpt)

RSMeans uses a system called MasterFormat (MF04) developed by the Construction Specifications Institute (CSI) to organize information in a hierarchy from very broad (called divisions or level 1 information) to very detailed, represented by Means' 12-digit line number. (We'll look at this in more detail in Chapter 16.) For each line item, specific price data is provided (reading from left to right): a coded standard crew size (in the case of gypsum board, 2 Carp = two carpenters); crew productivity (the quantity a crew can install in an eight-hour day and called Daily Output); labor productivity (how long it takes a single worker to install a single unit); unit (the standard unit measurement for the item, in our case, square feet); and bare material, labor, and equipment costs per unit (bare costs do not include overhead and profit). For the total cost per square foot, we'll move to the far right column (identified as Total Incl O&P).

In our problem, we've been asked to price 3,840 square feet of 5/8" fire resistant gypsum board. We can solve the problem by referring to the page detailed in Figure 11.4 – Gypsum Board. Let's see how the estimator might proceed.

We find the product we're pricing on line 2100 and, moving along from left to right, the costs for materials and labor (there are no equipment costs associated with this product). All the costs shown are per unit (in our case, this is square feet). The productivity rate for a single crew is 2,000 square feet per day. (The daily output is based on normal conditions: an eight-hour day, in daylight, with moderate temperatures.) On the far right, we get a total cost, including overhead and profit of $.81 per square foot. Our total cost is therefore:

3,840 SF x $.81/SF = $3,110

09 29 Gypsum Board										
09 29 10 – Gypsum Board Panels										
09 29 10.30 Gypsum Board		Crew	Daily Output	Labor-Hours	Unit	2010 Bare Costs Material	Labor	Equipment	Total	Total Incl O&P
2000	5/8" thick, on walls, standard, no finish included	2 Carp	2000	.008	S.F.	.28	.33		.61	.82
2050	Taped and finished (level 4 finish)		965	.017		.32	.69		1.01	1.41
2090	With compound skim coat (level 5 finish)		775	.021		.37	.86		1.23	1.72
2100	Fire resistant, no finish included		2000	.008		.27	.33		.60	.81
2150	Taped and finished (level 4 finish)		965	.017		.31	.69		1	1.40
2195	With compound skim coat (level 5 finish)		775	.021		.36	.86		1.22	1.71
2200	Water resistant, no finish included		2000	.008		.43	.33		.76	.98
2250	Taped and finished (level 4 finish)		965	.017		.47	.69		1.16	1.58
2290	With compound skim coat (level 5 finish)		775	.021		.52	.86		1.38	1.89
2300	Prefinished, vinyl, clipped to studs		900	.018		.71	.74		1.45	1.92

Figure 11.4. Construction cost data gypsum board (excerpt)

If the estimator wants only the cost for the materials or for labor, he multiplies the square footage by their respective costs ($.27/SF and $.33/SF). As with our residential problem, these cost figures reflect a national average. If asked to price the partitions for a particular location, we need to make a location adjustment.

If the estimator wants to know how long it will take to hang 3,840 square feet of drywall, he or she divides this area by the total daily output of a typical two-person crew:

3,840 SF ÷ 2,000 SF per day = 1.92 days (rounded up to 2 days)

The data sheet provides another handy cost figure. The vertical column titled "Labor Hours" represents the number of labor hours it takes to install one unit of whatever the product is. This figure can be used if the contractor anticipates a crew size different from the standard. Under the Labor Hours column for our 5/8" drywall, we see that it takes .008 hours (for one person) to install one square foot (units are identified in the column directly to the right). So here's how we determine how long our 3,840 square-foot job would take one worker to complete:

3,840 SF x .008 hours = 30.72 hours total for one worker

30.72 hours = 3.84 work days (rounded up to 4 days) for one worker

The estimate summary

Once the contractor has completed the estimate – quantities have been calculated, prices confirmed, and indirect project costs determined – he or she summarizes the data on an estimate summary sheet such as that shown in Figure 11.5 and, assuming costs have been calculated using in-house data and do not yet include overhead and profit, adds these costs plus applicable sale taxes and labor burden.

On a competitively bid job, the contractor submits the final number (in figure 11.5 summary, $1,795,979) as the bid estimate. (This is also called the quote.) For a fixed price project, the owner sees only the bid amount; for projects that reimburse the contractor for actual costs, the owner has access to all these numbers.

Division	Work	Materials	Labor	Equipment	Subcontracts	Total
1	Gen'l Conditions	$72,340.00	$46,560.00	$2,040.00	$0.00	**$120,940.00**
2	Site work	$4,320.00	$3,675.00	$2,200.00	$162,500.00	**$172,695.00**
3	Concrete	$76,540.00	$66,800.00	$4,323.00	$0.00	**$147,663.00**
4	Masonry	$0.00	$0.00	$0.00	$56,400.00	**$56,400.00**
5	Metals	$4,300.00	$3,200.00	$0.00	$0.00	**$7,500.00**
6	Wood & Plastics	$234,000.00	$176,000.00	$0.00	$0.00	**$410,000.00**
7	Thermal & Moisture protection	$0.00	$0.00	$0.00	$76,000.00	**$76,000.00**
8	Doors & Windows	$34,566.00	$22,311.00	$0.00	$2,211.00	**$59,088.00**
9	Finishes	$0.00	$0.00	$0.00	$220,000.00	**$220,000.00**
10	Specialties	$6,400.00	$5,430.00	$0.00	$0.00	**$11,830.00**
11	Equipment	$0.00	$0.00	$0.00	$0.00	**$0.00**
12	Furnishings	$0.00	$0.00	$0.00	$0.00	**$0.00**
13	Special Const.	$1,240.00	$765.00	$1,200.00	$0.00	**$3,205.00**
14	Conveying Systems	$0.00	$0.00	$0.00	$52,000.00	**$52,000.00**
15	Mechanical	$0.00	$0.00	$0.00	$78,000.00	**$78,000.00**
16	Electrical	$0.00	$0.00	$0.00	$86,775.00	**$86,775.00**
	SUBTOTALS	**$433,706.00**	**$324,741.00**	**$9,763.00**	**$733,886.00**	**$1,502,096.00**
	Sales tax @ 7.75%	**$33,612.21**	$0.00	$0.00	$0.00	**$33,612.21**
	Payroll tax @36%	$0.00	**$116,906.76**	$0.00	$0.00	**$116,906.76**
	SUBTOTALS	**$467,318.21**	**$441,647.76**	**$9,763.00**	**$733,886.00**	**$1,652,614.97**
	Overhead @ 5%					**$82,630.74**
	SUBTOTAL					**$1,735,245.71**
	Profit @ 3.5%					**$60,733.57**
	TOTAL ESTIMATE					**$1,795,979.28**

Figure 11.5. An estimate summary

The contractor identifies each broad scope of work by number (again, often following the MasterFormat divisions) and these are listed along the left vertical column. To the right are columns for material, labor, and equipment costs incurred by the general contractor. In our example, costs for subcontracts are identified as a separate column. (Remember, the general contractor is responsible for the costs for his own crews *plus* the costs for subcontracted crews.)

To see how to read the summary, let's look at item 3 – Concrete. In the columns to the right, we see that there are costs identified for materials, labor, and equipment but zero for subcontracts. This means that the GC's crews will do 100 percent of the concrete work. Conversely, under Masonry (item 4), there are zero costs identified for materials, labor, and equipment but $56,400 for subcontractor costs. The general contractor will do *none* of the masonry work using his or her own crews. Costs along the horizontal are added and the total cost for the item is on the far right. The total estimate for item 3 = $147,663 and the total for item 4 = $56,400.

Once the indirect project costs and direct costs are subtotaled, the estimator adds in applicable sales and payroll taxes. This last number is not actually a tax (or much of it isn't) but includes everything included in fringe benefits (such as vacation and health) as well as social security and other taxes. Sometimes this figure is called the **labor burden**. The total payroll tax, expressed as a percentage, varies from company to company and location to location. In our example, the sales tax (on materials only) is 7.75 percent. The payroll tax (on labor only) is 36 percent.

After adding in the taxes, the estimator adds a percentage to cover business overhead. As we've learned, this number is also variable. In our example, we've added 5 percent ($82,630).

The final number added to the estimate is profit. The profit is the amount of money left over after all expenses have been paid. The contractor's profit is paid as a fixed dollar amount or a percentage of the construction cost. As noted earlier, in jobs with fixed price contracts, the profit is included in the bid estimate. In jobs with reimbursable contracts, such as a cost plus contract, the profit is added to the overhead and is called the **fee**.

The amount of profit (or fee) the contractor can charge depends on many factors, including the amount of risk the contractor feels the project carries (higher risk jobs should have higher profit) and the volume of work the contractor does. Contractors who do high volumes of work can have a smaller profit per job. The competitiveness of the current construction environment can affect the profit a contractor can charge and still get the job. Profits are typically lower when jobs are scarce and there is a lot of competition than they are when there is less competition.

There is no clear answer to what the profit should be; it can range from zero percent when a contractor hasn't enough work and wants to keep crews busy, up to whatever the market will bear. Typically, the larger a job is the lower the profit percentage. Conversely, small jobs often carry a higher profit relative to the overall cost of the job. In our example, we use 3.5 percent ($60,733).

With all the figures totaled, the estimator now has a total project cost: $1,795,979. This is the number presented to the owner as the bid.

The contractor will make every effort to "bring the project in" on budget, in other words, to meet the estimated costs. A major role for the contractor is to manage the job to ensure that this occurs.

Chapter Vocabulary

Bid estimate (final, detailed, unit price estimate) – a cost estimate based on the most detailed design information developed by the contractor (or bidding contractors) after the design drawings and specifications are completed.

City location factor – used to adjust the national average costs of materials and installation shown in RSMeans cost data publications to those at specific locations.

Conceptual estimate – a cost estimate based on very little design information and using gross unit pricing to determine the project cost.

Detailed estimate (bid, final, or unit price estimate) – a cost estimate based on the most detailed design information developed by the contractor (or bidding contractors) after the design drawings and specifications are completed.

Detailed estimate (bid, final, or unit price estimate) – a cost estimate based on the most detailed design information developed by the contractor (or bidding contractors) after the design drawings and specifications are completed.

Estimate summary – a summation of final project costs prepared by a contractor prior to submitting a bid.

Final estimate (bid, detailed, or unit price estimate) – a cost estimate based on the most detailed design information developed by the contractor (or bidding contractors) after the design drawings and specifications are completed.

Labor burden – costs that are added to the direct wage of a worker, including fringe benefits (such as vacation and health) as well as social security and other taxes.

Preliminary estimate – a cost estimate developed after some design is known and decisions are still being made.

Rough-order-of-magnitude (ROM) estimate – a conceptual cost estimate that is completed early in the planning phase by the owner to determine if the project is affordable and to help define the scope of work.

Square foot estimate – an estimate that uses floor area to calculate costs after some design detail is available.

Unit price estimate (bid, final, or detailed estimate) – a cost estimate based on the most detailed design information developed by the contractor (or bidding contractors) after the design drawings and specifications are completed.

Test Yourself

1. What is the value to an owner of a rough estimate?
2. When are square foot estimates completed?
3. What is the most common source of published cost data?
4. What are the square foot costs for a 1,200-SF, two-story residential project with wood siding over wood frame? Refer to figure 11.1.
5. Why is a location factor used?
6. Refer to Figure 11.2: Is it more costly to build in Los Angeles or in Washington DC? What is the cost difference?
7. What are three types of estimating systems and write a sentence about each.
8. What sort of estimate is developed for a bid proposal?
9. The owner develops the bid estimate. True or false?
10. Refer to Figure 11.5: Which is the most expensive subcontract for this project? How much were the costs for the general contractor's crews for item 4?

PART 4

The Contract Documents

- Chapter 12: Introduction to Contracts
- Chapter 13: Construction Contracts
- Chapter 14: Contract Documents: The Agreement
- Chapter 15: Contract Documents: General and Supplementary Conditions
- Chapter 16: Contract Documents: The Specifications

Andrea Young

CHAPTER 12

Introduction to Contracts

The delivery method describes the manner in which a construction team is *organized* for a project. A contract, on the other hand, describes the *legal structure* for the project. A **contract** is a legally binding agreement between parties.

But what exactly is a construction contract? A construction contract is an agreement made up of different documents that, together, form a legally binding promise between the parties. On a typical project, the "parties" are the owner and a general contractor. Other parties also have contracts. For example, the contractor has separate contracts with subcontractors and the owner typically has a separate contract with an architect. Having a contract means that the parties are legally obligated to meet the terms outlined in the documents that make up the contract. This, in turn, means that if you don't have a contract, you may have to pay compensation to the other party.

There are different types of construction contracts, which we'll discuss later. But first, let's talk about why contracts are important and what makes something a contract.

Why are contracts important?

When you make a promise to someone, that person may rely on you to keep your word. For example, let's say you promise an owner that you will build him a garage for a certain price by a certain date. The owner has a new car coming and needs the garage to be completed when the car arrives. The owner is relying on you to keep your promise. At the same time, you expect the owner to fulfill his promise to pay you. A contract is a legally binding agreement between you and the owner that describes the promises you have made to each other. If one of you fails to uphold your end of the agreement, the wronged party has recourse – taking the other to court.

In addition to providing the parties with legal protection, a contract outlines the expectations – the rights and obligations of each party. If you have agreed to build the garage, the contract provides you with clarity regarding what you must do for the owner and how you will be reimbursed. The documents that make up your contract detail your promises to each other.

When we make a contract, it stays in effect until the responsibilities are performed (the job is done) or the contract is terminated (it is ended). If either party fails to perform an obligation agreed to in the contract, that party may have breached the contract. To **breach** a contract (default) is very serious and can result in one party being sued by the other party. When someone is sued, it means they have to go to court and a judge or jury may determine what happens.

Primary ingredients of a contract

There are many types of contracts (not just in construction), but all of them share certain general characteristics. In order to be valid (legally binding), a contract must meet certain conditions. These conditions are:

- **Mutual agreement**: both parties must agree to the terms of the contract.
- **Capacity**: both parties must be able to understand the terms of the contract.
- **Consideration**: there must be an exchange of something of value.
- **Lawfulness**: the terms of the contract must be allowable by law.

Let's look at each of these conditions in more detail.

Mutual agreement

Mutual agreement indicates the fact that both (or all) parties to a contract agree with what it says. The key is that everybody agrees to *exactly the same thing.* In construction, one party (a contractor) makes an offer, or a bid, to do work and the other party (the owner) may or may not accept that offer. If an offer with definite terms is accepted, there is evidence of mutual agreement. Once an offer is accepted, and other possible conditions are met, the parties will have a contract and the offer cannot easily be withdrawn. (The same is true for subcontractors who submit a bid to a contractor.) *Be sure you want the job before you submit a bid because it might be accepted!*

Mutual agreement example – You're a contractor and have given me a price to build a bay window on the north wall of my living room. I agree to your price but say I'd like you to build the bay on the south wall instead. Unless you agree to that change, we don't have mutual agreement; the terms are not exactly the same, and therefore there is no contract.

Capacity

Capacity refers to the competency or ability of each party to have mutual agreement. If one party can't fully understand what they're agreeing to because, for example, they are mentally insane, or intoxicated, or too young or too ill, then the law says they shouldn't be held to the terms of a contract. The goal is that a person entering into a contract has the ability to understand fully what they're agreeing to. This is the reason, for example, that children can't enter into contracts (in most states, you must be 18 years old).

Capacity example – You have signed a contract with an old man to make several renovations to his home. He seems to be somewhat dotty and keeps asking you to make odd changes in the scope of work, such as tearing out the kitchen and putting it in the living room. You need the work and he has agreed to pay you whatever it costs, so you do what he asks. Before the work is complete, and before he pays you, he dies. His children refuse to honor your bill, claiming that their father was demented and didn't know what he was doing. You sue the children for your payment and end up in court. Unhappily for you, the judge rules that the diminished mental capacity of the owner (together with your awareness at the time of that diminished capacity) meant that you did not have a valid contract. You may not get paid or may get paid less than the price in the contract.

Consideration

Consideration is something of value given by one party to another as an exchange for something else. When you make a promise to do something, that promise is generally only legally binding if there is some kind of exchange and you are both receiving a benefit from the arrangement. In construction, the consideration is typically a building (a benefit flowing to the owner) and payment (a benefit flowing to the contractor). The courts generally don't care about the amount of consideration, so long as there is some.

Consideration example – Sometimes not having consideration works to the contractor's advantage. Let's say your local church needs a new fence and you agree to build it at no cost to the church. You and the church write out a simple statement regarding the appearance of the fence, how the materials will be purchased, and when you will do the work. The day you do the job you are feeling sick and grumpy and don't do your best. The church says you didn't follow the agreed plans, the result is unacceptable, and asks you to redo the work. You refuse and the church tries to get the courts involved. Because there was no consideration, you had no contract and no legal obligations; the church is out of luck. If you had received even a token payment from the church, your obligations to them would likely have been legally enforceable.

Here's another example: The local Women's Guild meets in the church basement every Tuesday night and, in exchange, they pay the church $1 a year. The consideration is the basement (benefit to the guild) and $1 (benefit to the church.) The guild and the church have a contract; the church can't just change its mind and decide to let another group use the basement on Tuesday nights.

Lawfulness

The object of a contract must be lawful. In other words, the law will not enforce a contract when it is for something that is not legal.

Lawfulness example – You have a contract to build a second unit on a property in town. Due to zoning regulations, the building cannot be larger than 840 square feet. The owner has decided he wants a larger structure and therefore decides against getting a building permit. You agree to do the work anyway. When the job is done, the owner fails to pay you and you take him to court. The courts may not uphold your right to be fully paid because you built an illegal structure, which can invalidate your contract with the owner.

There's another concern for contractors regarding the issue of lawfulness. This has to do with whether the contractor is properly credentialed. Let's say you are an unlicensed contractor and you sign a contract with an owner to re-roof his house. All goes well and you finish the work according to the terms of the contract. The owner fails to pay you so you take him to court. The court may very well deny you full reimbursement because you were not licensed and thus did not have an enforceable contract.

Summary

Contracts are important for both the contractor and the owner as they state the rules for a project and identify the individual rights and obligations of the parties. The contract provides a legal framework for addressing disputes and has serious legal implications. Because of this, both parties must be fully aware of what is included in the contract. (Imagine how distressing it would be for the contractor to be surprised to learn, after construction starts, for example, that he will be paid every *other* month instead of the more typical once a month!) Beyond providing the owner and the contractor with legal protection, the contract outlines exactly what has been agreed to. When agreements are clearly stated, misunderstandings, confusion, and disputes can be avoided.

Chapter Vocabulary

Breach of contract (default) – failure to live up to the terms of a contract.

Capacity – the ability and skill of a contractor to complete a project; also, the competency or ability of a party to understand the terms of a contract.

Consideration – something of value promised by one party to another in exchange for something else; consideration is one of the requirements for a valid contract.

Contract – a legally binding agreement between parties.

Lawfulness – a condition of contracts that says the law will not enforce a contract for something that is not legal.

Mutual agreement – a key ingredient of contracts under which all parties must agree to the terms of the contract.

Test Yourself

1. What is a contract?
2. What does mutual agreement mean?
3. What are the primary ingredients of a contract?
4. What is the primary document that identifies that you and an owner agree to the terms and conditions of the contract?
5. You are building a house for someone. What is the consideration?
6. Why is it important for contractors to understand what makes a contract valid?
7. Why would it matter to a contractor if a project does not have the required building permits?
8. What does it mean to breach a contract?
9. What might happen if you failed to have the necessary contractor's license and an owner failed to pay you?
10. You signed an agreement with a friend to build an addition on his house. He was drunk when he signed the agreement. How might this cause problems if you ever have to take him to court for non-payment?

Andrea Young

CHAPTER 13

Construction Contracts

In the construction industry, agreements are made daily between various parties: owner with contractor, owner with designer, contractor with subcontractors, and contractor with suppliers. Each of the agreements between these parties is a separate contract that defines the specific obligations between the parties. Although each contract is a unique document (or set of documents), there are several *types* of contracts used in the industry. Typically, the owner chooses which type of owner-contractor agreement to use. This selection is important because the agreement used partially determines how much risk each party assumes. Let's see why this is so.

Basis for selecting a contract type

The primary distinguishing characteristic of contracts is how the contractor gets paid and how financial risk is distributed between the owner and the contractor. (Bear in mind that as the risk of one party increases, the risk to the other party decreases.) There are many ways that contracts can be crafted, but it helps to remember that each one is basically either **fixed price** (the contractor is paid according to the estimate he or she provided to the owner and therefore the total amount is known up front) or **reimbursable** (the contractor is paid for actual, as opposed to estimated, costs). Sometimes a contract incorporates both characteristics.

The owner develops an overall contractual strategy that is chosen after analyzing project objectives and restraints. For example, if a project's primary restraint is a very tight budget, the owner will likely choose a contract in which construction costs are fixed. This is called a lump-sum contract. On the other hand, if a project is undefined (as it might be with a renovation project, for example), the owner will likely prefer a contract that is flexible and pays the contractor for actual costs as design decisions are finalized.

Issues that impact the choice of contract include the following:

- **The project's delivery method**. Different delivery methods lend themselves to different contractual arrangements. For example, jobs that are competitively bid under a design-bid-build delivery method typically use lump-sum contracts, which we'll discuss momentarily. Other types of delivery methods might call for different contract types.
- **Whether the job is competitively bid or negotiated**. Competitively bid jobs tend to use contracts that have a fixed price; negotiated projects are more likely to use a different type of contract.
- **Risk allocation**. Which type of contract allocates financial risk fairly and encourages efficiency? Contracts distribute risk differently between the owner and the contractor; the owner balances this risk against the needs of the project. For example, a contract in which the contractor doesn't provide the owner with a fixed price up front is riskier for the owner but may be the best choice for the project (see the example to follow).
- **The quality of the design information**. Projects that have many design unknowns, such as renovation projects, are more suited to a contract that is able to adjust to changes. For example, when a contract is based on a competitively bid fixed price from the contractor, and adjustments and changes are made, the changes are typically much more costly than they would be if they had been part of the original bid. In addition, it is very difficult for a contractor to give a low fixed price on such a project because of the risk to *him*. This also argues for a reimbursable contract.
- **The type of project**. Public projects typically have fixed price contracts; private projects often do not. Similarly, the contract used for a

simple and straightforward project might be different from that used for a highly technical project.

Types of construction contracts

There are four types of contracts commonly used in construction; each is based on either a fixed-cost or reimbursable-cost payment to the contractor. The four are:

- **Lump-sum** (also called fixed price, fixed cost, or stipulated sum)
- **Cost plus a fee** (also called time and materials)
- **Cost plus with a guaranteed maximum price (GMP)**
- **Unit price**

Lump-sum and its variation, unit price contracts, pay the contractor a fixed price based on a cost estimate provided before construction to the owner by the contractor. Cost plus a fee and its variation, cost plus with a GMP, reimburse the contractor for actual costs. Let's take a look at these four and see how they differ.

Lump-sum contract

In a **lump-sum contract**, a specified amount of work is provided by the contractor for a set price that is known up front. The contractor estimates the labor, material, and equipment costs, and adds on a dollar amount for overhead and profit. The resulting number is submitted to the owner as the fixed price for the work. This price is the bid price and includes all the work *reasonably inferable* as being necessary to produce the intended results. (For example, even if a contractor's fixed price does not include carpet for the entry hall [because it wasn't shown on the drawings], it is reasonably inferable that the owner intended that it match the rest of the house and be more than just a plywood subfloor.)

Because of the fixed nature of the contractor's reimbursement, this type of contract is generally considered the *riskiest for the contractor*. If a mistake is made on the bid estimate, or if there are no provisions in the contract to account for unexpected situations, the contractor could find him- or herself responsible for costs that were not included in the price given to the owner. For example, if the contractor failed to notice that the drawings showed a higher quality carpet in the living room than in the rest of the house, and the cost estimate was therefore too low, he might have to pay the difference. If he misjudged the time it would take to complete the foundation and it took three days longer than was anticipated, that's too bad. If a mistake on the quantity of materials was off or he got the price wrong, then the added costs are his. The owner pays the contractor a fixed amount; if it comes in under that amount, the contractor makes money, but if it comes in over budget, he loses.

In addition to identifying the final cost up front, lump-sum contracts have several other characteristics:

- The lump-sum contract is familiar to people and is sometimes preferred for this reason.
- Projects that are competitively bid use lump-sum contracts. With competitively bid lump-sum contracts, the owner has the advantage of being able to examine bids and choose the one that suits him best.
- A fixed cost contract has a low risk for the owner and is well suited to an owner on a strict budget.
- A lump-sum contract that has thorough design documents can result in a lower cost project due to competitive bidding.
- This type of contract is well suited to small or formulaic projects (such as fast-food restaurants or single family homes, for example).

Lump-sum contracts also have limitations:

- A lump-sum contract is relatively inflexible and changes are costly.
- Lump-sum contracts are based on a cost estimate completed by the contractor. This is the bid amount, which we have discussed elsewhere. An accurate bid is absolutely dependent on complete design information. If the contract documents are incomplete or poorly executed or the scope of the work is unknown (as with a renovation project, for example), the contractor will have many questions during the bid process and during construction. Confusion typically leads to conflict and increased costs.

See Figure 13.1 for a graphic description of how a lump-sum contract impacts a contractor and an owner. Note that if the project costs more than the contractor's bid, the contractor loses money. Conversely, if the project costs less than the contractor's bid, the contractor makes additional money.

Contract amount	Actual cost	Impact on Contractor	Impact on owner
$500,000	$525,000	Contractor has $25,000 loss	No impact as contract price was fixed
$500,000	$475,000	Contractor realizes a $25,000 gain	No impact as contract price was fixed

Figure 13.1. Implications of lump-sum contracts

With a fixed price contract, an owner can put virtually all the financial risk onto the contractor's shoulders. There are ways, however, that the risk can be more evenly distributed and thus create a fairer contract. For example, language can be added that specifically limits the contractor's financial liability in certain circumstances (say, in case of unexpected underground conditions). This means the contractor will get paid if there are problems and won't need to carry so much extra money in the bid to cover unexpected situations that may arise.

Cost plus a fee contract

In a **cost plus a fee contract**, the owner reimburses the contractor for actual costs and pays a fee (which has been bid or negotiated) for overhead and profit. The contractor assumes little financial risk (assuming the fee is adequate) and, in exchange, makes complete cost information available to the owner.

Owners often don't like this type of contract because final costs aren't known until the project is complete, with the possibility of excessive expenditures. (It's not hard to imagine what can happen if a contractor has no strict budget!) And contractors don't like the extensive paperwork required of them when they have a cost plus contract. With a lump-sum contract, the contractor gets payments (typically based on a percentage of completed work) on a regular basis. With a cost plus contract, the contractor needs to justify each payment with documentation of the work completed during that billing period.

Why would an owner choose a cost plus contract?

- Sometimes the schedule takes precedence and it's important for construction to start on a job before the design is complete. (This is called *fast-tracking*, which we talked about in Chapter 6. It is not possible to get a fixed price up front for a fast-track job unless they are phased and each phase is separately bid.)

- Cost plus contracts are very flexible and changes can be made easily during construction.
- When complete design information is not known, an owner can often get a better price with a cost plus contract than with a fixed price contract.
- When a project is very complex or involves unquantifiable risks, a cost plus contract is often used.

Const. budget	Actual cost	Fee at 5% of cost	Final project cost (actual +fee)	Impact on contractor	Impact on owner
$450,000	$475,000	$23,750	$498,750	The contractor earns $1,250 more than expected	Final cost is $25,000 over budget and the owner pays this + the fee on that additional amount.
$450,000	$425,000	$21,250	$446,250	The contractor earns $1,250 less than expected	The owner pays $25,000 less than the budgeted cost and saves the fee on that amount

Figure 13.2. Implications of a cost plus a fee contract

The fee – A contractor's **fee** is the money a contractor gets from the owner to cover his business overhead plus a profit. (Overhead is also called indirect costs and includes home office expenses such as rent; see Chapter 10.) The fee is typically either a fixed amount or a percentage of the construction cost. The latter can be anything from 2 or 3 percent to whatever the market will bear. The amount added to a contract price to cover overhead costs and profit will be carefully analyzed by the contractor's estimator; if the fee is too high the contractor may not get the job. As we learned in Chapter 11, in a lump sum contract the overhead and profit are rolled into the bid amount. In a cost plus job these costs are separated out and the owner will know exactly what they are.

With the cost plus a fee contract, the owner pays all the direct and indirect project costs plus a separate fee to the contractor. If the contractor's fee is a fixed percentage of costs, he or she will earn more as the actual costs increase.

Cost plus with a guaranteed maximum price contract

Many owners are uncomfortable with cost plus contracts and feel the financial risk is too great. One way to reduce the owner's risk is to have the contractor provide a cap on the cost, which is called a **guaranteed maximum price** (GMP). With this type of cost plus contract, the owner is invoiced for actual expenditures, as he is with a standard cost plus contract. The difference is that the owner can be assured that there is a maximum cost that will not be exceeded. If the contractor goes above the cap, he has to cover the costs. If costs come in below the cap, the owner and the contractor typically share the difference. The contractor's fee is generally on a lump-sum basis.

For large and complex projects requiring flexibility, a cost plus contract with a reasonable GMP and a sharing clause that provides incentive to the contractor is generally superior to other contract types. These projects can be fast-tracked.

GMP contract (including fee)	Actual cost (including fee)	Impact on contractor	Impact on owner
$450,000	$475,000	Contractor has $25,000 loss.	No impact as maximum contract price was fixed.
$450,000	$425,000	No impact as contractor has guaranteed to keep total costs at $450,000 maximum. May split the savings with owner.	Owner receives benefit of $25,000 savings (which may be split with contractor)

Figure 13.3. Implications of cost plus with fixed fee and GMP

Unit price contract

There are certain classes of construction work that can be specified by a designer but for which it is difficult to determine in advance the exact amount of work required. Unit price contracts are typically used for these projects. Projects that use unit price contracts are typically engineered projects such as highways that do not use materials that can be precisely counted ahead of time (such as the quantity of soil excavated). The quantities are imprecise and the work is often done with heavy equipment such as bulldozers. Unit price contracts are common on public transportation jobs.

In a **unit price contract**, the contractor bids a fixed unit price and, at the completion of the job, the total quantities are determined and payment is made to the contractor based on actual quantities. The owner provides a *projection* of what she expects the quantities to be (such as tons of gravel or cubic yards of fill) and bidding contractors base their quotes on those projections.

This system provides for competitive bidding even though the exact contract amount isn't known until completion of the project. In addition, if the owner's quantities are off, she, not the contractor, is responsible for the added costs. To understand more fully what this means, see Figure 13.4.

Work item	Owner's estimated quantities	Contracted unit prices	Bid amount	Actual quantities	Actual cost
Excavation	10,000 CY	$ 6.00	$ 60,000	12,000 CY	$ 72,000
Pipe	1,000 LF	$20.00	$ 20,000	1,000 LF	$ 20,000
Backfill	10,000 CY	$ 5.00	$ 50,000	13,525 CY	$ 67,625
Total			$130,000		$159,625

Figure 13.4. Implications of a unit price contract

In the example detailed in Figure 13.4, the owner estimated 10,000 cubic yards (CY) of trench excavation and provided this figure to contractors interested in bidding for the job. Contractors then bid fixed unit prices. In our example, our contractor bid $6.00 per CY for a bid price of $60,000 for the trench excavation (10,000 CY x $6.00/CY). When the trenches were excavated, however, the actual quantity was slightly more, 12,000 CY. The contractor is paid his bid price of $6.00 per CY times the total actual cubic yards ($6.00 x 12,000 = $72,000). The other parts of the job were similarly bid for a total estimated project cost of $130,000. When all the actual quantities were calculated, however, the owner's projected quantities were low and our contractor was paid $159,625 instead of his total bid price of $130,000. The owner paid $29,625 more than expected, because the job required greater quantities than expected of excavation and backfill. (Only the pipe lengths were accurately projected by the owner.)

Unit price contracts are hybrids, as the contractor bids a price like a lump-sum contract but is paid for actual quantities like a cost plus contract. Financial risk is spread between the owner and the contractor.

Risk management and contracts

Most risk in construction is ultimately financial in nature. Both an owner and a contractor are motivated to reduce their risk on a job. There are different ways to manage risk; bonds, insurance, and hiring subcontractors are some of them. How a construction contract is structured is another primary way of allocating (and reimbursing) risk.

We have learned that different contracts distribute risk between the owner and the contractor in different ways. When an owner seeks a contractor, he does so not only for the contractor's expertise but so that the contractor can carry some of the risk as well. A good contract, however, distributes risk equitably and compensates each party for their risk.

In a lump-sum contract, the contractor is paid to assume most of the financial risk. This is the riskiest type of contract for the contractor because he is giving the owner a price for the building and hoping the estimate on which he based his bid is accurate. If the contractor makes a mistake and the costs turn out higher than expected, the contractor can't count on additional funds from the owner. Conversely, a well-estimated lump-sum project that is efficiently managed can result in increased profit for the contractor. A cost plus contract is riskiest for the owner because the contractor does not quote a firm price up front and the owner pays all the actual costs for the work. Risk is increased for the owner because the contractor's fee is typically based on construction costs – a situation ripe for abuse by an unscrupulous contractor!

Figure 13.5 identifies how risk shifts between the owner and the contractor based on the type of contract selected for the project.

	Lump-sum	Cost + fee with GMP	Unit price	Cost + fee
Owner	Least risky	Less risky than CP but riskier than LS	Less risky than CP but riskier than LS	Riskiest
Contractor	Riskiest as price is based on fixed bid	Riskier than CP but less so than LS when there's a sharing clause	Less risky than fixed bid	Least risky

Figure 13.5. Risk comparison

Within different types of contracts, there are a variety of ways, such as sharing cost overruns or savings, used to equalize the risk between the contractor and the owner. Why would it be desirable to equalize the risk? It's often better for a project if the parties feel that they are carrying a fair and not excessive portion of the risk and that one party is not benefiting at the expense of the other. A good contract is typically one that pays a fair price for the work and appropriately rewards the risks assumed.

Note:

Figures 13.1-13.5 are based on similar figures created by Barbara Jackson for her book *Construction Management JumpStart*. Her method of explaining the implications for both the owner and the contractor of different contract types is something I could not improve upon.

Chapter Vocabulary

Cost plus (a fee) contract – a type of contract in which the owner reimburses the contractor for actual costs and pays a bid or negotiated fee for overhead and profit to the contractor.

Fee – the amount paid as remuneration for services. In construction, the fee is typically overhead plus profit.

Fixed price contract (lump-sum contract, stipulated-sum contract) – a type of contract in which a specified amount of work is provided by the contractor for a set price that is known up front.

Guaranteed maximum price (GMP) contract – a cost plus contract which has a cap on the final cost.

Lump-sum contract (fixed price contract, stipulated sum contract) – a type of contract in which a specified amount of work is provided by the contractor for a set price that is known up front.

Reimbursable contract – a contract in which the contractor is paid for actual cost, as opposed to estimated costs.

Risk – something that can go wrong on a project, leading to potential financial loss.

Stipulated-sum contract (lump-sum contract, fixed price contract) – a type of contract in which a specified amount of work is provided by the contractor for a set price that is known up front.

Unit price contract – a type of contract in which the contractor bids a fixed unit price and, at the completion of the job, the total quantities are determined and payment is made to the contractor based on actual quantities.

Test Yourself

1. What is the primary distinguishing characteristic of the different contract types?
2. You are a contractor with a cost plus a fee contract and the project ends up costing $50,000 more than the budget. What is the impact on you?
3. What type of contract would an owner on a very tight budget probably prefer? Why?
4. What type of contract is riskiest for the contractor? Why?
5. What type of contract is riskiest for the owner? Why?
6. If you are a contractor and have a lump-sum contract, what happens if the final project cost is less than what you bid?
7. What type of contract is generally used on small or formulaic projects?
8. What type of contract is considered inflexible in the sense that it's costly to make changes?
9. How does a guaranteed maximum price reduce an owner's risk?
10. How does a unit price contract reduce a contractor's risk?

Andrea Young

CHAPTER 14

Contracts Documents: The Agreement

In Chapter 8, we looked at the bid documents – the documents and instructions the contractor uses to price and submit a bid. Once the owner and contractor have entered into a contract, the bid documents are now called the *contract documents*. Typically, those bid documents that provide information on the *process* of bidding are not considered contract documents. Not every bid document becomes one of the contract documents, but most do:

Bid Documents	Contract Documents
Bid forms	N/A
Instructions to bidders	N/A
Bidder qualifications	N/A
Agreement	Agreement
Drawings	Drawings
Specifications	Specifications
General conditions	General conditions
Supplementary conditions	Supplementary conditions
Addenda	Addenda
N/A	Change orders

The **contract documents**, taken together, form the legal basis for the contract between the owner and the contractor and describe the project, the rights, and the obligations of each party, and the terms and conditions (the rules) for how the project will be administered. If either the owner or the contractor fails to live up to the terms outlined in the contract documents, the other party can terminate (end) the contract and take the offending party to court. (This is also true of contracts entered into between the general contractor and subcontractors.)

The bid documents are put together during the design phase under the supervision of the architect (see Chapter 7). Some of the documents (such as the architectural drawings) are developed by the architect. On most projects, consultants hired by the architect supply many of the documents. Examples are the construction drawings developed by the structural or electrical engineers and the specifications prepared by a specifications consultant. Some of the documents (such as the *agreement* and the *general conditions*) may be standardized forms published by organizations such as the American Institute of Architects.

Summary: – The **bid documents** are the collection of documents used to make and obtain bids and to define the requirements of the work and the process that the contractor must follow when she submits a bid. Bid (and therefore contract) documents consist of both graphic and written elements. All bidding contractors must have access to all the bid documents. If a contractor doesn't follow the requirements set forth in the bid documents, she will typically not be awarded the job. Once a contract is awarded, most of the bid documents become the **contract documents** and define the legal terms of the contract. The contracts between general contractors and subcontractors typically reference these documents.

Contract documents are part of every project. On large jobs, all the documents (with the exception of the drawings) are compiled in a project manual; on small jobs, some of the documents may simply be added as notes on the drawings. No matter what form, the documents describe the obligations of the parties.

Review of the contract documents

The contract documents typically include some or all of the following separate documents, described briefly:

- **Agreement**. Although often referred to as the *contract*, the agreement is only one of the various documents that make up the contract. The agreement legally obligates the signing parties (such as the owner and the contractor) and states certain contractual facts about a specific project such as the contract price and when the project must be completed. The agreement is the subject of this chapter.

- **General conditions**. The general conditions identify the obligations, the rights, and the responsibilities of the contractor and the owner. Unlike the agreement, the general conditions can be used on multiple projects, as many of the terms are "boilerplate" and do not change from project to project.
- **Supplementary conditions**. Supplementary conditions are used to modify the general conditions to take into account special requirements for a specific project. If, for example, the general conditions state a procedure for making changes to the work that is unacceptable to the owner, the supplementary conditions can be used to change this term. Additional project requirements such as liquidated damages may be identified in the supplementary conditions. We'll look at the general and supplementary conditions in the next chapter.
- **Drawings**. The drawings are the graphic representation of the project, which describe the quantitative aspects of a project and are made up of plans, elevations, sections, and details (see Chapter 7).
- **Specifications**. The specifications are written descriptions of the work that define the materials, the processes, and the quality of products and systems. The specifications and the drawings work together to provide the information contractors need in order to price and build a project. We'll look at the specifications in Chapter 16.
- **Addenda and Modifications**. Changes made to the work before the bids are submitted are called *addenda*. Once a construction contract has been signed, changes are called *modifications*. Most modifications are change orders, as we'll see in Chapter 22.

In this chapter, we focus on the agreement between a general contractor and an owner. As mentioned, the agreement is the document that consists of facts about the individual project being built. *It is the most important contract document and takes precedence over all the others*. This means that if there is a conflict between documents, the terms identified in the agreement will rule. For example, if the general conditions and the agreement identify different payment procedures, those identified in the agreement would be considered correct. The agreement is the most important document because it contains evidence, through the parties' signatures, that both agree to the terms and conditions of the entire contract.

What is the agreement?

As noted, the agreement is one of the documents that make up a contract and is sometimes referred to as the contract because it includes, by reference, all the other documents.

The agreement can be quite brief but always consists of statements of fact about the *specific* project: it identifies who the parties are, what the scope of work is, and what the terms of payment will be. Each project has its own, separate agreement. Both parties to the contract (the contractor and the owner) sign the agreement as evidence that they both agree to all the terms and conditions of the contract. Typically, once both parties have signed and dated the agreement, the parties have entered into a legally enforceable contract.

Components of all agreements

All agreements contain the same type of project information including:

Names, addresses, and signatures of the contractor and owner

The agreement clearly identifies the parties to the contract – the contractor and the owner. By signing the contract's agreement, both parties accept the obligations set forth in the agreement form and, by extension, the other referenced documents (such as the drawings). The signatures are evidence of mutual agreement.

Address of the project and brief description of the work

There should be no confusion regarding the project, so the description needs to clearly (although briefly) summarize the work and state the project location. A description might be as follows: *"The Contractor will provide all labor, materials, and equipment to complete the residence located at 200 Main Street, Haverford, PA."*

How much the contractor will be paid & the payment terms

The project sum is the amount of money the contractor can expect to receive for doing the work described in the contract. In most cases, this figure is the amount of the contractor's bid. For example, language in the agreement regarding payment might be as follows *"The contractor will be paid a fixed sum of*

$225,500 to be paid monthly based on work completed the previous month." This means that the contractor will be paid a total of $225,000 for the work and that he will be paid in monthly installments based on how much work was completed during the previous payment period.

List of documents referenced by the agreement

The agreement identifies which drawings or other documents have been provided by the owner, and are therefore part of the contract. A simple way to do this is with language such as the following: *"The Work will be done according to the plans dated May 25, 2010, Specifications prepared by Spec Writers Inc. and dated April 12, 2010, and Soils Test Data provided by Soil Testing Associates, dated February 19, 2010."*

Time for completion

Typically, the owner requires specificity from the contractor regarding how long the project will take. Time is generally identified in total number of days to complete the work. A projected start date might be included. For example, *"The Work to be performed by Contractor shall be commenced within five (5) days from receipt of the building permit and will be completed within 185 days thereafter."* Failure to complete a job on time can result in liquidated damages. (If specific information regarding time is not included, the assumption is that the work will be completed in a "reasonable" period of time.)

On many jobs, there are items that the contractor will not or does not want to be responsible for and they should be identified in the agreement. It is often advisable for a contractor to add potential problems as **exclusions**. An exclusion is a piece of work or service that is outside the contractor's scope of work and is so identified in the contract. For example, the contract might state:

- *"Permits, soil tests, and disposal costs are not included in this work."* This exclusion states that the contractor will not be responsible for getting or paying for any of these three items.
- Maybe the contractor is concerned about possible, unavoidable damage to the roots of a tree in the client's front yard. He or she could state the following as an exclusion: *"Contractor is not responsible for any damage to existing fruit tree in front yard."*
- Other examples of possible exclusions are uncovering unexpected underground conditions that might increase foundation costs, or an unreasonable increase in material expenses.

Exclusions are a way for the contractor to reduce the need to increase the bid to take care of *possible* problems.

The agreement entered into between a general contractor and a subcontractor includes similar information to that between the GC and owner: a brief description of the work and the location of the project, the names and addresses of the parties, a list of documents, a time frame for completion of the subcontractor's work, and how the sub will be paid. The agreement between the GC and a sub, as that between the GC and the owner, must meet the standards for a valid contract: there must be evidence of mutuality, consideration, capacity, and lawfulness.

Forms of Agreements

There is no set form for agreements. Some owners write their own; some use standardized, off-the-shelf forms; some are published by professional organizations such as the Associated General Contractors of America and the American Institute of Architects. On small private jobs, the contractor typically provides the owner with the agreement. On larger projects and those that are publicly funded, the owner typically determines the contract that will be used. What is important is that sufficient information (as previously described) is included in order to reduce misunderstandings, to show mutual agreement regarding the work that is to be done, and to clarify the rights and responsibilities of the owner and the contractor.

The agreement that is selected is typically dependent on the delivery method and how payment will be made (i.e., is payment to the contractor based on a fixed price or reimbursable costs?).

Letter agreements

Contracts do not have to be complicated to be valid and enforceable, nor do they have to be written by a lawyer and filled with legal language. In the case of small construction jobs, a written contract can be made simply by the exchange of suitable letters. This is called a **letter agreement**.

Let's see how this works, using a straightforward project as an example. Mr. Owner has requested that ABC Construction submit a cost proposal for completing a trellis/arbor and fence repair project at the owner's home in Santa Rosa, California. The work for this project includes building a redwood trellis/arbor, replacing several sections of an existing fence, and adding two small hinged gates. There is planting shown on the drawings, but the owner has indicated with a note that he would like to take care of this part of the work himself.

The owner has shown ABC the site and provided the contractor, Jane Smith, with two simple drawings detailing the scope of work. (As is typically the case with design drawings or sketches, each sheet is titled, dated, and numbered. ABC will want to refer to these specific drawings in their proposal.)

Jane Smith and the owner have agreed that ABC will submit a cost estimate in letter form and that if the owner agrees to the price and terms, he will sign the letter and return an original to ABC. Once the owner signs the contractor's letter, the two of them have an agreement and a contract is formed. Figure 14.1 is an example of how this letter might be structured. Bear in mind that even such a simple proposal should contain all the important elements of an agreement.

ABC Construction Company, Inc.
Post Office Box 2345 Windsor, CA 95407 License #23456

May 28, 2010

Mr. Owner
431 Main Street
Santa Rosa, CA 95404

Dear Mr. Owner:

We have examined the site and the drawings (No. 1 & No. 2 dated April 30, 2010) for the trellis/arbor and fence repair work at the above address. We are pleased to offer this bid to provide all labor and materials to construct and complete the following work:

- Installation of redwood arbor and adjustment of south fence as required
- Installation of redwood gates at south and east elevations as shown
- Installation of pavers at the south entry as shown

This bid does not include adjustments to the existing concrete patio except as noted on the drawings nor does it include any plumbing or irrigation.

We propose to complete this work for $3,350. Payment in full will be due at completion of the work. Work will commence three days after acceptance of this offer by owner. Contractor anticipates the work will be complete in five business days. Kindly indicate your agreement to these terms by signing and dating below and returning one original copy to our offices.

We are pleased to have the opportunity to provide you with this bid and look forward to working with you. Thank you.

Sincerely,

Jane Smith, President
ABC Contractors

________________________ ____________

Owner's signature here Date

Figure 14.1. Letter agreement

A letter agreement is sufficient for only the smallest projects; a more extensive and detailed agreement form is typical on most projects.

Standardized agreements

Figure 14.2 is an example of a simple, standardized agreement form between an owner and a contractor that can be purchased at a stationery store. All the components identified previously are included: names and addresses of the parties, description and address of the project, project sum, completion time, and signatures. The signatures indicate mutual agreement, and unless both parties sign, there is no contract. In this simple agreement, the general conditions are included right on the agreement form.

Several professional organizations and government agencies publish blank agreement forms. Some of the most frequently used are from the American

PRIME BUILDING CONTRACT

(Not to be used for Residential Remodeling or Swimming Pools)

THIS AGREEMENT IS BETWEEN: RE PROJECT:

(Contractor's Name) (Owner's Name)

(Contractor's License Number) (Owner's Home Address)

(Contractor's Address) (City, State & Zip)

(City, State & Zip) (Project Address)

(Contractor's Telephone - FAX) (City, State & Zip)

CONSTRUCTION LENDER: Name and address of construction fund holder is: ________

(Name And Branch Address Of Bank, Savings And Loan Assn., Escrow Agent, Joint Control Or Other)

DESCRIPTION OF PROJECT (according to the plans and specifications, including materials to be used or installed): Contractor shall furnish all labor, materials and equipment to perform in a workmanlike manner: ________

(Describe Labor, Materials, And Equipment To Be Furnished)

Work will commence approximately on or about ________ (Approximate Start Date)

TIME FOR COMPLETION: The work to be performed by Contractor pursuant to this Agreement shall be substantially completed within ________ ( ) days or approximately on ________ (Date).

PAYMENT: Owner agrees to pay Contractor a total cash price of $ ________ (Total Contract Price).

Down Payment (if any) $ ________.

Payment Installments As Follows:

1. $______ (Work or Services to be Performed) (Date)
2. $______ (Work or Services to be Performed) (Date)
3. $______ (Work or Services to be Performed) (Date)
4. $______ (Work or Services to be Performed) (Date)

INTEREST: Overdue payments will bear interest at the rate of 1½% per month.

Contractors are required by law to be licensed and regulated by the Contractors' State License Board which has jurisdiction to investigate complaints against contractors if a complaint regarding a patent act or omission is filed within four years of the date of the alleged violation. A complaint regarding a latent act or omission pertaining to any structural defects must be filed within 10 years of the date of the alleged violation. Any questions concerning a contractor may be referred to the Registrar, Contractors' State License Board, P.O. Box 26000, Sacramento, California 95826, 1-800-321-2752.

You, the buyer, have the right to require the contractor to have a payment and performance bond. However, the contractor can require you to pay for that bond.

☐ NOTICE TO OWNER: IF YOU AGREE TO ARBITRATION, REVIEW THE "ARBITRATION OF DISPUTES" SECTION ON THE REVERSE SIDE OF THIS PAGE (PROVISION 13) AND PLACE YOUR INITIALS ON EACH COPY OF THIS CONTRACT.

Owner: X______ (Owner Sign Here) ____ (Date) Firm Name: ______ (Contractor's Firm Name)

Owner: X______ (If More Than One Owner, Please Sign Here) ____ (Date) Contractor or Agent: X______ (Contractor or Agent Sign Here) ____ (Date)

TERMS AND CONDITIONS: The terms and conditions on the reverse side are expressly incorporated into this Agreement.

Figure 14.2. Standardized agreement
Form 202-1, 2003. Builder's Book Inc., Canoga Park, CA

Institute of Architects (AIA), the Associated General Contractors (AGC), and the Engineers Joint Contract Documents Committee of the National Society of Professional Engineers (EJCDC). These forms are quite extensive but may be modified, if necessary, for specific project requirements. Using standardized forms has several advantages: They save preparation time and users can be fairly confident that the forms are complete and accurate. In addition, some standardized forms have been used for so many years they are widely accepted within the industry and have been upheld in the courts. (Although standardized forms may reduce misunderstandings and misinterpretation, we'll see in the next chapter that there may still be problems with various aspects of some of these forms.)

Standardized forms are typically preferred because they are very familiar to those in the industry and many have been tested in the courts. Only the simplest projects use a form such as that shown as Figure 14.2; larger and more complex work benefit from a more extensive agreement such as the AIA form shown in Figure 14.3.

Whether the agreement is a simple letter signed by the contractor and the owner, or a much more extensive, standardized form, this document provides evidence that both the contractor and the owner agree to the terms and condi-

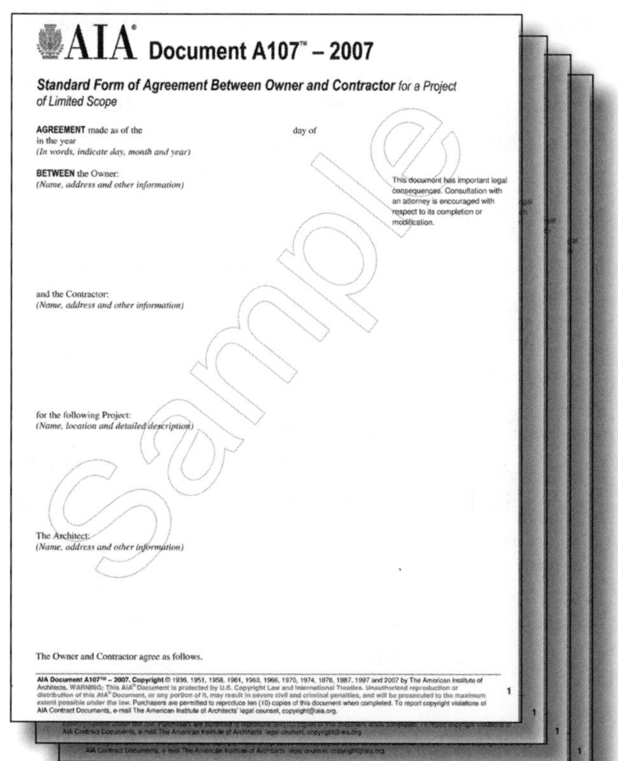

AIA® Document A107™ – 2007

***Standard Form of Agreement Between Owner and Contractor** for a Project of Limited Scope*

AGREEMENT made as of the day of
in the year
(In words, indicate day, month and year)

This document has important legal consequences. Consultation with an attorney is encouraged with respect to its completion or modification.

BETWEEN the Owner:
(Name, address and other information)

and the Contractor:
(Name, address and other information)

for the following Project:
(Name, location and detailed description)

The Architect:
(Name, address and other information)

The Owner and Contractor agree as follows.

1

Figure 14.3. Owner-contractor agreement excerpt, AIA Document A107-2007

tions set forth in all the contract documents. If there is no written and signed agreement, it is often difficult to enforce a contract.

Written vs. unwritten agreements

Sometimes a project is so small and straightforward that the owner and the contractor assume a written contract is unnecessary. But even with the simplest projects, things change and misunderstandings can arise. Unanticipated situations can lead to disputes and the resolution of disputes often requires reference to the terms of a contract. The larger and more complex the project, the more critical this becomes.

Usually, contracts do not have to be in writing to be legally valid or sufficient. If a contract is not in writing when the law requires that it be, then the contract will not be valid. If a contract is not in writing, but the law doesn't require it to be in writing, the contract may be valid but unenforceable. This is a difference worth noting.

Here's an example of why this is important for owners as well as contractors. An owner has made an oral agreement with you that you will replace the windows in his bedroom for $2,000. Before you are scheduled to begin work, you realize that your bid was too low so you don't show up. When the owner calls you, you deny that you ever had an agreement, claiming that you provided him only with an estimate. What's the owner to do? You may have a valid contract, but there were no witnesses and the owner is basically out of luck. There is no way for the owner to enforce the contract. The same thing can happen to the contractor. You do the work for an agreed-to price, but the owner fails to pay you the entire amount. If nothing is in writing, it will be difficult for the courts to determine what was agreed to. You may not be fully paid. Beyond the issue of enforceability, when agreements are in writing, misunderstandings and confusion regarding expectations are reduced.

The law is complicated, and whether a contract is legally required to be in writing varies from state to state, depending on the project type and size. In some states, small projects (typically defined in dollar terms) do not require written agreements. Generally, if a project cannot be completed within a certain time (for example, a year), the law requires that there be a written contract. In some states, contracts for specialized work, such as home improvement work, also need to be in writing.

Chapter Vocabulary

Agreement – the contract document that legally obligates the signing parties (such as the owner and the contractor) and states certain contractual facts about a specific project, such as the contract price and completion date.

Bid documents (bid package) – the collection of documents (including drawings, specifications, agreement forms, general conditions, and other documents) used to make and obtain bids and to define the requirements of the work and the process that the contractor must follow when submitting a bid. When a construction contract is executed, most of the bid documents become contract documents.

Contract documents – the information that defines the legal terms of a contract.

Exclusion – a piece of work or service that is outside the contractor's scope of work and is so identified in the contract.

Letter agreement – a contract in the form of a letter between the parties. Letter agreements contain the elements of standardized agreements.

Test Yourself

1. What is the difference between bid documents and contract documents?
2. Who is responsible for developing the bid documents?
3. Who is responsible for developing the contract documents?
4. Why are there more bid documents than contract documents? What kind of information is included in the bid documents that is not (typically) included in the contract documents?
5. Why is the agreement considered especially important?
6. Why should contracts be in writing, even if the law doesn't require it?
7. What are four pieces of information that should always be included in an agreement?
8. Why might a contractor include an exclusion in an agreement?
9. Why are some valid contracts not enforceable?
10. Why do the contractor and the owner both sign the agreement?

Andrea Young

CHAPTER 15

Contracts Documents: General & Supplementary Conditions

As we have learned, construction contracts are made up of several (complementary) documents. The most important of these is the agreement, which is brief and contains statements of fact about the specific project. All contracts also include conditions that define the basic rights, obligations, and relationships of the parties. There are two conditions documents: general conditions and supplementary conditions.

The **general conditions** are "boilerplate" standards (a standard is a norm or a requirement) that apply to the project as a whole and which can be applied to multiple projects. The general conditions are modified by the **supplementary conditions** to reflect the needs of individual projects. As with all the contract documents, the architect is (typically) responsible for developing or coordinating the development of the general and supplementary conditions to make sure that they meet the needs of the project and are clear and complete. Conditions are an inherent part of a contract and are included as part of the bid package. After a contract is finalized between the owner and the contractor, the general and supplementary conditions become part of the contract documents.

What are the general conditions?

When contractors, owners, and designers are working together to complete a project, it is important that there be understanding regarding responsibilities and procedures. The conditions of a contract refer to the agreed-upon rules under which the project will be built and establish the rights, authority, and obligations of the owner, the owner's representative (often the architect), and the contractor. This information is contained in the general conditions.

The general conditions are standards that can be used on multiple projects (hence the word "general") and are provided in conjunction with the agreement. They outline the broad rights and responsibilities of the parties; outline terms for making changes to the work; specify the procedures for contractor payment; provide guidance for dealing with disputes or delays; and much more.

Forms

On small projects, the general conditions may be included as part of the agreement document itself. Sometimes the conditions are added as simple notes on the drawings. On most projects, however, the conditions are extensive enough to require a separate document. As is true with the agreement, many owners prefer to use standardized forms. (This is typically not true of public agencies, which often supply their own agreements and general conditions documents.) Standardized general conditions have the same advantages as standardized agreements: they are typically very familiar to the parties involved and some have been tested in the courts so that there is clarity regarding their language and meaning.

Irrespective of the form of the general conditions or how extensive they are, they are an important component of the contract and it is critical that all parties clearly understand what they contain.

Excerpts from the AIA General Conditions

Although the various forms of general conditions published by different agencies and organizations have similar language, when owners are using the services of an architect, the preferred document is typically one published by the American Institute of Architects. On projects where the lead designer is an engineer (such as a utility project, for example), a form published by the Engineers Joint Contract Documents Committee (EJCDC) is more typically used. There are others as well. In this text, we'll refer to the AIA version.

The American Institute of Architects form AIA Document A201- 2007 General Conditions of the Contract for Construction (that's the formal name; most people refer to it as "A201") is very detailed and information is organized into 15 articles as follows:

1. General Provisions
2. Owner
3. Contractor
4. Architect
5. Subcontractors
6. Construction by Owner or by Separate Contractors
7. Changes in the Work
8. Time
9. Payment and Completion
10. Protection of Persons and Property
11. Insurance and Bonds
12. Uncovering and Correction of Work
13. Miscellaneous Provisions
14. Termination or Suspension of the Contract
15. Claims and Disputes

As the reader can see, different categories are covered in A201. The document begins, in Article 1, with basic definitions – of the contract, the work, the contract documents, and more – and moves on to identify the major players (the owner, the contractor, the architect, and subcontractors) and their roles, rights, and obligations (Article 2, 3, 4, and 5). Procedures for how changes are made to the contract (Article 7), how payments are made (Article 9), how the contract can be terminated (Article 14), and how disputes are to be handled (Article 15) are among the issues described by the general conditions. Each article is divided into multiple sections.

Work – In contract documents, you might see the term Work with a capital W. This refers to the very specific work, called the scope of work, that the contractor has agreed to perform. In A201, Work is defined in Section 1.1.3 as the following: *"the construction and services required by the contract documents, whether completed or partially completed, and includes all other labor, materials, equipment and services provided or to be provided by the Contractor to fulfill the Contractor's obligations ..."* In other words, the Work is what the contractor is obligated to complete. In this text, we do not, as a rule, capitalize work.

Let's look at some of the articles and the provisions included in A201 to introduce a few of the important items addressed in this part of a construction contract. Note that each of the excerpts to follow are only a small portion of the total document and are offered only as samples. In many cases, the same items are covered, though somewhat differently, in non-AIA general conditions.

Article 2: The owner

It's important for the owner and the contractor to understand what their rights as well as their responsibilities are to each other and to the project. This section of the AIA General Conditions identifies what information and services the owner must provide to the contractor and gives information regarding the owner's right to stop or carry out work or make changes to the work. Here's a small part of the rights the AIA General Conditions give to an owner. This concerns what the owner may do if a contractor fails to perform.

> "*If the Contractor fails to correct Work which is not in accordance with the requirements of the Contract Documents ... or persistently fails to carry out Work in accordance with the Contract Documents, the Owner may issue a written order to the Contractor to stop the Work, or any portion thereof until the cause for such order has been eliminated ...*" A201 Section 2.3

Article 3: The contractor

Article 3 specifies the contractor's responsibilities regarding review of the contract documents and the jobsite, supervision and construction procedures, the contractor's obligations regarding labor and materials, procedures regarding shop drawings and product data, permits and fees, cleaning the site, and more. Here are two examples of what Article 3 says.

> "*The Contractor shall be responsible to the owner for acts and omissions of the Contractor's employees, Subcontractors ... and other persons or entities perform-*

ing portions of the Work ..." A201 Section 3.3.2 [In other words, the general contractor is responsible for everyone who performs work for or supplies materials or equipment to the job.]

"*If the Contractor performs Work knowing it to be contrary to applicable laws, statutes, ordinances, codes, and rules and regulations, or lawful orders of public authorities, the Contractor shall assume appropriate responsibility for such Work and shall bear the costs attributable to correction.*" A201 Section 3.7.3 [If the general contractor knows that something is not allowed under the local building code, for example, and does it anyway, he may have to pay for correcting the problem.]

Article 4: The architect

On every job, someone must administer the construction contract to make sure everyone is doing what they're supposed to be doing and procedures are being followed. On small projects, it may be the owner who performs this role. On larger projects, this is typically one of the responsibilities of the architect (and is so stated in the general conditions). As administrator, the architect is the owner's agent to make sure the work is progressing and that the contractor is performing according to the requirements of the contract documents. One of the roles that the administrator serves is of particular interest to the contractor: reviewing and approving (or denying) the contractor's pay requests. The architect's role in this important activity is stated in the general conditions.

"*Based on the Architect's evaluation of the Contractor's Application for Payment, the Architect will review and certify the amounts due the Contractor and will issue Certificates for Payment in such amounts.*" A201 Section 4.2.5

Article 5: Subcontractors

As we have already learned, a subcontractor is a person or entity that has a direct contract with another contractor to perform a portion of the work. There are several points regarding subcontractors in the general conditions. One is that the general contractor must, under certain circumstances, inform the owner of who he intends to hire as subcontractors. The owner is obligated to accept the general contractor's choices unless he (the owner) has reasonable objections to a subcontractor.

"*The Contractor shall not contract with a proposed person or entity to whom the Owner or Architect has made reasonable and timely objection. The Contractor shall not be required to contract with anyone to whom the Contractor has made reasonable objection.*" A201 Section 5.2.2 [In other words, the general contractor is not free to hire any subcontractor he wishes.]

Article 7: Changes in the work

The general conditions state that the owner has the right to make reasonable changes in the work and that the contractor has the obligation to make those changes. This section of the general conditions defines the three types of changes or modifications (change orders, change directives, and minor changes in the work) and the responsibilities of the parties with each. We can see from the following excerpt that, in the A201 General Conditions, all three primary players – the owner, the contractor, and the architect – agree to and sign change orders. (Note that on many jobs that do not use the AIA general conditions, only the owner and the contractor sign change orders.) If there is disagreement regarding changes, the general conditions provide guidance regarding how to proceed. Here are a couple of excerpts from the section on Changes in the Work.

"*Changes in the Work may be accomplished after execution of the Contract, and without invalidating the Contract* ..." A201 Section 7.1.1

"*A Change Order is a written instrument prepared by the Architect and signed by the Owner, Contractor and Architect stating their agreement upon all of the following: The change in the Work, The amount of the adjustment, if any, in the Contract Sum, and The extent of the adjustment, if any, in the Contract Time.*" A201 Section 7.2.1

Article 9: Payment and completion

As noted, the contractor will be very interested in the payment procedures: what date invoices are due each month, how many days the owner has to make payment, what happens if the architect denies an invoice or an owner doesn't pay, and so on. This section of the general conditions provides the parties with specific information on the payment process, procedures for withholding payment, and how the contractor will receive final payment.

"*The Architect will, within seven days after receipt of the Contractor's Application for Payment, either issue to the Owner a Certificate of Payment ... for such amount as the Architect determines is properly due or notify the Contractor ... in writing of the Architect's reasons for withholding certification in whole or in part ...*" A201 Section 9.4.1

"*Upon receipt of the Contractor's written notice that the Work is ready for final inspection … the Architect will promptly make such inspection and, when the Architect finds the Work acceptable … and the Contract fully performed, the Architect will promptly issue a final Certificate for Payment …*" A201 Section 9.10.1

Article 14: Termination or suspension of the contract

Under certain circumstances, both the owner and the contractor can end the contract and Article 14 identifies the conditions under which this can happen. Here are just a few of several situations that can result in termination or suspension of the contract.

"*The Contractor may terminate the Contract if the Work is stopped for a period of 30 consecutive days through no act or fault of the Contractor … {or} Because the Architect has not issued a Certificate for Payment…*" A201 Section14.1.1

"*The Owner may terminate the Contract if the Contractor: 1. persistently or repeatedly refuses or fails to supply enough properly skilled workers or proper materials; 2. fails to make payment to Subcontractors …; 3. persistently disregards laws … regulations …; 4. otherwise is guilty of substantial breach of a provision of the Contract Documents.*" A201 Section 14.2.1

Article 15: Claims and disputes

A claim is filed (typically) by the contractor when he feels he is owed additional money or time or, conversely, by the owner against the contractor over contract performance. If agreement cannot be reached, the claim will become a dispute. The general conditions provide guidance regarding how the parties may (or must) proceed when there is a claim or a dispute.

"*The parties shall endeavor to resolve their Claims by mediation … A request for mediation shall be made in writing …*" A201 Section 15.3.2

Other provisions

Other provisions are also included as general conditions. These include, but are not limited to, procedures for addressing delays in the work, responsibilities for cleaning the jobsite, requirement for a jobsite safety officer, insurance and bonds, and correction of work.

Some standardized forms of general conditions have their critics. It has been noted, for example, that certain provisions of the A201 General Conditions aren't clear: they state that the architect has the right to reject "non-conforming" work but don't spell out what that means. Others complain that provisions in the AIA document don't always match state requirements, and some contractors express annoyance that the documents appear to favor the architect over the contractor. All the standard forms have strengths and weaknesses and it is wise for all parties to read all documents carefully so that adjustments can be made (in the supplementary conditions) if necessary.

Supplementary conditions

Often there is a necessity to adjust the general conditions to meet the needs of a specific project. Sometimes the owner has requirements that are not adequately covered by the boilerplate nature of the general conditions. In both of these cases, adjustments can be made to the general conditions. These adjustments are made in a separate document called the supplementary conditions. The supplementary conditions modify the general conditions and add information *specific to the particular job*.

Not all provisions of the general conditions are suitable for every job. The supplementary conditions are used to delete or re-word portions of the general conditions and to make appropriate modifications. For example, an owner has hired a construction manager and adds language into the supplementary conditions that identifies the CM, instead of the architect, as administrator of the contract. Or the work is being done at a hospital and can only happen during certain hours, or deliveries can only be made at night. These conditions would all be spelled out as supplementary conditions.

As noted, many construction contracts include a specific completion date. The general conditions might identify that if the contractor fails to deliver the project on time, he will have to pay the owner a certain amount of money, called liquidated damages. The supplementary conditions would be the document that identifies the conditions under which liquidated damages will be paid on the job, along with the dollar amount.

There are no rules about what might or might not be suitable for inclusion as a supplementary condition and not all projects use supplementary conditions. If there's an issue that's important to the job and/or the owner, it can be included. Here are several other items that a contractor might find in the supplementary conditions:

- Damage to the work or jobsite (For example, the supplementary conditions could identify specific requirements regarding procedures for replacing plants that might be damaged during construction.)

- Special requirements regarding pedestrian flow around the jobsite such as might exist in an urban area or at a school
- Scheduling and determination of progress (Maybe the owner will require special progress reports.)
- Permits (such as any that the owner will secure)
- Special testing
- Meeting requirements
- Access to the site and maintenance of street traffic (Perhaps the owner will request that all workers access the jobsite off of a particular street, for example.)

The general and supplementary conditions (along with the agreement), form important parts of the contract documents. In the next chapter we'll take a look at another important component; the specifications.

Chapter Vocabulary

AIA A201 – General Conditions published by the American Institute of Architects.

Claim – a demand by one party seeking an adjustment in the terms of a contract.

Conditions, general and supplementary – the parts of a contract that define the basic rights and responsibilities of the parties.

Dispute – a claim that has not been satisfactorily resolved.

General conditions – the contract document dealing primarily with the terms and conditions of the work that apply to the work as a whole and that can be applied to multiple projects.

Liquidated damages – a previously agreed-upon amount of money the contractor is required to pay an owner if construction is not completed on time.

Supplementary conditions – the conditions of a contract used to modify or expand the general conditions to reflect the needs of individual projects.

Termination (of a contract) – the voluntary or involuntary end of a contract.

Work, the (scope of work) – the obligations defined by the contract documents.

Test Yourself

1. What are the general conditions?
2. Why is it important that a contractor thoroughly understand what is contained in the general conditions?
3. Why are standardized general conditions such as those published by the American Institute of Architects often preferred over those written by the owner?
4. On small projects, where might the general conditions be found?
5. Who is responsible for ensuring that the general conditions are included as part of the bid documents?
6. Which construction document modifies the general conditions?
7. Does the owner have the right to stop the work, and if so, under what circumstances?
8. In the A201 General Conditions, who is responsible for verifying and approving a contractor's application for payment?
9. What right does the owner have when a contractor proposes that a specific subcontractor be hired?
10. Give a specific example of when supplementary conditions might be used.

Bob Moore Construction

CHAPTER 16

Contract Documents: the Specifications

As we have already learned, projects are described by both drawings (the "plans") and written descriptions. An important segment of the written descriptions are the specifications.

The drawings describe the project graphically; they provide instructions to the builder regarding the size, layout, and detailing of the structure. The drawings show anything measurable: for example, how many cubic yards of concrete are required in the foundation, the quantity of carpeting in the living room, and the number of doors onto the patio.

In contrast, the **specifications** describe, in written form, what cannot be conveyed by the drawings alone; they detail materials, processes, and quality, such as the type of concrete; the brand, color, and weight of carpeting; and the manufacturer, material, or glazing for the doors. The specifications add critical information to the architects' or engineers' drawings.

The project manual – As we know, there are many written documents necessary for every project. Often these documents are collectively referred to as "the specifications." But the specifications we're talking about in this chapter specifically describe the characteristics of and qualitative requirements for products, materials, and workmanship (and are sometimes referred to as "the technical specifications," although this term is not preferred). The specifications are bound together with the other written documents – the agreement, the general and supplementary conditions, and the modifications to the contract – into a **project manual**. The project manual provides an organizational framework for *all* the written documents, in fact, for everything except the drawings. Some projects have such large amounts of written information the project manual may include multiple volumes.

The specifications are typically the responsibility of the architect and may be written in-house or by a specification consultant hired by the architect. The specifications are compiled before the project goes out to bid, and form part of the information the contractor uses for bidding. Contractors study the specifications to determine the *quality* of products and installation (the measurements or *quantity* of which appear on the drawings) and other standards related to the product or work.

What do the specifications identify?

Explanatory notes of various sorts are usually included on the drawings. These notes are short and general and for very small projects may be sufficient to explain the work fully. For example, the specifications for a sink faucet on a small bathroom project might consist of a simple note on the drawings: "*Kingsley high arc widespread lavatory fixtures by Moen.*"

On larger projects, however, short notes are inadequate and must be supplemented with more complete and thorough written information. Here's an example of how this works. You are a specialty trade contractor and are putting together a price for supplying and installing roofing for a new building. The drawings show where and how much roofing you'll need and include a note stating that the tiles are concrete. There are some detail drawings that identify flashing requirements and so on, but you can't tell from the drawings who manufactures the tiles, what color and quality they need to be, or if there are any special installation requirements. The specifications will answer these questions. Let's see what sort of information you might find in them.

Quality of materials and products

Let's say that the note on the drawing reads "concrete roof tiles." You will need additional information in order to purchase and install the correct tile. The specifications might more fully explain the product in the following way: "*Provide standard weight extruded concrete roofing tiles, Old World Slate manufactured by Hanson. Color selected by Architect.*"

Quality assurance

This refers to the procedures for guarding against defects and deficiencies, and might include language regarding standards, such as: "*Conform to NRCA (National Roofing Contractors Association) – Steep Roofing Manual.*"

Special installation requirements

The architect has determined that she wants specific installation procedures: "*Install underlayment with 2 inch side laps and 6 inch end laps.*" You will take into account all special installation instructions when you price the labor.

Submittals

The specifications identify requirements for information submittals that will assure the team that the contractor will provide the correct products. For example, there might be a requirement that you provide the following: "*Product data including tile properties, configurations, jointing methods and locations, fastening methods and locations, and installation details.*" You might also be required to provide a physical sample of the tile: "*Three samples of tiles to illustrate color, profile, and finish.*"

Specifications are necessary so that the contractor can order the proper products and materials and accurately assess the labor necessary to install a product. Again, in our tile example, the drawings identify where the roofing tiles go and how many there are (the *quantity*), but the specifications give the contractor detailed information on what type of tile (the *quality*). It is not possible for a contractor to provide a complete or accurate cost estimate without referring to the specifications.

As we shall see, specifications are organized so that they describe products, systems, materials, and work results. Wood windows, cast-in-place concrete, and toilet accessories, for example, each have their own section in the specifications. There are four ways of identifying product requirements in sections: descriptive, performance, reference standard, and proprietary. Each describes requirements in a different way, as follows:

- **Descriptive specifications** may be the most common, and provide product details without specifically mentioning a brand name; example: *Sand for grouting shall pass a 30-mesh screen.*
- **Performance specifications** identify the ends to be achieved, but not how the ends are achieved; example: *Capacity of 500 CFM.*
- **Reference specifications** identify a required standard such as ASTM, State of New York, Federal, and so on; example: *Conform to ASTM C150.*
- **Proprietary specifications** identify the desired product by manufacturer, brand name, model, and so forth; example: *Floor tiles to be "Contempo" manufactured by Kentile Corp.*

No matter which of these four ways the designer uses to describe something in a specification section, there are general guidelines for how the information is to be presented.

How the specifications are organized

Written documentation has been used on projects for centuries. By the beginning of the twentieth century, the building process had become more complex and expanded written specifications became routine. Until about 60 years ago, however, project information was not organized or standardized.

In 1948, a group of specification writers formed the **Construction Specifications Institute (CSI),** a membership organization founded to improve specification practices in construction and related industries. Over the following years, they published (in conjunction with the Construction Specifications Canada) several specification-writing standards. One of these was **MasterFormat**, a master list of numbers and subject titles that organizes information about a project, based on the type of work. Although there are several organizational standards used in the industry, many projects follow MasterFormat, and contractors, architects, and engineers are very familiar with the system.

CSI MasterFormat[1]

Until 2004, when the standards were revised and expanded, MasterFormat[1] organized information about a project (including both administrative and work categories) into 16 divisions. The divisions, unchanging in name and number, represent broad categories of materials, products, and systems, for example, concrete, metal, mechanical, and electrical. The following are the 16 divisions with examples of what might be found in each:

Division 01 General Requirements
The requirements and procedures for administering the project, such as submittals, mobilization, and quality control. (Nothing that is left behind when the job is over is included in Division 01.)

Division 02 Site Construction
Site demolition, grading, excavation, irrigation, landscaping

Division 03 Concrete
Cast-in-place concrete, concrete forms/finishing, reinforcing steel

Division 04 Masonry
Brick, concrete block, stone, mortar

Division 05 Metals
Steel beams, girders, columns, ornamental iron, metal decking

Division 06 Wood and Plastics
Rough carpentry, interior trim, cabinets, shelving, stairs

Division 07 Thermal/Moisture Protection
Insulation, roofing, waterproofing, gutters, flashing, caulking

Division 08 Doors and Windows
Doors and frames, wood doors, overhead doors, windows, skylights

Division 09 Finishes
Drywall, paint, carpet, tile, acoustic ceiling

Division 10 Specialties
Toilet partitions, flagpoles, bathroom accessories, fire extinguishers

Division 11 Equipment
Kitchen appliances, medical equipment, recreational equipment

Division 12 Furnishings
Draperies, art, bookcases, benches, stadium seating

Division 13 Special Construction
Swimming pools, tennis courts, kennels, security systems

Division 14 Conveying Systems
Elevators, escalators

Division 15 Mechanical
Plumbing, heating, and air conditioning

Division 16 Electrical
Electrical wiring, fixtures, transformers, communications, AV (audio/video)

Any contractor would know to look in Division 09 – Finishes – for information on carpets or paint; Division 08 for doors and windows; Division 03 for concrete work, and so on. In MasterFormat, the division numbers are unchanging: Division 09 is *always* Finishes, Division 08 is *always* Doors and Windows, Division 03 is *always* Concrete, and so on.

Divisions are, in turn, subdivided into related products or units of work, called **sections**. For example, Division 08 – Doors and Windows – includes the following sections:

- Metal doors and frames
- Wood & plastic doors
- Specialty doors
- Steel windows
- Wood windows

Within the sections, information is broken down even further if required by the project. For example, if a contractor is looking for information on access doors, he can find it under Specialty Doors in Division 08. He knows where to look because, under MasterFormat, information on access doors is *always* found under Specialty Doors, which is *always* found in Division 08.

Digits are used to describe increasingly detailed scopes of work. The division number is always the first two digits, with three additional digits added as needed. Using the access door again as an example, under the MasterFormat system, access doors are assigned the number 08305: 08 is the division number, 08300 is the section number for specialty doors and 08305 identifies the particular specialty door that we're looking for – access doors. Each digit represents a narrower or more detailed scope of work.

As buildings and their products have become increasingly complex, however, the 16-division and section format has proven too restricted and inflexible. Whole new technologies, new products, and new areas of specialization have evolved and the old system (referred to as MasterFormat 1995) doesn't have the capacity to accommodate these changes and the additional topics that are often required. Basically, MasterFormat has run out of room.

CSI MasterFormat 2004

In response, the CSI introduced a new expanded and updated version in 2004 that increased the number of divisions from 16 to 50; some divisions stayed the same, some names were changed (for example, Division 08 is no longer called Doors and Windows but Openings), others were split up, and still others were added (including new divisions for Communication, Electronic Safety and Security, Pollution Control Equipment, and more). The 50 divisions were also organized into subgroups that further define where information is located. Here's what the updated MasterFormat 2004 (MF 04) looks like (note that the first 14 divisions remain unchanged except for Division 02 – Site Construction – which was expanded into multiple divisions):

GENERAL REQUIREMENTS SUBGROUP

Division 01 General Requirements

FACILITY CONSTRUCTION SUBGROUP

Division 02 Existing Conditions

Division 03 Concrete

Division 04 Masonry

Division 05 Metals

Division 06 Wood, Plastics, and Composites

Division 07 Thermal and Moisture Protection

Division 08 Openings

Division 09 Finishes

Division 10 Specialties

Division 11 Equipment

Division 12 Furnishings

Division 13 Special Construction

Division 14 Conveying Equipment

Division 15-19 Reserved for future use

FACILITY SERVICES SUBGROUP

Division 20 Reserved

Division 21 Fire Suppression

Division 22 Plumbing

Division 23 Heating, Ventilating, Air Conditioning

Division 24 Reserved

Division 25 Integrated Automation

Division 26 Electrical

Division 27 Communications

Division 28 Electronic Safety and Security

Division 29 Reserved

SITE AND INFRASTRUCTURE SUBGROUP

Division 30 Reserved

Division 31 Earthwork

Division 32 Exterior Improvements

Division 33 Utilities

Division 34 Transportation

Division 35 Waterway and Marine Construction

Division 36-39 Reserved

PROCESS EQUIPMENT SUBGROUP

Division 40 Process Integration

Division 41 Material Processing and Handling equipment

Division 42 Process Heating, Cooling and Drying Equipment

Division 43 Process Gas and Liquid Handling, Purification, Storage Equipment

Division 44 Pollution Control Equipment

Division 45 Industry-Specific Manufacturing Equipment

Division 46 Reserved

Division 47 Reserved

Division 48 Electric Power Generation

Division 49 Reserved

MasterFormat 2004 didn't just expand the number of divisions, it also increased the number of section digits from five to six to enable increasing levels of detail. Two further digits can optionally be added to accommodate more detail. Here's how access doors would be handled with the new system:

08 00 00	=	Openings
08 30 00	=	Specialty doors and frames
08 31 00	=	Access doors
08 31 13	=	Access doors and frames
08 31 13. 53	=	Security access doors and frames

It's easy to see that the expanded MasterFormat system provides opportunities to describe levels of detail in a way that the old system could not. This is especially important on complex projects. (Note: MasterFormat has been further refined and updated in 2010.)

CSI SectionFormat[2]

Now that we have an idea of how MasterFormat groups information into divisions and sections so that contractors and others can find the information, let's look at how the sections themselves are organized.

Within the MasterFormat divisions, information is organized and presented according to a uniform system called SectionFormat, also a creation of the Construction Specifications Institute. Each section is divided into three parts with each containing the following types of information:

- Part 1 – General
  This portion of the section includes administrative, procedural, submittal requirements, temporary requirements, quality assurance, delivery, storage, handling, and warranties.
- Part 2 – Product
  Describes materials, products, systems, equipment, fabrication, manufacturer, tests and inspections, and more.
- Part 3 – Execution
  Describes installers, verification of conditions and pre-installation testing, surface preparation, erection, installation, application, testing and inspections, system start-up, cleaning, close-out activities, protection (such as from weather), and more.

Not everything for every part is included; the specification writer (the specifier) selects what is most suitable for the particular product being described. Figure 16.1 is an example of a section for asphalt paving; each of the three parts identifies only the information considered necessary for that product.

SECTION 32 12 16
ASPHALT PAVING

PART 1 GENERAL

1.01 SECTION INCLUDES
A. Repair and patching of existing asphalt paving.
B. Surface sealer.

1.02 RELATED REQUIREMENTS
A. Surface applied detectable warning materials, see Section 32 12 13.

1.03 QUALITY ASSURANCE
A. Perform Work in accordance with Sonoma County Public Works.
B. Mixing Plant: Conform to State of California Public Work's standard.
C. Obtain materials from same source throughout.

1.04 FIELD CONDITIONS
A. Do not place asphalt when ambient air or base surface temperature is less than 40 degrees F, or surface is wet or frozen.

PART 2 PRODUCTS

Reference specification

2.01 MATERIALS
A. Asphalt Cement: ASTM D 946.

Descriptive specification

B. Aggregate for Base Course: Angular crushed washed stone; free of shale, clay, friable material, and debris.
C. Primer: Cut-back petroleum asphalt.
D. Tack Coat: Homogeneous, medium curing, liquid asphalt.
E. Seal Coat: AI MS-19, sand type.

2.02 ASPHALT PAVING MIXES AND MIX DESIGN
A. Use dry material to avoid foaming. Mix uniformly.
B. Base Course: 3.0 to 6 percent of asphalt cement by weight in mixture in accordance with AI MS-2.
C. Binder Course: 4.5 to 6 percent of asphalt cement by weight in mixture in accordance with AI MS-2.
D. Wearing Course: 5 to 7 percent of asphalt cement by weight in mixture in accordance with AI MS-2.

PART 3 EXECUTION ← Requirements for on-site work activity

3.01 EXAMINATION
A. Verify that compacted subgrade is dry and ready to support paving and imposed loads.
B. Verify gradients and elevations of base are correct.

3.02 BASE COURSE
A. Place and compact base course.

3.03 PREPARATION—PRIMER
A. Apply primer in accordance with manufacturer's instructions.
B. Apply primer on aggregate base or subbase at uniform rate of 1/3 gal/sq yd.
C. Use clean sand to blot excess primer.

3.04 PREPARATION—TACK COAT
A. Apply tack coat in accordance with manufacturer's instructions.
B. Apply tack coat on asphalt or concrete surfaces over subgrade surface at uniform rate of 1/3 gal/sq yd.

3.05 PLACING ASPHALT PAVEMENT—SINGLE COURSE
A. Install Work in accordance with Sonoma County.
B. Place asphalt within 24 hours of applying primer or tack coat.
C. Compact pavement by rolling to specified density. Do not displace or extrude pavement from position. Hand compact in areas inaccessible to rolling equipment.
D. Perform rolling with consecutive passes to achieve even and smooth finish without roller marks.

3.06 SEAL COAT
A. Apply seal coat to surface course and asphalt curbs in accordance with AI MS-19.

Figure 16.1. Section courtesy of Michael Chambers, FAIA, MCA Specifications

Although some firms still use the old 16 division MasterFormat. MasterFormat 2004 is now widely used and has been voluntarily adapted by major organizations such as the Associated General Contractors and the American Institute of Architects, companies such as McGraw-Hill Construction and Reed Construction, vendors, building products manufacturers and government agencies. Much industry software now uses MF 04.

But no matter how skillfully organized the information for a project might be – everything appears to be in its proper place – problems can and do arise. Often there are conflicts between the drawings and the specifications, and the issue for the contractor, the architect, and the owner is what can be done about it?

Resolving contradictions in the documents

It is easy to understand why conflicts arise: people are human, projects are complex, and it's not possible for *everything* to be 100 percent correct. Sometimes a detail is forgotten on a drawing, or information regarding a product differs between the drawings and the specifications. Maybe the drawings indicate that all the windows are vinyl-clad casements, but the specifications indicate painted wood. Or maybe the roof tile is identified as Spanish tile on the drawings but as concrete tile in the specifications. Sometimes the specification writer makes a change, and the architect's draftsperson isn't informed or fails to note the change in the drawings. Confusion often follows the mistake of putting information in multiple places. It's easy to imagine errors occurring when information is included on the drawings and again in multiple places in the specifications.

When the drawings say one thing and the specifications say another, or two drawings conflict, how is the conflict resolved? There is no universally accepted rule for which document takes precedence over another. Generally, a more-detailed drawing takes precedence over a less-detailed drawing. But when the conflicts are between documents, it's less clear. Many owners choose to include a preferred order of precedence in the general conditions. More typically, the architect is identified as the arbiter in such situations and must take into account all the relevant information from the documents and make a determination. This determination often results in an adjustment to the time or cost of a project and requires a real test of the architect's ability to be fair to both the owner and the contractor.

The best way to deal with conflicts in the documents is of course to avoid them in the first place: say something exactly once, and say it in the right place.

---

1 MasterFormat™ 1995

2 The Groups, Subgroups, and Divisions used in this textbook are from MasterFormat™ and the three-part SectionFormat™/PageFormat™ published by The Construction Specification Institute (CSI) and Construction Specifications Canada (CSC), and are used with permission from CSI. For those interested in a more in-depth explanation of MasterFormat™ and its use in the construction industry visit www.csinet.org/masterformat or contact CSI at 110 South Union Street, Suite 100, Alexandria, VA 22314 @ 800-689-2900/703-684-0300 www.csinet.org.

Chapter Vocabulary

Construction Specifications Institute (CSI) – a membership organization founded to improve the specification practices in construction and related industries.

Descriptive specification – a method of specifying that provides product details without mentioning a brand name.

Divisions – broad categories of construction (such as concrete, masonry, finishes, etc.) as defined by the Construction Specification Institute's MasterFormat™.

MasterFormat™ – a work-based master list of numbers and subject titles, developed by the Construction Specifications Institute, that organizes information about a project.

Performance specifications – a method of specifying that identifies the ends to be achieved, not how the ends are achieved.

Project manual – a binder containing all the written documentation for a project.

Proprietary specifications – a method of specifying that identifies the desired product by manufacturer, brand name, model, and so forth.

Reference standards – a method of specifying that identifies a required standard, such as ASTM, state, or federal.

SectionFormat™ – the organization of related units of information within the MasterFormat™ divisions.

Sections – drawings that graphically represent a structure by showing vertical cuts through the entire building or a portion of the building.

Specifications – written descriptions of the work that define the materials, the processes, and the quality of products and systems. The specifications and the drawings work together to provide the information contractors need in order to price and build a project.

Test Yourself

1. What are the specifications?
2. What does CSI stand for and what is it?
3. How does MasterFormat assist the contractor?
4. Information about carpet is shown in Division 09 (Finishes).Where would information on the carpet's manufacturer be found?
5. What is a section?
6. What was the reason for developing MasterFormat 2004?
7. There are four ways of writing specifications: descriptive, performance, reference, and proprietary. Which type was used for identifying the asphalt cement in Figure 16.1?
8. Sections are presented in a three-part format. In which part would the contractor find information regarding the manufacturer of a product?
9. In which part of the section for roofing would a subcontractor find information regarding the correct installation procedures?
10. The drawings identify linoleum floor covering in the washrooms. In which part of the specifications would the contractor find information regarding the requirement to submit samples to the architect?

PART 5

Construction

Andrea Young

CHAPTER 17

Pre-construction & Mobilization

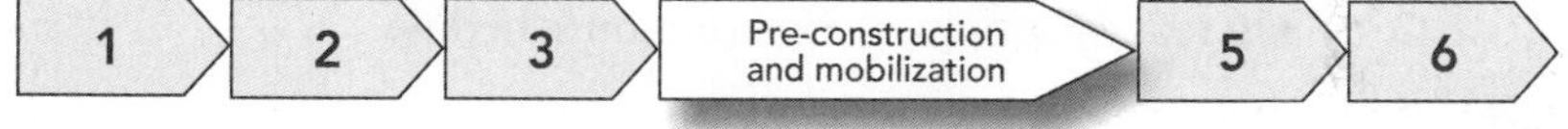

Pre-construction

Construction doesn't always begin simultaneously with the awarding of the job. In fact, it usually doesn't. The contractor has much planning and organizing to do before the physical work can start. This period is called pre-construction. In addition, moving workers, material, and equipment onto the jobsite (called mobilization) typically waits until the owner issues a document to the contractor, called the notice to proceed, that provides the contractor with legal access to the site. At first glance, this delay seems silly; the contractor and the owner have signed an agreement, why can't the contractor just get going? The contractor wants to be absolutely sure the job is going ahead before money is spent mobilizing. Waiting until there is formal notification from the owner reduces the contractor's risk.

There are several situations that could cause a job to be postponed or cancelled: the owner may have last-minute issues to resolve or finish; crucial easements or permits may not yet be in hand; or loan documentation may not have been completed by the bank. If a contractor starts working before the notice to proceed is issued, he is taking the chance that if for some reason the job doesn't happen, he may not be reimbursed for start-up costs.

Although the award of subcontracts, procurement of materials, and mobilization onto the project site typically don't take place until the notice to proceed has been issued, planning for construction begins as soon as the contractor gets confirmation that he has won the contract. Thorough planning up front enables the contractor to begin work immediately upon receipt of the notice to proceed.

There are several pre-construction planning activities that happen at this stage of a project; the general contractor's project manager, working closely with the superintendent, typically takes the lead. The more complex the project, the more complicated this stage becomes. The following are typical pre-construction activities, not necessarily in this order:

- Organizing the contractor's team
- Determining the means, methods, and techniques of construction
- Adjusting the bid estimate
- Buying out the job
- Creating a master construction schedule
- Pre-construction submittals
- Jobsite layout plan
- Permits
- Pre-construction meeting

Let's see what each of these activities entails for the contractor.

Organizing the contractor's team

Up until the job is won, the contractor's estimator (who is either an employee or a consultant) is the primary person involved in the project. During pre-construction, the team expands and the contractor's project manager is in charge of putting together a team that will (it is hoped) work effectively to meet project goals. Some members of the team are drawn from permanent employees of the contractor; others are hired on an as-needed basis. Members vary depending on the complexity of the project, the size of the construction company, the availability of the personnel, and how much of the work will be done by the contractor's crews and how much will be subcontracted. (See Chapter 3 for a review of the contractor's team and the members' individual roles.)

The general contractor assigns a superintendent to work at the jobsite (in the field), who will be responsible for coordinating all the production aspects of the job, including the performance of the contractor's own crews and the subcontractors. The superintendent is typically at the jobsite on a full-time basis; in fact, some general conditions identify this as a requirement. Sometimes there is also an assistant superintendent. The project manager may be involved with multiple projects and is not typically located full-time at the jobsite. The PM works closely with the superintendent, especially during this critical planning stage, and with the other members of the contractor's team to identify how best to complete the work. They are supported by others back at the home office, such as estimators, accountants, administrative assistants, and senior management.

Determining the means, methods, and techniques of construction

The plans and drawings tell the general contractor what has to be done; her job is to decide how to do it. According to the AIA General Conditions, "*The contractor shall be solely responsible for, and have control over, construction means, methods, techniques, sequences and procedures and for coordinating all portions of the Work under the Contract, unless the Contract Documents give other specific instructions ...*" (AIA Document A201-2007 Article 3.3.1) This makes sense; after all, the owner is paying for the general contractor's expertise. The contractor has the skill and both the right and the responsibility to determine how the drawings and specifications are going to be realized: how the structure will actually be constructed.

Everything that happens on the jobsite is under the control of the contractor: she is the one who determines when materials should arrive at the site, what equipment is to be used, the sequence of activities, and what parts of the work will be subcontracted and what parts will be completed using the contractor's own crews. Here's an example. An architect has designed a roof that is made up of 4FT X 8FT panels. His thinking is that the contractor could build the panels in her shop and bolt the pre-assembled panels together on-site. But the contractor prefers to construct the panels in place. The architect has no right to insist that a particular construction method be used.

Decisions regarding how the process of construction will happen are made during this planning period. These decisions are reflected on a master construction schedule as well as on cash flow projections.

Adjusting the bid estimate

Once the contractor knows the job is his, he does an internal review of his bid estimate and makes adjustments as necessary and as subcontracts are signed. For example, the GC may have estimated (and included in his total bid for the job) $50,000 for a particular portion of the work that he anticipates subcontracting. His assumption is that he will receive sub-bids equal to or less than that amount. When sub-bids for this work are received, however, he finds that his earlier assumptions were wrong and this section of the job will actually cost $54,000. In order to maintain his profit, the GC will need to make up this $4,000 difference elsewhere on the job. A new budget reflecting these changes will be developed. The numbers contained in this adjusted estimate become the baseline against which the contractor evaluates actual costs as the job progresses and additional subcontracts are signed, materials are purchased, and work proceeds.

All the items and activities identified in the estimate are coded and tracked throughout the job. Using codes to track costs against a baseline enables the contractor to make on-going and accurate assessments of how well he is keeping to his budget estimates. We'll discuss tracking costs in more detail in the next chapter.

Buying out the job

During pre-construction, the contractor begins the process of buying out the job: finalizing subcontracts, and issuing purchase orders for material and equipment and some short-term specialty labor. Although on some jobs subcontractors are identified before the contractor submits his or her bid to the owner, buyout typically takes place during pre-construction and extends throughout construction.

The contractor negotiates, with subcontractors and suppliers, the terms of their contracts prior to making final selections. Several items are covered during these negotiations, including:

- Ensuring that the complete scope of work is included
- Ability of the sub or supplier to meet the contractor's schedule
- Responsibility for delivery and storage costs
- Submittal responsibilities
- Price escalation terms
- Discounts (suppliers often offer discounts for prompt payment; this

discount may be identified, for example, as 2 Net 10, which means the contractor will receive a 2 percent discount if payment is made by the tenth of the month).

We'll look at the process of buying out the job in detail in Chapter 21.

Creating a master construction schedule

An initial schedule based on the owner's tentative time frame identified during the bidding process was probably prepared by the contractor when he developed his bid estimate. The purpose of this schedule is primarily to plot the length of the construction period so that a complete estimate can be made. Once the contractor knows the job is hers, the schedule needs refinement and adjustment. After the contractor has made decisions regarding how the work will proceed, she links this strategy with the estimated activity durations and creates a final, detailed, computer-generated master schedule. This schedule is used as a baseline and is updated on a regular basis, typically as required by the contract documents. The master schedule is used much as the budget is, to help the contractor manage the job and measure progress. We'll talk about scheduling in much greater detail in Chapters 19 and 20.

Pre-construction submittals

Typically, the contractor does not begin the construction until she has supplied the owner with certain documents or submittals. Pre-construction submittal requirements are identified in the contract documents and might include but are not limited to the following items:

- Surety bonds. The owner determines the bonding requirements for a project. If a bid bond is required, it is submitted with the bid. Other surety bonds, such as payment and performance bonds, are submitted before construction begins.
- List of proposed subcontractors. Contractors cannot hire subcontractors to which the owner or architect have made a reasonable (and timely) objection. Some owners require a list of proposed subcontractors when the bid is submitted; more typically, it is part of the pre-construction submittals.
- Schedule of values. During pre-construction, the contractor develops an outline of what he expects each portion of the work to cost. These

estimates are used as a basis for applications for payment. We'll discuss this in more detail in Chapter 23.

- Certificates of insurance. Insurance is bought to reduce the risk of loss or damage to the contractor, to property, and to equipment from theft, accident, fire, floods, and so on. Some insurance is carried on an ongoing basis by the contractor; some is purchased for a specific job, with the requirements typically identified in the contract documents. Sometimes the law even requires coverage, such as workers' compensation insurance.

Insurance – The types and the amount of insurance coverage used on a construction job are important and can be very complicated. The contractor balances potential risks, what the construction contract and law require, and what good sense indicates. Sometimes the owner establishes minimum insurance requirements for the job. In either case, the owner generally requires evidence of insurance coverage prior to the start of construction.

There are many different types of insurance policies. The following are ones commonly used in construction.

Builders risk insurance protects the builder, the subcontractors, and the owner from losses while a specific project is under construction. A builders risk policy may include all risks or be limited to damage caused by specific risks such as fire, storms, and theft. (Often losses due to floods or earthquakes require a separate policy.) Damage to materials stored on- and off-site are generally covered. Example: a fire breaks out on the jobsite and destroys the work that has been completed. Typically, builders risk insurance will pay for replacement costs. Here's another example: there is a break-in on the jobsite and someone walks off with an expensive piece of equipment. Builders risk is the policy likely to cover the loss.

General liability insurance provides protection against third-party claims of injury or property damage. Example: a friend of the owner is visiting the site and breaks his foot when he trips over a pile of wood. The contractor's general liability insurance will cover the costs.

Property damage insurance protects the contractor against damage to his property caused by the job. Example: the contractor's truck is damaged when a tree on the jobsite falls in a storm.

Umbrella liability insurance provides coverage for losses that exceed the standard policy amounts. Example: a contractor is concerned that his general liability policy (written for a maximum of, say, $2 million) may be insufficient in the event of a catastrophic occurrence, so he purchases (a less costly) umbrella policy that covers specific occurrences up to a much higher amount, say, $25 million. If the owner's friend in the previous example is accidentally killed or seriously injured and the family sues for $10 million, the umbrella liability policy will cover the difference between the contractor's $2 million policy and the amount awarded.

Workers' compensation insurance protects workers who are injured on the job by covering medical and hospitalization expenses, plus a percentage of wages lost because of the injury. Serious injuries, such as a lost limb, are compensated on a set lump-sum basis. In exchange for this coverage, workers give up their right to sue their employers for additional compensation when they are injured on the job. The employer's insurance company pays the injured party's costs. Workers' compensation is very expensive; rates vary depending on the type of job, and increase the more claims a contractor makes. Companies with a higher accident rate pay higher premiums. Workers' compensation insurance is administered through the state and can typically be purchased through a state fund or through a private insurance company; some states allow contractors to self-insure.

Jobsite layout plan

Before the contractor moves onto the jobsite, decisions need to be made regarding how people, materials, and equipment will move around the site, where the job trailer will be located, where materials will be stored, how to get temporary power onto the site, and so on. The superintendent is responsible for all aspects of moving onto the jobsite, including the development of a jobsite layout plan. (Sometimes the layout plan is included as a required pre-construction submittal.)

The jobsite layout plan shows existing conditions such as adjacent buildings, utility lines, and streets and indicates planned locations for all temporary jobsite facilities including trailers, bathrooms, fences and gates, utilities, erosion control, and drainage. Clear pathways for the efficient and safe movement of materials, equipment, and labor are identified, as are areas for material handling and storage, equipment staging, and worker and visitor parking.

A good site layout helps:

- Eliminate any bottlenecks to equipment movement on the site
- Locate material storage areas as close as possible to where the material will be used
- Place the primary project office trailer near the main entrance for visitor control

- Provide turn-around areas for delivery vehicles
- Minimize traffic and pedestrian impacts on adjacent streets

Permits

One of the most important pre-construction tasks is to secure the necessary construction work permit from the "authority having jurisdiction" (AHJ), such as a city's Building Inspections Division. Most jurisdictions require some kind of permit before work can begin on a project. The type of permit depends on whether the owner is public or private, the type of structure, the type and value of the work, the location of the project, and other characteristics. Jurisdictions typically require that permits be secured for one or more of the following:

- New construction
- Alterations and additions
- Garages
- Decks and fences
- Any mechanical, electrical, or plumbing work

How does one get a permit? Again, the process varies from jurisdiction to jurisdiction, but, typically, the general contractor secures the building permit (subcontractors may be responsible for securing permits in their trades). The process usually begins with submittal of a permit application (with a fee) and several sets of construction drawings to the AHJ issuing the permit (such as the local building department). In order to secure a permit, the AHJ will require that drawings be included; requirements vary depending upon the type of structure and local AHJ requirements. The drawings required for a permit for a new building, for example, would likely include the following:

- Site plan identifying where the building will be placed on the property; this will demonstrate, for example, that zoning regulations are met (such as distance from an adjoining property)
- Grading plans identifying drainage, soil excavation, walkways, and curbs
- Architectural drawings (floor plans, elevations, sections, and details)
- Engineering drawings: structural, electrical, mechanical, and plumbing

Additional documents, such as engineering calculations, energy data, soils and geotechnical reports, and landscape irrigation plans, may be required. Sometimes several agencies (such as planning, engineering, fire, and utilities) are required to review the application before a building permit is issued.

At completion of the work, the AHJ will review it for compliance with codes and safety requirements. The AHJ must "sign off" on all permits before a certificate of occupancy can be issued.

Pre-construction meeting

Nearly all construction projects begin with a pre-construction conference or meeting before the contractor has mobilized onto the jobsite. This is a formal meeting; sometimes the contract even states the items to be discussed. The pre-construction meeting is typically conducted by the architect or owner and includes representatives from the contractor's office, major subcontractors, and possibly other parties such as municipal authorities, utility companies, and others who may be impacted by the work. Minutes of the meeting are distributed to all attendees.

The objective of the pre-construction meeting is to open the lines of communication between the owner and the contractor, and to review the responsibilities and expectations of each of the project participants. Important administrative and communication procedures and policies are discussed, including such items as payment procedures, changes in the work, submittals, critical schedule milestones, and special requirements such as hours of operation, noise, and parking. Any matters of importance or concern to any of the parties are reviewed at this time. The record-keeping and documentation procedures are also reviewed.

Smaller jobs may not have a formal pre-construction meeting; in this case, the same information is provided to all players on an individual basis.

At the conclusion of pre-construction, the contractor is ready to go: the team is together, decisions have been made regarding how construction will proceed, and administrative procedures are in place. All that awaits is word from the owner that they can move onto the jobsite.

Mobilization

As noted earlier, moving workers, material, and equipment onto the jobsite is called mobilization, and typically does not happen before the owner issues to the contractor a document called the notice to proceed.

Notice to proceed

The notice to proceed not only gives the contractor access to the site, it also establishes the official start of construction time – the number of days the contractor has to complete the work. The notice to proceed starts the construction time clock running. (As we'll learn later, the end of construction time is marked by a document called the certificate of substantial completion.) Time is typically very important to owners (the contract may not only recite that "time is of the essence" but may really and truly mean it, because of some fixed external date by which the construction must be completed, such as the start of a school year). Often the contractor has to pay a pre-determined amount of compensation, called liquidated damages, if he or she does not finish the project on time.

So the notice to proceed is important. Sometimes the notice is a formal document such as shown in Figure 17.1. Even when a formal notice isn't provided, however, the contractor is advised to get written authorization from the owner regarding a start date for the physical work.

NOTICE TO PROCEED

To: Contractor
Address
City

Date: July 28, 2010

Project: Project name
Address

You are hereby notified to commence work on August 1, 2010 in accordance with subject contract dated July 10, 2010. You are to complete the work thereafter in 122 calendar days. Date of substantial completion shall be November 30, 2010.

Before commencing work Contractor is to submit to owner documents as required: Certificates of Insurance, Performance Bond, and Labor Bond.

By:____________________

(Authorized Signature)

Title:____________________

Figure 17.1. Notice to proceed

Mobilize

Once the contractor has completed required pre-construction activities – the team is in place, all owner-required submittals have been provided to and reviewed for compliance by the architect, and the jobsite layout plan has been implemented – then crews and equipment can be moved onto the site and construction can begin.

This move is the responsibility of the contractor's superintendent. The jobsite office/trailer is established and temporary utilities are installed according to the site layout plan. Site access is secured with fencing, gates are installed to provide access to workers and material deliveries, and a project sign is installed. Environmental protection measures such as erosion or sediment control or seeding may be put in place.

In addition to informing the contractor that he can mobilize onto the site and start work, the notice to proceed lets the contractor know that subcontracts can be finalized and the procurement of materials can begin.

Chapter Vocabulary

Buying out the job (procurement) – the process of finalizing subcontracts and issuing purchase orders for material and equipment.

Insurance – a means of protecting someone against a future loss.

Jobsite layout plan – a plan developed by the general contractor before mobilizing onto the site that graphically identifies existing conditions and locations for temporary utilities, fencing, access, and so forth.

Master construction schedule – a comprehensive and detailed schedule the contractor develops and uses as a baseline overview of the entire job and as a tool to control the job.

Mobilization – the process of moving personnel, equipment, and materials onto a jobsite so that the physical work can begin. Mobilization typically follows the owner issuing to the contractor a notice to proceed.

Notice to proceed – a document provided to the contractor by the owner that gives the contractor access to the site and establishes the official start of construction time.

Permit - authorization to proceed with a project according to regulatory requirements and issued by one or more authorities having jurisdiction.

Pre-construction meeting – a formal meeting, typically facilitated by the architect, that occurs after award of the contract but before construction begins, to review the responsibilities and expectations of each of the project participants.

Pre-construction – the period between award of the construction contract and the start of construction and marked by intense planning by the contractor.

Test Yourself

1. What is the document that indicates the contractor can move onto the jobsite and begin work?
2. What document establishes the start of construction time?
3. Why does it reduce a contractor's risk to begin construction only after receiving authorization from the owner?
4. What do the "means, methods, and techniques" refer to?
5. Why does the contractor adjust the job budget following award?
6. What does "buying out the job" mean?
7. What is the difference between a schedule developed during the bidding period and a master construction schedule in terms of how they're used by the contractor?
8. What purposes does insurance serve?
9. Who attends the pre-construction meeting?
10. What is the purpose of a jobsite layout plan?

Andrea Young

CHAPTER 18

Construction

We have a pretty good idea what construction is: it's building something. But, of course it's more than that: it's building something so that it meets certain requirements. Thus, we can define **construction** as the execution of physical work as outlined by contract documents. The physical construction begins at the completion of mobilization and at the completion of construction, the structure is ready for occupancy and use by the owner. For this process to proceed smoothly the contractor's role during construction extends beyond the physical work. In this chapter we'll look at some of the contractor's tasks during this period.

The general contractor is the entity or individual responsible for construction, but as we've seen in earlier chapters, this is a team effort that involves the active participation of all the major players. The owner, the designer, the contractor, and their team members (including consultants, subcontractors, suppliers and manufacturers, testing and inspecting organizations and agencies, and others) all have specific roles during the construction stage of a project.

The specific roles of each of the primary players during construction are determined by the project delivery method, contractual relationships, and the needs of the project. Although these roles may differ somewhat from project to project, they broadly include the following:

- The owner's primary responsibility is to make periodic payments to the contractor and approve modifications to the contract.
- The architect administers the owner-contractor contract and is responsible to the owner for verifying the performance by and payment to the contractor.
- The contractor is responsible for all the physical work and other requirements of the contract documents.

As noted, their roles vary depending on the type of delivery method. The architect's role as the owner's agent, for example, is typically different in a design-bid-build project than it is on an agency construction management project; the owner has a different role in design-build than he might in design-bid-build; the construction manager assumes administrative duties in an agency CM project that might otherwise be the responsibility of the architect.

Although the scope of the contractor's work varies from job to job – on some projects the general contractor does all the work, on others subcontractors do much of the work, on still others the general contractor simply coordinates the work – the contractor is *always* responsible for ensuring that the physical work is completed according to the requirements of the construction contract.

Contractor services during construction

The responsibilities of the contractor during construction include services and tasks that have been covered elsewhere in this text, but let's review what these include. This list is not exhaustive; small projects require fewer services and large projects significantly more, but unless the following are specifically excluded from the construction contract, the contractor is typically responsible for:

- The means, methods, techniques, and sequences of the work. The contract documents identify the scope of work – *what* is to be built - but the contractor has the right (and obligation) to determine exactly *how* the work will proceed
- Coordination and supervision of all the physical work, whether performed by his own crews or subcontractors
- Payment for all project-related labor and materials

- Hiring, contracting, and payment of subcontractors
- Submission of payment requests
- Preparation of a construction schedule and submission of periodic progress updates and reports
- Coordination of tests and inspections required by law and by the contract
- Obtaining of required permits such as the building permit
- Purchase and maintenance of insurance and bonds if required
- Warranty against defects of materials and equipment furnished under the contract
- Maintaining a safe and clean jobsite
- Correcting work that has been rejected by the owner or the architect
- Coordination of administrative procedures
- Tracking, evaluation, and control of the project time, project costs, and quality of materials and workmanship
- Management of subcontractors

Successful completion of the work requires that the contractor maintain control over all of these tasks. The final three items – coordination of administrative procedures; control of the time, cost, and quality of the work; and management of subcontractors – are particularly critical, so we'll look at them here in some detail. The other contractor tasks are discussed throughout this text.

Coordinating administrative procedures for the job

During pre-construction, the contractor develops procedures to manage the flow of the information and paperwork that is inevitably part of every job. Even modest projects require documentation: meeting minutes, notes, memos, tracking logs, field questions, and so on. Thousands of things happen on a job – from basic communication and daily events to contract negotiations and changes in the work – and the contractor makes a determination regarding what needs to be recorded, what forms of documentation are used, and how and to whom information is communicated.

Thorough record-keeping and effective communication and documentation procedures are important for several reasons. Good documentation reduces misunderstandings and provides the contractor with management tools, which enable him to maintain control over the progress of the work and the performance of subcontractors. Written records support the contractor if there are problems or delays and provide a basis for back-charging subcontractors should the need arise. (As we learned earlier in the text, a back-charge is an amount of money charged to a subcontractor for work that the general contractor was forced to complete with his or her crews because the subcontractor failed to do so.)

Back-charges – There are two common ways that a subcontractor can incur back-charges: she can fail to perform the work she was hired to do or she can cause damage and fail to make the necessary repairs. In either case, the general contractor should provide sufficient notification to the subcontractor of the consequences of not completing required work. *(Notification might state: "Be advised that failure to repair the damage your crew did to the drywall in the hallway and living room must be corrected by April 16, 2010, or our crews will correct the damage on Saturday April 17 on overtime and will administer a back-charge to you.")* If the sub fails to perform, the general contractor should then step in and perform the work with his own crews. Typically, written notification advises the subcontractor of the action. *("Because of your failure to repair the drywall in the hallway and living room per our letter to you of April 13, our crews have completed the work. We will advise you of total charges by next Friday, April 23, 2010.")* At the completion of the work, the contractor's superintendent submits a detailed accounting of labor and material costs to the accounting department. The total cost to the contractor is deducted from the subcontractor's next payment request.

Documentation provides the parties with a record of what occurred on the job and, importantly, may be used as evidence in court should that be required. Maintaining good documentation is a way for a contractor to reduce risk.

Although not all projects require the same type or quantity of documentation, there are several rules of thumb:

- Documentation should be retrievable and accessible, of course (for information to be of use, the team needs to be able to find it!). The documentation is often electronic.
- Documentation needs to be objective, accurate, complete, and timely. (Meeting minutes, for example, that don't accurately describe what occurred and aren't distributed in a timely manner may not be of much value.)

- Information should be appropriately distributed. (For example, a change by the architect needs to be communicated to all those who might be impacted by the change.)
- Documentation should be standardized. (A single format should be used for specific records. For example, it would be chaotic if change orders were sometimes issued on an AIA form and sometimes issued on a form developed in-house.)

Every job requires a variety of forms for record-keeping and documentation. Different projects have different documentation needs. Small, privately funded projects may require only a few forms; large projects that are publicly funded may use dozens of separate forms, from wage compliance forms, to product information and tracking logs, to field questions and change order forms, and more.

Some project forms are created in-house by the contractor, some are available through organizations such as the American Institute of Architects (AIA) and the Associated General Contractors of America (AGC), and some are available as part of software packages. The needs and requirements of the job and the preferences of the team determine which ones are used.

A review of all the forms that might be used on a typical project is beyond the scope of this book, although some are described in other chapters. There are several key documents, however, that are useful on any job and we'll take a look at them now. These forms (often created and used electronically) include:

- Daily job reports (also called construction reports or daily journals)
- Submittal tracking logs
- Meeting minutes

Daily job reports

The **daily job report** documents and records daily activities and conditions on the jobsite. The contractor's superintendent completes a pre-printed blank at the completion of each workday; it is used to track activities, provides documentation for back-charges and claims, and serves as a historical record of the job.

Several important items are typically included in the daily report:

- Number and types of workers on the job and a brief description of work accomplished. This can provide a record of whether a subcontractor is sufficiently staffing the project and how the work is progressing.

- Daily weather summary. Weather data can provide information regarding temperature-linked product performance. For example, a product's ability to set or adhere under certain conditions can be verified based on weather data. In addition, unexpected storms might justify a time extension for the contractor and the daily report can provide backup for this claim.
- Identification of the rental equipment at the site. The contractor can use this information to verify that necessary equipment has been delivered and/or installed on a timely basis.
- Material and product deliveries are analyzed against purchase order requirements.
- Identification of visitors or inspectors.
- Problems, injuries, or other events that occurred that day.

Copies of the daily report are filed with those who have a need for the information such as the contractor's project manager. Sometimes the owner or the architect might also get copies. Even when completed electronically, a printed copy is typically filed chronologically in a binder.

Figure 18.1 is an example of a daily report form.

Superior Contracting Inc/Address

Daily Job Report

Project: Name & Address Superintendent: Name

Date: ____________ Day: ________________ Job #: __________

Today's weather: Temperature: ______________________

Conditions: ______________________

Activities completed: ______________________

Deliveries made/equipment rented: ______________________

Manpower:

Type/Sub: No. of each Hours Notes

Visitors: ______________________

Problems/Notes: ______________________

Figure 18.1. Daily job report form

Submittal tracking logs

Written records, called logs, are maintained to track and manage the flow of information and products. Almost everything is tracked, from the submittal of product samples, to questions asked in the field by subcontractors, to purchase orders. The logs are another important management tool and the contractor's project or field engineer is typically the person on the jobsite who is responsible for managing them.

Keeping track of submittals is especially critical for the contractor as materials and products often cannot be purchased or installed until they are reviewed by the architect. Let's look in some detail at submittals, since the process of getting them approved often involves several different participants and can be a source of delays.

During pre-construction, the contractor is typically required to provide the owner with several documents, called **submittals**, such as insurance policies, performance and payment bonds, a list of proposed subcontractors, and more. There are other types of submittals that the contractor is required to provide during construction. Construction submittals are product information sheets, physical samples, and mock-ups that are designed to demonstrate the way in which the contractor intends to conform to the requirements in the contract.

What sorts of things require submittals? Any product that involves special fabrication (ducts, casework, specialty hardware, for example); off-the-shelf products such as light fixtures, doors, pumps, and heaters; portions of the work that require special full-scale review, such as a curtain wall, stone detailing, and how a flashing system interfaces with a sliding patio door might require a mock-up. The specifications detail which products or systems require submittals.

In most cases, fabrication or installation cannot begin on any portion of the work requiring a submittal until it has been reviewed and accepted by the architect. The timing and procedures for submittals can be tricky, and delay of approval can cause problems for the contractor and work slowdowns. Managing the submittal process is an important part of the contractor's management responsibilities. Here's a representative process for submittal review:

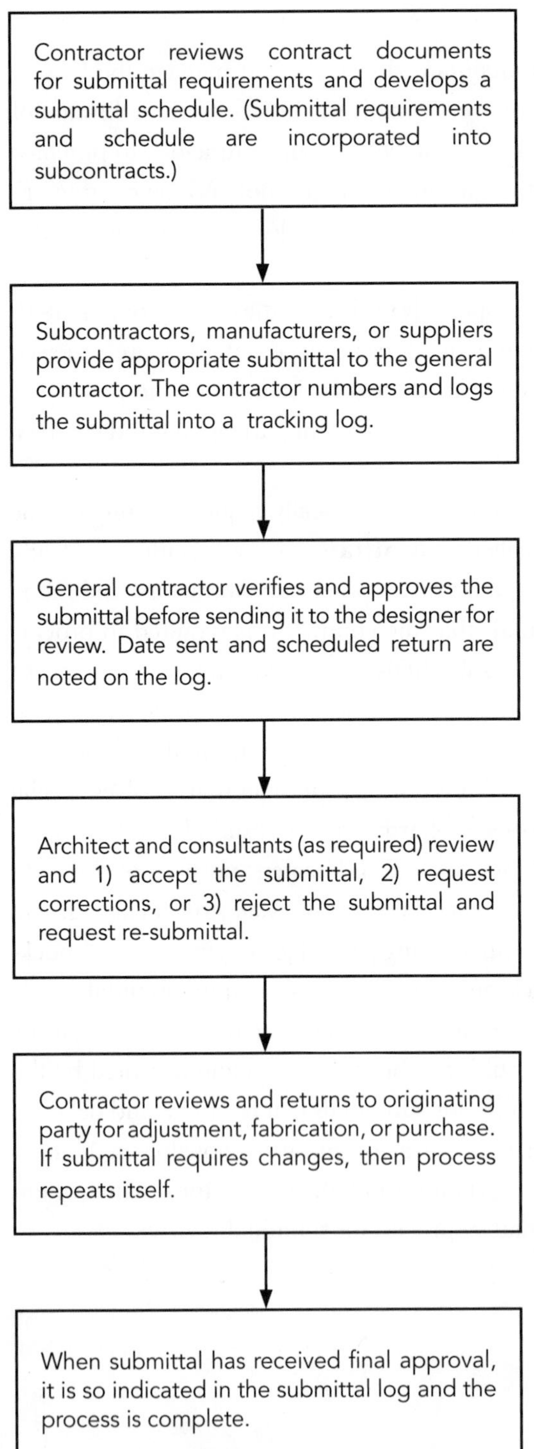

Figure 18.2. Submittal process

Typically the contract documents include a list of required submittals, and the contractor identifies when they must be submitted and reviewed. Because timely fabrication and installation is dependent on the review of submittals, the contractor carefully monitors and tracks the process on a log similar to the one shown in Figure 18.4.

As previously indicated, there are several different types of submittals; the major ones include shop drawings, product data, and samples.

• Shop drawings

Anything that requires special fabrication (in other words, it can't be bought off the shelf) requires a drawing, diagram, or illustration called a shop drawing, which will clarify fabrication or production details and identify material specifications, dimensions, details, and finishes. Shop drawings are commonly provided for such products as custom casework, structural steel connections, metal ducts, special hardware, roof trusses, and more.

When the contractor receives a shop drawing from a subcontractor or a manufacturer, he must *verify* and *approve* the shop drawing (as he does with all submittals): Are the materials correct and do they meet all contract requirements? Will the product fit as it is supposed to? Is the product in accordance with the specifications? After verification and approval by the contractor, the submittal is then forwarded to the architect who reviews the submittal for *intent*. For example, is it the right light fixture? Are the windows those that were specified? Are the bathroom colors correct? Fabrication or purchase cannot happen until sign-off from the architect has been received.

Figure 18.3 is a representative example of a shop drawing for a steel beam, showing how the fabricator intends to manufacture each individual steel beam. When appropriate, the architect forwards shop drawings to the appropriate consultant for review.

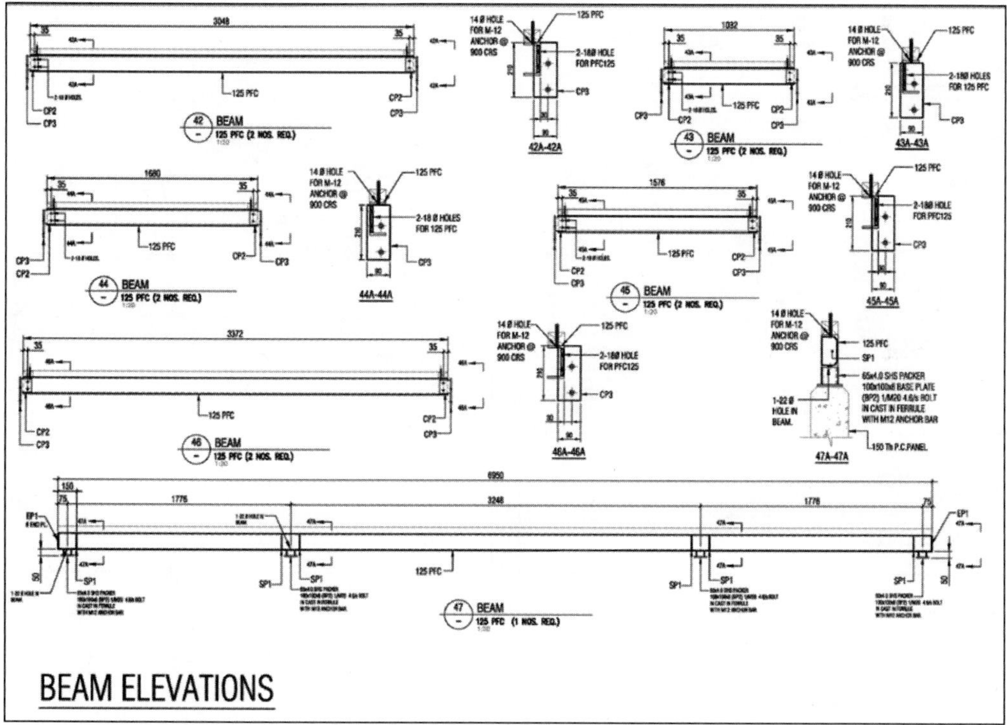

Figure 18.3. Shop drawing by High-Tech CADD service

- **Product data**

Manufacturers product data describe the model and type, physical characteristics, and performance information of a material or a product. Product data submittals can be brochures, information sheets, diagrams, or other forms that sufficiently describe the product. An example of something for which product data might be submitted is a pump or a boiler. Product data is typically submitted to the contractor from the supplier. Figure 18.4 is an example of a product data sheet for a roofing membrane. The information contained in the sheet includes: product and manufacturer data, product description, technical and installation data, availability, warranty, and maintenance and service specifications. Test data and a sketch are also included.

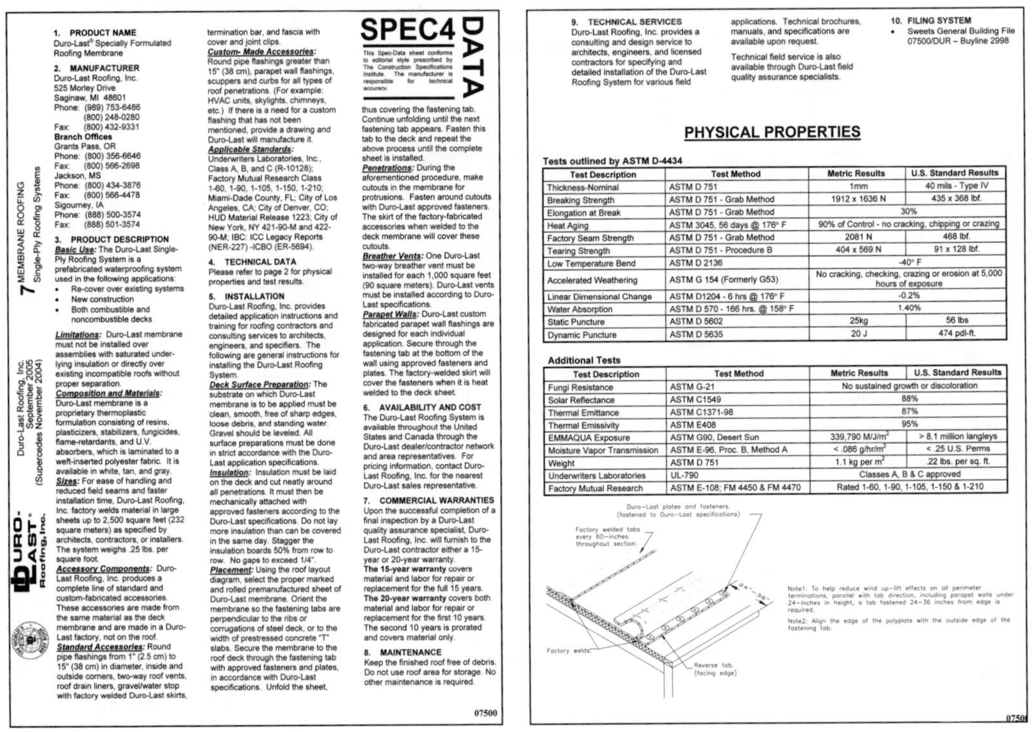

7 MEMBRANE ROOFING
Single-Ply Roofing Systems

Duro-Last Roofing, Inc.
September 2005
(Supercedes November 2004)

DURO-LAST® Roofing, Inc.

1. PRODUCT NAME
Duro-Last® Specially Formulated Roofing Membrane

2. MANUFACTURER
Duro-Last Roofing, Inc.
525 Morley Drive
Saginaw, MI 48601
Phone: (989) 753-6486
(800) 248-0280
Fax: (800) 432-9331
Branch Offices
Grants Pass, OR
Phone: (800) 356-6646
Fax: (800) 566-2698
Jackson, MS
Phone: (800) 434-3876
Fax: (800) 566-4478
Sigourney, IA
Phone: (888) 500-3574
Fax: (888) 501-3574

3. PRODUCT DESCRIPTION
Basic Use: The Duro-Last Single-Ply Roofing System is a prefabricated waterproofing system used in the following applications:

- Re-cover over existing systems
- New construction
- Both combustible and noncombustible decks

Limitations: Duro-Last membrane must not be installed over assemblies with saturated underlying insulation or directly over existing incompatible roofs without proper separation.
Composition and Materials: Duro-Last membrane is a proprietary thermoplastic formulation consisting of resins, plasticizers, stabilizers, fungicides, flame-retardants, and U.V. absorbers, which is laminated to a weft-inserted polyester fabric. It is available in white, tan, and gray.
Sizes: For ease of handling and reduced field seams and faster installation time, Duro-Last Roofing, Inc. factory welds material in large sheets up to 2,500 square feet (232 square meters) as specified by architects, contractors, or installers. The system weighs .25 lbs. per square foot.
Accessory Components: Duro-Last Roofing, Inc. produces a complete line of standard and custom-fabricated accessories. These accessories are made from the same material as the deck membrane and are made in a Duro-Last factory, not on the roof.
Standard Accessories: Round pipe flashings from 1" (2.5 cm) to 15" (38 cm) in diameter, inside and outside corners, two-way roof vents, roof drain liners, gravel/water stop with factory welded Duro-Last skirts, termination bar, and fascia with cover and joint clips.
Custom- Made Accessories: Round pipe flashings greater than 15" (38 cm), parapet wall flashings, scuppers and curbs for all types of roof penetrations. (For example: HVAC units, skylights, chimneys, etc.) If there is a need for a custom flashing that has not been mentioned, provide a drawing and Duro-Last will manufacture it.
Applicable Standards: Underwriters Laboratories, Inc., Class A, B, and C (R-10128); Factory Mutual Research Class 1-60, 1-90, 1-105, 1-150, 1-210; Miami-Dade County, FL; City of Los Angeles, CA; City of Denver, CO; HUD Material Release 1223; City of New York, NY 421-90-M and 422-90-M; IBC: ICC Legacy Reports (NER-227) -ICBO (ER-5694).

4. TECHNICAL DATA
Please refer to page 2 for physical properties and test results.

5. INSTALLATION
Duro-Last Roofing, Inc. provides detailed application instructions and training for roofing contractors and consulting services to architects, engineers, and specifiers. The following are general instructions for installing the Duro-Last Roofing System.
Deck Surface Preparation: The substrate on which Duro-Last membrane is to be applied must be clean, smooth, free of sharp edges, loose debris, and standing water. Gravel should be leveled. All surface preparations must be done in strict accordance with the Duro-Last application specifications.
Insulation: Insulation must be laid on the deck and cut neatly around all penetrations. It must then be mechanically attached with approved fasteners according to the Duro-Last specifications. Do not lay more insulation than can be covered in the same day. Stagger the insulation boards 50% from row to row. No gaps to exceed 1/4".
Placement: Using the roof layout diagram, select the proper marked and rolled premanufactured sheet of Duro-Last membrane. Orient the membrane so the fastening tabs are perpendicular to the ribs or corrugations of steel deck, or to the width of prestressed concrete "T" slabs. Secure the membrane to the roof deck through the fastening tab with approved fasteners and plates, in accordance with Duro-Last specifications. Unfold the sheet,

SPEC4 DATA

This Spec-Data sheet conforms to editorial style prescribed by The Construction Specifications Institute. The manufacturer is responsible for technical accuracy.

thus covering the fastening tab. Continue unfolding until the next fastening tab appears. Fasten this tab to the deck and repeat the above process until the complete sheet is installed.
Penetrations: During the aforementioned procedure, make cutouts in the membrane for protrusions. Fasten around cutouts with Duro-Last approved fasteners. The skirt of the factory-fabricated accessories when welded to the deck membrane will cover these cutouts.
Breather Vents: One Duro-Last two-way breather vent must be installed for each 1,000 square feet (90 square meters). Duro-Last vents must be installed according to Duro-Last specifications.
Parapet Walls: Duro-Last custom fabricated parapet wall flashings are designed for each individual application. Secure through the fastening tab at the bottom of the wall using approved fasteners and plates. The factory-welded skirt will cover the fasteners when it is heat welded to the deck sheet.

6. AVAILABILITY AND COST
The Duro-Last Roofing System is available throughout the United States and Canada through the Duro-Last dealer/contractor network and area representatives. For pricing information, contact Duro-Last Roofing, Inc. for the nearest Duro-Last sales representative.

7. COMMERCIAL WARRANTIES
Upon the successful completion of a final inspection by a Duro-Last quality assurance specialist, Duro-Last Roofing, Inc. will furnish to the Duro-Last contractor either a 15-year or 20-year warranty.
The 15-year warranty covers material and labor for repair or replacement for the full 15 years.
The 20-year warranty covers both material and labor for repair or replacement for the first 10 years. The second 10 years is prorated and covers material only.

8. MAINTENANCE
Keep the finished roof free of debris. Do not use roof area for storage. No other maintenance is required.

07500

9. TECHNICAL SERVICES
Duro-Last Roofing, Inc. provides a consulting and design service to architects, engineers, and licensed contractors for specifying and detailed installation of the Duro-Last Roofing System for various field applications. Technical brochures, manuals, and specifications are available upon request.

Technical field service is also available through Duro-Last field quality assurance specialists.

10. FILING SYSTEM
- Sweets General Building File 07500/DUR – Buyline 2998

PHYSICAL PROPERTIES

Tests outlined by ASTM D-4434

Test Description	Test Method	Metric Results	U.S. Standard Results
Thickness-Nominal	ASTM D 751	1mm	40 mils - Type IV
Breaking Strength	ASTM D 751 - Grab Method	1912 x 1636 N	435 x 368 lbf.
Elongation at Break	ASTM D 751 - Grab Method	30%	
Heat Aging	ASTM 3045, 56 days @ 176° F	90% of Control - no cracking, chipping or crazing	
Factory Seam Strength	ASTM D 751 - Grab Method	2081 N	468 lbf.
Tearing Strength	ASTM D 751 - Procedure B	404 x 569 N	91 x 128 lbf.
Low Temperature Bend	ASTM D 2136	-40° F	
Accelerated Weathering	ASTM G 154 (Formerly G53)	No cracking, checking, crazing or erosion at 5,000 hours of exposure	
Linear Dimensional Change	ASTM D1204 - 6 hrs @ 176° F	-0.2%	
Water Absorption	ASTM D 570 - 166 hrs. @ 158° F	1.40%	
Static Puncture	ASTM D 5602	25kg	56 lbs
Dynamic Puncture	ASTM D 5635	20 J	474 pdl-ft.

Additional Tests

Test Description	Test Method	Metric Results	U.S. Standard Results
Fungi Resistance	ASTM G-21	No sustained growth or discoloration	
Solar Reflectance	ASTM C1549	88%	
Thermal Emittance	ASTM C1371-98	87%	
Thermal Emissivity	ASTM E408	95%	
EMMAQUA Exposure	ASTM G90, Desert Sun	339,790 M/J/m²	> 8.1 million langleys
Moisture Vapor Transmission	ASTM E-96, Proc. B, Method A	< .086 g/hr/m²	< .25 U.S. Perms
Weight	ASTM D 751	1.1 kg per m²	.22 lbs. per sq. ft.
Underwriters Laboratories	UL-790	Classes A, B & C approved	
Factory Mutual Research	ASTM E-108; FM 4450 & FM 4470	Rated 1-60, 1-90, 1-105, 1-150 & 1-210	

0750

Figure 18.4. Product data sheet, courtesy of Duro-Last® Roofing, Inc.

• Samples

Some products require submittal of a physical and/or color sample. Examples include carpet, tile, paint, and light fixtures. The contractor or subcontractor responsible for providing the product submits samples to the contractor who, again, verifies for conformance with the specifications and forwards the sample to the architect for review.

Almost everything installed in a building requires some sort of submittal. (Different types of submittals are required as part of close-out too; we'll review those in the final chapter.) The contractor uses control logs to track all submittals: what is required, when the submittal is due, when it is received, when they are sent to the architect, response from the architect, and final action.

The logs used for tracking submittals are representative of other control logs. As with most administrative documentation, they can be developed in-house, published by outside organizations, or incorporated into software packages. Figure 18.5 is an example of a control log used to track the review of submittals.

CONTRACTOR SUBMITTAL TRACKING LOG

Project Name:____________________

Project Number:____________________

Item #	Description	Specification Section	Shop drawing	Sample	Product data	Date due	Originator	Date received	Date to Arch.	Due back from Arch.	Returned from Arch.	Approved	Rejected	Approved with notes	Revise & resubmit	Date ret. to originator
1	Silt Fence	31 25 13			X	9/9		9/9	9/13	9/17	9/18	X				9/18
2	Perforated pipe	33 46 16		X		9/13		9/13	9/13	9/15	9/15	X				9/15
3	Footing rebar	03 21 10	X			10/4		10/4	10/6	10/12	10/12	X				10/12
4	Structural steel	05 12 23	X			10/4		10/7	10/12	10/12	10/26			X		10/29
5	Access doors	08 31 00		X		11/17		11/17	11/17	11/18	11/19				X	11/19

Figure 18.5. Submittal tracking log

Note in Figure 18.5 that four different types of submittals are represented: #1 (silt fence) requires a product data sheet submittal, #2 (perforated pipe) and #5 (doors) both require that actual samples are submitted, #3 and #4 (rebar and structural steel) are described by shop drawings. When the contractor receives a submittal, he verifies that the product or material meets the specifications and that it will fit into the space. Following approval by the contractor and review by the architect, the submittal is stamped and returned to the originator (typically a subcontractor). Each submittal is tracked by date and the action is noted (such as approved, rejected, or approved with notes). If the architect chooses to make a change to a submittal (for example, selecting a different size rebar, or a pipe with a different gauge), a request for a change order proposal is submitted. The general contractor returns the approved submittal to the originating party who can then proceed with fabrication or procurement.

Meeting minutes

Any verbal communication regarding requests, understandings, and information should be documented in memos, minutes, diaries, or e-mails to reduce misunderstandings and confusion and to maintain records of agreements and actions.

Communication – One of the ways a project can get off track is for various parties to take action without the approval, or even the knowledge, of the contractor. It's easy to imagine things going awry if the owner requests that the plumbing subcontractor change the type of fixtures, or the architect re-details how the windows will be flashed, or the mechanical sub takes it upon himself to change the location of a duct without alerting the GC. One way to keep on top of such things is for the general contractor to maintain tight control over how communication flows on the job. This doesn't mean that people don't speak to each other—lots of communication occurs daily on a job—just that there are strict procedures for how action occurs and that all formal communication is recorded. There are some rules of thumb: communication between the contractor and the owner is through the architect; between the subcontractors and the architect, it is through the general contractor; between the consultants (such as the engineers) and the contractor, it is through the architect.

Numerous formal meetings between various parties occur during a project. Notes on these meetings are especially valuable and should be saved and distributed to participants and other interested parties.

Two important meetings are the progress meetings between the contractor and the architect and the contractor-subcontractor meetings (sometimes called the superintendent's meetings). The first are typically held in advance of the monthly payment requests and, in addition to the contractor and the architect, attendees may include the owner, major subcontractors, and sometimes the surety or the bankers who have funded the work. At these meetings, work progress, changes in the work, delays or problems, corrective actions, and more are reviewed.

The contractor-subcontractor meetings occur more often and may include all the major subcontractors or may be targeted to specific subs. Typically, the GC's project manager, superintendent or foreman, and subcontractor representatives attend these meetings.

If a meeting is justified, then an accurate record of what is discussed is also justified. The contractor typically facilitates these meetings and is responsible for summarizing the meeting clearly and accurately. Meeting minutes document communication and understandings and help track outstanding business.

Typical minutes include:

- Date, time, and location of the meeting
- Title of the meeting (for example, the monthly architect/contractor's progress meeting or the weekly contractor/subcontractor meeting)

- List of participants and list of others to whom the minutes will also be copied
- Identification of the person who prepared the minutes
- New to-do or action items with identification of the responsible party
- Unfinished or incomplete old business (that is, remaining to-do or action items from previous meetings)

Although several software programs have templates for minutes and other administrative operations, they can also be created in-house. Figure 18.6 is an example of the latter.

Meeting Minutes

Superior Contracting Inc.

Project Main St. Office — Meeting: OAC No. 35

Address — Report Date: 2/8/2010

By: J. Baker, SCInc

Arch/Cont. Meeting No. 35
Date: 2/8/2010 — Start: 01:35pm
Next Meeting: 2/15/10 — Time: 01:30pm

Attended by:	Copies to:
Jay Baker, SCInc	Sandra Guzman, Owner
Gail Burke, SCInc	Mike Nichols, SCInc
Mike Havsted, Ace Plumbing	Jim Balter Scaffolding Inc.
Nancy Myers, Key Mechanical	Rachel Schulman, Wright Architects

Item	Summary	By	Due	Resolution
OLD BUSINESS				
1-1	**THREE WEEK SCHEDULE** **Data due by subs every Friday**	**SCInc**	**weekly**	
30-1	**EXTERIOR FLASHING** **Wright needs to respond to proposed window details. Wright working on revised details.** **HIGH PRIORITY ITEM**	**Wright**	**1/20/10**	
33-1	**FENCE DESIGN** **Status?**	**Wright**	**2/3/10**	
34-1	**SCAFFOLDING/EXT. FRAMING** **Scaffolding will be put off until window issues are resolved by architect**	**ScafInc**	**1/25/10**	
NEW BUSINESS				
35-1	**INSTALLATION PV SYSTEM** **Wright to finalize details**	**Wright**	**2/10/10**	

All meeting minutes items are to be considered correct and accurate unless the Preparer is notified in writing prior to the next scheduled progress meeting.

Figure 18.6. Meeting minutes

Note that business is numbered according to the meeting (identified by week number) when it was brought up. The first item from *old business* is identified as item 1-1. This means that the item – a reminder that updated short-term schedules are due weekly – was the first item brought up at the first meeting and is kept on the minutes as an ongoing reminder. Another old business item, 30-1, refers to flashing details that have not yet (as of the current meeting) been submitted by the architect. Item 34-1 puts on record that the erection of scaffolding is on hold until 30-1 is resolved. This information will be of use at a later date if there is a time delay or cost increase due to the delay in getting flashing information to the contractor. The only new business (35-1) refers to mechanical equipment.

We've looked at three key examples of administrative procedures and documentation: daily reports, submittal tracking, meeting minutes. All of these are used to control the major responsibility of the contractor: to complete the work safely, on time, within budget, and according to the quality requirements identified in the contract documents. These are discussed below.

Tracking, evaluating, and controlling time, costs, and quality

Tracking (or **monitoring**) involves keeping up with how a project is doing: the determination of its current status. Once the contractor has this data, he can **evaluate** what the data means by comparing the current status with a baseline of where the project should be and then develop a strategy to **control** any problems so that the project can get back on track. There are different ways for the contractor to do this.

The contractor's detailed cost estimate and master construction schedule serve as targets for what the contractor anticipates the job will actually cost and how long it will take to complete. Measuring *actual* cost and performance against *planned* cost and performance provides the contractor with the data necessary to determine whether there are problems that need to be addressed.

Managing time

Updating the schedule against the master baseline schedule occurs on a regular basis and is important to the contractor for several reasons: if the work isn't completed according to the time requirements established in the contract documents, the contractor may be responsible for paying liquidated damages; accurate work updates alert the contractor to problems and indicate whether corrective measures are required; and understanding the differences between anticipated performance and actual performance assists in scheduling future jobs. An updated schedule provides a tool for monitoring work progress by comparing it to the targeted baseline. The contractor looks for problems as follows:

- Is each activity on target to meet its as-planned completion date?
- Where are there problems and are any of them along critical paths (see Chapter 20) that will lead to a delay in the entire project?
- Were there particular conditions such as severe weather or poor working conditions that caused inefficiencies?

and attempts to determine causes:

- Was the original schedule unrealistic?
- Did productivity suffer because of poor supervision?
- Are crews insufficiently skilled or understaffed?
- Is all necessary equipment available as needed?

and determines what actions can and should be taken in response:

- Are there any adjustments that need to or can be made in the sequence of the remaining activities?
- Will the contractor need to have his own crews step in and complete work because of a subcontractor's failure to perform?
- What are the most cost- and time-efficient ways to make up for delays? Can the schedule be accelerated by adding crews or overtime?

Crashing the schedule – If the updated schedule indicates there's a delay in the scheduled completion time, the contractor tries to figure out how to make it up. Accelerating an activity or activities in order to shorten project duration is called **crashing** the schedule. There are several ways this can be accomplished: overtime, additional crews, and/or multiple work shifts. Each strategy for crashing the schedule has cost implications that must be measured against time saved. The critical path method (CPM) schedule can identify to the contractor which activities, when accelerated, will have the desired effect in the most cost-efficient way. Crashing the schedule is intended to result in a time saving as well as a reduction in indirect project costs (the shorter the time a project lasts, the less the indirect project costs). But crashing also results in an increase in labor costs and these costs differ depending on how the contractor chooses to proceed. It might be more efficient and cost effective to add shifts rather than pay overtime. Perhaps increasing the size of crews makes more sense? Adding additional equipment? Savings must be balanced against costs to determine the best way to speed up the schedule.

Managing costs

During pre-construction and subcontractor buyout, the contractor's bid estimate is fine-tuned and results in a baseline for the project. As with the schedule, the estimate is monitored and evaluated to enable the contractor to review actual costs against the baseline, projected costs.

There are several reasons for the contractor's interest in how the project is doing in terms of the baseline budget: Is there any danger of exceeding the bid price and therefore reducing (or losing) his profit? Can any subcontractors be identified as responsible for excessive costs? What are the cost impacts for changes in the work? Updated cost figures are important to the owner as well and she will expect some kind of regular reporting on how the work is progressing. As with scheduling differences, a comparison of how actual costs varied from projected costs assists the contractor in estimating future jobs.

Once a job has been awarded, the contractor gives each work activity a **cost code** to use as a reference to track labor, material, equipment, subcontractor, and indirect costs. These codes typically incorporate the CSI MasterFormat division and section numbers (see Chapter 16), but can be based on the contractor's own coding system. All cost reports, subcontractor and supplier invoices, delivery slips, and purchase orders refer to the appropriate cost codes. On some jobs, separate cost reports are issued (such as labor cost reports and materials cost reports) On other jobs, all costs are rolled into a single report. Either way, the contractor's accounting department uses the codes to track costs for everything on the job.

In order to be a useful tool for evaluating problems with the budget, cost breakdowns need to be sufficiently narrow to allow the contractor to determine where a problem lies. For example, if a budget update shows that the costs for the slab on grade are $4,500 over budget, that information alone is limited. What was the cause of the problem? Was there a mistake on the take-off so that the quantities were incorrect? Which ones? Rebar? Formwork? Concrete? Was it a labor problem? Was there excessive waste? Unless the contractor breaks out costs beyond the broad category "slab on grade," he won't know.

Typically, cost progress reports are completed at least monthly as part of the data for the progress payment. A forecast of cash projections that include costs to date and costs to complete for all codes is also developed. This report assists the contractor's project manager in identifying problems and strategizing ways to improve productivity (labor costs are the most likely culprit in cost overruns). It is unrealistic to expect that every single cost item will come in exactly as it was estimated: some items will be over budget and some will be under budget. Even if there's nothing the contractor can do about a particular cost overrun, the goal is that *total* project costs stay within the baseline budget.

Managing quality

In contrast to time and cost, which are quantitative, the **quality** of a construction project is, well, qualitative. Quality can't be tracked and evaluated in quite the same way. But neither is quality some vague, subjective thing. The quality of a construction project is defined by the requirements called for in the contract documents. There are various levels of quality that can be specified – in products, materials, and workmanship – and the contractor's responsibility is to meet or exceed whatever is required. The design team and the owner determine the quality standards for the project; the plans and specifications are the primary tools for defining these standards.

It is not simply assumed by the designer or the owner that the contractor is building the structure according to the quality requirements. Certain procedures for determining the level of quality are typically written into the plans and specifications. **Quality assurance** procedures, such as fabrication and procurement standards, guard against defects and deficiencies before and during execution of work. **Quality control** procedures refer to those measures that can assist in verifying the quality of completed work. Examples of quality control measures are field testing, inspections, and submittals.

Some quality measures are determined by the owner (for example, which products require submittals and qualification requirements for manufacturers and installers), some are required by codes and are verified by inspecting agencies, and some are determined by good construction practice (such as doing additional testing).

The contractor has a major stake in ensuring that he meets quality standards. Most general conditions give the architect the responsibility for verifying performance (quality) and rejecting work that fails to meet performance standards. When this occurs, non-conforming work or materials must be replaced at the contractor's expense (with no extension of contract time for any impact this additional work has on the schedule). Perhaps even more critically, most contractors are dependent on good references or word of mouth for future work; those with a reputation for poor quality risk their business.

There are several measures that provide opportunities to verify that products and materials meet quality standards. These measures typically include (but are not limited to) the following:

- **Submittals**. As we have learned, the contract documents identify which products and materials require submittals to verify conformance to the contract requirements. If a submittal indicates non-conformance, correction can be made prior to purchase and installation.
- **Tests and inspections**. The contract documents typically identify testing requirements; codes identify others. Some occur at the fabrication site (steel welds, for example); others happen at the jobsite (for example, concrete design mix tests). Testing can also involve off-site analysis such as soil tests. Inspections involve visual observation for compliance with specific requirements such as flashing details or joint connections.
- **Qualification and fabrication requirements**. The contract documents might specify minimum expertise requirements for testing and inspection services, manufacturers and fabricators, and erectors and installers for certain products. There may also be fabrication specifications that establish a range of acceptability for certain products.
- **Visual inspection**. The contractor conducts daily inspection of the work. Typically, the architect is also responsible for making periodic inspections and verifies the contractor's performance as part of payment requests. (It is worth noting that failure by the architect to identify non-conforming work *does not* relieve the contractor of his obligations.) All materials and products are examined and verified against purchase orders at the time of delivery to the jobsite.
- **Commissioning**. Large projects typically hire independent commissioning inspectors to verify that all products and systems are working as intended and that facility managers are trained to maintain them. LEED-certified buildings are *required* to hire commissioning agents.

Managing subcontractors

Tracking, evaluating, and controlling are key aspects of management. For the general contractor, managing time, costs, and quality means not only overseeing his own crews, but also managing subcontractors and comparing their performance against a baseline. If need be, the contractor devises ways to get subcontractors back on track. It is the general contractor's superintendent who has the responsibility for managing all the specialty contractors that are on the job.

A project work schedule is coordinated with all of the trades and is generally included as part of each subcontract. On a regular basis, the subs update the schedule for their own portions of the work so that the superintendent can monitor and control the entire project. An important aspect of the schedule is ensuring that the jobsite is ready for subs as soon as they are expected to start work. The general contractor makes sure the preceding subcontractor is finished and out of the way, the site is cleaned, and required materials are on hand, so that the subcontractor who follows is able to start as soon as she arrives on the site. Although each subcontractor has agreed in advance to a schedule, exact start dates are confirmed and adjusted as necessary by the superintendent. If subcontractors are given adequate advance notice regarding when they can start their work, it helps keep the project moving and avoids an unnecessary last-minute rush.

Subcontractor performance

The general contractor or his superintendent must regularly (even daily) review the work of the trades so that feedback and requests for correction can be made. If the superintendent is unaware of a problem at the time it occurs, it may be harder and more costly to fix later. Careful and strict review of work so that the general contractor can gain (and keep) control over performance is especially important with a subcontractor that the GC hasn't worked with before.

As noted earlier, the superintendent facilitates frequent meetings (typically, weekly) between the GC and the subcontractors in which problems are discussed and mechanisms for resolving issues explored. There is an agenda for these meetings and notes are taken (which can be used as evidence in case of disputes, by the way). All attendees and other appropriate parties get copies of meeting minutes.

Part of open communication includes prompt dissemination of design changes and sketches. It is a common, and potentially serious, problem for subcontractors to be in the dark about a change that can impact their work. If, for example, the architect has forwarded a revised sketch for something, the general contractor needs to be sure to pass this along to all the subcontractors who might be affected.

Finally, the superintendent and the project manager do whatever they can to facilitate prompt review and approval of payment requests by subcontractors. This helps keep subcontractors financially viable and can provide additional benefits to the general contractor. When subcontractors are confident that they will be paid on time, it contributes to good relations on the job and may result in more favorable future bids.

Signs of trouble

Sometimes subcontractors get into financial trouble, which can result in trying to do the job "on the cheap" or even walking off. When a subcontractor appears to be in trouble, the general contractor's goal is to help the sub resolve his or her problems so that the project is not negatively affected. The signals that may indicate that a subcontractor is in financial trouble include:

- Failure to keep a sufficient number of workers on the job
- Delays in getting the necessary materials
- Delays in providing submittals such as shop drawings
- Requests to get paid faster than originally agreed to

If the contractor thinks a sub is failing, there are steps he can take to protect the job from delays and poor quality work. These steps include:

- Accurate assessment of any delays on the entire project
- Thorough documentation and identification of potential delays via meeting minutes and/or letters, as well as photographic documentation of the sub's work

- Making every effort to assist the sub in resolving problems, such as making equipment available or rescheduling the sub's work
- Notifying the subcontractor *in writing* of what the consequences will be if there are delays to the project, such as:
    1. Back charges assessed to the subcontractor for the costs of work that the general contractor must do to fulfill the subcontractor's responsibilities
    2. Assessment of penalties or liquidated damages for any delays
    3. Termination of the contract

Occasionally, a subcontractor faces such financial problems that he cannot afford to pay his employees or buy materials, and walks off the job. If this happens, the general contractor can and should do several things:

- Contact an attorney to be sure that the GC's actions are appropriate and legal
- Provide written notice to the sub that someone else will complete the job
- Look for solutions to complete the work such as using the GC's labor, or hiring other subs
- Take possession, and make an inventory of, the subcontractor's materials and supplies on the job
- Notify the subcontractor's bonding company (surety)

One subcontractor who fails can impact the success of the entire project. This reinforces the need for careful subcontractor selection (see Chapter 21).

We've seen that the general contractor has numerous responsibilities during construction. Before we look at several other important aspects of construction such as changes to the work, getting paid, and managing claims and disputes, we'll step back and look at the basics of scheduling. We've had several opportunities to mention the important role that scheduling plays *throughout* a project; in the next two chapters we'll delve into this topic in more detail.

Chapter Vocabulary

Back-charge – money charged to a subcontractor for work that the general contractor is forced to complete with his or her crews because the subcontractor has failed to do so.

Commissioning – a practice that involves a formal review of all parts of a building's systems to ensure that the project meets (and will continue to meet) certain energy objectives.

Construction – the execution of physical work as outlined by contract documents.

Construction time – the amount of time a contractor has to complete work.

Controlling – a key function of project management, in which, after tracking and evaluating, a project's schedule, cost, or quality are brought back in line with the project baseline.

Control log – a mechanism for tracking information and documents on a job.

Crashing the schedule – accelerating the work.

Daily job report – a form used to track the progress of work and daily activities on a jobsite.

Liquidated damages – a previously agreed-upon amount of money the contractor is required to pay an owner if construction is not completed on time.

Mock-up – a full-scale model built for testing or evaluating details.

Product data – information sheets that describe the model, type, physical characteristics, and performance details of a product.

Quality – the attributes or properties of something (a product, material, or workmanship) as defined by the requirements called for in the contract documents. There are various levels of quality that can be specified and the contractor's responsibility is to meet or exceed whatever is required.

Quality assurance – refers to procedures before and during execution of the work to guard against defects and deficiencies.

Quality control – measures and procedures, such as testing and inspections, for evaluating completed work.

Samples – physical examples of products such as carpet, tiles, and light fixtures.

Shop drawings – drawings that clarify the fabrication or production detail of an item, such as a roof truss or a metal duct.

Submittal – a document, product data, or physical sample that a contract requires the contractor to provide for review by the owner and/or designer. Submittals can include insurance certificates, manufacturers' product information and samples, and shop drawings.

Tracking – a key function of project management, in which current progress of a project is monitored.

Test Yourself

1. What is the definition of construction?
2. Construction is a team effort; who, besides the contractor, is involved and what typically determines their roles?
3. What does it mean to track, evaluate, and control? Give one specific example of something that would be tracked, evaluated and controlled on a project.
4. What are typically the roles of the owner and the architect?
5. What are three reasons for keeping records on a job?
6. The weather was stormy today at the jobsite. Where will this information be recorded?
7. What is the purpose of recording meeting minutes?
8. The shop drawings for the kitchen cabinets have been submitted. Who is responsible for verifying that the cabinets will fit? Who verifies that the cabinets meet the intent of the plans and specifications?
9. What is the purpose of crashing the schedule ?
10. Identify three ways to help ensure that products and materials meet quality requirements.

Andrea Young

CHAPTER 19

Fundamentals of Scheduling

Many factors influence a contractor's success or failure. Creating a realistic schedule is one of them. A **schedule** is a timetable, typically shown in graphic form, that identifies when, in what order, and how long project activities are going to take. A detailed schedule is developed by the contractor and is continually monitored throughout construction to identify how the work is progressing. Understanding how to schedule, and then using the schedule as a tool to monitor and adjust the progress of work, is one of the important ways for the contractor to maintain control over the job.

During feasibility and design, the owner and architect identify project **milestones**, important events that indicate turning points. Typical milestones might include: bidding, award of contract, notice to proceed, start of construction, substantial completion, and owner move-in. As part of preparing to submit a bid, a contractor analyzes these milestones and puts together a rough construction schedule. This rough schedule is called a **bid schedule**. Because a cost estimate for construction cannot happen without a time estimate (how long it will take to do the work), this is an important step in estimating a job. But this initial schedule is not detailed. As we learned in Chapter 17, once the contractor knows the job is his, he develops a much more comprehensive and detailed schedule, called a **master construction schedule**.

As with many parts of the construction process, the development of an accurate, realistic, and detailed schedule begins with careful planning. Planning for the schedule means setting objectives, or goals, and identifying strategies for accomplishing them. The architect and engineers identify (through the drawings and specifications) what the project will be in terms of quantities and quality. It is the contractor's job to determine the best way of meeting the design requirements – the **means, methods and techniques** of construction. Some of the questions the contractor answers during planning are: What is the best way of completing the physical work? How much of the work will be done by the contractor's own crews and how much will be subcontracted? Are there special requirements for inspections or testing? What sort of equipment will be necessary? How many crews need to be working to meet the owner's time frame? What are the budget restraints that need to be addressed? What are potential problems and obstacles? Once the contractor has identified how he intends to proceed to meet the design requirements, then detailed scheduling can begin.

As part of the planning process, the contractor identifies and lists broad activities (for example, HVAC rough-in, roofing, plumbing) that can then be broken down into more detailed activities according to subcontractor bid packages and the needs of the project. The contractor (typically with input from subcontractors) determines how long each activity will take and how activities fit logically with each other and with the work of other subcontractors. The general contractor adds this information to similar information for all the activities on the job and develops the detailed master construction schedule to be used to measure performance. We'll come back to this later in the chapter; for now, let's get a better understanding of why schedules are important.

The value of schedules

The typical project has hundreds (sometimes thousands) of activities and operations that need to be put in some kind of order and then coordinated with each other. How do all these job activities happen? Does everyone just know what to do and when to do it? As you might guess, the answer is definitely no! All of the activities required to construct a building need to be carefully organized and managed by the general contractor so that crews know where and when to go, and so that all work is completed in the correct order and on time. Most, if not all, work depends on the completion of other activities. For example, the painter doesn't want to show up and discover that the drywallers aren't quite finished and that painting can't begin. The primary tool used for coordinating the complicated processes that make up a construction project – the work – is the schedule.

As already discussed, the development of an accurate and effective schedule is dependent on careful up-front planning by the contractor. Let's look at a freeway reconstruction project as an example of how careful planning and the development of a master construction schedule based on that planning can result in a successful project.

The Northridge Earthquake, with a magnitude of 6.7, struck 20 miles from downtown Los Angeles on January 17, 1994. There was loss of life, thousands of injuries, and billions of dollars in damage. Several freeways, including the Santa Monica Freeway, were severely damaged, and the loss of their operation risked seriously damaging the Los Angeles economy.

Caltrans, the California agency responsible for overseeing the freeway reconstruction, set up a bidding procedure whereby pre-qualified, experienced highway contractors were invited to bid on rebuilding the Santa Monica Freeway. (Then-governor Pete Wilson relaxed certain procurement regulations to expedite the process and the federal government contributed emergency funding. In addition, after construction began, a Caltrans representative was made available throughout to expedite decision-making.) Invited bidders were informed that if their work was completed after an agreed-upon date established by Caltrans and the winning bidder, they would be penalized, and if the work was completed prior to that date, they would receive bonuses. The penalty/bonus incentive was set at $200,000 per day.

The rebuilding contract for the freeway was awarded to C. C. Myers of Sacramento at a cost of $14.9 million and a contract time of 140 days. Myers figured that if they carefully planned and scheduled the work, they would be able to shave about 40 days off the schedule and receive an $8 million bonus. Careful analysis of project goals and resources resulted in strategies for accomplishing this goal, including the following:

- Acceleration of the work.
- Identification of problems associated with an accelerated schedule and strategies for overcoming those problems; for example, how could multiple crews be scheduled so that they didn't interfere with each other?
- Using materials and processes that might result in faster fabrication and/or delivery of materials and products to the jobsite.

- Developing an incentive plan for subcontractors and material suppliers through a share of the bonus money.
- Maximizing equipment availability.

Once planning was completed and Myers had identified strategies for meeting project goals, they were ready to develop a detailed schedule of work and procurement activities. Here are some of the ways the schedule reflected the goals set up in the planning phase:

- Crews (Myers' own and those of their subcontractors) were scheduled 7 days a week, 24 hours per day, with up to 400 workers on the job. Time durations were carefully calculated and crews coordinated to maximize efficiency.
- Fabrication of modularized sections of the road was carefully scheduled so that delivery to the site was efficient and timely.
- Key pieces of equipment were scheduled to be at the jobsite on a standby basis to ensure ongoing availability and thereby reduce downtime.

As a consequence of careful planning and scheduling, Myers broke all expectations by completing the work in 66 days, 74 days ahead of schedule. Their bonus was $14.8 million rather than the expected $8 million, an amount that almost matched their original contract price.[1] Not only did Myers and their subcontractors and suppliers do extremely well, the City of Los Angeles came out ahead too. The governor's office had calculated that closure of the Santa Monica Freeway was costing the Los Angeles economy $1 million per day in lost wages, business revenues, and increased transportation costs. Thus, although the speediness of completion cost the city more than anticipated, it may have saved the local economy as much as $34 million.[2]

The Santa Monica Freeway reconstruction is an extraordinary example of how careful planning and scheduling can benefit a project and its contractor.

There are several excellent reasons why scheduling is an important part of good project management. Schedules can assist contractors and provide value to the job in several ways. They:

- Force thinking about and planning for the work
- Help the contractor set goals and maximize efficiency

- Help control the job
- Improve communication and clarify work goals
- Are used to evaluate the effects of changes in the work
- Provide documentation and can be used as evidence in court

We'll look at each of these in more detail.

Schedules force thinking about and planning for the work.

The process of planning and scheduling provides the key opportunity for the contractor to think about how the work will proceed. It's not possible to develop the schedule without mentally building the project, and this process of defining and sequencing tasks provides an opportunity to think through the labor, equipment, and materials the contractor will need as well as potential problems that the project may face. This process helps reduce mistakes caused by doing tasks out of order and can save money by maximizing productivity. Projects that are well organized have fewer mistakes and less need for expensive rework or overtime. This results in a more cost-efficient (and profitable) job.

Help contractor set goals and maximize efficiency.

We know from the Santa Monica Freeway example that good planning and scheduling can reduce construction time. A clear schedule sets milestones that can become goals for everyone on the job and can act as an incentive to improve productivity. (A schedule that identifies a building inspection for the following week, for example, will likely spur everyone on!)

If the contractor needs to adjust the work to make up for delays, the schedule can provide guidelines for the allocation of resources. For example, if the project is delayed, the contractor must identify the most efficient way to make up the lost time. He or she can simply accelerate *all* the work and pay a premium for overtime. But not every task, if speeded up, will result in a savings in the overall project time. Schedules can identify which tasks *must* be accelerated in order to complete the work on time.

Schedules are used to help control the job.

As we know, the task of a contractor is to complete the contracted work on time, within budget, and according to the requirements of the specifications. The schedule, and its continual evaluation, is one of the contractor's major tools for maintaining control over the progress of the physical work and the project costs. The schedule establishes a checklist of key dates, activities, and resources and the master construction schedule is a baseline against which actual progress is measured. The contractor will refer to and evaluate the schedule on an ongoing basis to anticipate and identify problems. When the schedule shows that progress is slipping, the contractor can take steps to get back on track.

Schedules improve communication and clarify work goals.

On many jobs, the primary causes of frustration can be traced to poor communication. The contractor may get frustrated because the architect doesn't respond to requests for information in a timely fashion; the subcontractors get frustrated with the contractor because they haven't been given sufficient lead times; the contractor gets frustrated with the suppliers because deliveries are delayed; the owner gets frustrated with the contractor because the contractor doesn't seem to appreciate the owner's goals; the contractor gets frustrated with the owner because the owner keeps changing his mind and doesn't appreciate the consequences; and so on. Schedules help reduce this frustration by presenting the contractor's thinking to all the parties and setting clear timelines. It's more difficult for one party to claim ignorance when a realistic schedule has been developed and agreed to by all parties. The schedule is the primary mechanism for communicating expectations and for clarifying time goals.

Schedules help evaluate the effects of changes in the work.

Schedules provide a means for evaluating the effect of changes and delays and provide a written record of what happened on a job. For example, if the contractor is claiming that delays have occurred through no fault of his own, and that the construction completion date should be adjusted, the schedule can provide proof.

Schedules provide documentation and can be used as evidence in court.

Lots of things can happen on a job that might result in changes to the initial master schedule, such as: the owner makes design changes; deliveries are delayed; a subcontractor fails to provide sufficient manpower; the architect does not make prompt product selections. Updated schedules are generated to reflect the impact of changes on the progress of work and assist the contractor in identifying why the work has been delayed and who is responsible. In some cases, schedules can be used as evidence in a court of law.

In addition, the schedule (and any updated versions) is a record of what actually happens on a job. This information provides historical data to the contractor so that future jobs can benefit from lessons learned.

Types and forms of schedules

There are different types of projects, with various needs, and they require different types of schedules. A schedule can take various forms and include various levels of detail. The way the schedule is intended to be used determines both its form and its level of detail. A master construction schedule, for example, is very detailed and is used by the contractor as a baseline overview of the entire job and as a tool to control the job. It is not necessary for every member of the team to have the master schedule, however. A **summary schedule**, typically in the form of a much simpler bar chart, is developed to show progress in broad areas or milestones and can be used for presentation purposes to the owner or funders. Often the GC will use a summary schedule for subcontractors and suppliers too. Once construction begins, updated short-term schedules are put together on a regular basis. These schedules, called **look-ahead schedules**, are typically developed every two or three weeks by the superintendent using data provided by the foreman and each subcontractor.

The owner of a large project may not be interested in knowing when each room is being framed or the drywall installed. A simple summary schedule that identifies milestones may be sufficient. Bar charts (also called Gantt charts) are very good for this. The superintendent, on the other hand, *does* need to know when the framing and drywall take place; his need is for a far more detailed construction schedule that will provide up-to-date information on work progress. Due to these different needs, schedules are shown in different ways; some of these ways are simple, some are complex. There are three that are especially common, however, and these are the ones on which we will focus:

- **Bar charts (Gantt charts)**
- **Network diagrams**
- **Network bar charts (time-scaled logic diagrams)**

Let's see how these schedules compare.

Bar charts (Gantt charts)

Bar charts are simple graphic representations of schedules that relate progress of activities to a timeline. This type of schedule was developed in 1910 by a mechanical engineer named Henry Gantt (hence the term "Gantt chart") and was used on large infrastructure projects such as the Hoover Dam. Bar charts are readily adaptable to construction scheduling and, despite serious limitations, are widely used today because they are so easy to understand. Figure 19.1 shows a basic bar chart for a landscape project. It was drawn using Excel.

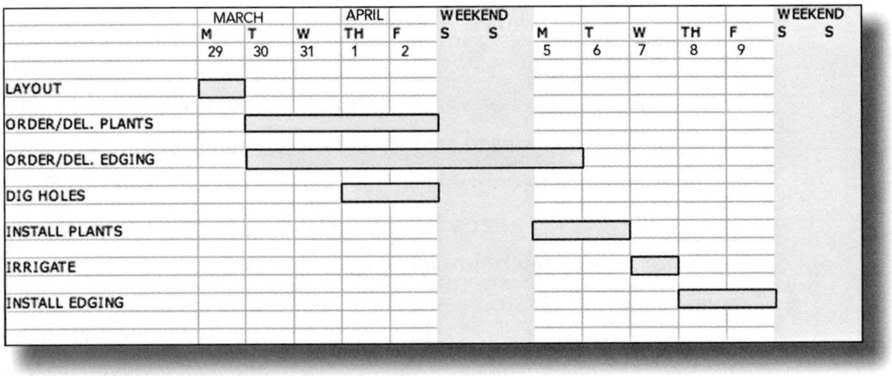

	MARCH			APRIL		WEEKEND							WEEKEND	
	M	T	W	TH	F	S	S	M	T	W	TH	F	S	S
	29	30	31	1	2			5	6	7	8	9		
LAYOUT														
ORDER/DEL. PLANTS														
ORDER/DEL. EDGING														
DIG HOLES														
INSTALL PLANTS														
IRRIGATE														
INSTALL EDGING														

Figure 19.1. Bar chart

You can see that a bar chart can be simple and even easily drawn by hand. With readily available software packages for scheduling, however, charts are more often computer generated. Figure 19.2 shows the same landscape project bar chart drawn using Microsoft Project 2007, which is a commonly used program.

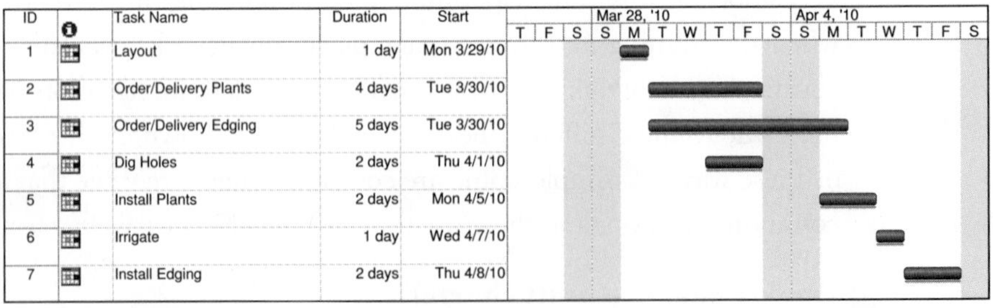

ID	Task Name	Duration	Start
1	Layout	1 day	Mon 3/29/10
2	Order/Delivery Plants	4 days	Tue 3/30/10
3	Order/Delivery Edging	5 days	Tue 3/30/10
4	Dig Holes	2 days	Thu 4/1/10
5	Install Plants	2 days	Mon 4/5/10
6	Irrigate	1 day	Wed 4/7/10
7	Install Edging	2 days	Thu 4/8/10

Mar 28, '10 — Apr 4, '10
T F S S M T W T F S S M T W T F S

Figure 19.2. Bar chart using Microsoft Project 2007

On both bar charts, project tasks run vertically down the left side of the chart and the task duration (the time it takes to complete the task) is identified along the horizontal axis. A horizontal bar or line is drawn opposite each activity to represent when the activity is scheduled to start and when it is scheduled to finish.

The charts are read from the top down and left to right. In our example, we can see that the project is scheduled to begin Monday, March 29, with the task "Layout" and on Tuesday the contractor will place orders for both the plants and the edging material. Delivery of the plants is due Friday, April 2, with the edging following on Monday, April 5. The contractor has scheduled digging the holes to finish in time for the delivery of plants. Installation of the plants begins Monday, April 5, followed by irrigation and installation of the edging. The project is due to be completed on Friday, April 9. (Note that task durations are identified in work days, not calendar days. Saturdays and Sundays are shaded and may or may not be scheduled as workdays.)

Many activities (tasks) in construction depend on each other and must be completed in a particular sequence or order. For example, you can't put the reinforcing steel in a foundation trench before the trench is dug, or start to frame the walls before the foundation is poured. In our example, the plants can't be installed before the holes are dug. Although the bar chart can show these activities and identify start and completion dates, it leaves many unanswered questions about the interrelationship of the various activities. For example, can a task be started early? What happens if there is a delay in starting a task? Will other tasks be impacted? And, critically, what is the effect on the overall schedule if an activity is delayed? These questions cannot be answered with a simple bar chart and this is one of its most severe limitations.

Our landscape example is a simple one. Projects that are more complicated present more challenges and it is easier to see the limitations of a simple bar chart in those cases. Although one can readily identify start and finish dates for individual activities, other essential data are unknowable from these charts.

Though the information that can be presented in a simple bar chart is quite limited, this type of schedule does have advantages. Bar charts are easy to create and to read and everyone can see the progress of work at a glance; they are therefore useful as presentation tools to owners and others. As already mentioned, simple bar charts can fairly quickly and easily be created by hand and provide the contractor and others with a quick overview of timelines and activity progress.

Network diagrams

Network diagrams (also called precedence, logic, or PERT diagrams) are both a tool for making scheduling decisions and a way of representing the schedule. They are an improvement on the bar chart because they show the dependencies between activities. Network diagrams show the flow of activities and their logical ties to each other as networks instead of items along an axis. Computer-based network diagrams can also be expanded to provide early and late start and finish times, slack in the schedule and, critically, the impact on other activities and the project as a whole if an activity is delayed.

Network diagrams were developed in the 1950s simultaneously by the DuPont Company to track plant maintenance and by the U.S. Navy to assist in the development of the Polaris missile system. By the 1960s, network diagrams were beginning to be used in construction; they are now very common, in large part due to the prevalence of computer technology.

There are different ways of drawing network diagrams but the most popular is called **activity-on-node** (AON). In this type of diagram, activities are represented by a single node (either a box, circle, or bar with milestones identified as diamonds) and these activity nodes are connected by arrows to other activity nodes with which they have a dependency. Figure 19.3 shows what a basic activity-on-node network diagram of our landscape project looks like. Again, this was developed using Microsoft Project 2007.

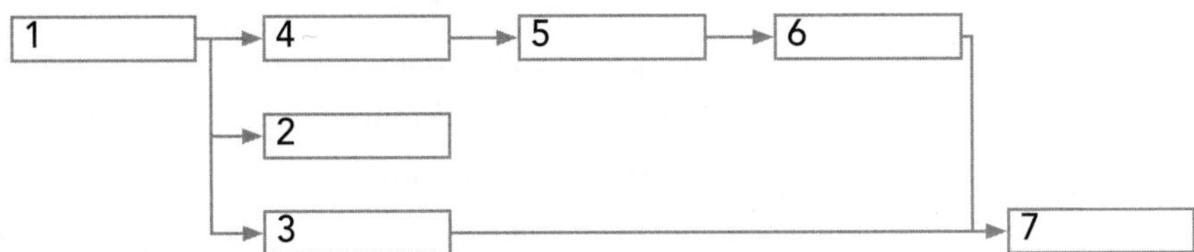

Figure 19.3. Landscape project network diagram based on Microsoft Project 2007

Each box represents one of the seven broad activities identified by the contractor as necessary to complete the work, from layout through the installation of edging. Some activities are linked because they have some kind of dependency. For example, activities 2, 3, and 4 are all dependent on activity 1 and cannot begin until it is finished. Activity 6 is dependent on the completion of activity 5 and must be finished before activity 7 can begin. This network diagram gives the user a quick overview of dependencies but otherwise isn't terribly helpful because it contains so little information. The software used to develop it, however, has the capability of expanding the amount of information available to the viewer. Figure 19.4 shows an expanded form of the network diagram, with additional information including the activity name, start date, and other data helpful to the contractor.

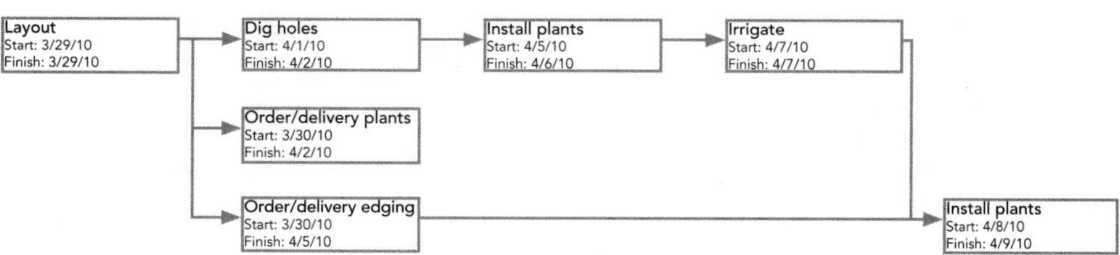

Figure 19.4. Landscape project expanded network diagram based on Microsoft Project 2007

Network diagrams can also be developed using the critical path method (CPM). A **CPM network diagram** identifies those critical activities that *must* be completed on time or the project will be slowed down. A project's **critical path** is the unbroken chain (or chains) of activities that have no extra time built in and which, if delayed, will cause the entire project to be delayed. Because of their importance to job completion, contractors typically pay special attention to the progress of critical activities. There is a scheduling method used to identify the critical path and we'll talk about this a bit more in the next chapter.

A network diagram is used as the basis for creating other, computer-based schedules, such as the network bar chart, which we'll look at next. Even with the extensive use of computers, however, network diagrams are not simple: they are time consuming to create and difficult to read. Though many managers use them to control a job, they are not particularly suitable as a quick and easily understandable presentation tool or for general use on a jobsite, as many people cannot accurately read them.

Network bar charts (time-scaled logic diagrams)

Because network diagrams allow for enhanced graphic representation of dependencies, they can provide valuable information for the general contractor. Unfortunately, many people can't read them! Conversely, the bar chart is clear and easy to read but gives insufficient information regarding linkages between activities. **Network bar charts** solve the problems inherent in network diagrams and simple bar charts by using interconnected lines and arrows to show how tasks relate to each other along a timeline. A time-scaled network bar chart can identify start times and completion dates, and indicate which tasks depend on each other and which tasks can happen at the same time. It answers the question of whether an individual activity delay will cause an overall project delay.

Let's take a look at our landscape project again, this time as a network bar chart (see Figure 19.5).

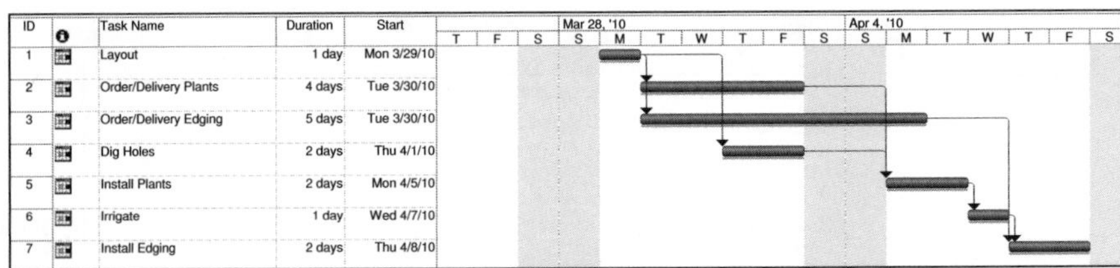

ID	Task Name	Duration	Start
1	Layout	1 day	Mon 3/29/10
2	Order/Delivery Plants	4 days	Tue 3/30/10
3	Order/Delivery Edging	5 days	Tue 3/30/10
4	Dig Holes	2 days	Thu 4/1/10
5	Install Plants	2 days	Mon 4/5/10
6	Irrigate	1 day	Wed 4/7/10
7	Install Edging	2 days	Thu 4/8/10

Figure 19.5. Landscape project network bar chart using Microsoft Project 2007

Here's how to read the example: as we have learned, project tasks or activities, and their identification numbers (in our example, called activity ID), are shown on the left side of the chart, followed by the scheduled duration in days for each, and their scheduled start time and finish time. Dates are shown horizontally along the top of the chart and each activity is represented by a bar that extends for its expected duration.

Activities are listed in chronological order and each activity is connected with lines and arrows to other activities. Activities that are linked mean that they have a dependency. For example, the arrows tell us that "*Order/Delivery Plants*" (activity 2) and "*Order/Delivery Edging*" (activity 3) are both linked to and dependent on "*Layout*" (activity 1). The arrows tell us that they cannot begin until activity 1 is complete. Similarly, activities 2 and 3 are linked to other activities that occur later in the project. Activities can be linked to each other in different ways and we'll learn more about this important characteristic in the next chapter.

Through symbols or color, many network bar charts also indicate to the contractor which activities are along the critical path. For most jobs, this is crucial information that can provide the contractor with direction regarding where to put resources in order to make up for project delays.

Due to the ability of network bar charts to show a wide range of data, their flexibility regarding how they can be formatted, and the wide use of personal computers, network bar charts are now extensively used in the industry. The accuracy of computer-based schedules is dependent on the data that is input, however, and most schedulers begin the process of developing computer-based schedules by drawing the linkages by hand. The process of creating the schedule is the subject of the next chapter.

---

1 C.C.Myers, Inc., Rancho Cordova and Anaheim, CA

2 Peter Philips, "Lessons for post-Katrina reconstruction," October 6, 2005, Economic Policy Institute Briefing Paper #166.

Chapter Vocabulary

Activity-on-node (AON) – a type of network diagram in which individual activities are represented by a node connected by arrows to other activities with which they have a dependency.

Bar chart (Gantt chart) – a simple graphic representation of a schedule that relates the progress of activities to a timeline.

Bid schedule – a rough schedule, based on project milestones, that a contractor puts together in order to develop his or her bid.

Critical activities – activities that if delayed, will delay the entire project.

Critical path – the unbroken chain (or chains) of activities that have no extra time built in and which, if delayed, will cause the entire project to be delayed. The critical path determines the minimum project duration.

Critical path method (CPM) network diagram – a network diagram that identifies activities that must be completed on time or the entire project will be delayed.

Gantt chart – see Bar chart.

Look-ahead schedules (three-week, updated schedules) – short-term schedules, typically developed every three weeks by the superintendent, that provide information on upcoming activities.

Master construction schedule – a comprehensive and detailed schedule the contractor develops and uses as a baseline overview of the entire job and as a tool to control the job.

Means and methods – the contractor's approach to meeting the design requirements.

Milestone – an important event that indicates an event or point in time. Typical milestones are bidding, award of contract, notice to proceed, start of construction, substantial completion, and owner move-in.

Network bar chart – a diagram that uses interconnected lines and arrows to show how tasks relate to each other along a timeline.

Network diagram (precedence diagram, logic diagram, PERT diagram) – a tool for making scheduling decisions and a way of representing a schedule that shows the flow of activities and the dependencies between them.

Schedule – a timetable, typically shown in graphic form, that describes the order in which project activities will happen, details how long each activity will take, and tracks the progress of the work.

Summary schedule – a schedule developed to show progress in broad areas or milestones that can be used by those not requiring detailed information, such as an owner or funder. Summary schedules are typically in the form of a bar chart.

Test Yourself

1. Why would a contractor need to develop a schedule before submitting a bid?
2. What is the difference between a master construction schedule and a summary schedule? How is each used?
3. How does the schedule assist the contractor in controlling a job?
4. What are three commonly used graphic forms used for schedules?
5. Which form of schedule is the most easily understood and is therefore often used for presenting information to owners?
6. How do network diagrams solve the primary problem with bar charts?
7. What do the arrows indicate in Figure 19.5?
8. What is one advantage and one disadvantage of network diagrams?
9. How does a network bar chart address the problems of bar charts and network diagrams?
10. What happens if an activity along a project's critical path is delayed?

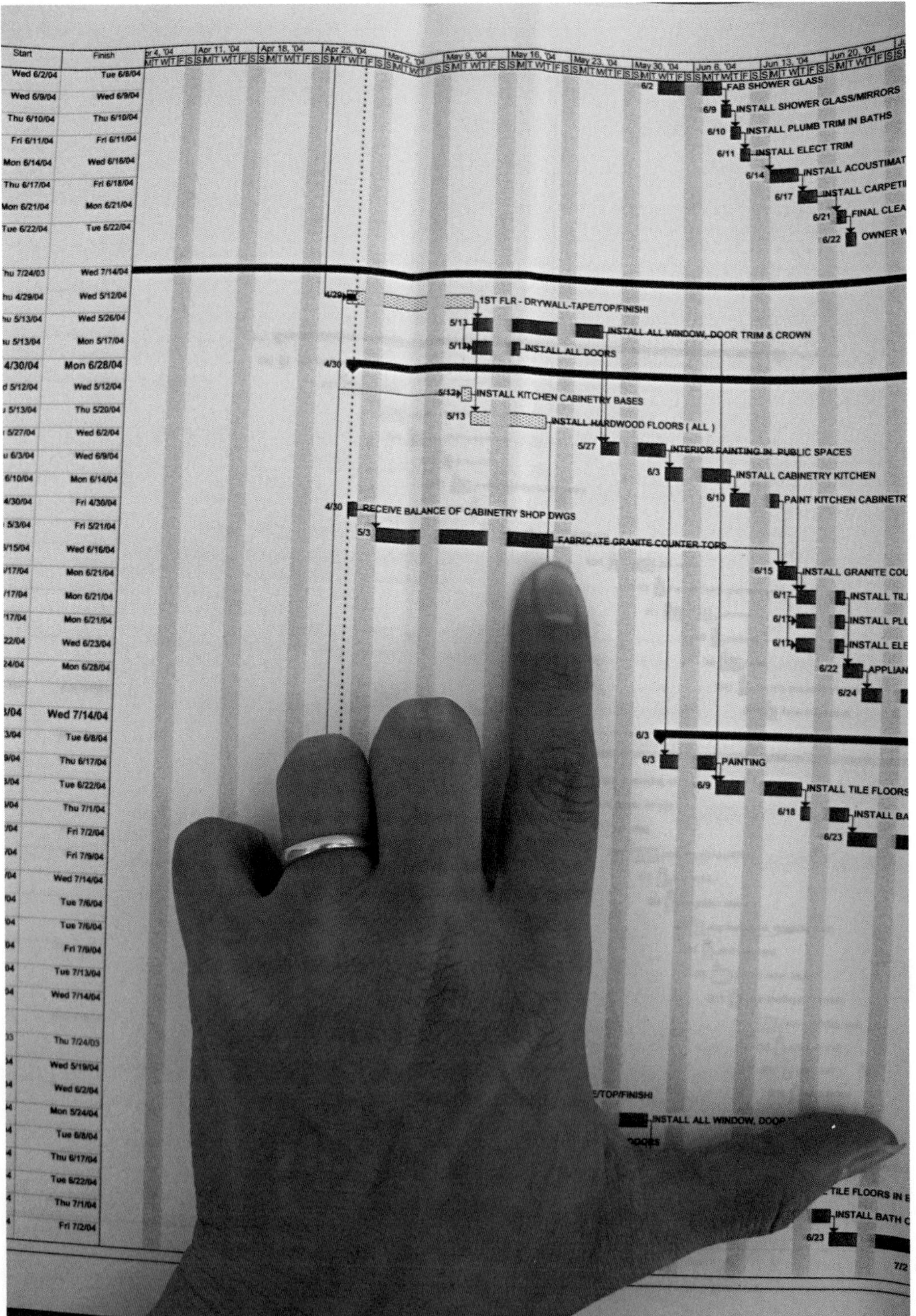

Andrea Young

CHAPTER 20

Creating and Using the Schedule

We've learned that the master construction schedule is a refinement of the schedule the contractor developed as part of the bidding process. Although the bid schedule (which is typically based on a time frame set by the owner) provides the contractor with sufficient information to create a bid estimate, it is insufficiently detailed to serve the needs of the job once the project is under construction. The contractor needs a detailed master schedule to highlight:

- Day-to-day work activities on the jobsite with the start and finish dates for activities and the relationship between activities
- Milestone events and procurement deadlines
- Administrative activities such as inspections and testing deadlines

Steps in creating a schedule

We know that the three schedule types that we looked at in the last chapter – bar charts, network diagrams, and network bar charts – serve different purposes and are different ways of graphically representing scheduling information. In this chapter, we'll learn the basics of how a contractor might approach the development of a schedule and take a look at its components: *activities*, *logic*, and *durations*. Finally, we'll explore the techniques for linking activities into a network diagram and look at updating and using a schedule.

There are several steps required to develop a master construction schedule. For the contractor, these include:

1. Identify work activities (tasks)
2. Sequence the work activities
3. Estimate activity durations
4. Hand-draw the schedule
5. Input the data into a computer

Let's see what's involved in each of these steps. Although some of this work is done during the bid preparation phase, more detailed analysis by the contractor's team occurs after the contract is awarded, as it plans for construction.

Step 1. Identify the project work activities

The first step in creating the schedule is for the contractor to create a list of work activities that can be organized and controlled. The way that activities are organized is called the **work breakdown structure** (WBS) and this breakdown provides the framework for the rest of the scheduling steps. The amount of detail in the work breakdown reflects several things, including the complexity of the project, what aspects of the work are to be subcontracted, and the amount of control desired by the general contractor.

Before we look at the work breakdown structure, let's make sure we understand what an activity is. All construction projects are made up of a variety of activities or tasks to be completed and these activities must be organized in a logical way. In Chapter 3, we looked at the characteristics that define projects. Projects are made up of activities, but both share the following characteristics:

- They consume time.
- They consume resources such as labor, equipment, and/or money.
- They have a definable scope of work: "Paint 1st Floor" and "Excavate Foundation Trench" are examples; each of these activities is a project within the whole project.

- They have a beginning (called the *start*) and an end (called the *finish*). The activity "Form Concrete Wall," for example, starts with formwork and ends when the forming is complete.
- They are measurable and the progress of work must be trackable so that the contractor can clearly determine if an activity (and the project) is on schedule.

The CSI MasterFormat that we learned about in Chapter 16 provides a commonly used format that divides activities into broad work divisions such as Concrete, Masonry, Finishes, Plumbing, and so on. The WBS might identify these very broad categories of tasks, but only on the smallest jobs are they sufficient. With most jobs, a more detailed breakdown of activities is necessary. This is to provide a manageable way to subcontract parts of the work and to control the progress of the work.

Let's look at two ways of identifying a work breakdown: a rough, broad scope breakdown and a more detailed, narrower scope breakdown. In Figure 20.1, the top bar (task 2) identifies *Complete Garage* as a single activity with a duration of 30 days and a construction time frame that starts on March 22 and finishes at the end of April; this as a very broad activity. The absence of detail shown in this figure is not sufficient for most jobs, however. Below it, the activities required to complete the garage have been broken into a narrower set of tasks: *Order/Delivery Brick, Excavation, Footing/Foundation*, etc. It's easy to imagine how this more detailed breakdown might provide more useful information regarding progress of the work.

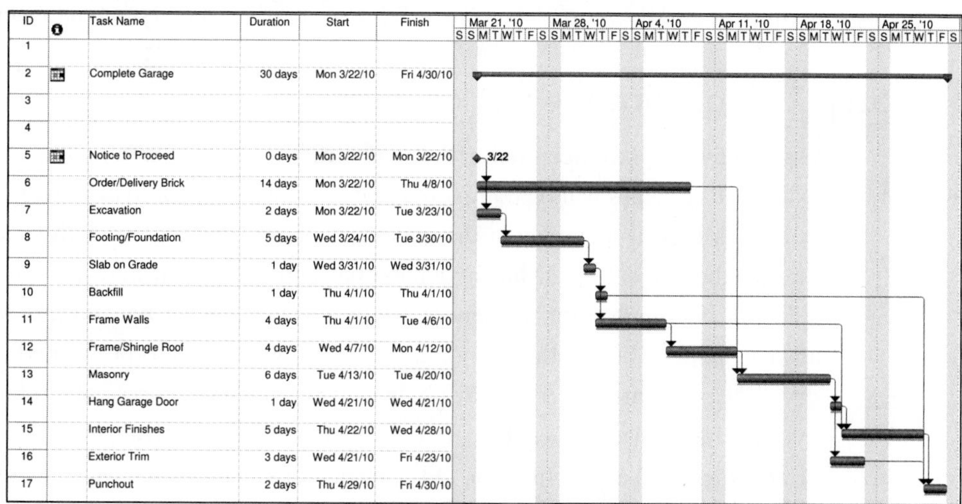

ID	Task Name	Duration	Start	Finish
1				
2	Complete Garage	30 days	Mon 3/22/10	Fri 4/30/10
3				
4				
5	Notice to Proceed	0 days	Mon 3/22/10	Mon 3/22/10
6	Order/Delivery Brick	14 days	Mon 3/22/10	Thu 4/8/10
7	Excavation	2 days	Mon 3/22/10	Tue 3/23/10
8	Footing/Foundation	5 days	Wed 3/24/10	Tue 3/30/10
9	Slab on Grade	1 day	Wed 3/31/10	Wed 3/31/10
10	Backfill	1 day	Thu 4/1/10	Thu 4/1/10
11	Frame Walls	4 days	Thu 4/1/10	Tue 4/6/10
12	Frame/Shingle Roof	4 days	Wed 4/7/10	Mon 4/12/10
13	Masonry	6 days	Tue 4/13/10	Tue 4/20/10
14	Hang Garage Door	1 day	Wed 4/21/10	Wed 4/21/10
15	Interior Finishes	5 days	Thu 4/22/10	Wed 4/28/10
16	Exterior Trim	3 days	Wed 4/21/10	Fri 4/23/10
17	Punchout	2 days	Thu 4/29/10	Fri 4/30/10

Figure 20.1. Broad and narrow WBS using Microsoft Project 2007

On larger projects, the WBS will often be even further broken down. For example, a contractor might choose to schedule HVAC (heating ventilating, air conditioning) not as a single broad activity, but according to more specific work tasks: *fabricate duct, install main trunk, install branch lines, install diffusers*. The more detailed breakdown will provide the subcontractor with helpful scheduling information, and the general contractor with a better tool for measuring progress.

Identifying project activities is not always simple. The activity list needs to be sufficiently detailed so that the contractor can track progress but not so detailed that every nail is counted and there is information overload. For example, the framing of a simple house could be one activity, "frame." Or it could be broken down into a few more activities such as "frame floor," "frame loadbearing walls," " frame roof," "frame interior partitions." It could also be broken down into needless detail: "place mudsill on foundation," "mark location of foundation bolts," "drill 5/8" hole," "apply sill sealer," "put mud sill on top of foundation and sill sealer," and so forth.

It is good practice to keep trades separate and to identify more than a single activity per trade. For example, instead of "electrical" being identified as a single activity throughout a project, having additional details such as "sub-slab electrical," "rough electrical," "electrical service," and "finish electrical" linked to a time frame provides the subcontractor with more direction and the general contractor with more control. Maybe even that level of breakdown is insufficient for the job and additional detail is required, such as "electrical rough-in 1st floor" or "finish electrical east wing."

Sometimes a summary WBS is provided to the superintendent and the subcontractor and the more detailed breakdown is used for day-to-day management.

Step 2. Sequence the work activities

Once activities have been defined, the contractor must determine the order in which the activities will be completed. This is called **task sequencing.** Every task has a logical sequence in the overall work and, unless an activity starts or finishes the project, each has activities that come before it and activities that follow it. Although some sequences are pre-determined or natural (excavation always happens before the foundation is built; walls need to be framed before drywall can be installed, etc.), the contractor usually has a choice about how activities relate to each other. The goal of the scheduler is to arrange the sequence of activities to meet the timeline in the most efficient and effective way possible.

What criteria will the contractor use to determine the sequence of activities?

There are several guidelines:

- Some activities have a *natural sequence*, such as the example that excavation always happens before the foundation can be built.
- Some activities can be run *concurrently*. For example, rebar can be laid in trenches while the excavation is being completed; the contractor can start pulling electric wires before all the studs are in place.
- Some activities have a relationship because it's more efficient and less costly to link them. For example, multiple tasks may share a piece of equipment.
- Some sequences might result in unsafe working conditions and are to be avoided. For example, on a multi-story building, it may be hazardous for a crew to be working below another due to the potential for falling debris from the work above.
- Sometimes the size of the work area limits the tasks that can be done at any one time.
- Most contractors have preferences regarding how to sequence certain activities. For example, is the gravel for the slab on grade being installed before or after the underground plumbing?

Part of the job of sequencing is to determine which activities have direct links to other activities – to determine the *exact* relationships between activities. The contractor needs to answer the following questions:

- Which activities *immediately* precede (come before) each activity?
- Which activities *immediately* succeed (follow) each activity?
- Which activities can occur at the same time (concurrently)?

An activity that comes immediately before another activity is called a **predecessor activity**. An activity that immediately follows another activity is called a **successor activity**. What does *immediately* mean? On a typical construction project, drywall certainly follows building the foundation, but it does not immediately follow. Drywall, however, does **immediately** follow rough wiring; it is therefore drywall's predecessor. Similarly, excavation precedes wall framing but does not *immediately* precede it. The predecessor to wall framing is more likely to be building the foundation. The links between activities and their predecessors and successors is critical information when constructing the schedule.

How the activities link together, their sequencing, is called the **job logic**.

Activity durations, which the contractor determines next, are based on the logic.

Step 3. Estimate activity durations

Duration is the amount of time required to complete an activity. Although the contractor can use any units for duration, on most projects time is defined in days. This is because the activities on most projects are too broad to fit conveniently into hourly units but too small to fit into weekly units on the master schedule. (Sometimes projects require such precision that the contractor develops specialty schedules that identify work in hourly units. There are also situations in which the use of an expensive piece of equipment – a tower crane, for example – might need to be scheduled in 15-minute increments! But these are not typical situations.)

After determining the sequence of activities, the contractor identifies the duration for each activity. The primary considerations used for determining activity durations are the total available time, the available resources (labor and equipment), and expected levels of productivity (the quantity of work that can be completed in a certain amount of time).

Usually, the contractor starts with the anticipated completion date and, based on job logic, blocks out "windows" within which specific tasks must be completed. Working with subcontractors, the general contractor identifies start dates and finish dates for each activity within the given time window. The contractor's goal is to maximize the efficient allocation of labor and equipment to complete the activity within the identified number of days. Activity durations are estimates and can be inaccurate for many reasons: maybe the crews aren't as productive as anticipated, perhaps there is a lack of necessary equipment or an earlier activity was delayed, maybe too many workers are assigned at one time and got in each others way, or maybe the quantity of work was miscalculated. These factors can all impact duration.

Step 4. Hand-draw the schedule

Although some contractors immediately sit at their computer and enter the work breakdown structure and duration data and let the software create the schedule, this is often a mistake. Hand-drawing a rough network diagram on a large piece of paper using erasable markers or sticky labels so that the overall logic can be viewed enables the contractor to identify possible gaps or mistakes in how the job has been laid out and enables adjustments to be made before construction begins. The computer cannot pick up mistakes in logic; inputting data from a hand-drawn rough schedule leads to a more accurate final schedule. As the contractor draws the rough schedule, he gains a thorough understanding of how the project will proceed.

As we learned in the last chapter, in an activity-on-node (AON) type of network diagram, which is the easiest to draw by hand, activities are represented by nodes (which can be circles, squares, or bars). Each node represents a single activity and is connected by arrows to those with which it has an immediate dependency. Viewed as a whole, these dependencies, or linkages, make up the job logic. The process of drawing the linkages provides the contractor with an opportunity to develop a job logic that best meets his goals and those of the project.

The contractor draws the project diagram in the same way he will build the structure: from the ground up. The first activity starts the diagram on the left side of the page and the final activity completes it on the right. All activities identified in the WBS are drawn.

There are certain conventions that the contractor follows when developing his network diagram:

- Every activity – except the first (start) and the last (finish) – has at least one predecessor activity (an activity that immediately precedes it) and at least one successor activity (an activity that immediately follows it).
- Each node represents only one activity.
- No activity can start until predecessor activities have been completed or have met a linkage requirement. For example, the rough wiring can be started when the wall framing is 75 percent completed. There is a way to show this relationship in an AON diagram.
- Diagrams are not drawn to scale.
- Diagrams are developed (and read) left to right and top to bottom.

Figure 20.2 shows how a simple network diagram is constructed. The contractor created a list of job activities (identified by letters) and indicated the predecessor activity or activities associated with each.

Activity	**Predecessor Activity**
Contract	None
A	Contract
B	Contract
C	A, B
D	A, B
E	D
F	C, E

Signing the contract starts the job and tasks A and B happen right away; they are concurrent activities. Signing the contract is the predecessor to both A and B which means that neither activity can begin until the contract is signed.

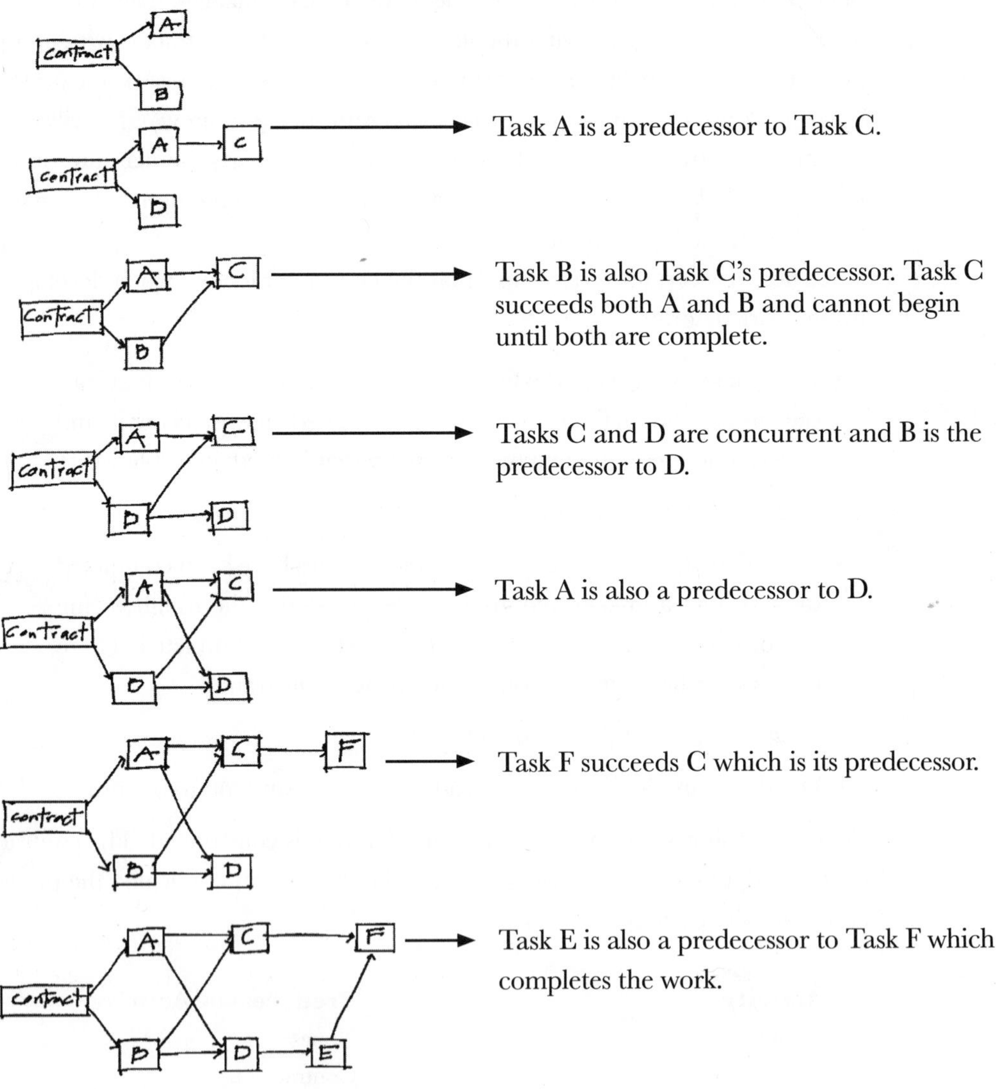

Figure 20.2. Development of a simple network diagram

Once the hand-drawn network diagram is complete, the contractor reviews the activities and linkages to be sure that the logic is correct and that no activities are missing. At this point in the process, it's relatively easy to identify problems and make corrections.

When the contractor is satisfied with the logic and adjusted the network diagram as necessary, the scheduler is ready to enter the data into the computer. Software programs are sophisticated and have the capability of displaying schedules with varying levels of detail. This means that the contractor can customize schedules for various purposes, thus improving his or her ability to manage and control the job.

Software – There are many software programs that take input data to create a variety of schedule types. Some programs have the capability of handling huge volumes of data and have extensive performance capability. Oracle's *Primavera P6*, for example, is designed to handle almost any type or size project, can group different projects together, and displays a large variety of reports and other related graphic representations. The capability of this software is reflected in its cost and it is not typically used on small projects. In this text, we use *Microsoft Project* 2007, a much less costly program that is well suited to smaller projects. Much of its popularity is due to its ease of use, similarity to other Microsoft programs, and relatively low cost.

Linking activities

The network diagram in Figure 20.2 represents activities that all show a *finish-to-start* link from a predecessor activity to a successor activity. That means that no activity can begin until its predecessor activity (or activities) has been completed.

The real world is complicated, activities don't always neatly fit into a finish-to-start model, and the project manager will require a more detailed diagram to identify the different linkages possible between activities. Finish-to-start linkage is only one of four ways that activities can be linked to each other. Possible linkages include:

- Finish to start
- Start to start
- Finish to finish
- Start to finish

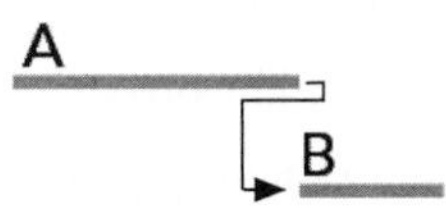

Finish to start: An activity cannot begin until its predecessor activity is finished. Our diagram indicates that Activity B can start when Activity A is completed. For example, in the garden, the tree can't be planted until the hole has been dug. This is the most common way that activities are linked to each other.

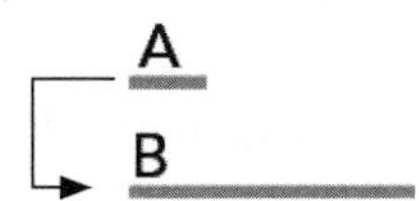

Start to start: Activities can begin together. For example, if Activity A is Start Project and Activity B is Project Management, then project management begins as soon as the project does.

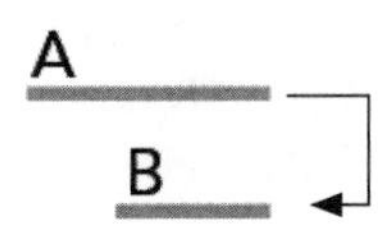

Finish to finish: Links are used to show the relationship between the completion of activities. For example, when Forming the Slab on Grade is complete, the Reinforcement can also be finished.

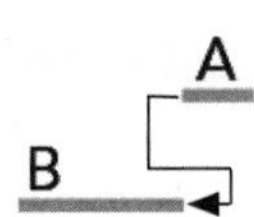

Start to finish: The start of one activity forces the end of a second activity. If Activity A is Grand Opening and Activity B is Advertising for that event, then when the grand opening starts, the advertising ends.

Figure 20.3. Types of activity linkages

Setting up a diagram to show accurate activity linkages provides a more realistic picture of what will happen in the field and these linkages will be incorporated into the contractor's final schedule.

Critical path scheduling

On every job, there is a set (or multiple sets) of activities that have the potential to create bottlenecks in the work and delay the entire project. For example, if the bricks don't arrive on time, the mason can't begin the task of laying them and the entire project could therefore be delayed. Or the specially sized windows can't be manufactured as anticipated, delaying other tasks, which, in turn, delay the whole project. These activities are termed critical and every project contains several such activities or series of activities.

One of the major advantages of network diagrams is that they can depict a project's **critical path**. The *critical path* identifies activities that, if delayed, will delay the entire project. Thus, if any task on the critical path finishes late, then the whole project will also finish late. There is always at least one critical path.

Figure 20.4 shows the critical path identified by a darkened line. There are three separate activity paths on this diagram. The top path extends from *Start* through tasks 1, 2, and 3 and is completed at the *Finish*. The middle path (which can occur at the same time as the top path) also begins at *Start* but extends through tasks 4, 5, and 3 to the *Finish*. The bottom path includes two tasks, 6 + 3. Durations (in days) are indicated under each task and identify the minimum number of days necessary to complete each task. For example, task 1 requires

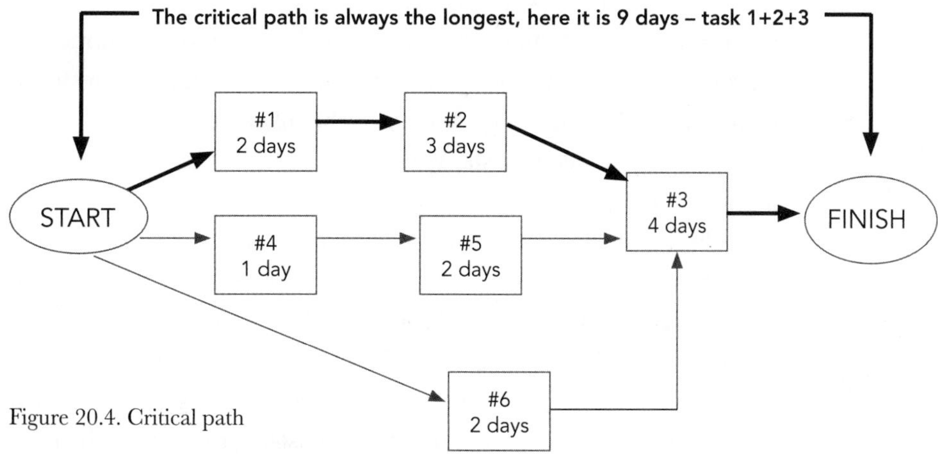

Figure 20.4. Critical path

2 days to complete; task 2 requires 3 days; task 4 requires 1 day, and so forth.

In our example, the top path requires 9 days to get from *Start to Finish* (2 days + 3 days + 4 days). The middle path requires only 7 days (1 day + 2 days + 4 days) and the bottom only 6 days (2 days + 4 days). This means that the overall project can't possibly be completed in less than 9 days and any delay along the top path will extend that time. Conversely, any delay up to two days along the middle path will not impact the overall schedule and a delay up to 3 days along the bottom path can be absorbed without delaying the entire job. (These extra days are called **float**. Activities on a critical path have no float.)

Using little information (activities, logic, and durations), computer software can identify a project's critical path, thus giving the contractor important information, including early and late start and finish dates, available float for each activity, the critical path(s) through the project, and the minimum total project duration. Although some might argue that having a computer calculate the critical paths is the fastest and most accurate way to proceed, others argue in favor of using the hand-drawn network diagram to calculate the critical path manually. The reasoning is that if a contractor doesn't fully understand where data come from, it's difficult to assess the accuracy of the computer output. Explaining how to calculate the critical path is beyond the scope of this text, but there are several good resources. One of the most helpful is *Computer Integrated Construction Project Scheduling*, by John Buttelwerth (Prentice Hall, 2005).

Updating the schedule

As we have seen, the schedule is one of the important tools used by the contractor to control and manage a job. It is not possible for a contractor to manage a project effectively unless he understands how work is progressing. This is accomplished by comparing a baseline schedule of target dates with an updated (and dated) schedule that shows what level of progress has been made in meeting those targets.

The contractor's first task is to create a baseline schedule from the master construction schedule that identifies planned start and finish dates. This baseline remains unchanged throughout the project and is useful as a historical document for future projects. The baseline schedule can be a simple bar chart, but the key is that it reflects accurately the contractor's original time projections. Updated schedules are compared to the baseline to see how the job is going.

Figure 20.5 is the baseline schedule for the garage that was shown in Figure 20.1. The timeline runs horizontally across the top, tasks are identified vertically on the left; projected activity duration and start and finish dates are shown on the right vertical columns. Each activity is represented by a horizontal bar and is linked to its predecessor and successor activities (if there are any). The garage project starts on March 22 with one milestone - *Notice to Proceed* - and two activities - *Order/Delivery Bricks* and *Excavation* which are scheduled to take 14 days and two days respectively. (Note: tasks 1, 2 and 3 are all scheduled to begin March 22 but because there are linkages from 1 – *Notice to Proceed* – to the other two we know that they cannot begin unless or until 1 happens. Because *Notice to Proceed* is a milestone - an event without a duration - it is identified, not with a bar, but with a diamond. *Punchout* is the final activity and is scheduled to complete the job on April 30.

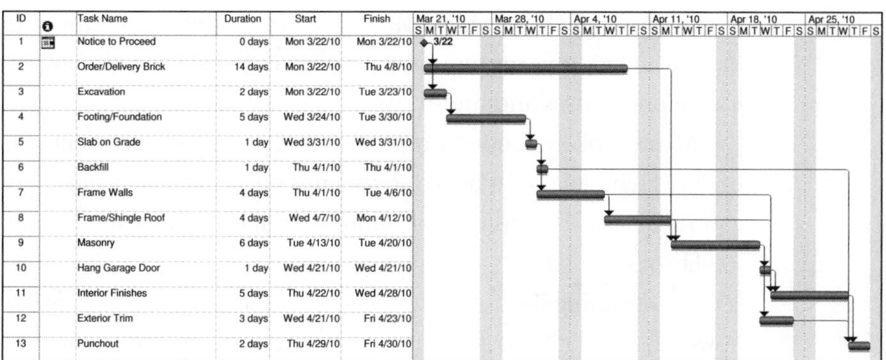

ID	Task Name	Duration	Start	Finish
1	Notice to Proceed	0 days	Mon 3/22/10	Mon 3/22/10
2	Order/Delivery Brick	14 days	Mon 3/22/10	Thu 4/8/10
3	Excavation	2 days	Mon 3/22/10	Tue 3/23/10
4	Footing/Foundation	5 days	Wed 3/24/10	Tue 3/30/10
5	Slab on Grade	1 day	Wed 3/31/10	Wed 3/31/10
6	Backfill	1 day	Thu 4/1/10	Thu 4/1/10
7	Frame Walls	4 days	Thu 4/1/10	Tue 4/6/10
8	Frame/Shingle Roof	4 days	Wed 4/7/10	Mon 4/12/10
9	Masonry	6 days	Tue 4/13/10	Tue 4/20/10
10	Hang Garage Door	1 day	Wed 4/21/10	Wed 4/21/10
11	Interior Finishes	5 days	Thu 4/22/10	Wed 4/28/10
12	Exterior Trim	3 days	Wed 4/21/10	Fri 4/23/10
13	Punchout	2 days	Thu 4/29/10	Fri 4/30/10

Figure 20.5. Garage baseline schedule

On a regular basis, an updated schedule is created, identifying how much of each activity has been completed to date. On a computer-based bar chart, tasks that have not yet started or been completed are shown as solid lines; tasks, or portions of tasks, which are completed are indicated with a split bar. Figure 20.6 shows the work progress on the garage as of April 8 (indicated by a dotted vertical line). If we compare this schedule to the baseline we can see that there's been a delay and that the delivery of the bricks is now expected to take 17 days instead of 14. All other tasks appear to be on schedule: task 1 (*Notice to Proceed*) through task 7 *(Frame Walls*) have been completed and are so indicated with a split bar and, on the left, a checkmark; task 8 *(Frame/Shingle Roof*) has just begun and all other tasks are yet to start. Because the masonry can't begin until the brick is at the jobsite, however, the anticipated project completion date is now May 3 instead of April 30 and the start dates for tasks 8-13 have all been adjusted accordingly (and automatically).

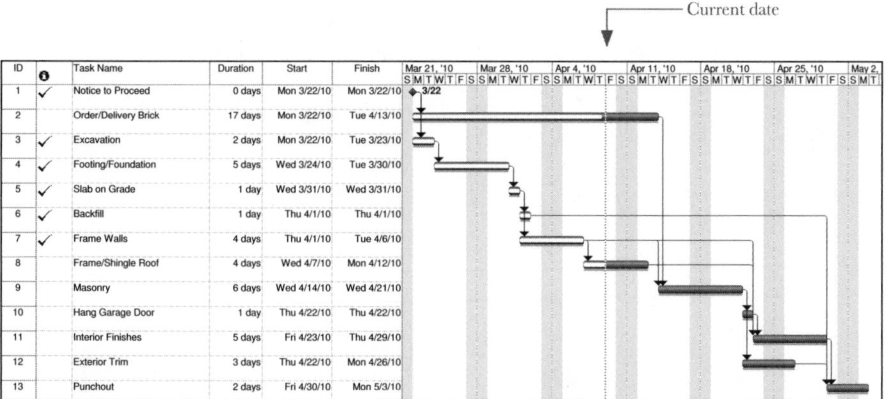

ID		Task Name	Duration	Start	Finish
1	✓	Notice to Proceed	0 days	Mon 3/22/10	Mon 3/22/10
2		Order/Delivery Brick	17 days	Mon 3/22/10	Tue 4/13/10
3	✓	Excavation	2 days	Mon 3/22/10	Tue 3/23/10
4	✓	Footing/Foundation	5 days	Wed 3/24/10	Tue 3/30/10
5	✓	Slab on Grade	1 day	Wed 3/31/10	Wed 3/31/10
6	✓	Backfill	1 day	Thu 4/1/10	Thu 4/1/10
7	✓	Frame Walls	4 days	Thu 4/1/10	Tue 4/6/10
8		Frame/Shingle Roof	4 days	Wed 4/7/10	Mon 4/12/10
9		Masonry	6 days	Wed 4/14/10	Wed 4/21/10
10		Hang Garage Door	1 day	Thu 4/22/10	Thu 4/22/10
11		Interior Finishes	5 days	Fri 4/23/10	Thu 4/29/10
12		Exterior Trim	3 days	Thu 4/22/10	Mon 4/26/10
13		Punchout	2 days	Fri 4/30/10	Mon 5/3/10

Figure 20.6 Progress schedule

Software such as Microsoft Project can produce a variety of useful, and more detailed, reports and can track the progress of costs, equipment, administrative procedures and more.

Most publicly funded projects, and many private projects, specify that an updated schedule be attached to the monthly progress payment requests. Many contractors find it easier and, ultimately, more useful to update the schedule weekly or even daily.

Determining the amount of work completed isn't as easy as it might appear, however, and the contractor has to determine how to define progress. Is it best to identify percentage of work completed or number of days remaining? Will completion be based on the quantity of materials installed or the percentage of labor hours expended? For example, if 50 percent of the bricks have been installed, does that translate to 50 percent completion? Maybe the remaining bricks have extensive cutting that will result in a reduction in worker productivity. Although the contractor can use any approach to defining progress, the most common method is percent complete based on actual quantities physically in place.

The reader is encouraged to review Chapter 18 in which we discussed how the contractor uses schedules to monitor, evaluate, and control the project.

Chapter Vocabulary

Activity – an individual task.

Activity-on-node (AON) – a type of network diagram in which individual activities are represented by a node connected by arrows to other activities with which they have a dependency.

Concurrent – activities that can happen at the same time.

Duration – the amount of time required to complete an activity.

Finish to finish – a project dependency in which one task cannot be completed before some other task has also been completed.

Finish to start – the most frequently-used type of project dependency, in which one task cannot be started before some other task has been completed.

Float – the amount of time that a task can be delayed without affecting the completion time of the overall project.

Job logic – the sequence of activity linkages.

Precedence diagram (network diagram, logic diagram, PERT diagram) – a tool for making scheduling decisions and a way to represent a schedule showing the dependencies between activities.

Predecessor activity – an activity that comes immediately before another activity.

Start to finish – a type of project dependency, in which one task cannot be completed, until some other task has been started.

Start to start – a type of project dependency, in which one task cannot be started until some other task has also been started.

Successor activity – an activity that comes immediately after another activity.

Task sequencing – the order in which work activities are scheduled for completion.

Work breakdown structure (WBS) – the way that work activities are organized.

Test Yourself

1. Activities are not typically definable. True or false?
2. Sequencing identifies a job's logic. True or false?
3. What is a linkage? Give an example.
4. What is a work breakdown structure? What is the difference between a broad-scope work breakdown and a narrow-scope work breakdown? Give an example of each.
5. What does natural sequencing mean?
6. Why should a contractor hand-draw a schedule?
7. What does a start-to-start linkage mean? Give an example.
8. What does it mean if an activity is determined to be critical?
9. When is a baseline schedule used?
10. Finish to start is the most common relationship link. True or false?

Andrea Young

CHAPTER 21

Buying Out the Job: Subcontracting

As we've already learned, on typical projects most of the physical work is done not by the general contractor but is subcontracted out to specialty contractors. (Remember: a subcontractor is defined as a contractor who is hired by another contractor.) Because so much of a project may be completed by subs, it's not hard to see why the general contractor would be concerned about their performance; a single subcontractor who fails to show up on time, or does shoddy work, or is uncooperative can wreck a job. For this reason, the process of hiring and managing subcontractors eats up a large portion of the general contractor's time and energy.

It is the owner's responsibility to define the extent of the general contractor's work (scope of work), which is detailed by the drawings and the specifications. It is the general contractor's responsibility (and right) to determine how the work will be completed and which parts of the job will be subcontracted to others. The general contractor, therefore, determines the scope of work for the first-tier subcontractors who, in turn, determine the scope of work for their subcontractors.

Subcontractor scope of work

As soon as the general contractor knows that he will be bidding for a job, he develops a plan that identifies which portions of the work will be self-performed and which portions will be subcontracted to others. There is no right or wrong way to designate subcontracted work; it depends on the skills and workload of the contractor, the type and complexity of the job, and the requirements of the owner.

Subcontractors are hired to provide different levels of service. Sometimes it makes sense (for any number of reasons) for the general contractor (or even the owner) to purchase the materials and have the subcontractor do just the installation. Sometimes subcontractor services include everything to complete their portion of the job: labor, equipment, and materials. And in some cases, the subcontractor is asked to design and install a system on performance requirements. Examples of this are a specialized type of heating system or a building's elevator system. The general contractor makes the determination regarding what services the subcontractors will be hired to provide.

Once the contractor has determined what work will be subcontracted, he develops separate bid packages that identify the individual "scopes" for which subcontractors will be hired. There are separate bid packages for each piece of work that will be bid by, awarded to, and performed by separate subcontractors.

The general contractor is careful to ensure that nothing is omitted, that every task is covered by somebody. Additions that are part of the contractor's obligations but weren't included in any subcontractor's scope of work can be expensive for the general contractor who will have to get the work done somehow. Similarly, if there are overlaps in the work, this too can cause delays and unnecessary costs.

The term buying out a job (also referred to as procurement) refers to the process of securing subcontractors and issuing purchase orders for materials and equipment. Buying out subcontracts follows a process much like bidding for the prime contract and results in the GC and subcontractors entering into contracts. (Note: the GC has a separate contract with each subcontractor.)

Solicitation of bids

Once the general contractor has developed the sub's packages, he solicits bids. Although subcontractors identify potential work the same way that general contractors do – through advertisements in journals, newspapers, and other sources – many general contractors use preferred subcontractors and issue invitations to bid (requests for quotations) to multiple potential bidders for each work package. The general contractor will want to get at least three bids, ideally five or six, from specialty contractors for each scope of work.

Review of bids

While the general contractor is putting prices together for self-performed work, the specialty subs who intend to bid are pricing their scopes. After receiving the sub-bids, the general contractor analyzes them to be sure they are complete. This involves comparing bids for different scopes of work to ensure that no details have fallen through the cracks (for example: is the plumber responsible for vent stack boots at the roof or are they included in the roofer's bid package?). Although some bids come in early, the general contractor typically receives subcontractor quotes just before he submits his bid. The GC inserts the winning sub-bid in the final bid estimate that goes to the owner, but details with the winning subcontractor won't be confirmed until after the GC knows the job is his.

Awarding subcontracts

Negotiations are typically part of the buying-out process and can include price, scope of work, payment, warranty issues, and more. Clarity regarding goals and objectives for both the general contractor and the subcontractor are part of the negotiations. Before signing a subcontract, the GC needs to be satisfied that everything is covered and all important issues are included. Some concerns might be:

- Clarification regarding responsibility for items that can fall between trades. For example, some plumbers expect to set and hook up dishwashers; on other jobs, the plumber hooks it up, but the general contractor sets it in place first.
- Responsibility for securing necessary permits
- The schedule, along with notification requirements regarding start dates
- Process and procedures for pricing and completing change orders
- Consequences for failure to perform
- Clean-up responsibilities and expectations
- Procedures for warranty work

When the general contractor is satisfied that all the details have been addressed, the subcontract is finalized.

Subcontract agreements tend to be much shorter than prime contracts and typically combine the agreement and conditions into a single form. Several standardized contracts are available, including from the American Institute of Architects and the Associated General Contractors. There are less formal, off-the-shelf subcontract forms available, and some contractors prefer to create their own. As with the prime contract, subcontracts include the signatures of the parties, description of the scope of work, and references to the appropriate contract documents. Figure 21.1 is an example of a subcontract.

The terms of the general contractor's contract with the owner are typically incorporated into subcontracts. For example, if the general contractor has a clause in her contract with the owner that says progress payments will be made every five weeks, then the subcontracts will likely have the same clause. Another example: if the prime contract requires a three-year warranty on all work, the general contractor is going to require that subcontractors have a similar warranty. Terms included in one contract (such as the prime contract) that are referenced in a subcontract are called flow-through clauses. (Language of a flow-through clause might be as follows: "*the provisions of the prime contract, plans, specifications, addendums, change orders, and other documents that comprise the prime contract are incorporated into this subcontract* ") Similar terms are typically included in the second-tier subcontracts as well.

The subcontract, just like the prime contract between the general and the owner, is a serious legal document and both parties should be fully aware of their rights and obligations under the contract. Having an agreement that clearly lays out the expectations for each party will reduce confusion, misunderstandings, and potential disputes.

SUBCONTRACTOR'S AGREEMENT

(Between Subcontractor and General (Prime) Contractor)

This Subcontract Agreement is entered into this _____ day of ________________, ________, in ________________, California.

Subcontractor, ________________________________, hereinafter called "Subcontractor" agrees to provide the following described labor, materials and construction in accordance with plans and specifications as may be referred to herein by reference, upon the following described property.

Owner: ________________ (Owner's Name) Lender: ________________

________________ ________________ (Lender's Address)

________________ ________________ (City, State & Zip)

LEGAL AND COMMON DESCRIPTION OF JOBSITE: ________________________________

Prime Contractor, ________________, hereinafter called the "Contractor," agrees to pay to the Subcontractor for the satisfactory performance of the Subcontractor's work the sum of $________________ (________________ **dollars**) in accordance with the following terms and conditions.

DESCRIPTION OF WORK: ________________________________

SCOPE OF WORK: All work necessary or incidental to complete work for the project in strict accordance with this subcontract and all terms and conditions hereof and as more particularly specified as (in): ________________

with the following additions or deletions: ________________

OTHER SPECIAL PROVISIONS: ________________

SCHEDULE OF PAYMENT(S): ________________

and for extra work, if any, as follows: ________________

This schedule of payment(s) is strictly construed and is not conditioned upon Contractor(s) first being paid by owner. Contractor's obligation to pay Subcontractor when payments are due is independent of Contractor receiving payment from owner.

TIME AND SCHEDULING WORK: Subcontractor shall not deliver any materials to the jobsite or commence work until notified to do so by Contractor. Subcontractor shall commence work within ______ days after written notice from Contractor. After Subcontractor commences work, he will then complete the work within approximately _______ working days thereafter, subject to excusable delays. Working days are defined as Monday through Friday, inclusive, holidays excluded. Scheduling of work, as provided for in this subcontract, is based on acceptable industry standards.

The subcontract provision for price and time included herein shall be void at the option of the Subcontractor, if Subcontractor is not called upon to commence work within six (6) months from the date of the signing of this contract. Should this situation arise, subcontractor is relieved of any responsibility to perform under this subcontract agreement and shall be held harmless by Contractor of any liability associated with his/her refusal to perform. Any amounts that are not paid when due shall bear interest at a rate of 1 1/2% per month until paid or the maximum rate permitted by law, whichever is higher. The Contractor's supervisor of this project shall be the designated agent for the Contractor.

SOLE AGREEMENT: This Agreement, including all terms and conditions hereof, is expressly agreed to and constitutes the entire Agreement as of this date. No other Agreement or understandings, verbal or written, expressed or implied, are a part of this Agreement unless specified herein.

IN WITNESS HEREOF the parties have accepted this Agreement the day and year first above written.

Subcontractor: ________________ Contractor: ________________

By: x ________________ (Title) By: x ________________ (Title)

License Number: ________________ License Number: ________________

Figure 21.1.GC/subcontractor agreement by Builder's Books, Inc.

Often the owner reserves the right to approve or reject the contractor's selection of subcontractors. The AIA General Conditions states the following regarding this issue: "*the Contractor, as soon as practicable after award of the Contract, shall furnish in writing to the Owner or the Architect the names of persons or entities … proposed for each principal portion of the work. The Architect may reply within 14 days to the Contractor in writing stating whether the Owner or Architect has any reasonable objection to any such proposed person or entity … Failure … to reply within the 14-day period shall constitute notice of no reasonable objection.*" (AIA document A201-2007, Article 5.2.1)

Bid shopping – Bid shopping is a familiar term to many, but what exactly does it mean? This is an unethical practice that involves a contractor sharing subcontractor bids with other subcontractors in an effort to get lower prices. Bid shopping (also called price shopping) may occur before or after bids have been submitted to the GC and may be instigated by either the sub or the GC. The impact of bid shopping is that a contractor who engages in this practice may have a difficult time getting solid, well-priced bids on future jobs. If you're a subcontractor and you know the general contractor bid shops, what would you do next time they ask for a price?

Criteria for selecting subcontractors

Although some general contractors select subcontractors solely on the basis of price, this approach is often shortsighted and may not, in fact, result in the best price. The ideal subcontractor has other strengths that could be of great benefit to the general contractor and to the job. In analyzing a potential subcontractor's bid, there are three broad criteria that the general contractor typically uses to evaluate a subcontractor (much the same as an owner uses to evaluate a potential general contractor):

- Business competency
- Trade competency
- Price

Business competency

Business competency refers to the subcontractor's business and financial background and status.

- How long has the subcontractor been in business? A new business is at higher risk for failure than one that has shown itself to be resilient.
- Does the specialty contractor have sufficient working capital (cash reserves)? The general contractor wants to feel confident that if something unexpected happens, the sub will be able to weather the storm financially.
- Does the sub have a reputation for communicating effectively and promptly? The general contractor wants a subcontractor who responds quickly to issues and problems.
- Does the subcontractor qualify to purchase the required bonds? Most jobs that require general contractors to purchase bonds have similar requirements for the subcontractors.
- Does the sub have appropriate insurance coverage?
- Does the sub pay his subcontractors and suppliers on time? If the sub isn't paying suppliers and sub-subcontractors, there may be a holdup on the job. In addition, this could put the owner at risk of a lien placed on the property. (See Chapter 24 for information on mechanic's liens.)
- The subcontractor represents the general contractor on the job: does he look and act professional?

Trade competency

The general contractor is especially interested in the subcontractor's ability to produce a product of expected quality within the project schedule.

- Can the subcontractor deliver the required quality? Is he experienced with similar jobs? The general contractor wants to be sure that the subcontractor is "up to the job."
- Does the potential subcontractor deliver his work on time? The last thing the contractor wants is a sub who doesn't live up to scheduling agreements. A sub who is delayed may delay others on the job and may, in fact, delay the entire job.
- Does the sub supply jobs with appropriate labor? If the number of workers is too low, the job cannot be completed efficiently. The gen-

eral contractor wants assurance from the subcontractor that his job will get the necessary workers.

- Does the sub complete a job before moving to the next one? The GC doesn't want to fight to get the sub to complete her work.
- What sort of attitude does the sub bring to the job? A construction project is a team effort. Uncooperative, unhelpful contractors can negatively impact the entire job.
- Is the subcontractor appropriately licensed? Subcontractors without the required license can cause a job to be shut down.
- Is the sub responsive to claims that his work was not up to the requirements of the contract? If the sub is uncooperative about doing follow-up warranty work, the general contractor is going to hear about it from an unhappy owner. Poor warranty response can sour an otherwise positive experience for an owner and do serious damage to a contractor's reputation.

Price

On most projects, subcontractors quote a bid price. Typically, the contractor who submits the lowest bid gets the job. But, as noted earlier, the lowest bidder is not always the best, or even, ultimately, the lowest bidder! A very low bid can result in expensive change orders and/or efforts to reduce quality and workmanship. If a bid comes in way too low, the general contractor must take an especially close look to make sure the bidding subcontractor included everything and omitted nothing. A low bid – say 15 percent lower than the rest – is great. A bid that comes in 20 or 30 percent lower than everyone else's may be incomplete, or the contractor may have made an estimating error. Items that are missed in a bid will either generate change orders or create an environment in which the subcontractor might try to make up for underestimating the costs. This can result in poor quality and/or delays to the job that can be costly. Sometimes unscrupulous subcontractors deliberately under-bid a job in order to be awarded the contract and then make up for it with expensive change orders.

Because working cooperatively, with mutual respect, is important, many general contractors have a list of preferred subcontractors with whom they have developed good working relationships. In turn, subcontractors who feel fairly treated and respected are more likely to give the general contractor favorable pricing on future jobs. But there are also disadvantages to using the same subs on every job. If other subcontractors feel as though a general contractor has a "stable" of subcontractors that she always uses, then they might be discouraged from bidding, assuming that subcontractor "A" will get the job anyway. This can result in less competitive bidding and perhaps higher costs. In addition, if a subcontractor feels that repeat business from a general contractor is unlikely, he may not give his all if he does get the job.

Advantages of hiring subcontractors

Contracting is a risky business and successful contractors are skillful at identifying effective ways to reduce their risk as much as they can. Hiring subcontractors reduces a contractor's risk in two major ways:

- Shifting financial risks and costs
- Added quality and efficiency

Let's look at how specialty subcontractors help the general contractor in these ways.

Shifting financial risks and costs

Hiring a subcontractor has the advantage of shifting some of the financial risks of doing a project off the shoulders of the general contractor and onto those of the subcontractor. When a general contractor enters into a contract with a specialty contractor, that specialty contractor is now assuming the risk of properly pricing the labor, the material, and the equipment for their portion of the construction. If there is a mistake in the bidding, the risk belongs to the subcontractor.

Financial risk is also present for the general contractor due to the need to provide warranty services following the completion of a project. The subcontractor carries the responsibility for this warranty on her portion of the job, thus reducing the general contractor's liability.

It is very costly for a contractor to keep expensive workers with specialty skills on the payroll. If the general contractor can rely on others to perform some parts of a job, the GC does not have to maintain specialized labor and can thus reduce his overhead costs.

Added quality and efficiency

Specialty contractors provide crews that are experienced in a particular skill and can typically perform a task better and more efficiently than the general contractor. Because someone who repeats a task over and over is generally more productive as well as more experienced than someone who does not, using subcontractors typically results in both lower costs and a higher quality job.

Other advantages of subcontracting

In addition to the benefit to individual contractors, subcontracting also benefits the construction industry as a whole. When a general contractor subcontracts out some of the work on a project, it provides opportunities for smaller contracting firms. Many specialty contractors don't have the volume of business to qualify for the bonds typically required for large projects. Subcontracting means, therefore, that a greater number of smaller firms, with limited capital, can enter the field. This creates a more vibrant and competitive industry, which in turn, means better pricing and a reduction of overall construction costs.

Disadvantages of hiring subcontractors

Subcontracting is not all positive; there are several disadvantages both for general contractors, and, ironically, for the specialty contractors themselves. Some of the challenges to the general contractor in hiring subcontractors include the following:

- Administrative and oversight challenges
- Financial challenges
- Quality assurance

Administrative and oversight challenges

The presence of subcontractors on a project adds administrative and oversight complications for the general contractor. Each sub represents a separate business, with their own perspective and way of doing things, with their own employees, and with differing company goals and objectives. The general contractor is responsible for ensuring that a potentially disparate group of subcontractors is adequately coordinated and scheduled and that lines of communication are open and clear with each.

There can be practical oversight problems too. On big jobs, subcontractors can get in each other's way physically if their work is not carefully coordinated. In addition, the work of most subcontractors is directly linked to that of another contractor, so if there is a slowdown with one subcontractor, others down the line may be impacted. For example, if the electrical subcontractor has not finished installing the rough wiring, the drywall subcontractor will be unable to complete his work. And what if there is damage done on a site with multiple subs? It may be almost impossible for the general contractor to sort out the responsibility and therefore sort out who has to pay the costs.

In addition, and importantly, the general contractor is responsible for the work of the subcontractors so she must be on constant alert for poor workmanship and must be prepared to address problems quickly and effectively.

Financial challenges

Contracting with specialty firms can cause financial problems for the general contractor who may face delays in getting monthly progress payments from an owner. A payment that is delayed does not relieve the general contractor from his obligation to pay the subcontractors on time.

Let's look at the Superior Construction Company again to illustrate why this might be a problem. Superior is the general contractor and is owed $100,000 by the owner for the work that was completed this month. Superior owes $60,000 to their subcontractor ABC Contractors. Superior's contract with ABC states that ABC will be paid the same day that Superior is scheduled to be paid by the owner, which is the fifteenth of every month. (Although the general contractor typically adds a clause into subcontracts delaying payment to the subs until the contractor receives payment from the owner, in some situations the subcontractors may not agree to this clause.) For whatever reason, the owner delays payment to Superior and a check has not arrived by the fifteenth. Superior has to get a loan from the bank in order to honor their obligation to pay ABC on that date.

Quality assurance

When a contractor is required to be licensed, it provides some level of assurance to the public that she is qualified. But as we've just seen, many states have few, or no, licensing requirements for the specialty trades, so it can be difficult to determine qualifications. It also takes little money to start a subcontracting business, which means that in some situations it's easy to hire subcontractors without the necessary experience or knowledge. These problems are exacerbated if the general contractor is hiring subcontractors for a job that is located outside their normal location.

Procurement of materials

The purchase of building materials and products is a necessary part of any construction project. The general contractor purchases the materials required for self-performed work; the subcontractors are typically responsible for purchasing the materials to be installed as part of their work. Sometimes the general contractor buys materials or products that have special manufacturing or delivery requirements, called long-lead items. Early procurement ensures that materials that might take a long time to be manufactured are delivered close to the time that they are needed. Examples of materials that might require long-lead times include elevators, specially designed windows, and exotic granite countertops.

Sometimes materials are ordered very early in the construction process in order to lock in pricing too. Structural steel and special mechanical systems are examples.

Delivery of materials has several implications for the general contractor and project costs: the GC doesn't want to add congestion to the worksite; stored materials require protection from weather, damage, and theft; and in many contracts, the GC needs to pay suppliers as soon as goods reach the site but might not get paid by the owner until materials are incorporated into the project. In addition, many jobsites do not have excess area that can be used for material storage.

The normal procedure for the procurement of materials is for the contractor (or subcontractor) to select a material supplier. (Suppliers provide materials and equipment but not labor to a job.) After choosing a supplier (typically based on reliability and ability to quote reasonable costs), the contractor asks for firm prices before placing an order. Typically, the contractor tries to lock in prices for as long a period as possible to ensure against unexpected price increases.

Material orders are typically placed using a short contract form called a purchase order. Purchase orders (POs) are contracts for materials (and sometimes special labor) and reference project documents. POs may be standardized or written in-house, but all include important terms in addition to quantities and price such as taxes and freight, discounts and price escalation, submittal requirements, and a schedule. Purchase orders are dated and numbered and tracked via a log. The superintendent is responsible for verifying that material deliveries are scheduled, and that materials arrive as ordered and undamaged.

Generally, each contractor is responsible for ordering the materials necessary for his portion of the work and ensuring that materials are on the jobsite when they are needed.

Procurement of materials begins early in the process and typically continues throughout construction.

Chapter Vocabulary

Bid package (bid documents) – the collection of documents (including drawings, specifications, agreement forms, general conditions, and other documents) used to make and obtain bids and to define the requirements of the work and the process that the contractor must follow when submitting a bid. When a construction contract is executed, most of the bid documents become contract documents.

Bid shopping – an unethical practice that involves a contractor sharing subcontractor bids with other subcontractors in an effort to get lower prices.

Buying out the job (procurement) – the process of finalizing subcontracts and issuing purchase orders for material and equipment.

Flow-through clause – terms included in one contract that are incorporated into a subcontract.

Long-lead items – materials or products that have special manufacturing or delivery requirements that involve extra time.

Procurement – see Buying out the job.

Purchase order – a short contract form typically used to order materials and equipment.

Scope of work – the work as detailed by the drawings and the technical specifications.

Supplier (vendor) – a company that manufactures, distributes, or supplies products and services to a contractor.

Test Yourself

1. Who determines the general contractor's scope of work?
2. The general contractor has selected an electrical subcontractor that the owner doesn't like. Does the owner have the right to reject the GC's choice? Explain.
3. What is the difference between business competency and trade competency?
4. Why would the general contractor be careful to make sure that no pieces of the work are omitted from the subcontractors' scopes of work?
5. Why would the general contractor be concerned about a subcontractor's financial resources?
6. How might a subcontractor's poor attitude about warranty work impact the general contractor?
7. What is the risk to the general contractor in hiring the lowest bidder?
8. Why are flow-through clauses used?
9. What is a purchase order and when is it used?
10. Identify three issues that a general contractor would be concerned about when negotiating subcontracts.

Andrea Young

CHAPTER 22

Changes in the Work

Contract documents are never 100 percent complete or error-free; mistakes and omissions are inevitable. This means that changes are part of virtually all projects. Those that result in adjustment in the project cost or completion time are formally incorporated into the construction contract. Changes are difficult, however. They can cause anxiety, time, money, and, potentially, disputes and even lawsuits. One way to ensure that the process of making changes is as smooth as possible is to outline clearly, at the beginning of a project before the changes occur, the procedures and guidelines for handling them.

The term **change order** (CO, also called a **modification**) refers to a written agreement between the owner and the contractor (and, on most jobs, the architect) to make a change in the terms of the contract. A change order is one of the only legal means to change a contract after the award of a contract. (Changes made to contract documents during the bid period but before the award of a contract are called addenda.)

Change orders can be initiated by anyone on the team (but are typically issued by the architect), and are signed by the owner, the architect, and the contractor. Change orders are issued when there is a change in the scope of work, a change in cost, or a change in time. Changes can be **additive** – they add to the contract – or **deductive** – they reduce the scope, cost, or time. A change order is *not* required when the change is minor and does not involve a change in time or cost. An example of a minor change is the selection of a different paint color (assuming the change is made in a timely fashion). Of course, such changes should still be documented; but without an impact on project time, cost, or scope, there is no impact on the contract, and thus no change order.

Change order procedures are, ideally, outlined as part of the construction contract, and procedures for making changes are reviewed during the pre-construction conference by the contractor, the subcontractors, the architect, and the owner so that all parties understand the process.

Situations that cause changes in the work

Construction is a complicated business and contractors should expect some changes to be made on a job. These changes are not necessarily because architects don't know what they're doing, or because owners change their minds. Although both of these can, and do, occur, there are many other things that can cause changes to a project. Some of these situations can be managed by the contractor and some occur outside her control. Here are some common reasons for changes:

- **Errors/omissions in, or lack of coordination among contract documents**
- **Changes by the owner**
- **Cost changes due to market forces**
- **Delays**
- **Changes in sequencing of the work**
- **Cost-cutting adjustments**
- **Changes required by testing or inspection agencies**
- **Unexpected underground conditions**

See how each of these might result in cost or time changes.

Errors or omissions in, or lack of coordination among contract documents

Architectural drawings that show the layout of a structure must be coordinated with the drawings developed by the consultants, including the civil, structural, electrical, and mechanical engineers. It is not uncommon for a detail shown on one drawing or document to be inadvertently left off another. For example, a particular valve might be shown on the drawings but not mentioned in the specifications. Sometimes a detail has simply been forgotten and will need to be added to the work. Sometimes information is shown in multiple places and a later change made in one place doesn't show up on another. If the contractor bid one thing, but the owner expects another, a change order may need to be issued.

Changes by the owner

There are many situations in which an owner changes his mind regarding a design or a specification. For example, the owner wants to add a skylight in the bedroom, or decides to upgrade the carpet in the hallway. Projects are not set in stone: according to most contracts, the owner has the *right* to make changes (it's his building, after all) and the contractor has the *obligation* to complete reasonable changes.

Cost changes due to market forces

Changes in cost can add to or reduce project costs. For example, if the architect has specified a high-end Italian marble that is no longer available, the necessary substitution may result in a price adjustment.

Delays

Typical causes of delays include slow processing (of requests for information, of submittals, of decision-making) by any of the parties, interference and changes in the progress of the work, and severe weather. A delay that occurs along a project's critical path (see Chapter 20) will impact the completion date for a project and can cause serious conflict between the contractor and the owner. It is in the contractor's best interests to document carefully and thoroughly the causes for any delays.

Changes in sequencing of the work

The contractor has the right to determine how and in what order a project will be completed. But an owner might request, for example, that the sequence of construction be adjusted. (Maybe he needs to have the garage completed before the house, for example.) If the contractor agrees, this kind of change might result in an adjustment in completion time, and a change order is issued.

Cost-cutting adjustments

Owners often request that the contractor suggest ways to save money, either in initial construction costs or over the entire life of the building. Cost-cutting typically impacts purchase and/or installation costs. Value engineering is broader and takes into account the costs to operate and maintain a product or system over its anticipated life. A value-engineering study (typically conducted by the contractor or construction manager) might determine that a product that costs more initially may save money in the long run.

Why would the contractor be suggesting such changes now, rather than earlier? Although in some contract types, a contractor is brought on board at the time of design and can provide constructability reviews, in a lump-sum contract, a given contractor is not in a position to suggest such cost-cutting changes until after his bid is accepted and he is awarded the project.

Changes required by testing or inspection agencies

Regulatory or inspection agencies such as building or fire departments can make adjustments to a project, even after permits have been secured, if they believe that the public health and safety will be compromised. For example, a project's building inspector requires the contractor to substitute a higher grade conduit than was specified, or the fire chief insists on an additional smoke alarm at the top of the stairs, even though the alarm wasn't shown on the drawings. If the adjustment wasn't caused by contractor oversight, it will result in a formal change.

Unexpected underground conditions

Sometimes, through no fault of the contractor or the owner, conditions on a project site are different from what is shown on the drawings. For example, a project is being built on an archeological site that is only revealed during excavation and the project must be suspended while the remains are investigated. The discovery of an unexpectedly high water table, contaminated soil, or unknown utility lines are other examples of circumstances that can result in additional costs.

What is the process for making changes?

Anyone can initiate changes on the construction team – the owner, the architect, the general contractor, or the subcontractors. The process is slightly different depending on whether changes are initiated in the field or by the owner or architect.

Changes initiated in the field

Many change orders start out as a confusion or question about something in the field. Let's say that the pipes in the first-floor lobby are not shown in the drawings as being enclosed in conduit. The subcontractor questions whether this was intentional. There are established procedures that are typically followed in response to such a confusion. They are:

1. The subcontractor submits a **field question** to the GC, requesting clarification.
2. The GC may simply be able to answer the subcontractor's question. But if the GC does not know, a **request for information** is sent to the architect. (Note: subcontractors do *not* contact the architect without first going through the general contractor. This ensures that the GC stays in the loop and maintains control over the job.)
3. In some cases, the architect can immediately clear up the confusion, or the architect might determine that there was a mistake or omission in the drawings and that a change is required. The owner doesn't want a contractor to go ahead and make a change, however, without first knowing what the change will mean in terms of time or cost. The architect submits a **request for a change proposal** to the GC, asking for the impacts of the proposed change. Architectural sketches or other materials are attached to the request.
4. The contractor reviews the architect's request and, in consultation with the appropriate subcontractor(s), determines the impacts of the proposed change. When the contractor has gathered all the data, the contractor issues a **change proposal** (sometimes called a change order proposal) to the architect for review. (See Figure 22.1 for an example of a change proposal.)
5. The architect and the owner review the contractor's change proposal to determine what action to take. Not all change proposals are accepted: sometimes the contractor's proposed costs are too high; sometimes the owner decides against making the change. Proposals may be rejected or returned to the general contractor for adjustment.
6. Once a change proposal has been approved by the owner and the architect, the architect converts the proposal into a change order. As with proposals, change orders are logged in and tracked; they are typically numbered chronologically. An example of an executed **change order** is shown in Figure 22.2.

7. When signed by the owner, the architect, and the contractor, the change order becomes a formal part of the contract between the contractor and the owner. Work on the change can now proceed.

Changes initiated by the owner or architect

When an owner or architect initiates a change (for example, changing the countertops from tile to corian), there is no field question. The process begins with the request for a change order proposal to the contractor, which, as before, formally requests that the contractor determine the price for a change. The architect and owner review the contractor's change order proposal and do one of three things:

1. They determine that the costs (and sometimes schedule impacts) are satisfactory and they want the contractor to go ahead and make the change. In this case, the architect issues a change order as described.
2. The owner thinks the costs are too high and asks for an adjustment.
3. They decide against making the change (the tile will stay).

Let's assume that the architect realizes that a change needs to be made to the foundation and drainage detail on a project. He draws sketches to provide the contractor with information that will enable him to price and complete the work; in response, the contractor investigates and submits a change order proposal. An example of a contractor's change order proposal is shown in Figure 22.1.

Note that the proposal is dated and numbered (this is necessary so that it can be tracked), and briefly describes the work ("*Adjust foundation and drainage detail per architect's sketch SK3 and SK4*"). All relevant documentation, including the field question that initiated the change order or, as in this example, a request for a change order proposal from the architect, plus any additional information such as sketches are referenced.

In the contractor's proposal, direct costs for labor are itemized and costs for supervision, labor burden, and overhead and profit (O&P) are added as percentages. To the subcontractor's costs ($1,529), the general contractor adds a markup (in this example, 5%). Ideally, supervision, labor burden, O&P, and subcontractor markups are agreed to by the owner and the contractor early in the job and are the same on all change orders during the project. This eliminates the need for the contractor to justify these costs for each separate change order. The architect reviews the contractor's proposal and completes a change order based on the data provided by the contractor. In our example, the price adjust-

SUPERIOR CONSTRUCTION COMPANY
Address, Telephone number

PROJECT:	Main Street Office Building	JOB NO:
OWNER:	Geo. Smith Developers	
ORIGINATING DOCUMENT:	Change Order Request #1,	May 15, 2010 per Architect

CHANGE ORDER PROPOSAL NUMBER: 1 Date: May 17, 2010

DESCRIPTION OF WORK:

Adjust foundation and drainage detail per architect's sketch SK3 & SK4 dated May 15,2010

ATTACHMENTS:

Sketch # 3 and Sketch #4 dated May 15, 2010

ESTIMATE SUMMARY:		Subtotal	Total
Labor (SCC)		$1,450	
Supervision	15%	$ 217	
Labor burden	51%	$ 850	
Subtotal		$2,517	
15% Overhead & Profit on SCC labor		$ 378	
Total SCC Labor			$2,895
Subcontractor: (NAME)		$ 1,529	
5% markup on subcontractors		$ 76	
Total subcontractor			$1,605
Total			$4,500

The Date of Substantial Completion will be unchanged: August 10, 2011

Additional impact costs may not be fully realized at this time and contractor reserves the right to adjust this change order proposal should such costs be incurred.

Figure 22.1 Contractor's change order proposal

ment as proposed by the contractor has been accepted.

Figure 22.2 is an example of a change order published by the American Institute of Architects (AIA Document G701–2001). Whether the CO is completed on a form that is developed in-house or is purchased, however, several pieces of information should be included:

- Identification of the change order by number
- Description of the change (e.g., "*Adjust foundation and drainage detail*")
- Changed contract price if appropriate (either additive or deductive)

AIA® Document G701™ – 2001

Change Order

PROJECT: *(Name and address)*

MAIN STREET OFFICE
Address

TO CONTRACTOR: *(Name and address)*

SUPERIOR CONST. CO.
Address

CHANGE ORDER NUMBER: 1

DATE: May 18, 2010

ARCHITECT'S PROJECT NUMBER: 20104

CONTRACT DATE: April 12, 2010

CONTRACT FOR: General construction

OWNER ☒
ARCHITECT ☒
CONTRACTOR ☒
FIELD ☐
OTHER ☒

The Contract is changed as follows:
(Include, where applicable, any undisputed amount attributable to previously executed Construction Change Directives)

Adjust foundation and drainage detail per Architect's sketch SK 3 & SK4 dated May 15, 2010

The original (Contract Sum) (~~Guaranteed Maximum Price~~) was	$ 3,661,900
The net change by previously authorized Change Orders	$ -0-
The (Contract Sum) (~~Guaranteed Maximum Price~~) prior to this Change Order was	$ 3,661,900
The (Contract Sum) (~~Guaranteed Maximum Price~~) will be (increased) (~~decreased~~) (~~unchanged~~) by this Change Order in the amount of	$ 4,500
The new (Contract Sum) (~~Guaranteed Maximum Price~~) including this Change Order will be	$ 3,666,400

The Contract Time will be (~~increased~~) (~~decreased~~) (unchanged) by ( ) days

The date of Substantial Completion as of the date of this Change Order therefore is August 10,2011

(Note: This Change Order does not include changes in the Contract Sum, Contract Time or Guaranteed Maximum Price which have been authorized by Construction Change Directive until the cost and time have been agreed upon by both the Owner and Contractor, in which case a Change Order is executed to supersede the Construction Change Directive.)

NOT VALID UNTIL SIGNED BY THE ARCHITECT, CONTRACTOR AND OWNER.

LOCAL ARCHITECTS	SUPERIOR CONST. CO	GEORGE SMITH DEVELOPERS
ARCHITECT *(Firm name)*	CONTRACTOR *(Firm name)*	OWNER *(Firm name)*
ADDRESS	ADDRESS	ADDRESS
BY *(Signature)*	BY *(Signature)*	BY *(Signature)*
(Typed name)	*(Typed name)*	*(Typed name)*
DATE	DATE	DATE

CAUTION: You should sign an original AIA Contract Document, on which this text appears in RED. An original assures that changes will not be obscured.

Figure 22.2 Change order (AIA Document G701-2001)

- Completion date for the entire project (this date may change, or maybe unchanged as a result of the change order)
- Signatures of the owner, the contractor, and the architect

In our example, the change order adds $4,500 to the original $3,661,900 contract price and results in a new project cost of $3,666,400. There is no additional time required to complete the changes. Note that (as is typical) all three primary players – the owner, the architect, and the contractor – sign the form. These signatures indicate their mutual agreement regarding the change. (Remember, mutual agreement is one of the requirements for a valid contract.)

Tracking changes

Part of the process for successfully making changes on a job is the management of the paperwork. All changes involve documentation: architectural sketches and backup data on pricing and scheduling, as well as field questions, requests for proposals, change order proposals, and the change orders themselves. Jobs can have multiple outstanding change orders at any one time and the contractor must carefully monitor their progress. Logs similar to the submittal log we saw in Chapter 18 are used to track the development and routing of information related to all changes. Both the general contractor and the architect compile tracking logs, as do involved subcontractors.

Impact analysis

As we've already seen, changes often result in additional direct costs for materials, labor, and equipment, and sometimes in adjustments in the construction time for the whole project. Indirect project costs and overhead must also be included in the costs for a change. There may be other important impacts that are sometimes more difficult for the contractor to assess. The timing and volume of changes may adversely impact efficiencies and productivity on a job, or the change may have an impact on another part of the job in the future. These impacts may have cost or time implications that the contractor needs to acknowledge in the change order proposal so that he is not later unfairly penalized. Sometimes the contractor adds wording to a change order proposal to alert the owner that there may be other, as-yet undefined impacts. Wording such as that found in Figure 22.1 is often used: "*Additional impact costs may not be fully realized at this time and contractor reserves the right to adjust this change order proposal should such costs be incurred.*"

Industry guidelines

There are certain guidelines regarding changes that are typically observed by the industry. Following these guidelines can reduce potential disagreements and confusion around changes. They include the following:

- Even when the change doesn't rise to the level of a change order, changes should be executed only with written authorization. It's not hard to imagine a contractor making a cost or time change at the direction of the architect and the owner then refusing payment because there's no record of an agreement to the change.
- No changes should be included that are beyond the scope of the base contract. If, for example, the owner wants the general contractor to increase the size of the house greatly, the scope has changed significantly and a new contract should be executed.
- Those authorized to sign change orders should be identified at the start of the project and there should be clarity regarding the process for handling changes, for example, how costs will be determined, how deletions to the contract will be credited, and what the time requirements will be for performing a change.
- The formula that the contractor will use to calculate overhead and profit on changes should be understood. As noted earlier, the contractor doesn't want to fight the owner for markups on each change. Ideally, they have negotiated how costs will be determined before construction begins.
- The scope of the change must be clear, with adequate information to enable the contractor to make an accurate and complete estimate of all costs. (This typically means that the architect needs to provide sufficiently detailed drawings.)
- The contractor should carefully review changes for possible impact costs and delays as these may not be reimbursable after the change order is executed.
- All parties should make an effort to expedite the handling of changes: the contractor should issue change order proposals in a timely fashion; the architect should review them as soon as possible; and the owner should make a decision so that the contractor can proceed with the change.

Change directives and minor changes in the work

The owner has the right to make changes to the work. The contractor may protest the changes or the contractor and the owner might not agree on the costs for making a change. Sometimes there simply isn't enough time to process, review, and execute a change order. (For example, an emergency situation may require immediate attention.)

The mechanism for making a change to the contract in such situations is a construction change directive.

AIA® Document G714™ – 2007

Construction Change Directive

PROJECT: *(Name and address)*
Main Street Office Bldg.
Address

TO CONTRACTOR: *(Name and address)*
Superior Construction Co.
Address

DIRECTIVE NUMBER: 3
DATE: September 13, 2010
CONTRACT FOR: General construction
CONTRACT DATED: Aprill 12, 2010
ARCHITECT'S PROJECT NUMBER: 20104

OWNER ☒
ARCHITECT ☒
CONSULTANT ☒
CONTRACTOR ☒
FIELD ☐
OTHER ☐

You are hereby directed to make the following change(s) in this Contract:
(Describe briefly any proposed changes or list any attached information in the alternative)

Redirect drainage at rear entry per architect's sketch SK 14 and replace faulty sump pump

PROPOSED ADJUSTMENTS

1. The proposed basis of adjustment to the Contract Sum or Guaranteed Maximum Price is:
   - ☐ Lump Sum (increase) (decrease) of $
   - ☐ Unit Price of $ per
   - ☒ As provided in Section 7.3.3 of AIA Document A201-2007
   - ☐ As follows:

2. The Contract Time is proposed to (be adjusted) (remain unchanged). The proposed adjustment, if any, is (an increase of days) (a decrease of days).

When signed by the Owner and Architect and received by the Contractor, this document becomes effective IMMEDIATELY as a Construction Change Directive (CCD), and the Contractor shall proceed with the change(s) described above.

Contractor signature indicates agreement with the proposed adjustments in Contract Sum and Contract Time set forth in this CCD.

Local Architects	George Smith Developers	Superior Construction Co.
ARCHITECT *(Firm name)*	OWNER *(Firm name)*	CONTRACTOR *(Firm name)*
Address	Address	Address
ADDRESS	ADDRESS	ADDRESS
BY *(Signature)*	BY *(Signature)*	BY *(Signature)*
(Typed name)	*(Typed name)*	*(Typed name)*
DATE	DATE	DATE

CAUTION: You should sign an original AIA Contract Document, on which this text appears in RED. An original assures that changes will not be obscured.

Figure 22.3 Change directive (AIA Document G714-2007)

The owner and the architect, but, initially, not the contractor, sign the change directive. This document indicates that the contractor is to proceed with a change and, once the contractor and owner agree to the terms and the change directive is signed by the contractor, the change becomes part of the contract. In our example, there is an emergency drainage problem at the rear of the building that requires immediate attention. Because there is no time to get complete cost figures, the contractor is being directed to complete the change and costs are to be determined at a later date, according to the procedures outlined in Section 7.3.3 of the AIA General Conditions. These procedures state:

If the Construction Change Directive provides for an adjustment to the Contract Sum, the adjustment shall be based on one of the following methods:

1. *Mutual acceptance of a lump sum properly itemized and supported by sufficient substantiating data to permit evaluation;*
2. *Unit prices stated in the Contract Documents or subsequently agreed upon;*
3. *Cost to be determined in a manner agreed upon by the parties and a mutually acceptable fixed or percentage fee; or*
4. *As provided in Section 7.3.7* (This Section outlines the procedures in case the contractor disagrees with the method for adjustment to the contract.)

As with our change order example, Figure 22.3 is a form published by the American Institute of Architects (AIA Document G714–2007) that is completed by the architect.

A minor change can be made without issuing a formal change order. A change is considered minor if it results in no change in cost or time to complete the project; there should be a written notice from the architect identifying the change. AIA Document A201 identifies procedures for making minor changes in the work:

> *The Architect has authority to order minor changes in the Work not involving adjustment in the Contract Sum or extension of the Contract Time and not inconsistent with the intent of the Contract Documents. Such changes will be effected by written order signed by the Architect and shall be binding on the Owner and the Contractor.* (AIA Document A201–2007 Section 7.4)

Summary

To summarize, a change order is a written authorization from the architect and the owner to the contractor to make a change to the contract sum, time, or scope. Change orders are prepared by the architect and signed by the architect, the owner, and the contractor. The signed change order states their agreement to the change. Minor changes that have no impact on contract sum or time (such as a timely change in paint color) do not require a change order.

Another way to make changes is through a document called a change directive. The owner has the right to make changes within the general scope of the work. A change directive is a means of ordering a change when the owner and the contractor have not agreed to the proposed cost or time impacts of a change. A change directive is prepared by the architect and signed by the architect and the owner, not by the contractor. (There is no agreement.) The contractor is obligated to perform the work and the architect determines the amount of the adjustment. Once the parties have reached an agreement regarding impacts, the directive is recorded as a change order and becomes part of the construction contract.

Chapter Vocabulary

Additive change – a change that adds to the scope, cost, or time of a contract.

Change directive – a mechanism for making changes in the work without the contractor's prior agreement regarding price and/or scope of work.

Change order (modification) – a written agreement between the owner and the contractor (and, on most jobs, the architect) to make a change in the terms of the contract. A change order (including a change directive) is the only legal means of changing a contract after the award of a contract.

Change order proposal – a contractor's proposal for cost and time impacts of a proposed change in the work.

Change order request – a document from the architect asking for a change order proposal from the contractor.

Deductive change – a change that reduces the scope, cost, or time of a contract.

Field question – a request for clarification made to the architect.

Minor change – a change that results in no adjustment in cost or time.

Modification – a change to the contract price or time. A modification can be a change order, a change directive, or a minor change in the Work.

Request for a change proposal – a request from the architect that the contractor determine the cost and time impacts of a proposed change.

Request for information – a request for clarification or information resulting from a field question.

Test Yourself

1. What is a change order?
2. What information does an architect want when she submits a request for a change order proposal to the contractor?
3. Who signs change orders?
4. What document is be used in the absence of total agreement on the terms of a change order?
5. Why is it important that changes be authorized in writing?
6. There is confusion regarding what floor covering to use in the lobby. What document does the floor subcontractor submit to initiate the process of determining the correct product? To whom is this document submitted?
7. Why might an owner request that a contractor propose their markup rates before the work begins?
8. What is the dollar amount of the change order shown in Figure 22.2?
9. Who signs change directives?
10. A project needs an extra 10 days to complete, but there is no extra cost required. Assuming the owner agrees to the extension, is it necessary to complete a change order?

Andrea Young

CHAPTER 23

Getting Paid

Contractors may love their work but getting paid is what it's all about. Like most businesses, construction depends on cash flow. It's no wonder the terms of and procedures for payment are of extreme interest to all concerned. It's not just the contractors who are interested; the owner's primary responsibility during construction is to pay for the work. Most contracts specify the procedures for submitting an application for payment and specify when the owner must pay the contractor. The same is true of contracts between general contractors and subcontractors. Failure to follow the procedures agreed to in the contract can result in consequences for both parties. Importantly, the contract documents also outline the contractor's recourse should he or she not be paid. There are two primary ways that payment is made to the contractor:

- A pre-determined amount is linked to milestones and paid to the general contractor when each milestone is reached. For example, completion of the foundation, closing in the structure, or completing a floor might all generate payments. The milestones are determined and agreed upon at the time the construction contract is signed.
- A more standard approach is for progress payments to be made on a regular basis for work completed and materials delivered during that

> period. Typically, the general contractor is paid monthly for all work completed during that billing period and the monthly application for payment includes costs for his own crews, plus all subcontractor costs, plus (depending on the terms of the construction contract) the costs for material delivered to the jobsite and installed. Payment is made by the owner the following month on a pre-determined schedule.

Coordinating the payment process is usually the responsibility of the contractor's project manager and can be quite complicated. It is important that payment requests are accurate and complete so that there are no delays. Typically, the contractor submits progress payment requisitions at the end of the month, the architect reviews and certifies them, and the owner pays them sometime in the following month. Because timely payment is critical to the contractor, there is usually a meeting with the architect in advance of the submittal date to be sure there are no problems.

The contract specifies exactly when submittal, review, and payment are due. This means the contractor has a predetermined date when all the required requisition forms and attachments are due to the architect for review and when payment will be made. Subcontractors submit their pay requests to the general contractor according to the terms of *their* contracts, typically, a few days before the GC's submittal is due. This gives the general contractor time to review the subcontractor's requests before making the application for payment to the architect.

The contractor is obligated to pay subcontractors and vendors when he gets paid by the owner. The AIA General Conditions (Document A201–2007) states: "*The Contractor shall pay each Subcontractor no later than seven days after receipt of payment from the Owner … The Contractor shall, by appropriate agreement with each Subcontractor, require each Subcontractor to make payments to Sub-subcontractors in a similar manner.*" Some subcontracts have "**pay when paid**" clauses, which means that subs will be paid when the owner pays the GC. It's not difficult to see the problem that a delayed payment to the general contractor potentially presents for subcontractors! Sometimes the general contractor and the subcontractor have an agreement that requires payment at a predetermined time whether or not the owner has paid the GC. Just as "pay when paid" can present problems for subcontractors, it's not hard to imagine the potential financial difficulties for the general contractor if he is required to pay subcontractors before he receives payment from the owner.

How does everyone know how much is due each month? The basis of all progress payments is a determination, in the field, of the actual quantities of work that have been completed as of the date that the payment request is submitted. The accuracy required of these field measurements is determined by the type of contract involved.

Contract types and payment

We saw in Chapter 13 that construction contracts are differentiated largely by how the contractor gets paid. Let's see how each of the major contracts – lump sum, cost plus a fee (with or without a GMP), and unit price – differ in this regard.

Payment under lump-sum contracts

As we have already learned, under a lump-sum contract, the general contractor gives the owner a single price for the whole job (exactly how much each portion of the work costs is proprietary to the GC and is known only to him). When monthly payments are made, the owner's concern is that the payments more or less reflect the amount of work completed and that there are adequate funds to finish the work. For example, if the total price for the job was bid at $500,000 and the contractor is around 50 percent complete, approximately $250,000 in payments should have been made. The contractor's overhead and profit are rolled into activity costs and are therefore pro-rated on each progress payment. So, if the request for payment identifies that the work is 50 percent complete, the contractor is entitled to be paid 50 percent of his total contracted amount for overhead and profit.

Although verification of the contractor's payment request can occur in different ways, typically, the architect completes a visual inspection to make her own assessment of the amount of work completed. On lump-sum contracts, the owner's concern is not that every month every dollar is exactly accurate; his concern is that there are sufficient funds to complete the work adequately and that at the end of the project the total paid is the bid amount.

One of the advantages of a lump-sum contract is that although the contractor needs to be vigilant to ensure a level of accuracy, monthly applications do not have to reflect exactly the costs incurred during the billing period. As a consequence, the contractor need not include detailed documentation, which he needs to do with a cost plus contract.

Payment under cost plus a fee contracts

On a cost plus contract, the contractor gets reimbursed for all actual costs, up to a capped amount if there is a guaranteed maximum price (GMP). The agreement identifies which costs the owner reimburses to the contractor and which costs are covered by the contractor's overhead and profit. Reimbursable costs typically include all the (documented) direct and indirect project costs for the billing period. Payment to the contractor for indirect business expenses (overhead) and profit are added onto each progress payment as a fixed fee or percentage of the construction cost. Unlike lump-sum contracts, where monthly payment is based on a rough approximation of work completed, and where slight disparities can be adjusted at the end of a job, with cost plus contracts (including GMP contracts) the contractor is invoicing for actual costs incurred during the payment period. The contractor must verify his requisition with labor and delivery reports, rental slips, and invoices.

Payment under unit price contracts

As we saw in Chapter 13, a unit price contract is a hybrid form of construction contract that uses fixed prices for units of materials but reimburses the contractor for actual quantities used during the billing period. The bid documents identify anticipated quantities; the contractor provides the owner with a firm price for each of the identified units, such as lengths of pipe, cubic yards of soil, or linear feet of trim. The contractor's unit price bid is multiplied by the actual in-place quantities to determine payment amount, and quantities are verified for each payment requisition. For example, if the contractor bid a unit price of $1.50 per linear foot (LF) for pipe, and 1,256 linear feet have been installed during the billing period, the contractor will be paid $1.50/LF x 1,256 LF = $1,884.00 in that payment period. If 200 LF are installed the following month, the contractor's payment will be $1.50 x 200 = $300. The unit price remains constant for the duration of the project, but quantities must be documented each month for payment to be made. Because the quantities provided by the owner in the bid documents are projections only and the final contract amount will reflect *actual* quantities, there may be a significant difference between what the contractor bid and what he ends up being paid.

Payment procedures

The agreement and/or the general and supplementary conditions outline the time frame and procedures for payment. Several of the payment procedure terms are important to both the contractor and the owner and are typically negotiated as part of the owner-contractor agreement. These terms might include:

- What day of the month the contractor's application for payment must go to the architect
- The number of days allowed for the architect to review the application
- When the owner must pay the contractor
- The conditions under which payment can be withheld
- The contractor's recourse if the owner doesn't pay
- Procedures for final payment at completion of the contract
- Procedures for the release of withheld funds, called retainage (discussion to follow)

Developing the payment request (application and certificate for payment)

It is in everyone's interest that the monthly pay request be accurate and thorough so that there are no holdups in payment. The process of gathering the data required for the general contractor to assess progress accurately during the billing period requires gathering costs from subcontractors, suppliers, and the general contractor's field staff and accounting department. This process can be lengthy and time consuming (imagine the complexity of gathering all the data for a very large project with multiple subcontractors and invoices of millions of dollars each month). As already mentioned, projects with cost plus or unit price contracts require the contractor to attach backup documentation with each pay request. But contractors for projects with lump-sum contracts still need to compile the data in order to understand the figures they will submit. Despite the differing requirements of the various contract types, the procedures for determining monthly pay requests are quite similar:

1. At the beginning of the job, the general contractor submits to the architect a breakdown of expected costs, called a **schedule of values** (SOV), as shown in Figure 23.1. This document, derived from the contractor's estimate, identifies the anticipated total amounts for each broad construction activity, such as site work, concrete, masonry, mechanical, and so forth. The schedule of values is used as a baseline for determining the monthly payments due. We'll look at it more closely later in the chapter.

2. The general contractor completes a take-off of the quantity of work completed (or expected to be completed) through the end of the billing month and determines the value of that work. Labor and material reports, delivery slips, and purchase orders are verified and reviewed. As noted, for cost plus or unit price projects, the contractor needs to determine exactly how much work was completed. For projects that have lump-sum contracts, the quantities are expressed as a percentage of anticipated totals.

3. The subcontractors complete a similar process for their portions of the work. In order to be sure that the GC's application and certificate for payment is submitted to the architect on time (typically by the end of the month), subcontractors are usually obligated to provide the general contractor with *their* payment requests in advance, say around the twentieth of the month. The GC reviews the subs' requests and verifies their accuracy. All subcontractor costs are included in the general contractor's request.

4. The GC compiles the required documents and data and assembles a draft payment request. The draft is typically reviewed by the architect in order to alert him to any potential problems and provide an opportunity for the contractor to adjust the request by the pre-determined due date.

5. The contractor submits the final application and certificate for payment to the architect on whatever form has been agreed upon with the owner. Often the contract requires additional attachments such as a schedule update and test reports. As noted, in the case of cost plus or unit price contracts, extensive documentation is included: labor and material reports, delivery slips and invoices, and purchase orders. There may also be a requirement that all contractors and suppliers provide partial lien release waivers proving that they have been paid. If the architect does not approve the application as submitted, he may refuse the application or, more typically, request that the contractor adjust the figures. The biggest problem is usually that the architect and contractor don't agree on the percentages of work completed during the billing period. The architect's role is to ensure that the owner's interests are protected, including that excessive payments are not being made to the contractor.

6. Once the architect approves the application, she signs it and submits the certified application to the owner for payment. The owner pays the contractor according to the terms of the contract.

7. The contractor pays subcontractors and suppliers.

Terms: contract wording can make a big difference – Contractors must make sure they understand all payment terms in their agreement with the owner. The author was the owner's project manager for a job on which the contractor submitted a payment request for $70,000 of steel, which was being stored off-site. The contract allowed payment for materials delivered to the site but not yet installed. It did not extend to materials stored off-site and the owner was within his legal rights to refuse payment. In the interest of keeping a well-regarded contractor solvent, however, a compromise was negotiated that did not financially compromise the contractor but upheld the spirit of the contract. A less flexible owner might have required the contractor to wait for any reimbursement until he could move the steel onto the site.

Payment documents

There are three documents that are typically part of the **payment application** submitted by the general contractor: the schedule of values, the payment continuation sheet, and the application and certificate of payment form. We'll now look at each of these documents.

Schedule of values

The schedule of values (SOV), based on the contractor's estimate summary, is developed early in the construction process and submitted to the architect before the first payment request. As noted earlier, this document is used as a basis for making payments. If the SOV is being used with a lump-sum job, each activity or line item represents a separate cost that incorporates the contractor's pro-rated indirect business costs (overhead) and profit. Cost plus and unit price contracts have separate categories for overhead and profit.

A	B	C
Item No.	Description of Work	Scheduled Value
1	Indirect Project Costs	$ 360,000
2	Site Work	$ 320,000
3	Concrete	$ 287,000
4	Masonry	$ 65,000
5	Metals	$ 344,000
6	Carpentry	$ 584,400
7	Thermal/Moisture Protect.	$ 102,800
8	Doors, Windows	$ 182,500
9	Finishes	$ 320,600
10	Specialties	$ 36,500
11	Equipment	$ 120,000
12	Furnishings	$ 85,000
13	Special Construction	$ -
14	Conveying Systems	$ 328,500
15	Mechanical Systems	$ 295,600
16	Electrical Systems	$ 230,000
	TOTAL CONTRACT	$3,661,900

Figure 23.1 Schedule of values

Figure 23.1 is an example of an SOV form that was generated in-house by the contractor for a lump-sum job. Each item of work includes a percentage to cover the contractor's overhead and profit. The numbered items (which may or may not follow the MasterFormat numbering system) and their scheduled values are approved by the architect prior to the start of construction. Let's look at the costs for Mechanical Systems and Finishes to see, briefly, how this document is used.

Mechanical Systems (Item 15) is valued at $295,600. If the current pay request reflects 65 percent of the total job completed, then the payment due is $192,140 ($295,600 x 65%) and a balance of $103,460 remains. The architect's concern will be that the balance is sufficient to complete the item.

On the same payment request, let's say that the contractor has identified that 10 percent of Finishes (Item 9) is complete. (This is a broad category that includes painting, drywall, carpet, tile, and the like.) On this job, the item is valued at $320,600, so, if 10 percent of the job is complete, the contractor can expect $32,060 in payment. Because the contractor (and the architect) must make a determination of percentages of work completed each month, it is often useful for the activities identified in the schedule of values to be broken into narrower scopes of work. For example, in Figure 23.1, site work (Item 2) is a single activity valued at $320,000. But site work has different components such as excavation, final grading, paving, and landscaping, and it might prove more useful for dollar values to be attached to each. Similarly, concrete (Item 3), valued at $287,000, might have been shown as concrete walls, slabs, and precast, with each activity carrying a portion of the total cost of concrete. Because this is a lump-sum contract, the general contractor is under no obligation to disclose his overhead or profit; as noted, these costs are incorporated into each line item.

Continuation sheet

The second document included as part of the application and certificate for payment is called a continuation sheet. The continuation sheet references the schedule of values and identifies current amounts due, how much has already been billed, and the balance remaining for each item. Figure 23.2 is an example of a continuation sheet representing the first payment request for the Main Street Office Building. Note that the item code, description of work, and scheduled value (from Figure 23.1) are identified in the first three columns. The reader can see that the only items invoiced as part of this (the first) payment request are: General Conditions (including mobilization, supervision, and other indirect project costs), Site Work, and Concrete. Each of these items has a total percentage of work that is (or is expected to be) completed as of the end of the current payment period. The balance remaining for each work item is identified, plus the amount of retainage being held. One change order has been ap-

AIA® Document G703™ – 1992

Continuation Sheet

AIA Document G702, APPLICATION AND CERTIFICATION FOR PAYMENT, containing Contractor's signed certification is attached.
In tabulations below, amounts are stated to the nearest dollar.
Use Column I on Contracts where variable retainage for line items may apply.

APPLICATION NO:
APPLICATION DATE:
PERIOD TO:
ARCHITECT'S PROJECT NO:

A	B	C	D	E	F	G		H	I
			WORK COMPLETED						
ITEM NO.	DESCRIPTION OF WORK	SCHEDULED VALUE	FROM PREVIOUS APPLICATION (D + E)	THIS PERIOD	MATERIALS PRESENTLY STORED (NOT IN D OR E)	TOTAL COMPLETED AND STORED TO DATE (D+E+F)	% (G ÷ C)	BALANCE TO FINISH (C - G)	RETAINAGE (IF VARIABLE RATE)
1	General Conditions	$360,000		$36,000		$36,000	10	$324,000	$3,600
2	Site Work	320,000		224,000		224,000	70	96,000	22,400
3	Concrete	287,000		114,800		114,800	40	172,200	11,480
4	Masonry	65,000						65,000	
5	Metals	344,000						344,000	
6	Carpentry	584,400						584,400	
7	Thermal-Moisture Protect.	102,800						102,800	
8	Doors, Windows	182,500						182,500	
9	Finishes	320,600						320,600	
10	Specialties	36,500						36,500	
11	Equipment	120,000						120,000	
12	Furnishings	85,000						85,000	
13	Special Construction								
14	Conveying Systems	328,500						328,500	
15	Mechanical Systems	295,600						295,600	
16	Electrical Systems	230,000						230,000	
	ORIGINAL TOTAL	3,661,900		374,800		374,800		3,287,100	37,480
	Change Order #1	4,500		4,500		4,500	100	-0-	450
	NEW TOTAL	3,666,400		379,300		379,300	10.3	3,287,100	37,930

Figure 23.2 Continuation sheet (AIA Document G703-1992)

proved during this billing period and its value, $4,500, has been added to the project cost at the bottom of the sheet. As additional change orders are agreed to, they are entered and are also carried forward each month.

The continuation sheet is updated with each payment request. It is easy for the team to see cash flows, amount of retained money, and balances for each item and the work as a whole. Although payment forms (like others) may be created in-house by the owner or by the contractor, many projects use documents published by the American Institute of Architects. Figure 23.2 is an example of one of the AIA published forms.

Application and certificate for payment

Cost figures from the schedule of values and the continuation sheet form the basis for the payment request presented to the owner on an **application and**

AIA® Document G702™ – 1992

Application and Certificate for Payment

TO OWNER: George Smith Developers
Address

PROJECT: Main Street Office Bldg.
Address

FROM CONTRACTOR: Superior Construction Co.
Address

VIA ARCHITECT: Local Architects
Address

APPLICATION NO: 1
PERIOD TO: May 31, 2010
CONTRACT FOR: General construction
CONTRACT DATE: April 12. 2010
PROJECT NOS: / /

Distribution to:
OWNER ☐
ARCHITECT ☒
CONTRACTOR ☐
FIELD ☒
OTHER ☐

CONTRACTOR'S APPLICATION FOR PAYMENT

Application is made for payment, as shown below, in connection with the Contract.
Continuation Sheet, AIA Document G703, is attached.

1. **ORIGINAL CONTRACT SUM** .... $ 3,661,900
2. **Net change by Change Orders** .... $ 4,500
3. **CONTRACT SUM TO DATE** (Line 1 ± 2) .... $ 3,666,400
4. **TOTAL COMPLETED & STORED TO DATE** (Column G on G703) .... $ 379,300
5. **RETAINAGE:**
   a. 10 % of Completed Work (Column D + E on G703) $ 37,930
   b. 10 % of Stored Material (Column F on G703) $

   Total Retainage (Lines 5a + 5b or Total in Column I of G703) .... $ 37,930
6. **TOTAL EARNED LESS RETAINAGE** .... $ 341,370
   (Line 4 Less Line 5 Total)
7. **LESS PREVIOUS CERTIFICATES FOR PAYMENT** .... $ -0-
   (Line 6 from prior Certificate)
8. **CURRENT PAYMENT DUE** .... $ 341,370
9. **BALANCE TO FINISH, INCLUDING RETAINAGE**
   (Line 3 less Line 6) $ 3,325,030

CHANGE ORDER SUMMARY	ADDITIONS	DEDUCTIONS
Total changes approved in previous months by Owner	$ -0-	$ -0-
Total approved this Month	$ 4,500	$
TOTALS	$ 4,500	$
NET CHANGES by Change Order	$ 4,500	

The undersigned Contractor certifies that to the best of the Contractor's knowledge, information and belief the Work covered by this Application for Payment has been completed in accordance with the Contract Documents, that all amounts have been paid by the Contractor for Work for which previous Certificates for Payment were issued and payments received from the Owner, and that current payment shown herein is now due.

CONTRACTOR:

By: ______________________ Date: May 31, 2010

State of:
County of:
Subscribed and sworn to before me this day of
Notary Public:
My Commission expires:

ARCHITECT'S CERTIFICATE FOR PAYMENT

In accordance with the Contract Documents, based on on-site observations and the data comprising this application, the Architect certifies to the Owner that to the best of the Architect's knowledge, information and belief the Work has progressed as indicated, the quality of the Work is in accordance with the Contract Documents, and the Contractor is entitled to payment of the AMOUNT CERTIFIED.

AMOUNT CERTIFIED .... $ ________

(Attach explanation if amount certified differs from the amount applied. Initial all figures on this Application and on the Continuation Sheet that are changed to conform with the amount certified.)

ARCHITECT:

By: ______________________ Date: ________

This Certificate is not negotiable. The AMOUNT CERTIFIED is payable only to the Contractor named herein. Issuance, payment and acceptance of payment are without prejudice to any rights of the Owner or Contractor under this Contract

Figure 23.3 Application and certificate for payment (AIA Document G702-1992)

certificate for payment form. The form in Figure 23.3 is also one published by the American Institute of Architects and is very commonly used. It is filled out using costs shown on the continuation sheet. Each future payment request will use the updated continuation sheet to calculate the numbers on the payment application. In our example (using the data from the continuation sheet in Figure 23.2), note that the original contract sum ($3,661,900) has been increased by the value of change order No. 1 and, as of the date of this application, is $3,666,400. As other change orders are added, the contract sum to date (No. 3) will be adjusted.

The application and certificate for payment form summarizes the payment request and provides space for the architect's approval. The contractor determines the gross amount due, deducts an agreed-to percentage of the total amount to be withheld (retainage), and identifies the net amount due.

When the architect signs the application, he forwards the certified payment amount to the owner.

Retention

A portion of the monthly pay request is commonly held back by the owner (and subsequently by the general contractor from the subcontractors). This is referred to as retention or retainage. Retainage requirements are identified in the contract. There are two reasons for such agreed-to temporary withholding of money owed to the contractor:

- As an incentive for the contractor to complete her work as quickly as possible.
- To provide a certain amount of money that can be available to the owner to satisfy lien claims should the contractor fail to pay subcontractors or suppliers. In the case of default by the contractor, these funds can be used to complete the work.

Retention amounts are typically 10 percent of each pay request. In some cases, these funds are withheld from every pay request for the duration of the project; in other cases, no additional retention is taken out after the work has progressed past a certain point. The owner pays all withheld funds to the general contractor after completion of the project. Subcontractors receive *their* retained funds at the same time. (This can result in real financial hardship for subs who might have to wait months beyond when they completed their work before funds are released. Many GCs are willing to accommodate subcontractors and release retainage earlier.)

Some argue that projects that carry performance and payment bonds should not also require retention. There is a growing consensus that, on large jobs that carry potentially hundreds of thousands of dollars as retainage, a reduction or an elimination of retainage at some point is appropriate. The U.S. government and the American Institute of Architects both view 10 percent during just the first half of a project as adequate to assure completion and to protect against claims. In cases where bonds are required, the surety is involved in all decisions regarding reduction of retention.

Profits through prompt payment – Construction is a financial revolving door; as soon as money comes in, it immediately goes back out. While the contractor begins incurring labor and material expenses on the first day of a project, requests for payment are made at the end of the month. Payment by the owner occurs sometime the following month. This means that the contractor typically needs to carry costs for more than a month before being paid by the owner. In addition, retention means that 10 percent of each pay request is withheld, adding further financial strain. Some general contractors have adequate resources to cover these expenses, but it's easy to imagine that small contractors can be especially hard hit by any delay in getting paid. As a consequence, there is often a premium for being paid promptly. Contractors with reputations for fast and fair payments to subcontractors often receive favorable bids, and material suppliers often give discounts for early payment. The converse is also true: if a contractor is consistently late in making payments, then future bids may be higher.

Given that most contractors don't have gobs of cash sitting around, how do they cover their cash flow needs? Most of those in the industry have **lines of credit**, loans through a bank, which can be used as short-term financing. A line of credit is a loan that can be accessed on an as-needed basis, and the borrower pays interest only on those funds that have been withdrawn. For example, a contractor has a $100,000 line of credit through his local bank. A current job isn't going well, the owner is late making payments, and the contractor is in danger of missing his contractual obligations to pay his subcontractors by an agreed-to date. In order to meet this obligation, he borrows the necessary funds (up to a maximum of $100,000) from his line of credit; his intention is to pay the loan back at such time as the owner pays *him.* Although the interest costs incurred in borrowing funds must be factored into the contractor's overhead costs, he is only borrowing the amount that he needs and, if he can pay it back quickly, his calculation is that the interest costs will be manageable. The line of credit is good for a pre-determined amount of time so the contractor knows that he can access funds again should the need arise

What happens if the owner refuses to pay?

As you may have guessed, sometimes the owner doesn't pay. Although the urge to heave a concrete block through the owner's window might be strong, there are procedures to follow. And sometimes the owner is within her rights to withhold payment. The general conditions and the supplementary conditions outline the situations that can result in the refusal of the architect to certify the contractor's payment request and the owner's withholding of payment. These situations include:

- Failure of the contractor to correct defective work
- Evidence that the work cannot be completed for the balance of the bid amount

- Repeated failure by the contractor to carry out the work according to the contract requirements

Some owners choose to include as contract terms other situations in which payment in full might be withheld, such as:

- Failure to follow the precise procedures for applying for payment (for example, submitting the payment request late)
- Incomplete or inaccurate applications for payment
- Failure to complete work (for example, change orders)
- Failure to pay subcontractors (thus exposing the owner to liens*)*

Sometimes the owner fails to pay the contractor without apparent cause. What can the contractor do? The contractor's primary recourse (after carefully following the procedures outlined in the general conditions) is to stop the work until such time as she gets paid. The AIA General Conditions, states the following:

> "*If the Architect does not issue a Certificate for Payment, through no fault of the contractor, within seven days after receipt of the Contractor's Application for Payment, or the Owner does not pay, within seven days of the date established in the Contract Documents, the amount certified by the Architect or the amount determined by dispute resolution, then the Contractor may, with seven days additional written notice to the Owner and Architect, stop the Work until payment of amount owing is received. The Contract Time shall be extended appropriately and the Contract Sum shall be increased by the Contractor's reasonable costs of shut-down, delay and start-up plus interest as provided for in the Contract Documents.*" (AIA Document A201-2007, Article 9.7)

There is at least one other important tool available to a contractor (or subcontractor or supplier) one a private job who does not get paid: the **mechanic's lien**. A mechanic's lien is an encumbrance, or limitation (like a mortgage), on real estate that can force the property to be sold to satisfy a debt. A lien can be placed on a piece of property when someone who has provided goods and/or services toward improvement of that property is not paid. The lien stays on the property until the debt is paid or otherwise resolved. We'll discuss mechanic's liens in more detail in the next chapter.

Chapter Vocabulary

Application and certificate for payment – the form on which a payment request is made by the contractor and certified by the architect.

Continuation sheet – a payment document that identifies current amounts due, how much has been billed, and the balance remaining for each item.

Line of credit – unsecured loan through a bank, which can be used as short-term financing.

Pay when paid clause – a clause in contract that specifies that payment will be made to one party (for example, the subcontractor) only after another party (the contractor) receives payment.

Progress payments – periodic payments made by the owner to the contractor. Progress payment procedures are outlined in the contract documents (the agreement and/or the general conditions); progress payments are typically made monthly.

Requisition – a request for payment from one party to another.

Retention – a portion of a pay request that is commonly held back by the owner (and subsequently by the general contractor from the subcontractors) until the end of the job.

Schedule of values – a budget outline created early in the construction stage that is not an accurate, detailed breakdown of costs but the expected payment amounts in the different categories; it is used to determine the monthly payments due.

Test Yourself

1. To whom does the contractor submit a monthly application for payment?
2. Referring to Figure 23.2, the continuation sheet, what is the SOV for Carpentry, how much is being billed in the current month, and what is the balance remaining?
3. Lump-sum contracts and cost plus contracts have different types of payment procedures. Which one is likely to have the most complicated and extensive monthly payment application process? Why?
4. How does the contractor know exactly when he can expect payment?
5. The contractor on a lump-sum contract invoiced for 80 percent of the work, but the architect feels that there is actually about 30 percent more work to be done, not 20 percent. What is the architect's likely response to the contractor's payment application?
6. When the architect agrees that the payment application is properly completed, to whom does he give it?
7. Which type(s) of contract relies on the measurement of approximate (as opposed to actual) quantities completed during each pay period?
8. Give two reasons why owners retain funds from a contractor's pay requests.
9. You are a subcontractor and have furnished the windows on a job but have not been paid. What can you do? What additional recourse does the prime contractor have?
10. Why is it good business for a contractor to pay subcontractors and suppliers promptly?

Alison Dykstra

CHAPTER 24

Claims, Disputes and Mechanic's Liens

Sometimes a problem occurs on a project and it becomes a **claim**, typically made by the contractor to the owner for additional time and/or payment. If a claim cannot be resolved among the project participants, it becomes a **dispute**, which, in extreme cases, can result in a lawsuit (litigation).

A claim is a demand by one party seeking an adjustment in the terms of a contract. Claims are initiated by written notice within a defined time following the event that caused a claim to be made. For example, a contractor has been asked to do extra work and he feels that the extra work has caused the project to be delayed. He submits a change order proposal (a claim) to the owner for an extension in contract time. The owner or the architect responds to the contractor by agreeing to the contractor's proposal, agreeing partially, or rejecting it. If the contractor does not agree with the decision, the claim becomes a contract dispute.

Disputes can often be settled fairly easily and without a lot of cost. When disputes aren't resolved, however, they can end in very expensive and time-consuming litigation. To avoid this, contracts typically identify specific procedures for settling disputes. These procedures are outlined in the general conditions and involve a series of steps that begin with negotiation. There are several methods for resolving disputes, but before we look at those, it's helpful to understand what sort of issues can cause disputes. The more the parties understand how disputes can arise, the more likely it will be that they can be avoided.

Situations that trigger disputes

Here are some common problems that can easily lead to disputes:

- Errors or omissions on the plans and/or the specifications
- Different conditions in the field from what was shown on the drawings
- Delays caused by the owner or architect
- Miscommunication or oral directives
- Scope of work changes (especially those initiated by the owner)

Let's see how each of these situations can lead to problems for the contractor (and the owner) on a job and how each might be prevented or resolved.

Errors or omissions on the plans and/or the specifications

As already noted earlier in this text, it isn't possible for construction documents to be 100 percent correct and coordinated. Errors (mistakes) and omissions (something that's not shown) are deficiencies in the drawings and the specifications. For example, the architectural drawings and the mechanical drawings have not been thoroughly coordinated and the drawings show an electric hot water heater while the specifications identify a more expensive demand hot water heater. The contractor will ask, "Which is it?"

Sometimes the contract includes guidelines that identify which of the contract documents "rule" in the case of a conflict among them. (This is called an order of precedence.) But often such specificity is lacking. Although there are no hard and fast rules about this, many assume that the information shown in the specifications takes precedence over the drawings, and that more detailed information takes precedence over less detailed information. Typically, the architect acts as the arbiter in such situations and makes a determination.

Field conditions that differ from the drawings

Many disputes arise when conditions on the site differ from what is identified in the contract. Subsurface conditions such as unexpected rocks, underground utilities, or soil contamination are all examples. If the contractor can show that she could not have reasonably anticipated an unexpected condition, she will typically qualify for additional time and/or money. The contractor and the owner may have differing opinions about what the contractor should have anticipated, however. This is one reason that the contractor is advised (and on some jobs, obligated) to visit the site before submitting a bid.

Delays caused by the owner or architect

Delay in reviewing submittals—product samples, shop drawings, and so on—can delay the work and is a common cause of disputes. The contractor depends on prompt review so that products can be fabricated or purchased in a timely manner. If there is a delay in completing a required review and the product cannot be ordered in a timely manner, the entire project could be delayed. Clarity regarding the process for reviewing submittals and change orders is best developed prior to the start of work and can help reduce conflicts.

Miscommunication or oral directives

There should be set lines of communication on a job. If an owner, for example, requests that the tiling subcontractor upgrade the tile, this directive must be issued as a written change order and be agreed to by the contractor. It is always advisable for all communication to go through the contractor, otherwise there is an increased risk of miscommunication (which can happen even with written directives).

Scope of work changes (especially those initiated by owner)

Some owners make changes to a job without clearly understanding the time and cost implications of that change. "Oh, just move the window over 12 inches" may be easy for the owner to request, but a shock when the cost is added! It is always best to have clarity regarding how changes will be processed and priced.

How are disputes resolved?

So what happens if a dispute arises? Let's say there is unexpected rock below grade that has required extra foundation work. The contractor submits a change order proposal (a claim) to the owner for extra money for this work. The owner contends that the soils report should have alerted the contractor to the possibility of subsurface rock and that he is therefore not entitled to extra reimbursement. With most contracts, there is a defined process for the contractor and the owner to resolve this type of problem.

There are several ways that disputes are resolved. These approaches vary from inexpensive and relatively quick to extremely costly and time consuming. The goal is to settle the dispute without going to court (litigating). Resolution methods include:

- Negotiation
- Mediation
- Arbitration
- Dispute resolution boards
- Litigation

Negotiation

When a dispute arises, the first (and best) approach is to negotiate a resolution among the parties. Negotiation is the process of reaching an agreement through discussion. Often a problem can be resolved through the normal give and take of talking something through, with both parties stating their positions and concerns and actively listening to the other. Negotiation offers the possibility of resolving a problem before it gets out of hand and positions on both sides have time to harden. There are several advantages to using negotiation to solve a conflict:

- Resolution can happen quickly
- Negotiators are in-house (typically the architect acts as the negotiator)
- There is minimal, if any cost
- Parties can take it or leave it, but an agreement is possible

Contracts typically require the GC to notify the architect immediately upon recognizing a situation that might lead to a dispute or claim. The architect, following the guidelines presented in the general conditions, tries to help the parties resolve the issue. If negotiations fail, then the parties typically move on to mediation.

Mediation

Mediation, often the first step after negotiation has failed, is the process of bringing the parties together with the aid of a trained mediator (facilitator) to discuss the problem and find a solution to which both parties can agree. The facilitator does not come up with a solution but listens to both sides and is trained to help them reach an agreement voluntarily.

Mediation has the following characteristics:

- It is a non-binding process – parties do not have to agree to the terms
- It is usually quick and easy
- The costs are typically lower than arbitration or litigation
- There is added moral pressure to reach an agreement

Mediation has another characteristic that makes it very effective: it's confidential. This means that what the parties say in mediation cannot be used against them should the dispute end up in arbitration or court. This fosters an atmosphere of honesty and creativity when trying to resolve issues.

Should the parties fail to reach an agreement through mediation, most contracts call for arbitration as the next level of resolution.

Arbitration

As with mediation, **arbitration** involves an outside neutral party skilled in dispute resolution processes. In arbitration, however, the facilitator not only hears the problem, but also makes a ruling, which may be binding (typical) or non-binding, depending on the terms of the contract; no jury is involved. In the United States, the American Arbitration Association is one of the major sources for arbitration services, and contracts often specify that an arbitrator from this association be used.

Arbitration has some advantages:

- Arbitration is less formal and typically (but not always) less costly than court action.
- An arbitrated ruling takes less time than going to court.
- It's possible, through language in the contract, to have an arbitrator who is very familiar with the construction industry and therefore more likely to issue a reasoned and informed judgement than might a judge who is unfamiliar with the industry.

Arbitration also has some disadvantages:

- The parties don't have some of the protections that a court would provide such as control over what evidence and testimony is presented. Arbitrators tend to allow much more evidence to be presented than in a court setting. In a courtroom, if a judge were to make a mistake, that mistake might be appealable. Arbitrated rulings cannot be appealed.
- Most contracts stipulate that the arbitration be binding (in other words, the parties must abide by the decision of the arbitrator).
- Procedures in arbitration aren't formalized as in a court proceeding which means they are less predictable than litigation.

Dispute resolution boards

Using a **Dispute resolution board** (DRB) is another resolution method. A DBR is organized before construction starts or any dispute arises, and consists of three industry experts: one member is nominated by the owner, a second by the contractor, and a third by the first two members. All board members must be acceptable to both the owner and the contractor. Board members sign an agreement obligating them to serve both parties fairly and equally. Because members are involved throughout the process, problems can often be resolved before they become disputes.

The members of the DRB familiarize themselves with the plans and specifications and visit the site regularly. Typically, they meet on the project site monthly or quarterly to review construction progress and hear any issues in dispute. Either the owner or the contractor can request a review by the DRB. After consideration of the facts, the board renders a written non-binding recommendation. The owner and the contractor may accept or reject the board's recommendation. If the recommendation is not accepted, the dispute will be resolved by either arbitration or litigation.

Litigation

If negotiation, mediation, arbitration, and the Dispute Resolution Board all fail to resolve the dispute, then the final resolution mechanism is **litigation**, which means referring the disputed issue to a court. In other words, one party sues the other. Litigation involves hiring legal counsel, preparing necessary documentation, and scheduling appearances before a judge. Litigation may or may not end in a jury trial. In general, litigation is the least desirable way to resolve problems on a job, as it is complicated, time consuming, and very costly. Furthermore, with litigation, an issue can take years to wend its way through the courts. Another major disadvantage with litigation is that the parties never communicate directly with each other; everything goes through attorneys.

The process of litigation can be quite predictable—there are very specific rules for entering evidence, and trials are generally well managed and understandable to the parties. For this reason, and the fact that decisions by a judge can be appealed, some prefer it to arbitration. But typically, the costs and time involved make litigation far less desirable than either mediation or arbitration.

Mechanic's Liens

A **mechanic's lien**, a technique unique to the construction industry, provides a way for someone who improves the value of real estate to get paid. Although who has lien rights varies from state to state, typically if a contractor, subcontractor, or supplier (or another) is owed money, he can attach an encumbrance to the owner's property. (An encumbrance is something that affects or limits title to a property.) If payment is not made within a certain time, the lien claimant can demand legal foreclosure of the property and have the obligation paid out of the proceeds of the sale of the property. In other words, if you work on a property and you don't get paid, the law gives you the right (after following a very specific process) to force the sale of the property to pay the debt.

Recording a mechanic's lien is only one of several ways for a prime contractor to satisfy a financial claim against an owner. Because the contractor has a legally enforceable agreement, she can take the owner to court, for example. For subcontractors and suppliers, however, who *do* not have a contract directly with the owner but who fail to get paid by the contractor with whom they do have a contract, filing a mechanic's lien may be their best recourse (depending on state law).

Because of the possibility of encumbering a property for which the owner has, in good faith, paid the contractor, anyone filing a lien must follow very strict procedures. In most states, for example, lien rights are greatly reduced or eliminated if steps are not taken early in construction to protect these rights. Although all states have mechanic's lien laws, the requirements and procedures *vary substantially* from state to state. The following are a few state requirements:

Recording requested by and returned to:

Name: ____________________
Company: ____________________
Address: ____________________
City: ____________________
State: _____ Zip: ____________
Phone: ____________________

Above this Line for Official Use Only

NOTICE AND CLAIM OF LIEN – INDIVIDUAL
(Civil Code § 3084)

Claimant, [name and address] ____________________ claims a Mechanic's lien on the real property and improvement in the City of ____________________ County of ____________________

located at ____________________ ("Property"). The following person(s) has/have or are reputed to have a property interest in said Property:

Said claim is for the sum of $__________ plus interest at the contract rate or the

legal rate, whichever is higher from ____________________ which is

due and unpaid to claimant (after deducting any just credits and offsets, if any) for labor, services, equipment and/or materials furnished by claimant and consisting of:

Claimant was employed to furnish the same by: ____________________

and furnished the same to: ____________________

Dated: __________ ____________________
[Signature of claimant or agent]

____
[Print or Type Name]

{Note: The claimant's signature is notarized on a separate sheet and attached}

Figure 24.1 California claim of lien

- In California, a Preliminary Notice with a description of labor, services, and/or materials supplied must be submitted to the owner within 20 days of first furnishing labor or materials. This notice puts an owner on notice that someone has lien *rights*.
- In Florida, subcontractors must file a Notice to Owner and a separate Notice to Contractor within 45 days of first providing services or materials.
- In Missouri, a prime contractor loses his lien rights if notification is not made prior to the first payment.
- In Texas, subcontractors must submit periodic notices to maintain their lien rights.
- Some states, such as Nebraska, have no mandatory notification requirements at all.

Putting an owner on notice that you have lien rights, however, is not the end of the story. After a project (or the contractor's or supplier's part of the project) is complete, the unpaid contractor or supplier must record the lien. As with notification laws, this process varies greatly from state to state. There are strict requirements for where and when this recording must take place, such as:

- In California, the general contractor has 60 days after a Notice of Completion is recorded by the owner, signaling that the work is complete, to file a lien claim. Subcontractors and others have even less time. (Note: it is in an owner's best interests to submit a Notice of Completion, as that reduces the period when liens can be recorded.)
- In Texas, the recording deadline is the fifteenth day of the fourth month after the date work is completed.
- Contractors on most private projects in New York have eight months to record a lien.

- In Maryland, a claimant has 120 days from the time the service was performed or materials were supplied to record a lien.

Having someone record a lien tends to make an owner sit up and take notice! Often payment is forthcoming and the claimant releases the lien. But if after a certain period of time, no payment is made, the claimant must file a lawsuit to begin the foreclosure procedure. This process can end in the sale of the property that was improved and payment of debts from the proceeds.

It is typically required that subcontractors and suppliers provide a document called a lien release (also called a lien waiver) for inclusion with a general contractor's regular progress payment requisition. These documents are used to waive lien rights in exchange for being paid and ensure the owner that subcontractors and suppliers have been paid for work up to that date. Upon final payment, the owner receives an unconditional waiver and release showing that the sub or supplier was paid in full.

Who has the right to file a mechanic's lien?

A list of who may claim liens is provided by state codes and, as always with lien laws, is highly variable among states. Here are some examples:

- In California, anyone performing labor or furnishing materials has lien rights, including mechanics, contractors, subcontractors, lessors of equipment, architects, engineers, land surveyors, and builders. Those with lien rights do not have to have a direct contract with the owner but must have a contract with an agent of the owner, such as a contractor or a subcontractor.
- In Kansas, only contractors with a direct contract with the owner or prime contractor have lien rights.
- In Pennsylvania, only contractors who have a direct contract with the owner and subcontractors who have a direct contract with the prime contractor have lien rights.

Anyone working on a project, or supplying material should research the lien laws in the state where the project is being built to understand the requirements.

How to avoid disputes

The best approach to dealing with disputes is to avoid them in the first place! Problems arise on every job; the successful contractor understands how to manage problems (and potential problems) so that they do not become disputes. Good project management leads to less conflict, and there are management tools and approaches available to the contractor that will increase the chance of a smooth job. Some of these include:

- Avoid the wrong jobs
- Understand the contract
- Communicate
- Maintain control
- Identify clear procedures
- Hire good subcontractors
- Stay educated
- Using partnering and integrated project delivery

Avoid the wrong jobs

The contractor should assess his ability to complete the work according to the contract requirements. An inexperienced contractor who doesn't understand his limitations is more likely to make mistakes and have trouble completing the job for the agreed price. This can lead to conflicts, disagreements, and disputes. Projects with unrealistic time frames and/or unrealistic estimates can result in both a contractor who cuts corners and an owner who is unhappy.

Understand the contract

Every contractor should follow two basic rules: 1) contracts should always be in writing, and 2) understand what the contract says! Having agreements in writing provides clarity and reduces misunderstandings. In addition, the contractor is legally required to complete the work according to the terms of the contract. If the contractor hasn't thoroughly read the contract or doesn't understand what it says, he may find himself obligated in unexpected ways. It often makes sense to hire an attorney to review the terms and conditions of a contract.

Communicate

Communication should be clear and in writing. There's a saying that has some truth behind it: "The party with the most paper wins." It is especially important for the contractor to document thoroughly all changes and their cost and time impacts and make these impacts clear to the owner and other interested parties.

Maintain control

Frequent and thorough review of work progress by the general contractor helps identify problems and assists in controlling the quality and progress of the work. Many superintendents walk through the entire jobsite daily. When problems are encountered, they should be confronted immediately.

Identify clear procedures

At the start of work, all parties should be sure there is clarity regarding processes and procedures, for example, with submittals and changes in the work. Confusion regarding processes can result in conflicts. This is the primary reason for having a pre-construction conference with major players: the owner, architect, general contractor, major subcontractors, and major suppliers.

Hire good subcontractors

The GC is responsible to the owner for the work of the subcontractors; hiring good subcontractors and maintaining control over them reduces problems.

Stay educated

Contractors who increase their education and level of experience are better able to avoid problems. For example, if a contractor decides to subcontract the geothermal heating system, it is important for him to make sure he understands the technology well enough to judge potential subcontractors and the quality of the work once installed.

Partnering and integrated project delivery

We should mention a couple of newer techniques for avoiding conflicts and for resolving conflicts, when they arise: **partnering and integrated project delivery**. Partnering was created in 1988 by the U.S. Army Corps of Engineers in an effort to find a better way to work together in general and to encourage the resolution of issues or disputes quickly and economically. Projects that are "partnered" are based on mutual agreement to work together toward a mission statement developed by all the parties and a recognition of the project's specific goals and objectives. The idea behind partnering is to break down barriers through increased understanding of each of the parties and their goals. The parties in such a collaborative approach typically include the major subcontractors as well as the owner, architect, and general contractor. A facilitator works with the parties to define their goals before the project starts and, together, they develop a process for quick resolution of differences. The facilitator works with the parties throughout the project to ensure that issues never get out of hand.

In Chapter 6, we discussed a type of delivery method that has recently been introduced called integrated project delivery (IPD). IPD is helpful in preventing and resolving disputes because all major players share equally in profits and losses on a job. Because projects with disputes may end up with losses, there is an incentive for all parties to avoid them if possible. The highly collaborative approach used on projects utilizing integrated project delivery can contribute to smoother-running jobs with fewer disputes.

Chapter Vocabulary

Arbitration – a dispute resolution technique that uses a trained arbitrator to make a ruling, which is binding (typical) or non-binding, depending on the terms of the contract.

Claim – a demand by one party seeking an adjustment in the terms of a contract.

Dispute – a claim that has not been satisfactorily resolved.

Dispute Resolution Board (DRB) – a board of three industry experts that works with disputing parties to resolve the dispute.

Integrated project delivery – a project delivery method in which all primary team members (the owner, architect, general contractor, engineers, and major subcontractors) are brought on board at the same time (during design), and, using sophisticated computer modeling and information sharing, are able to collaborate in unusually effective ways.

Lien – an encumbrance that affects or limits title to a property.

Lien waiver (release) – a document used to give up lien rights in exchange for being paid, typically submitted with a payment request.

Litigation – the process of using the court system to resolve a dispute. Litigation involves hiring legal counsel, preparing necessary documentation, and scheduling an appearance before a judge. Litigation may or may not end in a jury trial.

Mechanic's lien – a technique unique to the construction industry that provides a way for anyone improving the value of real estate to get paid by putting an encumbrance on the title to the property.

Mediation – a dispute resolution technique that brings the parties together with the aid of a trained mediator (facilitator) to discuss the problem and find a solution to which both parties can agree.

Negotiation – the process of reaching an agreement through discussion.

Order of precedence – the guidelines that identify which contract document "rules" in the case of a conflict among them.

Partnering – a dispute resolution approach based on mutual agreement by the parties to work together toward a mission statement developed by all the parties and a recognition of the project's specific goals and objectives.

Preliminary notice – notification to an owner that someone has lien rights.

Test Yourself

1. What are four potential causes of claims and disputes? Briefly explain how each can lead to a dispute.
2. What is the first thing the parties involved in a dispute will do to reach a resolution?
3. How does a dispute differ from a claim?
4. What are the six ways of resolving disputes and write a sentence about each.
5. You are contractor and there is confusion in the contract documents regarding structural requirements for the roof. The owner feels that you are obligated to provide a much more costly system than you bid and the architect agrees. This confusion has the potential of costing you your entire profit and you aren't about to give in. There are no requirements in the contract for exactly how the parties are to proceed; one option you have is to take the owner to court (to litigate.) Give two reasons why might you be reluctant to use litigation to resolve the problem. Explain.
6. Give two reasons why mediation is a good way to resolve conflicts.
7. What are the advantages of using arbitration to resolve disputes?
8. Why might arbitration be less desirable than mediation?
9. You are a general contractor who typically builds houses and you have decided to bid on a wing for the local hospital. Give two reasons why this job might lead to disputes.
10. Why is it important for the contractor to read and to understand her contract with the owner?

Andrea Young

CHAPTER 25

Close-out and Occupancy

By the end of construction, everyone is typically sick to death of the project and wants it to be over. The owner is tired of writing checks and wants to occupy the building. The contractor is anxious to finish so he can get his final payment and move on to the next job. But the contractor still has major responsibilities during this phase and, although the project has greatly wound down, there are endless small tasks to be completed. As with the start of construction, the end of the work must be carefully planned and managed. Typically a checklist will be used by the contractor to help answer "yes" to the following:

- Is all the physical work done?
- Have all the systems been tested and are they working as designed?
- Does the owner have all the manufacturers' information required to operate and maintain the building?
- Have subcontractors and suppliers submitted final payment requests?
- Is everything set so that the required regulatory agencies can issue final approval?

There are three related but different phases in finishing construction and closing out a contract. Each phase has its own focus and its own associated tasks:

1. **Construction close-out**: completion and approval of the physical work so that the structure can be turned over to the owner and occupied
2. **Contract close-out**: completion of the contract requirements and final payment to the contractor
3. **Contractor's close-out**: contractor's in-house project review and evaluation

Construction close-out

Construction close-out is the transfer of a project from the contractor to the owner. This transfer can be complicated; the contractor, architect, consultants, subcontractors, suppliers, and authorities having jurisdiction (AHJs) all have roles to play.

There are several important things that occur during construction close-out:

1. Completion of the physical work
2. Substantial completion
3. Systems testing
4. Certificate of occupancy
5. Demobilization and final cleaning

Let's look briefly at each of these.

Completion of the physical work

Toward the conclusion of work, the superintendent generates a list of all the work still to be finished. This list, called the **punch list**, identifies minor adjustments and repairs that must be completed prior to final payment by the owner to the contractor (or by the general contractor to a subcontractor).

What sort of items might be on a punch list? Their significant characteristic is that they are minor—last-minute details that have been overlooked or are still to be finished. Putting a new window in the living room or installing the plumbing fixtures would probably not be included. But sweeping the front walkway, installing switch plate covers in the living room, cleaning tile grout, and removing the dumpster might be. Punch list items won't prevent the owner from occupying the facility but typically need to be completed prior to final payment by the owner. The punch list is a result of a comprehensive inspection of the work by the contractor; the architect and their consultants may also add items to the punch list.

The contractor's superintendent tracks punch list progress in a log and holds regular meetings with subcontractors to monitor the work. The GC signs off on the work as it is completed. When the contractor's punch list is substantially complete, the architect does a pre-final inspection and, if she finds the work satisfactory, issues the certificate of substantial completion.

Punch list omissions – If a contractor fails to identify an item that was required by the contract and should have been picked up before project completion as a punch list item, it doesn't mean he's off the hook! According to the AIA General Conditions "*Failure to include an item on such a list does not alter the responsibility of the contractor to complete all work in accordance with the contract documents.*" (A 201 Article 9.8.2), Incomplete work can still be identified by the owner after close-out. Any defective or incomplete work will obligate the contractor as part of a correction period .

Substantial completion

There are two certificates of completion: one, generated by the architect, is called the certificate of substantial completion; and the other, generated by the authority having jurisdiction (AHJ) over the project, is called the certificate of occupancy. The second certificate gives the owner the right to move into or use the building (or a portion of the building). For the contractor, the more critical one is the certificate of substantial completion.

Substantial completion is when the work or a portion of the work is sufficiently complete that the owner can use the building for its intended purpose. Substantial completion is something short of total, or final, completion; rather, it is a *practical* completion. Although the owner cannot actually occupy a building until the building department says he can, the substantial completion certificate signifies that a project is ready for its intended use. It is an important milestone for several reasons:

- As the notice to proceed signals the start of construction time, substantial completion marks the *end* of construction time and the contractor's release from any (or any further) liquidated damages liability. When a contract states that the contractor will complete the work in, for example, 150 days, the contractor has 150 days from the notice to proceed to the certificate of substantial completion.

- Responsibility for the physical property, including all insurance requirements, shifts from the contractor to the owner when the certificate of substantial completion is issued. In addition to insurance, from this time forward, the owner is responsible for security, maintenance, and utilities.
- Substantial completion marks the beginning of the contractor's correction and **warranty** period. Owners are never in a position to absolutely determine whether the requirements of the construction contract are being met. Because of this, the contractor makes promises to the owner that materials, systems, and workmanship are as the owner reasonably should expect them to be. These promises comprise what is called a warranty.

Warranties – The most common expressed (written) warranties define the requirements of workmanship and products:

- All materials and equipment incorporated into the structure are of good quality and new (unless otherwise agreed to)
- All work is free of defects and conforms to the contract requirements

Most jurisdictions hold that a contractor provides certain warranties even if they are not explicitly expressed in the contract. The basis for these warranties is usually statutory (they're required by law). Any product that is sold—including a new building—has an implied warranty. Implied warranties are sometimes called manufacturers' warranties.

Most contracts stipulate a one-year warranty or correction period. Many manufacturers' expressed warranties are longer than that. The manufacturer's warranty often begins when the product is sold, which, in many cases, may be significantly before substantial completion. The contractor needs to verify the owner's requirements and purchase additional manufacturer's warranty coverage if necessary.

Once the parties sign the certificate of substantial completion and the surety agrees, the owner will release retainage to the contractor (less amounts to cover any outstanding punch list items). See Figure 25.1 for an example of a certificate of substantial completion.

AIA® Document G704™ – 2000

Certificate of Substantial Completion

PROJECT: *(Name and address)*

PROJECT NUMBER:

CONTRACT FOR:

CONTRACT DATE:

TO OWNER: *(Name and address)*

TO CONTRACTOR: *(Name and address)*

OWNER ☐
ARCHITECT ☐
CONTRACTOR ☐
FIELD ☐
OTHER ☐

PROJECT OR PORTION OF THE PROJECT DESIGNATED FOR PARTIAL OCCUPANCY OR USE SHALL INCLUDE:

The Work performed under this Contract has been reviewed and found, to the Architect's best knowledge, information and belief, to be substantially complete. Substantial Completion is the stage in the progress of the Work when the Work or designated portion is sufficiently complete in accordance with the Contract Documents so that the Owner can occupy or utilize the Work for its intended use. The date of Substantial Completion of the Project or portion designated above is the date of issuance established by this Certificate, which is also the date of commencement of applicable warranties required by the Contract Documents, except as stated below:

ARCHITECT	BY	DATE OF ISSUANCE

A list of items to be completed or corrected is attached hereto. The failure to include any items on such list does not alter the responsibility of the Contractor to complete all Work in accordance with the Contract Documents. Unless otherwise agreed to in writing, the date of commencement of warranties for items on the attached list will be the date of issuance of the final Certificate of Payment or the date of final payment.

Cost estimate of Work that is incomplete or defective: $ ______

The Contractor will complete or correct the Work on the list of items attached hereto within ( ) days from the above date of Substantial Completion.

CONTRACTOR	BY	DATE

The Owner accepts the Work or designated portion as substantially complete and will assume full possession at (*time*) on (*date*).

OWNER	BY	DATE

The responsibilities of the Owner and Contractor for security, maintenance, heat, utilities, damage to the Work and insurance shall be as follows: *(Note: Owner's and Contractor's legal and insurance counsel should determine and review insurance requirements and coverage.)*

Figure 25.1 Certificate of Substantial Completion

Systems testing

All equipment and systems, such as the mechanical and electrical equipment and systems, must be started up and tested to ensure that they are functioning properly. Manufacturers, suppliers, subcontractors, the general contractor, and the architect may all be involved in this process. The contractor notifies the architect so that he can observe the tests; the owner's facility manager might also be present.

Certificate of occupancy

Although substantial completion identifies the point when the building is ready to be used for its intended purpose, the owner can't actually occupy it until the authorities having jurisdiction, such as the building department and the fire department, sign off.

After the certificate of substantial completion has been issued, the contractor or the architect calls for final inspection by the AHJ. When the AHJ is satisfied that all code requirement have been met, and all agencies with jurisdiction over the structure are satisfied, they issue the **certificate of occupancy** (CO), a document certifying that a structure meets all applicable building codes and other requirements and that it is suitable for occupancy.

The requirements and procedures for obtaining a certificate of occupancy vary from jurisdiction to jurisdiction and with the type of structure. Generally, a CO is required whenever a new building is constructed or an existing building's use changes (such as the conversion of a manufacturing plant to housing). Inspections are conducted by the AHJ to ensure that the basic construction, wiring, plumbing, and other elements of the building are up to code, and can be certified as being safe for occupation. The certificate of occupancy is evidence that the building complies substantially with the plans and specifications submitted to and approved by the local authority. The CO complements the building permit, which is a document that must be filed by the applicant with the local authority before construction to indicate that the proposed construction will adhere to ordinances and codes and laws (see Chapter 5). Figure 25.2 is an example of how a very simple certificate of occupancy might read; jurisdictions create their own forms which may include additional data - special considerations such as the existence of a wetland, for example.

CERTIFICATE OF OCCUPANCY
{Name of jurisdiction}

Project Address: ____________________

Property Description & Parcel Number: ____________________

____

Permit Number: ____________________

This permit was issued and the structure was inspected based on the ______Edition of the

(appropriate) Code: ____________________

Owner's Name and Address: ____________________

____

Permit Holders Name and Address (if not the owner):

____

____

This structure has been inspected and complies with the applicable codes, regulations, and laws that were in effect at the time this permit was issued. All final inspections have been completed and this dwelling is approved for occupancy.

Signed this __________ **day of** ______________, __________

Code Compliance Official: ____________________

Figure 25.2 Certificate of Occupancy

Partial and temporary certificates of occupancy – An AHJ sometimes issues a partial certificate of occupancy (CO). When a project is built in phases, a partial CO allows the owner to use some of the facility while work on another area continues. Temporary certificates of occupancy may also be issued while the owner awaits the completion of something that does not have safety implications, such as the landscaping.

Demobilization and final cleaning

As work draws to a close, the contractor moves her operations physically off the site. This is called **demobilization**. The site office is closed and the jobsite trailer hauled to the next job, remaining materials and waste are removed, utility companies are notified that temporary power should be disconnected, and temporary security items such as fencing are removed. At the completion of demobilization, the contractor is responsible for a final cleaning of the site and the facility.

Contract close-out

The completion of construction marks the end of the physical work but the contractor will have additional obligations before he can expect to receive final payment from the owner. (Other than possible warranty work, when final payment is issued the contract has been *executed* or completed, indicating that both parties have met their contractual obligations.) The contract specifications typically identify close-out requirements and the project manager is often the person on the contractor's team who is responsible for completing these requirements. There are two categories of tasks during close-out: completion of contract requirements and application for final payment.

Completion of contract requirements

There are typically a number of submittals that need to be reviewed and approved by the architect as part of contract completion. As with the submittals required during pre-construction and construction, the scope and the procedures for review and approval of close-out submittals are outlined in the general conditions, supplementary conditions, or specifications. Some of these will likely include:

- Record documents such as **as-built drawings** (also called **record drawings**). Completed by the contractor on the original construction drawings, "as-builts" identify changes and field conditions such as where concealed pipes run, the location of underground utilities, and any adjusted dimensions. Because as-built drawings show conditions that are not specified on the construction drawings they are very helpful for future maintenance, renovation, or changes.
- **Operations and maintenance manuals** (O & M manuals) provide the owner (or his facility manager) with information on materials, finishes, equipment, and systems. These manuals typically include product data, maintenance, repair, and cleaning information, and are used for budgeting and maintenance purposes. On projects

with complicated systems, the contract may also require that the owner's facility manager receive training on the systems.

- Spare parts, extra materials, and keys. Often the contractor is required to provide spare parts such as fasteners, handles, and specialized tools and extra materials such as tile, carpet, paint, lubricants, and cleaners. These spare parts and materials will assist the owner in maintaining and cleaning the facility and are frequently required for materials in which finish, color or pattern is critical. During construction, temporary locks are put on doors. During close-out, the cylinders are replaced or re-keyed and the keys are turned over to the owner.
- Documents such as lien releases and manufacturers' and subcontractor warranties are additional submittals to be attached to the application for final payment.

Application for final payment

Once the punch list and all submittals are complete, the general contractor submits the final application for payment. The contractor's project manager makes sure that all documentation and necessary information is correct and complete so that the request can be submitted to the architect and payment released.

The form for the final payment request matches that of the monthly progress payments. The owner probably required conditional lien releases from the general contractor and subcontractors as part of the monthly application for payment. At the completion of the contract, the owner gets unconditional lien releases from everyone who worked on the job. These final lien releases indicate that the parties have been paid and end their rights to place a lien on the property.

If the project was bonded, the surety typically provides consent before final payment can be made.

As with all payment requests, the architect reviews and certifies the application and forwards it to the owner, who will pay the contractor in full per the terms of the contract. Any outstanding retainage is also paid in full. Construction and contract close-out are now complete.

But there's one final task for the contractor's team: the contractor's close-out.

Contractor's close-out

An important part of finishing up a project is an evaluation of how it went. As part of close-out, the contractor's team discusses what worked and what didn't, subcontractor performance is noted, and estimating and scheduling information is entered into the data bank for use on future jobs. The measurement of success is whether the project met both the owner's goals and the contractor's goals. Did the job meet expectations for cost, quality, and time? Was the owner happy with the contractor's performance? Finally, did the contractor meet his profit goals?

Occupancy

At the completion of construction comes a major milestone: the owner moves in. The authority having jurisdiction may have requirements that were not included in the construction contract but that must be completed prior to occupancy. These might include installation of signage or certain safety requirements. Once the AHJs have issued a certificate of occupancy, the facility's users can move in.

We've learned that, at the date of substantial completion, the owner has assumed responsibility for the building: maintenance, utilities, security, property insurance, and liability for the property. For large projects, there is a **facility manager** (also called a facility director or property manager) who assumes a variety of responsibilities. The facility manager is closely involved during construction and close-out; he takes part in systems testing and is trained by manufacturer representatives or suppliers to provide maintenance of products and systems. The facility manager will be in possession of all operations and maintenance manuals and drawings, should be very familiar with all warranties, should have a thorough understanding of operation and maintenance costs, and often works with the owner on projections of long-term use and needs of the facility.

Now, except for any future warranty issues that might arise, the project really is over. The process of taking a project from conception to occupancy is done: the owner can use the building and the contractors, the architects, the engineers, the subcontractors and suppliers have moved on.

Chapter Vocabulary

As-built drawings – drawings completed by the contractor that identify any changes made to the conditions or dimensions of the work relative to the original documents.

Certificate of occupancy (CO) – a document issued by the authority having jurisdiction that verifies that a structure meets all applicable building codes and other requirements and that it is suitable for occupancy.

Commissioning – a practice that involves a formal review of all parts of a building's systems to ensure that the project meets (and will continue to meet) certain energy objectives.

Demobilization – the process of physically moving off a construction site at the completion of construction.

Operations and maintenance (O&M) manual – a manual provided to the owner at the completion of the work that gives critical operation, maintenance, repair, and replacement information.

Punch list – a list of minor adjustments and repairs that must be completed prior to the owner's final payment to the contractor.

Substantial completion – when the work or a portion of the work is sufficiently complete for the owner to use the building for its intended purpose.

Warranty – a promise by the contractor that materials, systems, and workmanship are as the owner should reasonably expect them to be.

Test Yourself

1. What member of the contractor's team is responsible for project close-out?
2. What is the importance of substantial completion?
3. Who issues the certificate of substantial completion?
4. What is the purpose of a punch list?
5. Where does the contractor find information regarding close-out requirements?
6. What document lets the owner know that she can occupy the project? Who issues this document?
7. How do warranties protect an owner?
8. At what point does the contractor typically get paid all (or most) of the retainage?
9. At what point is final payment made to the contractor?
10. Why might a post-construction review of a job be helpful to the contractor?

GLOSSARY

A/E – see Designer.

AIA A201– General Conditions published by the American Institute of Architects.

Activity – an individual task.

Activity-on-node (AON) – a type of network diagram in which individual activities are represented by a node connected by arrows to other activities with which they have a dependency.

Addenda – formal changes or clarifications issued by the owner or architect during a bidding process.

Additive alternates – design adjustments that are priced as separate additions to a base bid.

Additive change – a change that adds to the scope, cost, or time of a contract.

Advertisement to bid (notice to bid) – a public solicitation for bids.

Agency construction management – a type of construction project delivery method whereby the CM, who is hired early in the process, works as the owner's agent but does not do any of the physical work.

Agreement – the contract document that legally obligates the signing parties (such as the owner and the contractor) and states certain contractual facts about a specific project, such as the contract price and completion date.

Alternates – design adjustments that are priced as separate additions or deletions to a base bid.

American Institute of Architects (AIA) – a professional organization for architects in the United States that provides education, advocacy and other support for the profession and the industry.

Application and certificate for payment – the form on which a payment request is made by the contractor and certified by the architect.

Arbitration – a dispute resolution technique that uses a trained arbitrator to make a ruling, which is binding (typical) or non-binding, depending on the terms of the contract.

Architect – see Designer.

As-built drawings – drawings completed by the contractor that identify any changes made to the conditions or dimensions of the work relative to the original documents.

Associated General Contractors of America (AGC) – a trade organization dedicated to supporting the commercial construction industry, improving jobsite safety, expanding the use of new technologies and strengthening contractor/owner dialog.

At-risk construction management – a type of construction project delivery method whereby the CM, who is hired early in the process, works as the owner's agent during pre-construction and as the general contractor during construction.

Authority having jurisdiction (AHJ) – an agency with designated authority to provide compliance inspections and approval for a project. Local building departments are often the AHJ.

Award – procurement of a contract; selection of a winning bidder.

Back-charge – money charged to a subcontractor for work that the general contractor is forced to complete with his or her crews because the subcontractor has failed to do so.

Bar chart (Gantt chart) – a simple graphic representation of a schedule that relates the progress of activities to a timeline.

Bid – a price quote presented by a contractor that identifies the price for which the contractor offers to complete work.

Bid bond – a construction bond that insures an owner against the financial risk of a low bidder not executing a contract.

Bid documents (bid package) – the collection of documents (including drawings, specifications, agreement forms, general conditions, and other documents) used to make and obtain bids and to define the requirements of the work and the process that the contractor must follow when submitting a bid. When a construction contract is executed, most of the bid documents become contract documents.

Bid estimate (final, detailed, unit price estimate) – a cost estimate based on the most detailed design information developed by the contractor (or bidding contractors) after the design drawings and specifications are completed.

Bid package (bid documents) – the collection of documents (including drawings, specifications, agreement forms, general conditions, and other documents) used to make and obtain bids and to define the requirements of the work and the process that the contractor must follow when submitting a bid. When a construction contract is executed, most of the bid documents become contract documents.

Bid schedule – a rough schedule, based on project milestones, that a contractor puts together in order to develop his or her bid.

Bid shopping – an unethical practice that involves a contractor sharing subcontractor bids with other subcontractors in an effort to get lower prices.

Bid submittal – a contractor's response to a bid package that typically includes the contractor's price for completing the work plus backup documentation. The bid submittal must be made exactly according to the requirements of the bid package.

Bidder's questionnaire – a form designed to determine a bidder's qualifications for a job.

Bidding – a process in which several contractors compete to get a job.

Bidding period – the period of time during which contractors develop bids.

Bond – a three-party agreement between a contractor, an owner, and a surety, that guarantees the surety will cover the obligations of the contractor.

Breach of contract (default) – failure to live up to the terms of a contract.

Builders (contractors or constructors) – individuals or firms that agree to construct a facility in accordance with contract documents.

Building codes – local building laws put in place to promote safe practices in the design and construction of a building.

Building information modeling (BIM) – a process of gathering and managing information that uses virtual (typically, 3D) models as a tool for design, construction, and facilities management. BIM software enables information on systems, costs, and scheduling to be incorporated so that design, budget, and installation assumptions can be extensively evaluated and tested prior to construction.

Buying out the job (procurement) – the process of finalizing subcontracts and issuing purchase orders for material and equipment.

Capacity – the ability and skill of a contractor to complete a project; also, the competency or ability of a party to understand the terms of a contract.

Capital – the amount of cash available to a contractor.

Certificate of occupancy – a document issued by the AHJ that states that a project is in compliance with regulatory requirements and may be occupied.

Change directive – a mechanism for making changes in the work without the contractor's prior agreement regarding price and/or scope of work.

Change order (modification) – a written agreement between the owner and the contractor (and, on most jobs, the architect) to make a change in the terms of the contract. A change order (including a change directive) is the only legal means of changing a contract after the award of a contract.

Change order proposal – a contractor's proposal for cost and time impacts of a proposed change in the work.

Change order request – a document from the architect asking for a change order proposal from the contractor.

Character – the integrity and honesty of the owners and the senior staff of the construction company and their proven willingness to meet their obligations and commitments.

Chronology (or stages) – the process of moving a project from an idea to use.

City location factor – used to adjust the national average costs of materials and installation shown in RSMeans cost data publications to those at specific locations.

Claim – a demand by one party seeking an adjustment in the terms of a contract.

Close-out – the process of completing the terms of a contract. In construction, close-out includes completion of the physical work (construction close-out), completion of fulfilling the terms of a contract (contract close-out), and final evaluation by the contractor (contractor close-out).

Closed projects – construction jobs that are negotiated or bid between a few select contractors.

Commercial sector – a sector of the construction industry that includes offices, large apartment complexes, theaters, schools, hospitals, and other such facilities. As with residential construction, commercial projects are usually designed by architects with engineers' support.

Commissioning – a practice that involves a formal review of all parts of a building's systems to ensure that the project meets (and will continue to meet) certain energy objectives.

Competitive bidding – the process of selecting a contractor that is based on several contractors competing against each other to be awarded a contract to do work. Typically (but not always), the contractor with the lowest bid gets the job.

Conceptual estimate – a cost estimate based on very little design information and using gross unit pricing to determine the project cost.

Concurrent – activities that can happen at the same time.

Conditions, general and supplementary – the parts of a contract that define the basic rights and responsibilities of the parties.

Consideration – something of value promised by one party to another in exchange for something else; consideration is one of the requirements for a valid contract.

Constructability review – review of materials, systems, and installation methodologies by experienced contractors to ensure that a project can be built efficiently.

Construction – the execution of physical work as outlined by contract documents.

Construction change directive – a mechanism for making changes in the work without the contractor's prior agreement regarding price and/or scope of work.

Construction documents – the written and graphic documents prepared or assembled by the architect for communicating the project design for construction and administering the construction contract.

Construction drawings (working drawings or plans) – the detailed plans developed by the architect that are part of the construction documents. These drawings identify the layout and dimensions of a project.

Construction management – the process of coordinating, monitoring, evaluating, and controlling a construction project; not to be confused with the specific delivery method known as Construction Management.

Construction Management (CM) delivery method – a delivery method in which a contract manager is hired early in the process and acts as the owner's representative. CM may be agency CM in which the CM manages the construction but does not do the work, or at-risk CM in which the CM performs as the general contractor following completion of design.

Construction Specifications Institute (CSI) – a membership organization founded to improve the specification practices in construction and related industries.

Construction time – the amount of time a contractor has to complete work.

Continuation sheet – a payment document that identifies current amounts due, how much has been billed, and the balance remaining for each item.

Contract – a legally binding agreement between parties.

Contract documents – the information that defines the legal terms of a contract.

Contract time – the amount of time the contractor has for completion of the physical work.

Contractors (constructors or builders) – individuals or firms that agree to construct something in accordance with contract documents.

Control log – a mechanism for tracking information and documents on a job.

Controlling – a key function of project management, in which, after tracking and evaluating, a project's schedule, cost, or quality are brought back in line with the project baseline.

Correction period – a period (typically, one year) during which a contractor is obligated to correct deficiencies and complete any work not previously noted.

Cost plus (a fee) contract – a type of contract in which the owner reimburses the contractor for actual costs and pays a bid or negotiated fee for overhead and profit to the contractor.

Cost plus guaranteed maximum price (GMP) contract – a cost plus contract which has a cap on the final cost.

CPM – see Critical path method network diagram.

Crashing the schedule – accelerating the work.

Critical activities – activities that if delayed, will delay the entire project.

Critical path – the unbroken chain (or chains) of activities that have no extra time built in and which, if delayed, will cause the entire project to be delayed. The critical path determines the minimum project duration.

Critical path method (CPM) network diagram – a network diagram that identifies activities that must be completed on time or the entire project will be delayed.

Daily job report – a form used to track the progress of work and daily activities on a jobsite.

Davis-Bacon Act – a law stating that labor on federal projects or federally assisted projects must pay workers no less than the local prevailing wages and benefits.

Deductive alternates – design adjustments that are priced as separate cost reductions to a base bid.

Deductive change – a change that reduces the scope, cost, or time of a contract.

Default (breach) – failure to live up to the terms of a contract.

Deliverable – an outcome; something specific that needs to be accomplished.

Delivery method – the organizational structure for completing a project.

Demobilization – process of physically moving off a construction site at the completion of construction.

Dependency – the connection or linkage between individual tasks that make up a project.

Descriptive specification – a method of specifying that provides product details without mentioning a brand name.

Design – the process of developing a project plan that meets an owner's vision within budget, site, regulatory requirements, and other constraints.

Design development – the stage of the design process in which a designer (an architect or an engineer) refines the design and makes decisions regarding layout, materials, and systems and takes the design to approximately 60 percent completion.

Design information – the information about a construction project provided to bidders or contractors in the plans and specifications.

Design phase – the stage of a project in which a designer (an architect or engineer) develops a design that meets the owner's vision and goals and creates the documents necessary to estimate the cost for the project and to enable a contractor to build it.

Design-bid-build (traditional) – a delivery method in which the GC is hired at the completion of design.

Design-build – a delivery method in which the owner has one contract with a single construction/ design firm.

Design-negotiate-build – a variation on design-bid-build, in which award of the general contract is made following negotiations between several general contractors and the owner.

Designer – architects or engineers (A/E), licensed professionals who provide planning, design, and construction administration services for a project. Architects are typically the designers of buildings; engineers typically design infrastructure and complex commercial and industrial projects.

Detailed estimate (bid, final, or unit price estimate) – a cost estimate based on the most detailed design information developed by the contractor (or bidding contractors) after the design drawings and specifications are completed.

Details – drawings that graphically represent blow-ups of specific elements to show how products or materials fit together.

Developer – a private owner who coordinates the tasks required to create a project.

Direct project costs – the labor, materials, and equipment expenses directly associated with the items that will become part of a physical structure.

Discount – a reduced price offered by suppliers for prompt payment by the contractor. A discount might be stated as "2 Net 10," meaning the supplier will give a 2 percent discount if payment is made by the tenth of the month.

Dispute – a claim that has not been satisfactorily resolved.

Dispute Resolution Board (DRB) – a board of three industry experts that works with disputing parties to resolve the dispute.

Divisions – broad categories of construction (such as concrete, masonry, finishes, etc.) as defined by the Construction Specification Institute's MasterFormat™.

Drawings (construction drawings, plans) – the portion of the contract documents that are the graphic representation of the work to be completed.

Duration – the amount of time required to complete an activity

Elevations – drawings that graphically represent a building as if the viewer is looking straight at it at eye level.

Estimate – an educated guess, based on the best available information, of what something is going to cost, usually in dollars or time.

Estimate summary – a summation of final project costs prepared by a contractor prior to submitting a bid.

Estimator – one who calculates the probable cost of something.

Exclusion – a piece of work or service that is outside the contractor's scope of work and is so identified in the contract.

Experiential information – a person's level of experience with a type of work.

Fast-track – a job in which construction starts before the design process is complete. Projects that are fast-tracked have compressed schedules and therefore can be completed faster than those that use sequential construction.

Feasibility – the process of assessing the desirability, cost, and potential of a project so that a decision can be made regarding whether to move ahead.

Fee – the amount paid as remuneration for services. In construction, the fee is typically overhead plus profit.

Field question – a request for clarification made to the architect.

Final estimate (bid, detailed, or unit price estimate) – a cost estimate based on the most detailed design information developed by the contractor (or bidding contractors) after the design drawings and specifications are completed.

Financial feasibility – a process of assessing a project's potential from a cost perspective.

Finish to finish – a project dependency in which one task cannot be completed before some other task has also been completed.

Finish to start – the most frequently-used type of project dependency, in which one task cannot be started before some other task has been completed.

First-tier subcontractor – a specialty contractor hired by a general contractor to perform specialty work on a project. First-tier subcontractors may hire their own specialty contractors (second-tier subcontractors).

Fixed price contract (lump-sum contract, stipulated-sum contract) – a type of contract in which a specified amount of work is provided by the contractor for a set price that is known up front.

Float (total float) – the amount of time that a task can be delayed without affecting the completion time of the overall project.

Floor plans – drawings that graphically represent a building using horizontal slices through the structure.

Flow-through clause – terms included in one contract that are incorporated into a subcontract.

Foreman – the person responsible for direct supervision of a contractor's workers.

Gantt chart – see Bar chart.

General conditions – the contract document dealing primarily with the terms and conditions of the work that apply to the work as a whole and that can be applied to multiple projects.

General conditions costs (general requirements costs, indirect project costs) – expenses that are directly linked to the cost of the work but not to a specific task or subcontract.

General contractor (GC) – an individual or firm hired by and responsible to an owner for coordinating the completion of a construction project. The GC hires subcontractors and suppliers.

General requirements costs (general conditions costs, indirect project costs) – expenses that are directly linked to the cost of the work but not to a specific task or subcontract.

Going out to bid – presenting a project to contractors so that they can submit a price to build it.

Green building (sustainable construction) – projects that seek to minimize or eliminate negative impacts on the natural and human environment.

Greenwashing – misrepresenting the environmental benefits of a product or structure.

Guaranteed maximum price (GMP) contract – a cost plus contract which has a cap on the final cost.

High performance – a term sometimes used interchangeably with "green" or "sustainable" but which tends to focus on energy systems.

Impact analysis – the assessment of the effect that some change will have on a project.

In the field – at a jobsite.

Indirect business costs (overhead) – costs associated with running the contractor's business and not directly billable to any specific job expense.

Indirect project costs – see General conditions costs.

Industrial sector – a sector of the construction industry that includes refineries, electrical stations, chemical processing plants, factories, and similar facilities. Industrial projects are typically highly technical and specialized.

Infrastructure – a sector of the construction industry that includes transportation and service projects such as roads, tunnels, bridges, ferries, and subways. Infrastructure is typically publicly owned and funded. These projects are designed by engineers and require specialized licensing of the contractors.

Instructions to bidders – one of the bid documents; it gives the exact requirements for prospective contractors' bids.

Insurance – a means of protecting someone against a future loss.

Integrated project delivery – a project delivery method in which all primary team members (the owner, architect, general contractor, engineers, and major subcontractors) are brought on board at the same time (during design), and, using sophisticated computer modeling and information sharing, are able to collaborate in unusually effective ways.

Interest – the money a lender charges to borrow money.

Invitation to bid – a solicitation for bids made by an owner to select contractors.

Job logic – the sequence of activity linkages.

Jobsite layout plan – a plan developed by the general contractor before mobilizing onto the site that graphically identifies existing conditions and locations for temporary utilities, fencing, access, and so forth.

LEED (Leadership in Energy and Environmental Design) – a voluntary rating system developed by the U.S. Green Building Council that provides a way to measure and give clarity to the definition of what makes a building green.

Labor burden – costs that are added to the direct wage of a worker, including fringe benefits (such as vacation and health) as well as social security and other taxes.

Lawfulness – a condition of contracts that says the law will not enforce a contract for something that is not legal.

Letter agreement – a contract in the form of a letter between the parties. Letter agreements contain the elements of standardized agreements.

License bond (contractor license bond) – a bond that contractors are required to purchase as a condition to being licensed.

Lien – an encumbrance that affects or limits title to a property.

Lien waiver (release) – a document used to give up lien rights in exchange for being paid, typically submitted with a payment request.

Line of credit – short term bank loans in which funds can be drawn as needed.

Linkages – a representation of task dependencies in the diagram of a project.

Liquidated damages – a previously agreed-upon amount of money the contractor is required to pay an owner if construction is not completed on time.

Litigation – the process of using the court system to resolve a dispute. Litigation involves hiring legal counsel, preparing necessary documentation, and scheduling an appearance before a judge. Litigation may or may not end in a jury trial.

Logic diagrams (network, precedence, PERT diagrams) – a tool for making scheduling decisions and a way of representing a schedule that show the flow of activities and their logical ties to each other as networks instead of items along an axis.

Long-lead items – materials or products that have special manufacturing or delivery requirements that involve extra time.

Look-ahead schedules (three-week, updated schedules) – short-term schedules, typically developed every three weeks by the superintendent, that provide information on upcoming activities.

Lump-sum contract (fixed price contract, stipulated sum contract) – a type of contract in which a specified amount of work is provided by the contractor for a set price that is known up front.

Master construction schedule – a comprehensive and detailed schedule the contractor develops and uses as a baseline overview of the entire job and as a tool to control the job.

MasterFormat™ – a work-based master list of numbers and subject titles, developed by the Construction Specification Institute, that organizes information about a project.

Means, methods, and techniques – how the contractor intends to complete the work.

Mechanic's lien – a technique unique to the construction industry that provides a way for anyone improving the value of real estate to get paid by putting an encumbrance on the title to the property.

Mediation – a dispute resolution technique that brings the parties together with the aid of a trained mediator (facilitator) to discuss the problem and find a solution to which both parties can agree.

Milestone – an important event that indicates an event or point in time. Typical milestones are bidding, award of contract, notice to proceed, start of construction, substantial completion, and owner move-in.

Minor change – a change that results in no adjustment in cost or time.

Mobilization – the process of moving personnel, equipment, and materials onto a jobsite so that the physical work can begin. Mobilization typically follows the owner issuing to the contractor a notice to proceed.

Mock-up – a full-scale model built for testing or evaluating details.

Modification – a change to the contract price or time. A modification can be a change order, a change directive, or a minor change in the Work.

Multi-prime contract – a project in which the owner has contracts with several prime contractors.

Mutual agreement – a key ingredient of contracts under which all parties must agree to the terms of the contract.

Negotiated contract – a method of selecting a contractor in which a few select contractors are asked to look at early design documents and put together a proposal. The owner then compares the proposals, interviews one or more of the contractors, and eventually selects a winning contractor.

Negotiation – the process of reaching an agreement through discussion.

Network bar chart – a diagram that uses interconnected lines and arrows to show how tasks relate to each other along a timeline.

Network diagram (precedence diagram, logic diagram, PERT diagram) – a tool for making scheduling decisions and a way of representing a schedule that shows the flow of activities and the dependencies between them.

Node – the representation of an activity in a network diagram.

Notice of award – notification made to a winning contractor that he or she has gotten the job and that the owner intends to enter into a contract.

Notice to bid (advertisement to bid) – a public solicitation for bids.

Notice to proceed – a document provided to the contractor by the owner that gives the contractor access to the site and establishes the official start of construction time.

Open projects – projects that allow any qualified contractor to bid.

Open shop wage rate – wages paid to workers who are not in a union or on a federal project, and as agreed to by the individual worker and his or her employer.

Operations and maintenance (O&M) manual – a manual provided to the owner at the completion of the work that gives critical operation, maintenance, repair, and replacement information.

Order of precedence – the guidelines that identify which contract document "rules" in the case of a conflict among them.

Overhead (indirect business costs) – costs associated with running the contractor's business and not directly billable to any specific job expense.

Owner – an individual, organization, corporation, business(es), or public agency that comes up with a project concept or idea, establishes the time and budget constraints, provides the site, figures out how to pay for the project, and hires many of the people who will help make it happen.

Partnering – a dispute resolution approach based on mutual agreement by the parties to work together toward a mission statement developed by all the parties and a recognition of the project's specific goals and objectives.

Pay when paid clause – a clause in contract that specifies that payment will be made to one party (for example, the subcontractor) only after another party (the contractor) receives payment.

Payment bond – a construction bond that provides assurance to an owner that subcontractors and suppliers will get paid by the contractor; typically issued with performance bonds.

Payment request – see Application and certificate for payment.

Performance bond – a construction bond that provides assurance to the owner that work will be completed in accordance with the plans and specifications at the bid price (plus any agreed changes).

Performance specifications – a method of specifying that identifies the ends to be achieved, not how the ends are achieved.

Permit - a document issued by one or more authorities having jurisdiction giving authorization to proceed with a project according to regulatory requirements.

PERT (Project Evaluation and Review Technique) diagram – see Precedence diagram.

Plug numbers – anticipated subcontractor expenses. Plug numbers provide the general contractor with a guideline for what the sub-bids should be and act as a price "placeholder" in case no sub-bids are submitted.

Pre-bid conference – a meeting, facilitated by the owner or architect, before bids are due, to answer any questions the contractors may have about the bid process and the project.

Pre-construction – the period between award of the construction contract and the start of construction and marked by intense planning by the contractor.

Pre-construction meeting – a formal meeting, typically facilitated by the architect, that occurs after award of the contract but before construction begins, to review the responsibilities and expectations of each of the project participants.

Pre-construction submittals – a document, product data, or physical sample that a contract requires the contractor to provide for review by the owner and/or designer before construction begins.

Pre-qualification – a determination by an owner that selected contractors have the necessary abilities to complete certain types of work.

Precedence diagram (network diagram, logic diagram, PERT diagram) – a tool for making scheduling decisions and a way to represent a schedule showing the dependencies between activities.

Predecessor activity – an activity that comes immediately before another activity.

Preliminary estimate – a cost estimate developed after some design is known and decisions are still being made.

Preliminary notice – notification to an owner that someone has lien rights.

Prevailing wage – pay rates set by the Department of Labor based on wages in a specific locality.

Price a job – to do a cost estimate.

Prime contractor – a contractor who has a direct contract with an owner.

Private owner – an individual, organization, corporation, or business(es) that pays for a project (typically, through short-term construction loans) without using public dollars.

Procurement (buying out the job) – the process of finalizing subcontracts and issuing purchase orders for material and equipment.

Product data – information sheets that describe the model, type, physical characteristics, and performance details of a product.

Productivity – how much a worker can accomplish in a given period of time.

Program – a document that provides design objectives and requirements as guidance to a project's designer.

Programming – the process of identifying specific project goals and objectives.

Progress payments – periodic payments made by the owner to the contractor. Progress payment procedures are outlined in the contract documents (the agreement and/or the general conditions); progress payments are typically made monthly.

Project – a unique activity that has a beginning and an end, uses resources, is not routinely done, and requires managing.

Project delivery – see Delivery Methods.

Project manager – the member of a construction team who is responsible for the business end of a project, in contrast to the superintendent who is responsible for production.

Project management – the process of coordinating, monitoring, evaluating and controlling , work in order to bring about the successful completion of a project.

Project manual – a binder containing all the written documentation for a project.

Proprietary specifications – a method of specifying that identifies the desired product by manufacturer, brand name, model, and so forth.

Public owner – a public entity such as a local, state, or federal government, or a certain institution, whose project is paid for with public funds.

Punch list – a list of minor adjustments and repairs that must be completed prior to the owner's final payment to the contractor.

Purchase order – a short contract form typically used to order materials and equipment.

Quality – the attributes or properties of something (a product, material, or workmanship) as defined by the requirements called for in the contract documents. There are various levels of quality that can be specified and the contractor's responsibility is to meet or exceed whatever is required.

Quality assurance – refers to procedures before and during execution of the work to guard against defects and deficiencies.

Quality control – measures and procedures, such as testing and inspections, for evaluating completed work.

Quantity sheet – a sheet developed by the contractor's estimator that tracks what has been measured in a take-off and the quantities of each material.

Quantity take-off – the process of itemizing the amount of materials required for a job.

Quote – see Bid.

RSMeans – a product line of Reed Construction Data, a primary supplier of construction cost data.

Rating – see Surety program.

Reference standards – a method of specifying that identifies a required standard, such as ASTM, state, or federal.

Request for a change proposal – a request from the architect that the contractor determine the cost and time impacts of a proposed change.

Request for information – a request for clarification or information resulting from a field question.

Request for payment – see Application and certificate for payment.

Requisition – a request for payment from one party to another.

Residential sector – a sector of the construction industry that includes both new construction and renovation of single- and multi-family residential properties such as houses, condominiums, and apartments. Buildings are often wood frame and fairly low-tech.

Responsible bidder – a contractor who meets the bid requirements regarding qualifications, experience, and any other criteria deemed necessary by the owner.

Responsive bid – a bid submittal that meets all the bidding requirements as outlined in the bid package.

Retention (retainage) – a portion of a pay request that is commonly held back by the owner (and subsequently by the general contractor from the subcontractors) until the end of the job.

Risk – something that can go wrong on a project, leading to potential financial loss.

Rough-order-of-magnitude (ROM) estimate – a conceptual cost estimate that is completed early in the planning phase by the owner to determine if the project is affordable and to help define the scope of work.

Samples – physical examples of products such as carpet, tiles, and light fixtures.

Schedule – a timetable, typically shown in graphic form, that describes the order in which project activities will happen, details how long each activity will take, and tracks the progress of the work.

Schedule of values – a budget outline created early in the construction stage that is not an accurate, detailed breakdown of costs but the expected payment amounts in the different categories; it is used to determine the monthly payments due.

Schematic design – the first phase of design, which focuses on developing an overall form and layout for the project. Schematic drawings are used for analyzing design alternatives.

Scope of work – the work as detailed by the drawings and the technical specifications.

Second-tier subcontractor – a contractor hired by a subcontractor to perform specialty work on a project. Second-tier subcontractors may hire their own specialty contractors (third-tier subcontractors).

SectionFormat™ – the organization of related units of information within the MasterFormat™ divisions.

Sections – drawings that graphically represent a structure by showing vertical cuts through the entire building or a portion of the building.

Self-performing – physical work that a general contractor performs with his own crews.

Sequential construction – a job in which each stage of a project is completed before the next stage begins. Projects that are sequential take the longest to complete.

Shop drawings – drawings that clarify the fabrication or production detail of an item, such as a roof truss or a metal duct.

Site – a piece of land on which something has been or will be located.

Site layout plan – see Jobsite layout plan.

Solicitation – see Invitation to bid.

Specialty contractor (trade contractor) – a contractor who performs specialized activities.

Specifications – written descriptions of the work that define the materials, the processes, and the quality of products and systems. The specifications and the drawings work together to provide the information contractors need in order to price and build a project.

Speculation – something completed (such as a building) for an unknown buyer or user.

Square foot estimate – an estimate that uses floor area to calculate costs after some design detail is available.

Standards – formal regulatory requirements (such as a building code) or a voluntary rating system (such as LEED).

Start to finish – a type of project dependency, in which one task cannot be completed, until some other task has been started.

Start to start – a type of project dependency, in which one task cannot be started until some other task has also been started.

Stipulated-sum contract (lump-sum contract, fixed price contract) – a type of contract in which a specified amount of work is provided by the contractor for a set price that is known up front.

Sub – a subcontractor.

Subcontractor – a person who has a contract with another contractor. In construction, subcontractors are specialty trade contractors.

Submittal – a document, product data, or physical sample that a contract requires the contractor to provide for review by the owner and/or designer. Submittals can include insurance certificates, manufacturers' product information and samples, and shop drawings.

Substantial completion – when the work or a portion of the work is sufficiently complete for the owner to use the building for its intended purpose.

Successor activity – an activity that comes immediately after another activity.

Summary schedule – a schedule developed to show progress in broad areas or milestones that can be used by those not requiring detailed information, such as an owner or funder. Summary schedules are typically in the form of a bar chart.

Superintendent – the person on the contractor's team who is responsible for the production of the project.

Supplementary conditions – the conditions of a contract used to modify or expand the general conditions to reflect the needs of individual projects.

Supplier (vendor) – a company that manufactures, distributes, or supplies products and services to a contractor.

Surety – a company (often an insurance company) that sells construction bonds.

Surety bond (construction bond) – a bond sold by a surety and used by an owner to manage risk on a project.

Surety program (rating) – a rating given by a surety that specifies the maximum bond amount that a contractor can qualify to purchase.

Sustainable construction (green building) – projects that seek to minimize or eliminate negative impacts on the natural and human environment.

Take-off ("doing the take-off") – the process of measuring construction drawings in order to quantify materials.

Task – an individual activity within a project.

Task sequencing – the order in which work activities are scheduled for completion.

Termination (of a contract) – the voluntary or involuntary end of a contract.

Tracking – a key function of project management, in which current progress of a project is monitored.

Tracking logs – written records, maintained to track and manage the flow of information and products.

Traditional delivery method – see Design-bid-build.

U.S. Green Building Council (USGBC) – the developers of the LEED rating system; a 501(c)(3) nonprofit organization working to make green buildings available to everyone within a generation.

Union rates – wages paid to workers who are members of a labor union and whose pay rate is established by the union and a project's management.

Unit cost – the cost of materials based on a typical unit for that product such as tons, square feet, linear feet, or cubic yards.

Unit price contract – a type of contract in which the contractor bids a fixed unit price and, at the completion of the job, the total quantities are determined and payment is made to the contractor based on actual quantities.

Unit price estimate (bid, final, or detailed estimate) – a cost estimate based on the most detailed design information developed by the contractor (or bidding contractors) after the design drawings and specifications are completed.

Value engineering – a methodical analysis of ways to reduce the costs of a project or structure over its entire life.

Vendor (supplier) – a company that manufactures, distributes, or supplies products and services to a contractor.

Wage rate – rate (typically, by the hour) for labor, including costs such as social security, unemployment taxes, and health benefits in addition to the worker's direct pay.

Warranty – a promise by the contractor that materials, systems, and workmanship are as the owner should reasonably expect them to be.

Work activity – a task.

Work breakdown structure (WBS) – the way that work activities are organized.

Work, the (scope of work) – the obligations defined by the contract documents.

Zero net energy building – building that provides all of its own energy on an annual basis from onsite renewable resources or offsite renewable energy purchases.

Zoning – a system of land use regulations.

Zoning map – a map of a specific zoning district that graphically identifies allowable uses for every piece of land within a zoning district.

Zoning ordinance – a law that describes what uses are allowed and what restrictions apply (such as maximum height and parking requirements) in a specific zoning jurisdiction.

BIBLIOGRAPHY

Abdulaziz, Sam K., and Kenneth S. Grosshart and Bruce D. Rudman (ed.). *California Construction Law*, 2009 Edition. Vista, CA: BNi Building News, 2009.

Abramowitz, Ava J. *Architect's Essentials of Contract Negotiation*. New York: John Wiley, 2002.

American Institute of Architects. *The American Institute of Architects Official Guide to the 2007 AIA Contract Documents*. Hoboken, NJ: John Wiley, 2009.

Balboni, Barbara (ed.). *RSMeans Square Foot Costs, 2010*. Kingston, MA: R. S. Means Company, 2010.

Bielefeld, Bert. *Construction Scheduling*, Basics series. Boston: Birkhaüser, 2009.

Buttelwerth, John. *Computer Integrated Construction Project Scheduling*. Upper Saddle River, NJ: Pearson/Prentice Hall, 2005.

Callahan, Michael T., Daniel G. Quackenbush, and James E. Rowings, *Construction Project Scheduling* New York: McGraw-Hill, 1992.

Civitello, Andrew M., Jr. *Construction Operations Manual of Policies and Procedures,* 3rd edition. New York: McGraw-Hill, 2000.

Coleman, Joseph D. *Construction Documents and Contracting* Upper Saddle River, NJ: Pearson/Prentice Hall, 2004.

Collier, Keith. *Construction Contracts*. Upper Saddle River, NJ: Pearson/Prentice Hall, 2000.

Construction Specifications Institute. *Project Resource Manual: CSI Manual of Practice,* 5th edition. New York: McGraw-Hill, 2005.

Fisk, Edward R., *Construction Project Administration*, 9th edition. Boston: Prentice Hall, 2010.

Gissen, David (ed.). *Big & Green: Toward Sustainable Architecture* in the 21st Century. New York: Princeton Architectural Press, 2002.

Glavinich, Thomas E. *Contractor's Guide to Green Building Construction: Management, Project Delivery, Documentation, and Risk Reduction*. Hoboken, NJ: John Wiley, 2008.

Gould, Frederick E. *Managing the Construction Process: Estimating, Scheduling and Project Control*, 3rd edition. Upper Saddle River, NJ: Pearson/Prentice Hall, 2005.

Gould, Frederick E., and Nancy E. Joyce. *Construction Project Management.* Upper Saddle River, NJ: Pearson/Prentice Hall, 2009.

Halpin, Daniel W., and Bolivar Senior. *Construction Management*, 4th edition. Hoboken, NJ: Wiley, 2011.

Hegazy, Tarek. *Computer-Based Construction Project Management.* Upper Saddle River, NJ: Prentice Hall, 2002

Helton, Joseph E. *Simplified Estimating for Builders and Engineers.* Englewood Cliffs, NJ: Prentice Hall, 1992

Hinze, Jimmie W. *Construction Planning and Scheduling*, 2nd edition. Upper Saddle River, NJ: Pearson/Prentice Hall, 2004.

Jackson, Barbara J. *Construction Management JumpStart*: The Best First Step Toward a Career in Construction Management, 2nd edition. Indianapolis, IN: Wiley/Sybex, 2010.

Kendrick, Tom, *Identifying and Managing Project Risk: Essential Tools for Failure-Proofing Your Project*, 2nd edition. New York: American Management Association/ AMACON, 2009.

Kibert, Charles J. *Sustainable Construction: Green Building Design and Delivery*, 2nd edition. Hoboken, NJ: John Wiley & Sons, 2008.

Kramon, Jim. *Smart Business for Contractors.* Newton, CT: Taunton Press, 2007.

LePatner, Barry B. *Broken Buildings, Busted Budgets: How to Fix America's Trillion-Dollar Construction Industry.* Chicago: University of Chicago Press, 2007.

Levy, Sidney M. *Project Management in Construction*, 5th edition. New York: McGraw-Hill, 2007.

Marchman, David A., and Tulio A. Sulbaran. *Scheduling for Home Builders with Microsoft Project.* Washington, D.C.: BuilderBooks.com, 2006.

Marchman, David A., and Tulio A. Sulbaran. *Scheduling with Suretrak.* Clifton Park, NY: Thomson Delmar Learning, 2006.

Meredith, Jack R., and Samuel J. Mantel. *Project Management: A Managerial Approach*, 6th edition. Hoboken, NJ: John Wiley, 2006.

Mincks, William R., and Hal Johnston. *Construction Jobsite Management*, 3rd edition. Clifton Park, NY: Delmar Cengage Learning, 2010.

Newitt, Jay S. *Construction Scheduling: Principles and Practices*, 2nd edition. Upper Saddle River, NJ: Prentice Hall, 2009.

Palmer, William J., James M. Maloney, and John L. Heffron III. *Construction Insurance, Bonding, & Risk Management.* New York: McGraw-Hill, 1996.

Peurifoy, R.L., and Garold D. Oberlender. *Estimating Construction Costs,* 5th edition. Boston: McGraw-Hill, 2002.

Pinnell, Steven S. *How to Get Paid for Construction Changes: Preparation, Resolution Tools, and Techniques.* New York: McGraw-Hill, 1998.

Ritz, George J. *Total Construction Project Management.* New York: McGraw-Hill, 1994.

Schaufelberger, John E., and Len Holm. *Management of Construction Projects: A Constructor's Perspective.* Upper Saddle River, NJ: Prentice Hall, 2002.

Schexnayder, Clifford J., and Mayo, Richard E. *Construction Management Fundamentals*, Boston, MA: McGraw-Hill Higher Education, 2004.

Sears, S. Keoki, Glenn A. Sears, and Richard H. Clough. *Construction Contracting: A Practical Guide to Field Construction Management*, 5th edition. Hoboken, NJ: John Wiley & Sons, 2008.

Waier, Phillip R. (ed.). *RSMeans Building Construction Costs Data, 2010.* Kingston, MA: R. S. Means Company, 2010.

White, Nancy J. *Principles and Practices of Construction Law.* Upper Saddle River, NJ: Prentice Hall, 2002.

Woodson, R. Dodge. *Be a Successful Green Builder.* New York: McGraw-Hill, 2009.

Yudelson, Jerry. *Green Building A to Z: Understanding the Language of Green Building.* Gabriola Island, BC: New Society Publishers, 2007.

Yudelson, Jerry. *The Green Building Revolution.* Washington, DC: Island Press, 2008.

INDEX

Q

R

About the Author

Alison Dykstra has a master's degree in architecture and has been a registered architect since 1983. She is a member of the American Institute of Architects and the Construction Specifications Institute, from which she received her CDT certification in construction documents technology. Her field experience ranges from project management for developers of mid-rise steel frame and townhouse complexes, to design and construction management of her own residential projects, to planning and organizing educational programs about solar and wind energy systems.

Dykstra began teaching construction organization and management in 1992 and is currently an adjunct faculty member at Santa Rosa Junior College in California. Her students range from those new to construction to general contractors with decades of experience in the field. Over the years, Dykstra has developed and refined techniques for conveying to both new students and seasoned professionals the complex information comprising construction management in a manner that enables students to grasp the subject, make it their own, and go on to become successful construction managers, superintendents, or architects. Dykstra's textbook *Construction Project Management: A Complete Introduction* is the direct result of this teaching experience and real-world practice.